Global Institutions a Development

The dearth of attention to ideas in multilateral institutions has prompted analysts to probe their role as intellectual actors. *Global Institutions and Development* is an insightful and welcome collection of essays exploring the nexus of ideas, institutions, and development policy.

Thomas G. Weiss, Presidential Professor and Director,
Ralph Bunche Institute for International Studies,
the CUNY Graduate Center

Global Institutions and Development's impressive scope covers a wide range of policy ideas and institutions, skilfully interweaving original case studies with cutting edge conceptual insights

Jonathan Fox, University of California, Santa Cruz

The impact that multilateral institutions have on development is hotly debated, but few doubt their power and influence. This book is about the role of ideas in such institutions: why some particular ideas are taken up; how they travel within the multilateral system; and how they are translated into policy, modified, distorted or resisted.

Global Institutions and Development argues that ideas are sometimes used, knowingly or unknowingly, to promote interests or worldviews favoured by powerful states or institutions. The book provides detailed case studies of selected ideas – such as social capital, sustainable development, reproductive health and governance – and a range of organizations, including the World Bank, UNDP, IMF, WTO, ADB, UNFPA, ILO and OECD.

It will be of interest to students and researchers in political science, development studies, economics, sociology and anthropology.

Morten Bøås is a Researcher at Fafo – Institute for Applied International Studies, Norway. **Desmond McNeill** is Research Professor, and former Director, at the SUM (Centre for Development and the Environment), University of Oslo, Norway.

RIPE series in global political economy

Series editors:

Louise Amoore — University of Newcastle, UK
Randall Germain — Carleton University, Canada
Rorden Wilkinson — University of Manchester, UK

Formerly edited by Otto Holman, Marianne Marchand (Research Centre for International Political Economy, University of Amsterdam), Henk Overbeek (Free University, Amsterdam) and Marianne Franklin (University of Amsterdam).

This series, published in association with the *Review of International Political Economy*, provides a forum for current debates in international political economy. The series aims to cover all the central topics in IPE and to present innovative analyses of emerging topics. The titles in the series seek to transcend a state-centred discourse and focus on three broad themes:

- the nature of the forces driving globalization forward
- resistance to globalization
- the transformation of the world order

The series comprises two strands:

The *RIPE series in global political economy* aims to address the needs of students and teachers, and the titles will be published in hardback and paperback. Titles include:

Transnational Classes and International Relations
Kees van der Pijl

Gender and Global Restructuring
Sightings, sites and resistances
Edited by Marianne H. Marchand and Anne Sisson Runyan

Global Political Economy
Contemporary theories
Edited by Ronen Palan

Ideologies of Globalization
Contending visions of a new world order
Mark Rupert

The Clash within Civilisations
Coming to terms with cultural conflicts
Dieter Senghaas

Global Unions?
Theory and strategies of organized labour in the global political economy
Edited by Jeffrey Harrod and Robert O'Brien

Political Economy of a Plural World
Critical reflections on power, morals and civilizations
Robert Cox with Michael Schechter

A Critical Rewriting of Global Political Economy
Integrating reproductive, productive and virtual economies
V. Spike Peterson

Contesting Globalization
Space and place in the world economy
André C. Drainville

Global Institutions and Development
Framing the world?
Edited by Morten Bøås and Desmond McNeill

Routledge/RIPE studies in global political economy is a forum for innovative new research intended for a high-level specialist readership, and the titles will be available in hardback only. Titles include:

* also available in paperback

Global Institutions and Development

Framing the world?

**Edited by Morten Bøås and
Desmond McNeill**

Routledge
Taylor & Francis Group

LONDON AND NEW YORK

First published 2004
by Routledge
2 Park Square, Milton Park, Abingdon, Oxon, OX14 4RN

Simultaneously published in the USA and Canada
by Routledge
270 Madison Ave, New York NY 10016

Routledge is an imprint of the Taylor & Francis Group

Transferred to Digital Printing 2005

© 2004 Morten Bøås and Desmond McNeill for selection and editorial
matter; individual contributors their contributions

Typeset in Baskerville by Taylor & Francis Books Ltd

British Library Cataloguing in Publication Data
A catalogue record for this book is available from the British Library

Library of Congress Cataloging in Publication Data
A catalog record for this book has been requested

ISBN 0–415–31289–2 (hbk)
ISBN 0–415–31290–6 (pbk)

Contents

Contributors

Morten Bøås is a Researcher at Fafo – Institute for Applied International Studies. His publications include *Multilateral Institutions: A Critical Introduction* (co-authored with Desmond McNeill) (2003), and *Ethnicity Kills?* (co-edited with Einar Braathen and Gjermund Sæther) (2000).

James J. Hentz is Assistant Professor of International Studies and Political Science at the Virginia Military Institute. His publications include *New and Critical Security and Regionalism: Beyond the Nation State* (co-edited with Morten Bøås) (2003).

Janne Jokinen was previously Research Fellow at the Department of Political History, University of Turku. He is currently working for the Finnish Ministry of Foreign Affairs.

Norman Long is Professor of Sociology of Development at Wageningen University. His publications include *Development Sociology: Actor Perspectives* (2001).

Ken Masujima is Associate Professor at the Faculty of Law, University of Kobe, Japan. His professional career includes experience as Associate Expert at OECD, Paris.

Desmond McNeill is Research Professor at the Centre for Development and the Environment, University of Oslo. His publications include *Global Sustainable Development in the 21st Century* (co-edited with Keekok Lee and Alan Holland) (2000), and *Multilateral Institutions: A Critical Introduction* (co-authored with Morten Bøås) (2003).

Knut G. Nustad is Associate Professor at the Department of Social Anthropology, University of Oslo. His publications include 'Development: the devil we know?', *Third World Quarterly* 22 (4): 479–89.

Ole Jacob Sending is Research Fellow at the Norwegian Institute of International Affairs (NUPI). His publications include 'The instrumentalisation of development knowledge', in Diane Stone (ed.) *Banking on Knowledge: The Genesis of the Global Development Network* (co-authored with Knut G. Nustad) (2000).

Alice Sindzingre is Research Fellow at the Centre National de la Recherche Scientifique (CNRS), Paris. Her publications include 'Les bailleurs de fonds en manqué de légitimité', *Esprit* 264: 116–27 (2000).

Asuncion Lera St Clair is Research Fellow at the Centre for International Poverty Research, University of Bergen.

Ian Taylor is a Lecturer at the Department of Political and Administrative Studies, University of Botswana. His publications include *South Africa's Multilateral Diplomacy and Global Change: The Limits of Reformism* (co-edited with Philip Nel and Janis van der Westhuisen) (2001).

Jonas Vevatne is a Researcher at the Centre for International Climate and Environmental Research, Oslo (CICERO).

Robert Wade is Professor of Political Economy and Development at the London School of Economics. His publications include 'US Hegemony and the World Bank: the Fight over People and Ideas', *Review of International Political Economy* 9 (2): 201–29 (2002), and *Governing the Market* (1990).

Foreword

At the Millennium Summit held at the United Nations in 2000, 147 heads of state and government agreed on goals for halving world poverty by 2015. Subsequently, almost all international agencies have declared active support for these goals to be among their highest priorities. But when it comes to action by the international agencies, in what sense can we assume that the goals have been adopted? When it comes to implementation, in what ways will the goals be modified, distorted or resisted? And what can be done to keep agencies more in line with what has been agreed?

These are key questions – on which the agency-focused chapters of this wide-ranging study present evidence, sometimes encouraging; often disturbing. Modification, distortion and resistance to ideas are inherent in the structure, personnel and professional approaches of all the international agencies, and this can undermine the simple implementation of even clearly agreed goals. But all is not lost. The studies also show some of the countervailing forces at work, especially well organized lobbying by the NGOs, which can help keep an international agency on track.

Some of the studies may seem academic, and indeed, the ambition of this book is to make a contribution to the literature of international relations. But I hope that my fellow economists working in the World Bank and other international agencies will read it, because they in particular have a lot to gain.

Ideas matter – but ideas are also interpreted differently in different institutions and the ideas and interpretations change over time, again in different ways in the different institutions. An example is how World Bank staff reacted to the new notion of social capital; there are gaps in thinking and approach between researchers and policy makers, between staff with different disciplinary backgrounds and between those applying the ideas in different policy contexts. Economists, in particular, regularly lead the way in adapting, modifying and distorting ideas, often with the best of intentions. Trained to high standards of precision in thought, and with methodologies purporting to be scientific and value-free, economists find it difficult to take aboard the perspectives and approaches of other disciplines. Yet as several of these studies show, concerns with environment, poverty and participation have frequently been significantly modified and distorted in the ways international agencies have adopted – and adapted – them.

Closely related to these modifications and distortions, and often underlying them, are the interests and dominating influence of the industrial countries, especially the biggest and most powerful. The orthodoxy of structural adjustment in the 1980s and of the Washington Consensus and the concept of good governance in the 1990s are supreme examples of this tendency. When allowed to have full rein, the dominating interests and influences can lead to the presentation of key ideas as common-sense approaches to rational economic management within countries, whereas they are in fact better explained as attempts by the North to reconstruct the South in its own image 'along decidedly neoliberal lines' and in ways which mostly match its own economic interests.

How does all this relate to the achievement of the goals for a major reduction of world poverty over a fifteen year period? For all the international agencies involved, supporting these goals involves a number of concrete steps: from defining the issues to monitoring and assessing results. Each of these involves ideas and concepts – and thus, as this study shows and warns, a process of adaptation and probably of modification and distortion of the ideas concerned. Even when top management is fully committed to the achievement of the goals, there is also likely to be resistance, especially when the very idea of supporting global goals for poverty reduction differs from past practice or from the professional training, paradigms and ideology of the main body of staff.

What can be done? Management consultants would no doubt say that this was a typical problem for any institution, with top management trying to ensure 'buy-in' among staff for new goals and new approaches. No doubt some of this is involved. But this book suggests there are much broader and more important and subtle problems behind the scenes, especially for international agencies. There is much to be learned from the case studies in this volume, for those ready to work through and ponder them with an open mind. The problem is not only bureaucratic resistance among staff to new ideas and goals, but how the very ideas and goals will be so adapted and distorted as to frustrate the realization of their underlying objective – the reduction of human poverty on a global scale, in ways which lead to the empowerment of the poor and marginalized in all countries and regions of the world. However, poverty reduction on a global scale is possible with empowerment, providing there are moves to some more democratic sharing of power, internationally and nationally.

The UN provides for this, far from perfectly but within a structure in which the voices of all countries can be heard. The UN also provides for the recognition of a wide range of human rights: political and civil rights which open the way to community empowerment as well as economic, social and cultural rights which open the way to equality, and to measures like education for girls which can open doors to strengthening personal capacities. Equally important, these rights and the many inter-government resolutions underpinning them, have served as focal points around which many NGOs, professional and activist, have rallied to press for more serious implementation. How NGOs mobilized action within the World Bank on environment shows their potential.

But for this to happen, there needs to be more recognition of the entire UN in the pursuit of poverty reduction. If the task is mainly left to the Bretton Woods institutions, with these being allocated the bulk of international resources for poverty reduction, the modifications, distortions and resistance noted in many of the case studies will undercut the effective achievement of the goals, even with committed leadership and sincere efforts from Bretton Woods staff to implement the goals as they perceive them. The rest of the UN needs to be fully involved, with their different perspectives and approaches strongly and fully represented. If this is done, the international effort will not only be stronger but less biased and distorted.

Richard Jolly
Fellow and Former Director of the Institute of Development Studies

Preface

There has been an increasing interest in the role of ideas among students of International Political Economy (IPE) over the last decade. This interest extends beyond IPE into the field of international relations and, as such, reflects a change of direction within the discipline. One can speculate as to why this sudden interest in ideas has emerged, but it appears that profound transformations engendered by globalization are an important contributing factor. Within this rapidly changing environment, dominant ways of seeing and doing are no longer taken for granted. As academics, we wish to understand why certain changes are occurring and what ideas guide their direction.

Global Institutions and Development: Framing the World? provides an unique contribution to the growing body of literature reflecting this cultural turn in IPE/IR. It is unusual in that it makes a conceptual contribution to the study of ideas by suggesting an eclectic approach informed by such diverse perspectives as realism, constructivism and neogramscianism. In choosing such an approach, the editors Morten Bøås and Desmond McNeill reject the institutional and expert-and-activist approaches to the study of ideas and associate themselves with constructivist and critical theoretical perspectives. Bøås and McNeill find that, within mainstream constructivist approaches, too little attention is being spent on the question of how the distribution of power influences the formulation and primacy of certain ideas. In the editors' view, neogramscianism, in contrast, sometimes errs on the side of materialism. However, the consensual underpinnings of hegemony in combination with the notion of the social construction of politics and while being attentive to the importance of power (distribution) provides a framework for studying the role of ideas, their importance and how they "travel" within multilateral institutions.

An additional reason for the importance of the present volume resides in the fact that it forces IPE scholars to seriously consider development issues and the field of development studies. As a topic, development has been rather marginalized within the fields of IR and IPE. In focusing on multilateral institutions and drawing on insights from IPE, development studies and other disciplines such as anthropology and economics, the contributions provide a microcosm of issues and concerns that resonate with the IPE community. Moreover, even within the field of development studies, the role of ideas generated by the multilateral institutions has received very little attention. The United Nations only recently started a project on its intellectual history (see foreword by Sir Richard Jolly). This is a clear indication that even within the multilateral institutions there now exists a need to reflect on the role of ideas, or as the editors have titled their project, on the Creation, Adoption, Negation, and Distortion of Ideas in Development Assistance (Candid).

Concepts central to the discourse surrounding multilateral institutions include social capital, sustainable development, good governance and poverty. As suggested, these ideas are not only important within the development community but are also central concerns for IPE, especially when taking into account the two underlying forces of neoliberal ideology and the economic–technocratic nexus which informs much of the way in which ideas are traveling through the institutions. Development and IPE scholars need to be aware of the power of these forces and how they can shape the policies emanating from the multilateral institutions.

The volume clearly shows that ideas are not coming from a single source such as the US treasury. However, in order to be "heard" and accepted, ideas need to comply with certain pre-requisites; in particular, they need to have a good fit with the two forces mentioned. If this is not the case, resistance against a particular idea will be developed and it will be transformed so as to provide a fit. This has happened, for instance, with the concept of sustainable development.

In short, *Global Institutions and Development: Framing the World?* by Bøås and McNeill is a must–read, not only for academics from the fields of IR, IPE and development studies but also by representatives of non-governmental organizations who are wondering why certain initiatives find such dogged resistance and others not. Moreover, those policy–makers and researchers working in the "world" of multilateral institutions will also find much useful information about how their own organizations work and why certain policy initiatives may not work as their underlying concepts have been distorted in the process of taking them on board. In sum, it is not only an excellent contribution to the RIPE Series in Global Political Economy but most importantly it is an unique and much needed contribution to the field of development studies and policy-making.

Otto Holman
Marianne Marchand
Henk Overbeek
Marianne Franklin
July 2003

Acknowledgements

This book is one output from the project on Creation, Adoption, Negation, and Distortion of Ideas in Development Assistance (CANDID). This project was financed by the Norwegian Research Council's programme on the multilateral system, and hosted by the Centre for Development and the Environment (SUM), University of Oslo. We would like to thank our colleagues at SUM for support, comments and criticism. So many people have contributed to this volume that it is simply impossible to list them all. We are very grateful to those of you who read some of our many drafts and took the time to share your insights with us.

There are also some persons we cannot avoid mentioning. Thomas Weiss, Richard Jolly, Louis Emmerij, Tatiana Carayannis, Jan Aart Scholte, Carlos Santiso, Richard Higgott and Robert Wade have in various ways made important impacts on the way in which we think about the relationship between ideas and international institutions.

As we started to develop this volume we have benefited immensely from Marianne H. Marchand's advice, comments and criticism. We would also like to thank the four anonymous reviewers. We still disagree with some of the comments they made, but they certainly also improved this volume. Finally we would like to thank Heidi Bagtazo at Routledge for her patience and professionalism.

Morten Bøås
Desmond McNeill

Abbreviations

ADB	Asian Development Bank
ADF	Asian Development Fund
AfDB	African Development Bank
CTE	Committee on Trade and Environment
DAC	Development Assistance Committee
DMCs	Developing Member Countries
EA	Environmental Assessment
ECOSOC	United Nations Economic and Social Council
EDF	Environmental Defence Fund
EMIT	Working Group on Environmental Measures and International Trade
ESAF	Enhanced Structural Adjustment Facility
FAO	Food and Agricultural Organization
GATT	General Agreement on Tariffs and Trade
GCI	General Capital Increase
GEF	Global Environmental Facility
HDI	Human Development Index
HDR	Human Development Report Office
HUDCO	Housing and Urban Development Corporation
IBRD	International Bank for Reconstruction and Development
ICPD	International Conference on Population and Development
IDA	International Development Association
IDS	Institute of Development Studies
IFIs	International Financial Institutions
ILO	International Labour Organization
IMF	International Monetary Fund
IPPF	International Planned Parenthood Federation
IWHC	International Women's Health Coalition
LDCs	Less Developed Countries
MDBs	Multilateral Development Banks
MOF	Ministry of Finance (Japan)
NAFTA	North American Free Trade Area
NBA	Narmada Bachao Andolan

NGOs	Non-Governmental Organizations
NIEO	New International Economic Order
NRDC	National Resources Defence Council
NWF	National Wildlife Federation
OCR	Ordinary Capital Resources
ODA	Official Development Assistance
OECD	Organization for Economic Cooperation and Development
PRC	People's Republic of China
SAF	Structural Adjustment Facility
SAPs	Structural Adjustment Programmes
UN	United Nations
UNCED	United Nations Conference on Environment and Development
UNCHE	United Nations Conference on the Human Environment
UNHCR	United Nations High Commission for Refugees
UNCTAD	United Nations Conference on Trade and Development
UNDP	United Nations Development Programme
UNEP	United Nations Environmental Programme
UNESCO	United Nations Educational, Scientific and Cultural Organization
UNFPA	United Nations Fund for Population Activity
UNHCR	United Nations High Commission for Refugees
UNICEF	United Nations Children's Fund
UNRISD	United Nations Research Institute for Social Development
USAID	United States Agency for International Development
WCED	World Commission on Environment and Development
WDR	World Development Report
WHO	World Health Organization
WTO	World Trade Organization

1 Introduction

Power and ideas in multilateral institutions: towards an interpretative framework

Morten Bøås and Desmond McNeill

Introduction

The impact that multilateral institutions have on development is hotly debated, but few doubt their power and influence. This book is about the role of ideas in such institutions. It is remarkable how little is known about this subject: why some particular ideas are taken up by the multilateral institutions; how they travel within the multilateral system; and how they are translated into policy, modified, distorted or resisted. This book seeks to redress this situation by offering perspectives that can be used to critically assess the political processes around some of the ideas that have informed the current development discourse, as evident in the policy prescriptions of the major multilateral institutions.

An 'idea' in this context is a concept which powerfully influences development policy. It is more than simply a slogan or 'buzzword' because it has some reputable intellectual basis, but it may nevertheless be found vulnerable on analytical and empirical grounds. What is special about such an idea is that it is able to operate in both academia and policy domains.[1]

The relationship between power and ideas is challenging. Do ideas have power in themselves? Or only to the extent that they are actively taken up by powerful individuals or groups? And what sort of power do ideas have: to motivate, or to alter the actions of individuals or groups? Clearly, their power must be tied up with the institutionalization of social action and the material capabilities that such kind of institutionalization is built upon. What then is the nature of the relationship; to what extent do ideas change institutions; or do institutions change ideas?

In this study we are concerned with multilateral institutions, and the exercise of what Gramsci calls hegemonic power. We suggest that powerful states (notably the USA), powerful organizations (such as the IMF) and even, perhaps, powerful disciplines (economics) exercise their power largely by 'framing': which serves to limit the power of potentially radical ideas to achieve change. The exercise of framing is composed of two parts: one, drawing attention to a specific issue (such as the environment or urban unemployment); two, determining how such an issue is viewed. A successful framing exercise will both cause an issue to be seen by those that matter, and ensure that they see it in a specific way. And this is achieved with the minimum of conflict or pressure. A good example, analysed at some length in this book, is the idea of governance. As George and Sabelli (1994: 150) put it: 'Being against good governance is rather like being against motherhood and apple-pie.' An effective 'frame' is one which makes favoured ideas seems like common sense, and unfavoured ideas as unthinkable. We suggest that a similar argument can be applied also to the other ideas because as Cox (1992a: 179) argues, 'hegemony frames thought and thereby circumscribes action'.

How and why does such 'framing' occur? A strong claim is that the most powerful multilateral institutions, in terms of the resources at their command, are controlled by the donor countries (and most particularly the USA), promote neoliberal ideas, and are dominated by an economic perspective; any challenging new ideas that arise, if not directly refuted, are distorted, in keeping with this worldview (and world interest). A weak claim is that multilateral institutions are necessarily consensual and technocratic; and that new ideas are diluted and distorted in the process of gaining broad acceptance for them, and putting them into operation. In this book we analyse a number of such framing exercises. But although the ideas concerned have been diluted and distorted in various ways, it is evidence of their potency that they have seldom been rejected outright. What emerges from the case studies is that the distortions that have occurred have been predominantly technocratic. There are, we suggest, two distinct, but partly related, forces at work: one is neoliberal ideology, the other what we call the economic–technocratic nexus. Whether and to what extent a specific idea is distorted as a result of the former depends on the type of idea; but all, we suggest, are subject to the latter. What is common to both is 'depoliticization': ideas are drained of any overt political content, even if they are not wholly drained of their power. This perhaps helps to explain the frustration of those who seek to oppose multilateral institutions and the policies they explicitly stand for; and why opposition to these institutions is increasingly taking an anarchistic form. All multilateral institutions are, of necessity, technocratic. In order for ideas to be used in such organizations they must be translated into terms which can be operationalized. This, we suggest, (together with the importance of achieving consensus), tends to involve a process of 'depoliticization', and a tendency for economics to become the dominant discipline. In short, we suggest that ideas that challenge the conventional wisdom become distorted as a result of a series of related pressures: depoliticization and 'economization' which may be – but are not necessarily – linked to neoliberal ideology and the material interests of those countries with most power in the system.

Institutions, ideas and approaches

Multilateral institutions, often in association with academia, seek to establish global consensus around certain ideas that they see as important for their policy purposes and international image. Indeed, in the introduction to *Ahead of the Curve* (the first major publication from the UN Intellectual History Project),

Emmerij *et al.* (2001) argue that ideas and concepts are the most important legacy of the UN.[2] Such ideas arise and are developed in the interplay between the two domains of academia and policy making, but they derive their credibility from their basis in the former. Examples include the informal sector, sustainable development, governance and social capital – which have contributed both to the development of new policy approaches and to institutional change. It is ideas such as these that are the focus of our interest here, ideas that are widely used by policy makers and have significant influence on them. Legitimacy in the making of development policy is often sought from grounding the proposals in a theoretical base and in supporting empirical analysis. In multilateral institutions, whose constituency is relatively ill defined, this is especially important. Moreover, originality in ideas seems to be highly valued – whether because of the beauty of new ideas or the hope that new policies will be more successful than old ones; hence the often heard critical comment on 'fashions' in development assistance policy.

This volume makes reference to all major multilateral development institutions: the World Bank and the United Nations Development Programme (UNDP); the regional development banks: the Asian Development Bank (ADB), the Inter-American Development Bank, and the African Development Bank. Also included are the International Monetary Fund (IMF), the World Trade Organization (WTO) and the Organization for Economic Cooperation and Development's Development Assistance Committee (OECD-DAC); because although not strictly development institutions, they have, to varying extents, played an important role in the multilateral system, and because they too are actively participating in the arena of ideas – at least with regard to some issues (e.g. governance in the IMF/OECD-DAC and sustainable development in WTO). To what extent do these institutions constitute a coherent group?

The term 'multilateral' suggests many member countries, but it is unspecific as to what number constitutes many. It can refer to anything from a minimum of three countries to an institution that encompasses all sovereign countries in the world (Caporaso 1993). Some of the institutions we are concerned with here have almost universal membership (for instance the World Bank and the IMF), whereas others have clear limitations to membership (e.g. the regional development banks and OECD-DAC).

When we talk about multilateral institutions we are also talking about social institutions. Institutions have been defined as 'recognised practices constituting of easily identifiable roles, coupled with collections of rules or conventions governing relations among the occupants of these roles' (Young 1986: 107). Or, to quote another definition, institutions are 'persistent and connected sets of rules (formal and informal) that prescribe behavioural rules, constrain activity and shape expectations' (Keohane 1989: 3). As social institutions, the multilateral institutions possess a clear coercive quality. The member states and the other actors in the institutions are expected to perform certain roles, and the costs to actors who opt out of participation are both uncertain and possibly very high. This is, as some of the case studies will reveal, one reason why some states have maintained their membership in particular multilateral institutions, even if highly disturbed by what was going on there. Multilateral institutions can thus be understood not only as socially constructed arenas for the facilitation of international order and cooperation, but also as battlefields between different actors (both state and non-state). This conflict aspect of multilateral institutions is, however, often hidden, largely because they have – ever since their establishment – adopted the doctrine of political neutrality. Most of the policies and statements from these institutions are (at least in rhetorical terms) founded on the functionalist logic that technical economic questions can be separated from politics. In the *Agreement Establishing the African Development Bank* and the *Agreement Establishing the Asian Development Bank* the principle of political neutrality is clearly present.

> The Bank, its President, Vice presidents, officers and staff shall not interfere in the political affairs of any members; nor shall they be influenced in their decisions by the political character of the member concerned. Only economic considerations shall be relevant to their decisions. Such considerations shall be weighed impartially in order to achieve and carry out the functions of the Bank.
> (AfDB [African Development Bank] 1964: Art. 38; ADB 1966: Art. 36)

Almost precisely the same text – word for word – is to be found in the World Bank's (1989a) Articles of Agreement, Article IV, Section 10. These statements of functionality and a technical, non-political approach to development are of course a facade. Every question concerned with development is a question concerned with planned social change and thereby also necessarily a political question. But multilateral institutions strive to avoid or minimize overtly political action. Important for our understanding of the role of ideas in the multilateral system is therefore the extent to which a technical, *depoliticized* approach to development has influenced the relationship between power and ideas; to what degree the technical discourse in the multilateral institutions has influenced the use of ideas taken up by the multilateral institutions.

Given that the focus of this book is on institutions, and the relationship between power and ideas, it is not surprising that the disciplinary focus of five of the contributors is that of political science; but the backgrounds of the others are quite varied. It is our view that important contributions to the study of institutions can be gained by incorporating insights from, for instance, economic sociology (the new institutionalism and the old institutional economics), anthropology (not only in relation to small and informal social groups, but also formal institutions such as development agencies), and from philosophy (certainly to the extent that the power of ideas derives from their moral content). In studying similar topics, these different disciplines also find themselves confronting similar theoretical issues, such as embeddedness and autonomy; the agency–structure question; and the issue of mutually constitutive phenomena. However, although this volume has benefited from insights from many disciplines, our work is located primarily in political science. More specifically, in terms of our theoretical approach, we locate ourselves within the nexus of realism, constructivism and neogramscianism. This implies that, in contrast to most of the literature on the role of ideas, we both seek to build a broader approach and place more emphasis on power and power relationships. To briefly illustrate our position, it is useful to refer to Weiss and Carayannis' (2001: 28–32) review of the ideational literature. They argue that the literature on the role of ideas can be grouped into three categories:

1   institutional approaches (e.g. Sikkink 1991; Goldstein and Keohane 1993)
2   expert- and activist-group approaches (e.g. Hall 1989a; Haas 1992; Risse and Sikkink 1999)
3   constructivist approaches and critical theory (e.g. Cox 1997, Ruggie 1998; Wendt 1999)

Our own approach falls mainly into the third of these categories. Within this, Weiss and Carayannis distinguish two rather different bodies of literature: that of Cox and others (the critical approach) and of Wendt, Ruggie and others (constructivism). We have much in common with Cox, although not all in this volume share his normative agenda. With regard to constructivists, we fully agree with their claim about the social construction of politics. However, we are also concerned that mainstream constructivist approaches (e.g. Ruggie 1998; Wendt 1999) put too much emphasis on shared ideas and the role of norms and legal institutions, and thereby neglect the real relationship between power and ideas. This is the main reason why we prefer to continue to flag the realist assumption that outcomes cannot be properly analysed in disregard of the distribution of power. And this is also our bridge to neogramscian critical theory. In particular, we find the neogramscian understanding of the consensual aspect of hegemony to be of value in our investigations. However, we also find clear limitations in neogramscianism. If we accept the central premise that both ideas (shared and contested) and the distribution of power (ideational and material) matter, then we need to study the interplay between actors and structures in the various power games that take place in relation to these material and ideational struggles in multilateral institutions.

Thus we believe that there is much to be learned from the work of Gramsci and Cox; the former for his theories of hegemony, and the latter for the application of such theory specifically to the field of international political economy. More generally, several of the chapters in this book relate to the so-called realist–constructivist debate within international relations theory, which is concerned with issues and questions that have implications far beyond the disciplinary borders of political science. In fact, we will argue that most of the authors in this book (political scientists or not) explicitly or implicitly seek to establish a middle ground in the realist–constructivist debate; not merely because the extreme positions in this debate are not sufficiently nuanced, but more specifically because neither perspective is well equipped to cope with the central issue: the relationship between power and ideas in multilateral institutions.

We claim that ideas have real power in the political world, but they do not acquire political force independently of the constellation of institutions and interests already present (Hall 1989b). Rather, 'the structure of any social system will contain three elements: material conditions, interests and ideas' (Wendt 1999: 139). Interest formation ultimately has both a material and a social basis. Materialist interpretations will give privilege to material conditions, under the assumption that they generally determine interests. By contrast, ideational interpretations will give privilege to ideas (Wendt 1999). These two contrasting approaches may be applied also at a deeper level. In other words, it may be claimed that material conditions directly influence ideas; or, alternatively, that ideas directly influence material conditions.

In discussing ideas, in this broader sense, Cox (1986) makes a useful distinction between ideas as inter-subjective meaning (i.e. shared notions of social relations which shape habits and expectations of behaviour),[3] and as collective images of social order (held by different groups of people). Collective images differ both according to the nature and legitimacy of prevailing power relations and structures, and with respect to the meanings attached to issues such as justice or the distribution of and access to collective public goods. The difference between ideas as inter-subjective meanings and as collective images is thus that whereas the former are generally agreed/shared throughout a particular historical period and constitute the common framework for social discourse (conflict included), the latter may be several and opposed (Cox 1986).[4] One may thus, drawing on both Wendt and Cox, suggest that interests are formed in part by ideas as inter-subjective meaning (independent of material conditions) and in part by ideas as collective images (influenced by material conditions). Ideas can be used, knowingly or unknowingly, to promote interests or even more deep-seated worldviews. Where these run counter to the interests or worldviews of others, they may be imposed not through the direct use of power, but through the exercise of what Gramsci calls 'hegemony'; through the adoption of shared ideas, and agreement concerning collective images.

Such a process depends crucially, we suggest, on institutionalization. From both a material and an ideational interpretation, this is a way of stabilizing and perpetuating one particular social order in the nexus between material conditions, interests and ideas. The current multilateral system can thus be seen as the institutionalization of the 'order of things'. The institutions within this specific system are particular amalgams of ideas, interests and material power which in turn influence the development of ideas, interests and material conditions. The approach in this volume is to see the multilateral system as a social construction, and not as a pre-existing entity. Thus, we interpret institutions within this system as institutions that take on a life of their own. They may become battlefields for opposed ideas, and rival institutions may reflect different ideas. The tensions between different interests cannot be wholly resolved, or even masked; and the distortion of ideas, with which this research is largely concerned, arises precisely from this.

Ideas and multilateral institutions: from informal
sector to social capital

In this book our aim is that each case study will make some contribution not only to our knowledge of the idea and the institution concerned, but also to the overall theoretical approach; and take up issues that arise also in other cases. For example, the study of social capital and the World Bank raises the issue of the power – or hegemony – of economics. And in seeking to understand the institutional context of the World Bank, it examines the interplay between different groups, with differing identities and differing norms: the researcher, the policy maker, the operations staff; and how individuals face incompatible norms in seeking to refer to more than one peer group.

In Chapter 2, Knut G. Nustad analyses the idea of development itself. His starting point is the observation that this idea, as it has been expressed in the multilateral system, has striking similarities with earlier conceptions of development: the concern with imposing order and preventing social unrest, and development as a process of social change emanating from the agency of elites. The form that development has taken in the multilateral system, he argues, implies an idea of trusteeship: that someone (multilateral institutions), who has the necessary overview, guides the process of development. From this perspective, popular proposals for reform, such as participatory approaches, look more like repeats of earlier efforts than true attempts to change the dominant development thinking among multilateral institutions.

In Chapter 3, Norman Long provides an anthropological perspective on the relationship between ideas, discourse and power – both in multilateral institutions and 'on the ground'. He emphasizes overlapping and multiplicity within the development discourse, and in particular he is concerned with the relationship between 'expert' and 'lay' knowledge. This relationship is related to the debate between the multilateral institutions and their opponents. Long argues the case for seeing this relationship as situated social practice. His point is that multilateral institutions are found in several arenas of social struggle on many levels of world politics, but they must be seen not in isolation but in relation to each other.

There follow a number of case studies, of specific ideas and institutions, beginning with the 'informal sector' which serves to introduce the *dramatis personae*: the multilateral institutions (such as the the World Bank and the ILO), the researchers and policy makers in North and South, etc. It introduces also some of the phenomena – such as international conferences, and visiting 'missions' – for those who are not already well acquainted with them. And it makes reference to the sorts of written materials which the different authors draw on: not only academic books and articles, but also consultants' reports, policy documents, annual reports, commissioned studies, etc. The story it tells is of an 'idea' which certainly became well established in both academic and policy arenas, though also disputed and distorted.

Following some of the same steps as Desmond McNeill in Chapter 4, Ole Jacob Sending's contribution (Chapter 5) is concerned with the relationship between knowledge and policy in the case of international population policy, where a major shift in approach – associated with a new 'idea' – was carefully orchestrated. His starting point is the observation that the International Conference on Population and Development (ICPD) held in Cairo in 1994 produced a new 'consensus' on international population policy; whereas the traditional policy approach of 'family planning' had defined population policy from its very beginning in the 1950s, the ICDP placed a 'reproductive health approach' to population policy at the core of its Programme of Action. This observation causes Sending to ask two important questions: (1) why did family planning remain the core term for population policy for over thirty years even though there were constant controversies within the field about whether and how to organize population policy; and (2) why did the change in population policy from family planning to reproductive health take place during the ICPD process. Sending's argument is that in order to understand processes such as this one, we must come to terms with the way in which the institution of science stabilizes international policy by legitimizing and validating certain facts, theories and concepts that form the foundation for certain specific policy approaches. In light of this understanding, policy change is interpreted as the production and usage of knowledge that creates space for the formulation of an alternative policy approach (in this case reproductive health).

The next three chapters (6, 7 and 8) deal with the environment in the World Bank (Robert Wade), the concept of sustainable development in the WTO (Morten Bøås and Jonas Vevatne) and the role of social capital in the World Bank (Desmond McNeill). These are quite closely related, although they also illustrate the differences between the institutions, and issues, concerned. A comparison of Robert Wade's discussion on the environment in the World Bank with Desmond McNeill's analysis of the discussion on social capital in the same institution shows us how the World Bank has in the former case been more reactive, in the latter more proactive, in dealing with ideas that do not immediately fit the traditional World Bank problem definition of development. Although the work of the World Bank on social capital might be interpreted as an attempt to move away from its previous technocratic approach to development, the case of sustainable development in the WTO reveals a clearly technocratic response. One reason might be that the WTO Secretariat's neoliberal approach to international trade also has defined the organization's approach to sustainable development.

The three following chapters (9, 10 and 11) represent not only three different institutions' approach to governance, but also different analytical approaches to the study of ideas in multilateral institutions. Ian Taylor's claim (Chapter 9) is that the promotion of *good governance* by the IMF is a powerful example of how certain ideas are constructed as common sense. In his analysis, good governance is seen as a hegemonic discourse pursued by the North to define the South in its own image, along neoliberal lines. Taylor's contribution clearly falls within the parameters of what is commonly referred to today as critical theory (akin to writers like Cox and Gill). The approach of Janne Jokinen (Chapter 10) and Ken

Masujima (Chapter 11) is different, and falls within the institutional literature (broadly defined). Nonetheless, seen together these three chapters cast an illuminating light on the role of an idea such as governance. The point of departure for Jokinen is the fact that the ADB was the first multilateral development bank (MDB) with a board-approved policy on governance (3 October 1995). The purpose of his chapter is therefore to look at the political and institutional environments in which the ADB's governance policy was created, and analyse how these environments influenced the content of the policy. One of the main arguments in this chapter is that the ADB's governance policy was in many ways a balancing act, in which it was necessary to find a way of defining the term so that the interests of Western donors, Japan, the regional borrowing countries and the Bank itself, at least temporarily, could be reconciled. Ken Masujima's chapter is concerned with the approach taken to the governance debate by the OECD-DAC. At first sight, it may look as if the DAC has a comparative advantage over other multilateral institutions concerning matters pertaining to governance, since DAC (unlike most other multilateral institutions) is not formally prohibited from interfering in the domestic affairs of non-member countries. However, as the discussion on governance became more sophisticated, the debate in the DAC was taken over by the World Bank. The OECD member countries preferred to continue this debate in what they perceived as the dominant (hegemonic?) multilateral institution. Thus, seen as a whole, these three chapters illustrate how issues concerning ownership structure (the ADB *vis-à-vis* the IMF) and perceptions about an institution's importance for policy debates, lead to differences in approaches, and also why some multilateral institutions (e.g. the World Bank) become the chosen arena for debate rather than others (e.g. OECD-DAC).

Chapter 12 (Alice Sindzingre) and Chapter 13 (Asuncion Lera St Clair) analyse the idea of poverty in the World Bank and the UNDP respectively. The idea of poverty has become one of the most recurrent concepts in the development discourse, and the World Bank and the UNDP have both made world poverty alleviation their main mission and reason for existence (i.e. legitimization). In Sindzingre's contribution she examines the different dimensions of the trajectory of the idea of poverty in the World Bank, and links it with the changes introduced to the concept by other institutions involved in development, where a 'consensus' also has emerged on the priority of poverty. This enables her to analyse the evolving meanings of the concept of poverty, and in particular the nascent shift in the World Bank from income poverty to inequality and multidimensionality. The World Bank has become more open to other voices under Wolfensohn's leadership, but a shift towards fuller participation of poor countries continues to be hindered by many cognitive and institutional constraints. Thus, as a broad concept allowing for multiple meanings and policies, 'consensus' around poverty reflects the tensions of the multilateralism-cum-hegemony characterizing the World Bank. The UNDP is clearly a very different institution from the World Bank. It was created in 1965 in order to function as the specialized agency for the coordination of all development assistance and technical cooperation programmes of the United Nations. St Clair's main claim is that the UNDP's conceptualizations of poverty are tied up not only with development theories, but also with the central values and principles of the UN and specific organizational changes that have taken place within the UNDP. The UNDP has evolved from an agency giving technical and scientific assistance to less developed countries to become a post-project agency, a policy agency with a significant concentration on governance issues (Brown 1999). Changes at the organizational level are parallel to changes in the UNDP's conceptual framework; in the ideas, concepts and theories that constitute the core of the institution's policies. The UNDP has seen itself as an important think-tank in the fields of development and poverty reduction, although this ambition of intellectual leadership has not been matched at the operational level, partly due to the discrepancies between the tasks given to the UNDP and the limited resources of the institution. If we compare St Clair's analysis of the UNDP with Sindzingre's chapter about poverty and the World Bank, it is interesting to hypothesize that the UNDP has become more political by default; given its lack of resources, the only viable alternative for the UNDP was precisely to become a post-project agency.

In Chapter 14, James J. Hentz takes up some of the issues which Long addressed in Chapter 3: the social construction of knowledge and patterns of dominance and subordination, but from a somewhat different perspective. His starting point is the observation that the West, and in particular the United States, controls the key multilateral institutions. However, he also acknowledges that multilateral institutions also play an autonomous role. In multilateral institutions, ideas do shape interests and thereby also policy, but the power of the policies of multilateral institutions can only effectively influence national policies if configurations of power at the domestic level can sustain such policies. Accordingly, Hentz's argument is that this demands bringing the state back in, not necessarily as an actor, but as an arena in the production and reproduction of a structure of dominant knowledge. In order for international relations theory to be able to deal with situations such as these, Hentz argues strongly for an understanding of the power of ideas that goes well beyond the constructivist–realist divide.

In the final chapter of this book (Chapter 15) the two editors return to the theoretical propositions of this chapter and seek both to evaluate them in the light of the various case studies and contributions, and to offer some concluding comments on the broader insights that can be extracted from this volume as a whole concerning the nexus between power and ideas in multilateral institutions.

Concluding remarks

All multilateral institutions were established in order to solve problems. Apart from the IMF and the WTO, the multilateral institutions we are concerned with in this book were established in order to promote development and reconstruction; first mainly in Europe after the Second World War (the World Bank) and then later, as the processes of decolonialization accelerated, in so-called Third World countries in Africa, Asia and Latin America.[5] Development was seen as a linear process towards increased prosperity and closer resemblance to Western societies, facilitated through improvements in the fields of communication and infrastructure, agriculture and industrialization. Originally, many of the issues discussed in this book fell outside their scope. But it is clear that the problem definition of development within and among multilateral institutions has changed considerably, as evidenced by the set of ideas referred to here: unemployment/unregulated economic activity (the informal sector), the environment, governance and the social fabric of society (social capital) and many others. But the question remains: how do ideas trigger new policies and transform institutional arrangements? What makes an idea attractive for multilateral institutions?

In addressing these two questions it must be recognized that multilateral institutions are intergovernmental organizations, and therefore dominated by political groups whose behaviour is subject to bounded rationality. And their survival as multilateral institutions has more to do with keeping their member governments happy than with their efficiency in a narrow sense.

> Because the states that are the masters and clients of international organizations are a heterogeneous lot, they present a similar heterogeneous *task environment* for organizational action. The *task* they jointly wish on the organizations represents the sum of possibly very different tasks each government faces at home.
>
> (Haas 1990: 55)

This means that in comparison to other social units, multilateral institutions confront certain specific challenges when faced with the demand for new ideas. Their mission is never simple and straightforward, because both their member states and other actors in their external environment disagree on the interpretation of their mission as well as on how the tasks of the mission are to be accomplished. As a result, conflict is an integral part of multilateral institutions. In social units that function under such circumstances, organizational routines and standard operating principles will be preferred to demands for change. For an idea to be attractive to multilateral institutions it must therefore be possible to adapt or distort it in accordance with already existing problem definitions of development. Moreover, according to the charters of most multilateral institutions, they were established in order to solve technical questions in a functional manner. Their programmes, projects and policies are therefore supposedly politically neutral. By defining various issue-areas and the approach to them in a technical manner, multilateral institutions seek to keep politics at bay. But these are, we assert, political institutions; and the twists and turns in the different case studies that follow can be understood only when this is recognized.

Notes

1   An 'idea' in this sense is thus distinct from a policy or programme such as import substitution, or the New International Economic Order (though it may be closely associated with one), and it is more specific than a paradigm such as Keynesianism or neoliberalism.

2   The UN Intellectual History Project is directed by Louis Emmerij, Richard Jolly and Thomas G. Weiss at the CUNY Graduate Center, and it is analysing the role of the UN in the evolution of key ideas and concepts about international economic and social development.

3   Such notions, although durable over longer periods of time, are historically determined. The order of the multilateral system has not always been represented in the same way as today, and may not be so represented in the future. It is possible in hindsight to trace the origin of such ideas, and also to identify the turning points of weakening or strengthening of them.

4   Thus collective images are not aggregations of fragmented opinions of individuals such as those compiled through surveys, but coherent mental types shaped by the *longue durée* (see Braudel 1969) and expressive of the worldviews of specific groups.

5   After the end of the cold war an additional field was opened up for the multilateral institutions when former communist countries were defined as countries in transition (i.e. from a socialist political economy to a market political economy). In this process it was widely assumed that they were in need of the guidance of the expert knowledge of multilateral institutions.

2 The development discourse in the multilateral system

Knut G. Nustad

Introduction

Development has been one of the most influential ideas of the last century, especially since the end of the Second World War. The idea is, however, beginning to lose its hegemonic position. Since the oil crisis in the 1970s, the agents in the multilateral system appear to have been more concerned with stabilizing the world market (as exemplified through the structural adjustment programmes) than actually attempting to alleviate poverty. This abandoning of faith in development has been reflected in academic writings in the field. Since the late 1980s, a group of authors writing from a poststructuralist perspective have begun to analyse development as a powerful discourse. Focus has been shifted to the way in which discourses of development help shape the reality they pertain to address, and how alternative conceptions of the problem have been marked off as irrelevant (see for example Cowen and Shenton 1995; Crush 1995; Escobar 1984; 1995a; Ferguson 1990; Sachs 1995).

This chapter has two aims: first, it is argued that the idea of development, as it has been expressed in the multilateral system, has important similarities with earlier conceptions of development. Although nineteenth-century ideas about development as formulated by the Saint-Simonians were different from the version adopted by the World Bank, there were also striking similarities: both were concerned with imposing order and forestalling social unrest, and both saw development as emanating from the agency of elites. After pointing out these constants in the idea of development, the second part of the chapter addresses the question of whether it is possible to reform the idea of development, by rethinking it as a people-driven process. This second part, then, explicitly addresses the question of the role of ideas in the multilateral system, and the relationship between the institutional framework within which the ideas are produced and the ideas themselves. The conclusion is somewhat pessimistic, and it will be argued that the structure of the multilateral system makes it unlikely that a radical new conception of development will emerge within its boundaries. Alternatives to development will have to be sought elsewhere.

Before turning to that argument, I want to introduce a dichotomy that I find a useful analytical tool. That is the distinction between the immanent and the

intentional meanings of the word 'development'. This conceptual pair, introduced by Cowen and Shenton (1995), seeks to distinguish between two *usages* of
the word development: as active intervention, as in a development project (intentional), and as a process that unfolds over time, as in 'the development of
capitalism' (immanent). It was when development in the immanent sense was
seen as creating problems that could be solved by active intervention, that intentional development was created. This historical transformation is discussed in the
next section.

Proposal for a Bank

The idea of development has a history that stretches back at least a century
before the emergence of a multilateral development system. Cowen and
Shenton's *Doctrines of Development* (1996) represents the first major attempt to
write a history of development discourse. According to them, intentional development emerged as a solution to the problems created by the immanent
development of capitalism in the first half of the nineteenth century. Capitalism
had alienated producers from the means of production, but not everybody was
reintegrated in the production process as wage-labourers. A surplus population
was therefore created and there was a real fear that it would be a basis for a revolution. It was the problem posed by this surplus population that intentional
development set out to solve.

The Saint-Simonians were, according to Cowen and Shenton, the first to
construct a doctrine of development aimed at solving the problems they believed
had been created by an immanent process of capitalism. Followers of Henri de
Saint-Simon, they are mostly known for establishing much of what later become
known as positivist thought. Auguste Comte, the most well known of the Saint-
Simonians, and the one who coined the term *positivisme*, worked for a time as
Saint-Simon's secretary, but later broke with his mentor and refused to acknowledge his obvious intellectual debt to him.

The Saint-Simonians divided human history into organic and critical epochs:
the organic epochs represented periods of stability and social equilibrium, and
the critical epochs the unstable and destructive transformations between them.
For the Saint-Simonians, capitalism was such a critical epoch that needed to be
transcended: it had succeeded in destroying the old social equilibrium but had
not led to the transformation to a new equilibrium. The problem, as they saw it,
was that the means of production were in the hands of irresponsible capitalists
driven by narrow profit-seeking. When an opportunity arose in the market, all
capital would rush to the new niche, thereby creating a competition which would
destroy all but the strongest. This, according to the Saint-Simonians, was an
enormous waste of resources. Also, the capitalist system was ineffective because
there was no overall structuring of society's resources. Thus when an industrialist
made a scientific discovery he would exploit it himself rather than make it
universally accessible. This lack of coordination led to a doubling of efforts
(Cowen and Shenton 1996).

The Saint-Simonians proposed a system of banks, headed by a national bank that would control the means of production (Cowen and Shenton 1996). These banks would then extend capital to those enterprises that were deemed worthy by those acting as *trustees* for society. In this way, the central bank would have the overall control of the rational planning of the productive efforts of the country. It would be 'the depository of all the riches, of the total fund of production, and all the instruments of work', in brief, 'of that which today composes the entire mass of individual properties' (1996: 26). The regional branches of this central bank 'would be merely extensions of the first, by means of which the central bank would keep in touch with the principal localities to know their needs and productive power' (*ibid.*). Development, then, was to come about as a result of the intentional acts of those *entrusted* with the welfare of society, here represented by the banks. *Intentional* development, Cowen and Shenton argue, was a strategy originally aimed at solving the problems perceived as stemming from the *immanent* development of capitalism. From its inception, the idea of development was intimately concerned with the creation of stability and order, and further, development was to come about as the result of the agency of elites.

The Bank realized

The system of banks proposed by the Saint-Simonians was never realized, but the idea had some striking similarities with the multilateral development system that emerged after World War II. The depression of the 1920s and 1930s had convinced the allies of the importance of reforming international trade after the war. Harry Dexter White, the first to propose a new economic world order based on a Bank, was convinced that the US needed to reconstruct Europe, and create a stable world market in the Third World to secure outlets for American products (Caufield 1996: 40). This would necessitate huge investments abroad. A World Bank, he reasoned, would be necessary to guarantee American investment. Simultaneously, Keynes was drafting a plan for a new international economic arrangement, based on a monetary union (*ibid.*). In 1945, after negotiations held at Bretton Woods, Truman signed the Bretton Woods Agreements Act, thus giving life to an institution which was an approximation of the idea suggested by the Saint-Simonians. There were important differences, though: while the original aim of the central bank suggested by the Saint-Simonians was to control all productive means of the nation, the World Bank was set up to lend money to developing countries. But the similarities were also striking, as we will see.

President Truman's inauguration speech on 20 January 1949 is commonly held to mark the beginning of modern development practice. There he held out scientific and expert knowledge as the solution to a world divided by poverty:

> We must embark on a bold new program for making the benefits of our scientific advances and industrial progress available for the improvement and growth of underdeveloped areas. For the first time in history, humanity possesses the knowledge and the skill to relieve the suffering of these people

... our imponderable resources in the technical knowledge are constantly growing and are inexhaustible. ... The old imperialism – exploitation for foreign profit – has no place in our plans. ... Greater production is the key to prosperity and peace. And the key to greater production is a wider and more vigorous application of modern scientific and technical knowledge.

(quoted in Porter 1995: 66–7)

Truman was explicit about posing development as an alternative to communism, 'the false philosophy which has made such headway throughout the world, misleading many peoples and adding to their sorrows and their difficulties' (Caufield 1996: 48). The Soviet Union had begun an industrialization process without adopting capitalism, and there was a real fear that Third World countries would follow the Soviet example. Development was in part launched to counter such a move. Some were more explicit about their political intentions than others. Rostow, for example, subtitled the work in which he introduced the stages of growth and the concept of 'take-off', *The Stages of Economic Growth: A Non-Communist Manifesto* (Rostow 1961). After spending the first half of the book outlining a universal model of the stages of economic growth, through which all countries would have to progress, he becomes explicitly political when he compares the Soviet Union with the United States:

> Russia was deeply enmeshed in its own version of a traditional society, with well-installed institutions of Church and State as well as intractable problems of land tenure, an illiterate serfdom, overpopulation on the land, the lack of a free-wheeling commercial middle class, a culture which initially placed a low premium on modern productive economic activity.
>
> (Rostow 1961: 98)

The USA, on the other hand, was the conceptual negation of this situation: 'The United States ... was born free – with vigorous, independent land-owning farmers, and an ample supply of enterprising men of commerce, as well as a social and political system that took easily to industrialization, outside the South' (*ibid.*: 98). The political dimension of development was stressed by McCloy, the first director of the World Bank. He promised that the Bank would be good for American Business, 'it would create markets for U.S. trade ... [and] stop Communism' (Caufield 1996: 53).

The Bank began with a strict focus on funding infrastructure in the countries to which it lent. This approach, which later became known as modernization theory, was most dominant in the 1950s and 1960s, but it is still influential today. Modernization theory was based on the belief that the poorer nations would eventually 'catch up' with the industrial countries. The remedy to their poverty was an infusion of what Hart (2000) has labelled the 'bourgeois package': elites, nation-states, capital, technology, democracy, education and the rule of law. Enduring underdevelopment was explained in terms of 'obstacles'[1] to this ideal, internal to the countries concerned, ideologically neutral and solvable by pragmatic means (Gardner and Lewis 1996).

The stress on the creditworthiness of the potential lenders soon created problems for the Bank, however: it ran out of countries to lend to. This happened both in its first years of operation and again in the mid-1960s. The predicament of the Bank led to a change in policy: from a concern with huge infrastructure programmes in the first decades, the Bank moved into the wider field of economic policy, directly seeking to influence the economic policy of its customers.

In the 1970s, it became increasingly clear that most of the debtor countries had no hope of repaying their loans. Money was being spent on projects that held no promise of future returns, or was stored away in international banking accounts owned by development country elites. To prevent an international crisis by defaulting loans, the so-called structural adjustment programmes of the 1980s, and their modified versions in the 1990s, sought to stabilize the situation by supplying further loans to pay off interest on debt. This went, as Caufield (1996) points out, directly against the original aim of the Bank. The granting of these programmes was, as is well known, conditional on a restructuring of economic policy in line with present neoliberal economic theory. The object of the Bank's operation has thus changed quite dramatically. From the granting of loans to large infrastructure programmes to advance modernization, present policies seem more concerned with stabilizing a world market than bringing about the long awaited development.

The original idea behind the proposal of national banks set forth by the Saint-Simonians found an expression in the World Bank in three important ways: first, the initial importance attached to investment in production; second, the implicit concern with order and stability and the forestalling of social unrest; and third, the connection of an idea of development with trusteeship. Development was from its inception intimately linked to the agency of elites: experts and scientists were given the responsibility for guiding the development of peoples seen as lacking it.

This version of development was challenged in the 1970s by a group of critics who established another important connection with Saint-Simonian development: the explicit link with capitalism. Like the Saint-Simonians, the dependency theorists saw capitalism as the problem and the cause of underdevelopment. But as we will see, their critique was trapped within the idea that they criticized. Modernization theory had created a condition, 'underdevelopment', that it set out to treat. Dependency theorists failed to question this diagnosis, instead they set out to find its real cause.

Dependency theory: bringing capitalism back in

The neo-Marxist and dependency-oriented critique of development argued that the First World 'underdeveloped' the Third World. Poverty was for them a political process, the result of an exploitative, capitalist, world economic system (Amin 1976; Frank 1967; 1978;[2] Wallerstein 1974). In the North, Andre Gunder Frank argued, the transition to capitalism separated producers from the means of production, but this process was matched by one in which they were reabsorbed into the production process as wage-labourers. This second process of reabsorption did not take place in the South (Cowen and Shenton 1996). What developed in the South as an immanent process, according to Frank, was the process of underdevelopment. The solution was therefore to withdraw from the capitalist world system.

Other writers were concerned with the futility of intentional development. They argued that capitalism was a reactionary force; the cause of poverty, not the solution, thereby echoing the Saint-Simonian critique. A capitalist development project thus became a contradiction in terms, and aid was seen as a means of perpetuating exploitative economic structures (see for example Lappé *et al.* 1980; Hayter and Watson 1985).

But this critique shows the extent to which 'development' had established itself as a hegemonic idea. It did not transcend the dichotomy of developed and underdeveloped countries; instead the theory was concerned with discovering 'the cause' of 'underdevelopment'. As Esteva puts it, 'the very discussion of the origin or current causes of underdevelopment illustrates to what extent it is admitted to be something real, concrete, quantifiable and identifiable: a phenomenon whose origin and modalities can be the subject of investigation' (1995: 11). Manzo uses Derrida's concept of logocentrism to make this point. Logocentrism denotes cases where a hierarchy is imposed on familiar dichotomies such as West and East, North and South, modern and traditional. The first term in such pairs belongs to the realm of logos, of the given, that which needs no explanation. The second term is defined solely in relation to the first, as its inferior form. It is natural, therefore, that the East should become like the West, the South like the North, the traditional like the modern (Manzo 1991: 8). According to Manzo, dependency theory, although challenging some of the modernist assumptions of modernization theory, failed to break free of logocentrism:

> Both [modernization theory and dependency theory] are trapped, albeit to varying degrees, within a modernist discourse which relies on the principles of nineteenth-century liberal philosophy, which treats the individual nation-state in the Third World as the sovereign subject of development, and which accepts the Western model of national autonomy with growth as the appropriate one to emulate. Because of this, the 'developed state' might be understood in both developmentalism and dependency as analogous to 'reasoning man' at the center of modernity, and the relationship between core/peripheral or modern/traditional states as implicitly akin to that between parent and child.
>
> (Manzo 1991: 6)

Dependency theory not only replicated the dichotomy of 'developed' and 'underdeveloped', it also reinforced the importance of elites in development. According to Hobart (1993), it replaced the idea of expert knowledge of development with an expert knowledge of underdevelopment. The underdeveloped could not understand the intricacies of the system that exploited them, and they were therefore unable to change it. The cause of underdevelopment was placed in factors external to the countries concerned. Here lay the weight of the criticisms raised against dependency theory: it subsumed local processes and distribution of wealth into a world-dominating system.

The object created by the World Bank as the single condition underlying all problems in the Third World, 'underdevelopment', was therefore further strengthened and made real by the critique of the dependency theorists. This division of the world into 'developed' and 'underdeveloped' has, however, been criticized in recent years. Through this dichotomy, Esteva (1995: 7) argues, 'two billion people ceased to be what they were, in all their diversity, and were transformed into a mirror of others' reality'. In mainstream development literature, Escobar holds:

> there exists a veritable underdeveloped subjectivity endowed with features such as powerlessness, passivity, poverty, and ignorance, usually dark and lacking in historical agency, as if waiting for the (white) Western hand to help subjects along and not infrequently hungry, illiterate, needy, and oppressed by its own stubbornness, lack of initiative, and tradition. This image also universalizes and homogenizes Third World cultures in an ahistorical fashion. Only from a certain Western perspective does this description make sense; that it exists at all is more a sign of power over the Third World than a truth about it.
>
> (Escobar 1995a: 8–9)

The conceptual pair of development and underdevelopment is therefore seen as mutually constitutive. The idea of development was established as the practice of addressing a problem, underdevelopment. It follows then, that a critique of the universal diagnosis of all the problems of the world (hunger, poverty, etc.) as resulting from underdevelopment, inevitably leads to a questioning of the idea of development itself. The question, then, is whether the idea of development can or should be salvaged. Below I will argue that a new and less dominating conception of development is unlikely to emerge within the institutional setting in which development now exists.

The role of ideas: can the idea of development be reformed?[3]

My doubt as to a fundamentally different idea of development arising within the multilateral development system is rooted in a conception of forms, and I want to pursue this argument by help of an analogy: the ideas of 'justice' and 'popular justice'. If we treat these two terms as analogous to development, as it is now practised, and a possible future true development, respectively, the exchange between Foucault and a Maoist about the possibility for reforming the present juridical system to an expression of popular justice after the revolution can clarify our thinking. Foucault argues that the judicial system cannot be adapted to a true expression of the will of the people (Foucault 1980). He points out that acts of popular justice in France and elsewhere in Western Europe have been profoundly anti-judicial, that the expressions they have been given are contrary to the very form of the court. This is because the form of the court, Foucault argues, is an expression of a bourgeois idea of justice. He asks us to consider the physical layout of a court:

> a table, and behind this table, which distances them from the two litigants, the 'third party', that is, the judges. Their position indicates firstly that they are neutral with respect to each litigant, and secondly this implies that their decision is not already arrived at in advance, that it will be made after an aural investigation of the two parties, on the basis of a certain conception of truth and a certain number of ideas concerning what is just and unjust, and thirdly that they have the authority to enforce their decision.
>
> (1980: 8)

The assumptions on which the physical layout of the court is based, that it is an expression of, is therefore in Foucault's view foreign to the very idea of a popular justice. It is this predominance of form that can be carried over to an examination of development. As the idea of popular justice involved a transformation of the old system for the Maoists, development organizations have in the last decade argued for a reformed development that has its origin in people's concerns. This bottom-up development seeks to avoid the failings of both modernization theory and dependency theory. We are presented with an image where development grows out of 'grassroots' concern, assisted and facilitated by development experts.

These theories advocate a transfer of power from experts to the people themselves. Thus the Human Development Report issued by the UNDP in 1993 states that in the face of the current challenges to development 'the best route is to unleash people's entrepreneurial spirit – to take risks, to compete, to innovate, to determine the direction and pace of development'. After informing us that this year's report has people's participation as its special focus, the authors go on to declare that 'people's participation is becoming the central issue of our time' (quoted in Mayo and Craig 1995: 2). A more radical approach is associated with the NGO sector: in addition to advocating an inclusion of the people to be developed in the process, they also argue for a transfer of power. Their task, as they see it, is one of 'empowerment'. Thus Nelson and Wright have argued that 'participation' must involve a shift in power to be more than a palliative (1995: 1). This shift involves an integration of local knowledge in the development process. In the same spirit, Edwards (1989) argues that development studies have been irrelevant to the practice of development since they are based on expert knowledge. The solution, he argues, is to deploy participatory research methods.

But using the language of participation does not in itself constitute a transferral of power (Nustad 1996; 1997). As Porter (1995) has pointed out, development since Truman has been the domain of technocrats, and with the construction of a technocratic discourse followed a denial of human agency. Hobart (1993) argues that the notion of the expert is closely related to what he calls the 'growth of ignorance' in the local population; the belief that an outside expert monopolizes the search for solutions presupposes the ignorance of the people she or he is helping.

This, then, is similar to the point made by Foucault. In the same way that the form of the court was the expression of a certain conception of justice, so the apparatus of development is, as Cowen and Shenton have pointed out, built on an idea of trusteeship. This was not a problem when intentional development was conceived as a state practice in the first half of the nineteenth century. At that time, those who saw themselves as developed self-consciously took it upon themselves to guide those who were less developed. This understanding of an elite-driven development was also carried into World Bank practices. The problem arises because the proponents of a bottom-up development argue for a rejection of trusteeship, yet this notion is embedded in the idea of intentional development. Cowen and Shenton (1996: 4) call this a tautology: 'Logically, the confusion arises out of an old utilitarian tautology. Because development, whatever definition is used, appears as both means and goal, the goal is most often unwittingly assumed to be present at the onset of the process of development itself'. According to them, to speak of 'bottom-up development' is to confuse the means and the goals of development. To assume that people have the knowledge necessary to guide their own development is to assume that they have reached the vantage point of a position that is commonly referred to as developed (*ibid.*).

The form of development therefore implies an idea of trusteeship: that someone who has the necessary vantage point guides the process of development. This is why I remain sceptical of attempts to reform the development apparatus to achieve a 'true' development from the bottom. For this reason, proposals for reform look more like recapitulations of old efforts than true attempts at reform. Culpeper (1997: 3), for example, argues that 'problems such as overpopulation, global warming and environmental collapse, mass poverty ... can only become more common in the absence of a rule-based, rule-abiding, and cooperative global community'. This community, further, 'requires viable and effective institutions to act on behalf of the common interest' (*ibid.*). As should be clear from the above, this is in effect a reinstatement of the trustee. The common interest referred to is the enlightened understanding of an elite.

The future of the idea of development

This is not a call for abandoning the academic interest in development and to bury the idea. There is, however, a need for a new focus. Discourse analysis of development has so far focused on the development apparatus, and this has indeed been an important first task. But by focusing the analysis on the practitioners of development and how they construct their object through the discourse of development, the reactions of the people to be developed are neglected (Nustad 1999). Much of this writing depicts development as a coherent system imposed on a passively receptive target population. What is left out of the account are the responses of the people thus constituted. Thus Kiely argues that 'post-development discourse tends to imply a passive Third World, simply having its strings pulled by an all-powerful West' (1999: 48). Kiely is not alone in this critique. It is rather an instance of a critique that has been levelled against discourse analysis more generally. The Italian Marxist and journalist Trombadori criticizes Foucault for a 'lack of individuating *real subjects* who are capable of determining a relation of power: in the context of the tension of a discursive formation or of a particular apparatus in which knowledge and power are intertwined', he asks, 'who struggles against whom?' (Foucault 1991: 18–19).

Everett (1997) has also argued along this line, pointing out that poststructuralists have ignored the agency of local elites as well as of 'target populations'. She introduces us to the example of a development project in Bogotá, Colombia, where the local elite used the language of 'sustainable' and 'participatory' development to secure their interests (controlling the spread of squatting near the city). She demonstrates that the residents were not fooled by this rhetoric. Instead they understood what was going on and mobilized against the development project. From this she argues that the post-structuralist critics of development 'have largely failed to reveal the agents of this repressive system. By leaving out or simplifying agency, they portray development as both more unified and more powerful than it is' (Everett 1997: 147). She agrees that those involved might misunderstand the consequences of development, but goes on to say that 'this fact does not mean that conscious actions and motivations have no role in shaping development interventions' (*ibid.*). Although she overstates the case, she has a valid point.

I believe that discourse analysis can be usefully extended by grounding it in the social reality from where the analysis began. This is also in line with Foucault's conception of power as he expressed it in *The History of Sexuality*, where power is seen as emanating 'from the bottom', as relational and intrinsic to other social relations (Foucault 1976). Instead of focusing on the institutions that have established a monopoly on the idea of development, we need to look to social groupings striving to bring about change outside the established institutional network. A good place to begin, I believe, would be the groups targeted by development projects. An examination of how people resist, undermine or use development interventions for their own ends will provide a useful contrast between institutional and popular approaches to change. Where better, then, to look for the 'power' in development than in concrete development encounters? This, indeed, is work that is being addressed at the moment (see for example Arce and Long 2000).

This does not, of course, supply an answer to those who want to salvage postdevelopment by deriving from it new ways of practising development. As I have argued, I do not see this as a task for critical development theory. This does not mean that nothing should be done about the problem which development discourses have colonized. Poverty is a very real problem. But I think it unlikely that the institutions that have so far made this problem their own, who for at least fifty years have supplied a shifting stream of solutions and remedies to it, are likely to solve it. Discourse analysis has helped clarify the problems with the development apparatus.

Where, then, is the solution to poverty going to come from? To continue the analogy with Foucault's discussion of popular justice, where the form of the court embedded an idea of bourgeois justice, it follows that an expression of justice that was truly popular would be very different in form than the court. It would probably not even be recognized as an expression of popular justice by those working within a court; and had a new court been set up, based on its principles, the form would have corrupted the content. The same, I believe, holds for development. Many critics of post-development have argued that putting one's faith in social movements is subject to both romanticism and naivety. But as I have argued, their call for practical solutions rests on the assumption that the apparatus now in place has the capacity for delivering a solution.

Notes

1 One example from anthropology is George M. Foster's (1962) description of 'the peasant image of limited good' as an obstacle to development.
2 *Dependent Accumulation and Underdevelopment* was written, according to the author in the preface, between 1969 and 1973.
3 The following two sections draw heavily on an article published in *Third World Quarterly* (Nustad 2001).

3 Contesting policy ideas from below

Norman Long

Introduction

Our lives are more than ever shaped by the global ideas and practices of multilateral organizations. The work we engage in, the incomes we receive, the commodities we consume, the goods we manufacture, the lifestyles we pursue, and the cultural identities we don, are all partly made possible, regulated and often transformed by the policy decisions, programmes, procedures and propaganda emanating from a core of multilaterals such as the World Bank, IMF and WTO, as well as – for many other people – from UN agencies such as the United Nations High Commission for Refugees (UNHCR). Much of this goes unnoticed until critical events affect us directly: for example, the laying-off of workers in industries that are no longer considered to have 'comparative advantage' in the global economy, or the failure of resource-poor rural and urban households to make ends meet in times of economic stringency and market volatility, or when the trading of certain goods is suspended because they fall below internationally defined quality standards, or when individuals are refused entry visas for a particular country due to the enforcement of strict immigration quotas. It is, of course, the poorer nations and social sectors that are disproportionately affected by these kinds of problems and processes.

Multilateral organizations such as the World Bank, IMF and WTO are constantly issuing pronouncements about their mandates, successes, promises for the future, and offering explanations for programme shortfalls, changes in direction, the continuance of controversial projects, and so forth. What is perhaps especially striking is that, despite differences in their responsibilities, operational domains and administrative make-up, they frequently convey a degree of consensus when it comes to more general goals and means of development. That is, they espouse a broadly common economic and political rationality. In the present era, this amounts to being a paid-up member of the neoliberal club of market-led development thinkers who assign the state a much reduced role in initiating and steering development, as compared to the space allotted to private enterprise and civic associations, both local and global. They are also dedicated to ordering the global economy through the establishment of formal rules for governing the commodity flows and financial exchanges that link countries, enterprises, producers and consumers. And over the last decade they have adopted the languages of 'good governance', 'participatory development' and 'empowerment' through civic associations to give greater credence to their policy agendas and to fend off their critics.

From this arise two central questions, namely where do these authoritative and influential ideas come from and how exactly are they transmitted and incorporated into the institutional thinking of specific multilaterals? Also, how do multilateral organizations share their ideas and experiences with each other in such a way as to create common ground in thinking and practice; or are these similarities only skin-deep, leaving many areas of disagreement, if not conflict?

These and other similar questions are explored in several of the contributions to this volume. On the basis of this, one can reach some empirical conclusions about the commonalities and differences between particular multilateral organizations. One should also be able to trace the origins, flows, transformation and consolidation of specific ideas and policies.

Yet, while all such dimensions and questions clearly merit systematic research, a necessary prior step involves taking a position on what exactly are ideas and how can we research them. Although seemingly a semantic problem, it is crucial that we situate the issue of ideas more generally in relation to processes of knowledge production and transformation. This lies at the heart of understanding how ideas travel, are relocated and reconstituted to acquire new meanings. The theoretical position I take – namely an actor-oriented/social constructionist view – can, I believe, offer a useful perspective on knowledge production and dissemination in respect to the policies and practices of multilateral organizations.

A further requirement for the elaboration of my argument – and one which is highly pertinent to the recent upsurge of global protest against the policies and ideologies of the World Bank, IMF and WTO – is that we must widen our perspective beyond the domains of policy making, academic research and development practice to include also all those actors (often considered 'non-experts') who are affected, directly or indirectly, by the actions of multilateral organizations and who, through their own actions, may themselves significantly mould the thinking and strategies of such organizations.

Expert domains and public policy

Discussions on the role of ideas in multilateral organizations mostly draw attention to the specific contributions made by recognized academic policy experts or schools of thought, such as 'Chicago'. The process is facilitated by the fact that organizations like the World Bank actively cultivate close links with academics (mostly economists on short- or long-term contracts) for advice on development policy and implementation measures. Of course, in the end, the particular policies and strategies adopted will have been significantly shaped by the strong presence and lobbying activities pursued by the more powerful coalitions of the US and European board members.

On the other hand, much less attention has been given to providing a full account of all the many circuits and flows of ideas that pass through and around the offices of the Bank or similar organizations. These diverse ideas are an important part of the everyday attempts of staff at various levels to accommodate the policy directives and to translate and concretize them in specific procedures and practices. It is also notable that almost nowhere do we find accounts of how everyday, non-expert or lay forms of knowledge and practice (both within and outside the Bank) influence these same activities, strategies and policies.

While several contributors to this volume attempt to fill these gaps by concentrating on the impact on multilaterals of certain key theoretical and ideological concepts, and others probe the internal politics of policy and administration, this chapter highlights the importance of considering how other actors, stakeholders and beneficiaries, engage with the ideas and actions of multilateral organizations. I am especially interested, therefore, in making the point that we also need to understand how ideas are transmitted, contested, reassembled and negotiated at the points where policy decisions and implementations impinge upon the life circumstances and everyday lifeworlds of so-called 'lay' or 'non-expert' actors.

What exactly are ideas?

In pursuing this line of inquiry, we must acknowledge the difficult conceptual problem of dealing with ideas. Some recent discussions simply attempt to resolve this empirically by distinguishing descriptively between various categories of ideas (e.g. theory, ideology, perceptions, principles, attitudes and values). Here, ideas are usually equated with mental events and refer to particular beliefs held by large numbers of people. Viewing ideas in this way leaves us with the problem of throwing together in the same basket all manner of ideas – from small atoms of information to organized worldviews or ideologies. Moreover, the stress on beliefs does not solve the problem either, because it often fails to distinguish between highly personalized beliefs that arise out of biographical experiences, and more institutionalized belief systems associated with membership of particular believer communities, whether religious or secular in nature. A bigger problem with this rag-bag of ideas and cultural beliefs is that each item is conceived of as some kind of object that can be detached from its practice and applied across the board. As I argue later, we need, through the notion of discourse, a way of contextualizing better the interconnections between ideas, beliefs and action.

Another problematic issue is the fact that interests are often seen as distinct from, rather than shaped by, ideas; they are usually assumed to come first and are considered therefore more foundational. As Laffey and Weldes (1997) rightly point out, this stance obstructs inquiries into the construction of interests. That is, interests are taken as 'given' and in isolation from ideas. Interests are non-ideational and somehow determined independently as if they come prior to ideas and beliefs. This position is often implicitly (if not explicitly) accepted by several schools of thought (both Marxist and non-Marxist). Despite the now-extensive literature on the interweaving of ideas, beliefs, interests, identities and social practice, the tendency persists (among policy makers in particular) to conceive of ideas as 'tools' to be used in the manipulation of various critical audiences (e.g. international elites, government bureaucrats and organized citizen groups).

As an alternative to these views, Greenblatt (1991) has proposed that we view ideas as 'symbolic technologies'. Although his use of this term might be questioned since it seems to resonate with the instrumentality of applied science, it does embrace the notion that ideas constitute and are constituted by forms of social action. Or, as he puts it in a more intricate way, symbolic technologies are 'most simply inter-subjective systems of representations and representation-producing practices'. Thus they are co-produced (though not necessarily 'collective') forms of practice or 'sets of capacities with which people can construct meaning about themselves, their world and their activities' (Laffey and Weldes 1997: 210). As capacities they enable and make possible certain kinds of action or 'ways of being in the world', and they also constrain or preclude other types of meaning and action. They also constitute forms of power through their capacity to produce or contest certain cultural representations. This focus on practices implies therefore that ideas cannot be conceptualized as discrete mental events or objects; nor should they be seen as separate from, but rather as constitutive and productive of, interests.

Knowledge production, dissemination and transformation

This social practice approach to understanding the production and dissemination of ideas has an affinity with discourse analysis, which concerns itself with how ideas are assembled and knitted together by means of framing and promoting (often contested) 'truths' or meanings. Both formulations emphasize the centrality of situated practical 'texts' and contexts, rather than abstract systems of thought or rationality.

Discourse analysis offers a useful way of exploring the significance of particular ideas and cultural repertoires and how they interact and interpenetrate situationally (see Long 2001: 50–3). By discourse is meant a set of meanings embodied in metaphors, representations, images, narratives and statements that advance a particular version of 'the truth' about objects, persons, events and the relations between them. Discourses produce texts – written and spoken – and even non-verbal 'texts' like the meanings embodied in infrastructure such as asphalt roads, dams and irrigation schemes, and in farming styles and technologies.

Discourses frame our understanding of life experiences by providing representations of 'reality' (often taken-for-granted) and shape or constitute what we consider to be the significant or essential objects, persons and events of our world. It is, of course, possible to have different or conflicting versions of the same discourse or incompatible discourses relating to the same phenomena. For example, discourse on development varies considerably depending upon the political or ideological positions of the organizations or actors involved.[1] As Escobar (1995b) shows in his account of the term, 'development' has its roots in the post-Enlightenment obsession for 'progress', 'social evolution' and the pursuit of 'modernity'. Following the Second World War, the idea of development as a form of social engineering, geared to designing and actively transforming so-called 'traditional' societies through the injection of capital, technology, and forms of bureaucratic organization, was added to the vocabulary of progress. This marked the beginnings of the period of massive state and international intervention in the 'developing countries', when development became largely synonymous with planned development and the aid industry. As Escobar (1995b: 213) explains:

> From this perspective, development can be best described as an apparatus that links forms of knowledge about the Third World with the deployment of forms of power and intervention. ... By means of this discourse, individuals, governments and communities are seen as 'underdeveloped' and treated as such. ... This unifying vision goes back only to the post-war period, when the apparatuses of Western knowledge production and intervention (such as the World Bank, the United Nations, and bilateral development agencies) were globalized and established their new political economy of truth.

Embodied in this history of development intervention were powerful narratives and images that represented the world in a particular way, offering a diagnosis of problems and their solutions. Although the general outcome was the widespread dissemination of 'Western' ideals and technology, resulting in post-colonial modes of exploitation, it also sowed the seeds for the emergence of counter-discourses that challenged established views and proposed alternatives to Western paradigms of development. The above text from Escobar also clearly hints at the existence of such countervailing discourses among subordinate groups, thus pointing to the significance of multiple discourses.[2]

It is important to unravel the discourses utilized in specific arenas of struggle, especially where actors vie with each other for control over resources in defence of their own livelihood concerns. As I emphasized above, it is essential to recognize that discourses (like Greenblatt's 'symbolic technologies') are not separate from social practice – hence the use of the phrase 'discursive practice' in the writings of Foucault (1972). Another critical point is that discourses may co-exist and intersect with each other, but may not always be fully elaborated in the form of abstract arguments, such as we find in formal plans or policy documents drawn up by development agencies or issued by other stakeholder groups. More often, bits and pieces of discursive text are brought together in innovative ways, or in strange combinations in particular situations, in order to negotiate or contest certain shifting points of view. Indeed, the multiplicity and fragmentation of discourses, especially in conversational and dialogical exchanges, is more often the case than the clash of well–defined opposing viewpoints, beliefs or rationalities. This also holds for the rhetorical content of official government statements drawn up by politicians and their 'spin doctors'.

On this basis one might argue that the advancement of any particular discourse depends on the strategic use of other discourses. This is illustrated, for example, by the way in which neoliberal policy statements with their stress on 'letting the market do its job' are now often accompanied by discourses that emphasize issues of 'equity', 'participation' and the problems of 'marginalization'. Indeed, structural adjustment measures have, in turn, given rise to 'social compensation' policies aimed at protecting the badly affected poorer and weaker social sectors. The World Bank, along with various national governments, has eventually been obliged to introduce the latter in order to counterbalance the growing evidence of marked decline in incomes and living conditions among these poorer sectors.

This brings out the important point that shifts in policy discourse and priorities are not simply provoked by the challenge of alternative development ideas or theories, but often by critical events that dramatically reveal the striking discrepancies that exist between the stated policy objectives/expectations and actual outcomes and social conditions. I will later return to this when I describe the new social movements that now act globally as a vanguard for change, using elaborate counter-discourses against various multilateral organizations such as the World Bank, International Monetary Fund and World Trade Organization, which they see as 'hegemonic' organizations.

Another self-evident but nonetheless crucial observation is that, although discourses may be said to 'belong' to organizations such as the state, the World Bank or the local community, it is actually specific actors (i.e. persons acting on behalf of themselves or as representatives of organizations or informal groups) who deploy them and recast them. Or, more precisely, it is the encounter between, or confrontation of actors and their ideas and values (such as farmers, extensionists, agricultural scientists, traders, international development experts and managers of transnational companies) that perpetuates or transforms particular discourses. Adopting such an actor-oriented approach is a good way to understand these processes, since it places emphasis on *situated* social practice, and provides a methodology for analysing discursive practice and development interface situations (for a full account of this theoretical perspective and its significance for development research, see Long 2001).

Escobar argues that the power of dominant representations of development is grounded in the way in which

> [t]hird World reality is inscribed with precision and persistence by the discourses and practices of economists, planners, nutritionists, demographers, and the like, making it difficult for people to define their own interests in their own terms – in many cases actually disabling them from doing so.
>
> (Escobar 1995b: 216)

An equally compelling view is that – in respect to specific issues such as sustainability, human rights, environmental pollution and health hazards – many groups (local and global) now contest expert views and are creating new discursive and political space for advancing 'counter-development' arguments (see Arce and Long 2000; Huq 2000). Actor-oriented analysis is especially appropriate for disentangling the complexities of these struggles at both the level of social action and of meanings and values.

The diffusion of development ideas – certainly from academia to the power-houses of international development policy – is often viewed as a relatively neutral, value-free process. That is, it is assumed that the most rational and convincing policy approaches are likely to be accepted. Of course this is an idealist view and ignores all the *realpolitik* of knowledge production and dissemination. As sociologists of science have forcefully shown, the diffusion and acceptance of particular ideas and findings depends crucially on the presentational skills of the scientists and the effectiveness of the organizations that they work for in transmitting and persuasively promoting ('selling') their knowledge products. As Latour's study of Pasteur and his laboratory vividly records, the right political and commissioning networks were essential for obtaining the necessary backing for the follow-through of experimentation (Latour 1988). Likewise, it seems that the 'Chicago School', the IDS (Institute of Development Studies) in Sussex, and other so-called 'blue-chip' development and research organizations have, through the close interpersonal networks of their senior staff, been able to reach out and influence policy making within multilateral circles, and concomitantly secure financial support for their own ventures from national (e.g. the Department for International Development, UK) and international bodies (predominantly the World Bank). We also witness the emergence of network consortia made up of a number of policy research units that respond to tenders for contracts put out by multilateral organizations. In addition to the institutional and network strengths that these applicants may have, each organization or group develops its own distinctive 'in-house' styles of research and policy discourse, which for the large part are geared to attract the attention of specific donors. In this respect, it has often been difficult for less well-connected groups with more open-ended and challenging agendas to make much headway. As ever, much depends on whether one can adjust one's points of view and line of work to fit in with current dominant development discourse. In this way the assessment of implemented programmes and the production of new policies are kept within established expert domains in which senior advisors play a key role.

Yet, although these political continuities are real enough, we must also note certain changing circumstances. As the years have progressed from the immediate post-Second World War situation dominated by the search for the magic formula of modernity with economic growth, to the much more insecure, risky and politically volatile situation of the 1980s onwards (marked by a realization that poverty was actually widening despite the efforts of international aid organizations, and by a concern for the deteriorating environmental situation and the negative outcomes of certain technological fixes), policy debates became anchored to how best to alleviate poverty without destroying the potential motor of development brought by technological innovation and well–placed financial injections. However, in many cases these efforts seemed to go nowhere. The reasons for this were manifold, but clearly linked to the persistence of an already established/entrenched group of experts and a well–organized, behind-the-scenes manipulative lobby of powerful post-industrial countries. Thus, roughly the same sets of interests guided the major policy shifts and the funding of development initiatives.

However, the world is now affected by the impact of globalization, rapid developments in information technologies and electronic communication systems and the advent of digitally organized internet facilities. While the powerful blocs of advanced capitalist states have been able to use these technologies to their best advantage, at the same time the internet has given life to a new sense of global communities, and has thus given local and civil-based organizations the chance to put their own points of view more forcefully and to enter the policy debate. This is combined with the use of more aggressive tactics for getting people onto the streets to engage in direct protest and confrontation with the organizations responsible for international agreements on environment, trade and finance. Here we should note the Seattle meeting of the World Trade Organization and the Prague meeting of the World Bank and the IMF. These street protests and attempts to force multinational organizations to debate with NGOs and other grassroots organizations and single-interest groups such as Greenpeace, together signify a new more global and heterogeneous people's movement, not based on existing recognized political bodies with specific aims and mandates, but on a more diffuse and self-organizing and transforming *modus operandi*. That these global counter-development movements are real in their actions and effects is seen by the various U-turns made recently by some of the world bodies. Note, for example, the somewhat surprising admission by the World Bank that structural adjustment and similar measures have not been able to address effectively the persisting patterns of poverty and the widening gap between rich and poor in the global scene. But whether this will result in concrete policy and implementation measures remains to be seen.

This emphasizes the point that discourses and strategies from below can be brought to bear on multilateral organizations. However, we must acknowledge that in fact there have always been counter-development discourses. Sometimes these have been couched in very general terms, such as questioning certain core values and practices of modernity (often backed by recourse to traditional counterposed views and institutional forms). At other times they have been rooted in more localized experiences of the effects of particular development policies and programmes of intervention. Hence, there has always been an ongoing critique of development practices and institutional ordering, as local people have sought space for change, sometimes aligning with local development workers and NGOs to exert pressure on the agencies of the state.

Before proceeding further with the discussion of counter-development processes, let me first provide a sketch of the centrality of knowledge and the role of ideas in the sociology of development. Through this I hope to provide a general rationale for considering the impact of non-expert lay knowledge and ideas on expert domains, bearing in mind the interest we have in addressing multilateral institutional ideas and practices. In order to do this we need to conceptualize the transmission and transformation of ideas and certain modes of discourse. I concentrate upon developing an actor-oriented perspective on this. After this I will illustrate briefly how one applies this to an extreme case of externally driven development that presents a set of major contradictions for dominant development thinking.

The rise of knowledge issues in the sociology of development

From about the early 1960s onwards, a number of social scientists interested in the theorization of uneven development, the transfer of technology, and the significance of cultural and institutional factors, turned towards modernization and, later, political economy models for an explanation of the dynamics of social transformation. While these approaches provided some important new insights into issues of class, 'traditional' versus 'modern' values, the role of the state and international capital, and thereby touched upon questions of power and knowledge, they failed to recognize the fundamental significance of 'expert' knowledge or science in the social construction of society and social change.

Knowledge and science were part of both modernization and neo-Marxist discourses, but they were perceived primarily as 'resources' and as part of the 'tool-kit' of a 'modernity' project aimed at isolating the central driving forces and mechanisms of social change.

Later, sociologists concerned with issues of popular education argued that 'external' forms of knowledge needed translation in order to become effective in local development. These translation tasks were the mission of so-called 'popular promoters', animators, 'change agents', and the like, whose assignment was linked to the overall goal of using knowledge for transforming society in an effort to achieve greater equity and political participation (see for example Freire 1970; Galjart 1980; Fals-Borda 1981). In this way the worlds of research and development practice became interconnected through the discussion of how to organize and use knowledge and science appropriately.

More recently, the sociology of knowledge has embraced a social constructivist perspective which provides fresh insights into how 'expert' and everyday forms of knowledge relate to development processes. For instance, Knorr-Cetina (1981), studying 'practical epistemologies' within science, has shown how expert scientific knowledge is produced and re-created not simply in the laboratories of research organizations, but also in the canteens and corridors of scientific establishments. Parallel views within the field of development studies have been expressed by Robert Chambers (1983) and Paul Richards (1985), who argue that the practical everyday knowledge of ordinary people can enrich 'science' and improve development practice. Thus two rather different research strands converge in insisting that rather than exploring the nature and epistemology of knowledge in an abstract and formalist manner, we should open the path to a re-evaluation of science-in-the-making. Such a perspective takes full cognizance of social actors, their values and understandings in the construction of knowledge, and in the scientific design for alternative or competing 'projects of society'. It also takes a stand against treating science and everyday knowledge as being onto-logically different.

The demystification of science through the ethnographic study of scientific practice and everyday knowledge brings into perspective a whole new set of images and representations of how the social world is constructed and orga-nized. From this new standpoint, a fresh panorama unfolds where the interplay and interfaces of local people and scientists become central to the production of more acceptable and 'human' solutions aimed at countering the 'supremacy' and 'excesses' of modern technological and economic development.

These various attempts to study and analyse expert science, scientists' interests, and people's knowledge and aspirations opened the way to detailed ethnographic studies on how knowledge is created and used by all sorts of actors in their prac-tical attempts to cope with issues of livelihood and planned intervention by outsiders. But the creation and transformation of knowledge, we argue, can only effectively be studied and analysed through an appreciation of how people – whether peasants, bureaucrats or scientists – build bridges and manage critical knowledge interfaces that constitute the points of intersection between their diverse lifeworlds (Arce and Long 1987; Long 1989). This requires paying close attention to the practices of everyday social life, involving actor strategies, manoeuvres, discourses, speech games, and struggles over identity networks and social imagery, since only in this way can one tease out the intricacies of how knowledge is internalized, used and reconstructed by the different actors. It is in this way that an actor-oriented perspective on knowledge and knowledge encoun-ters can help us go beyond earlier social constructivist views which tend to suggest a dichotomized representation of different forms of knowledge (i.e. in terms of 'modern science' versus 'people's science', 'external' versus 'local' knowledge).

This new focus concentrates upon exploring how practices are organized cognitively and enacted in everyday performances, not as self-contained cultural or institutional systems of social thought that frame or guide behavioural response. An actor-oriented perspective refuses to draw sharp distinctions between different kinds of knowledge on the basis of their origin, pedigree and so-called authority. Knowledge is generated and transformed not in the abstract but in the everyday contingencies and struggles that constitute social life. It is not given by simple institutional commitments or assumed sources of power and authority, but rather is an outcome of interactions, negotiations, interfaces and accommodations between different actors and their lifeworlds.

The lack of commonality in the concept of knowledge (i.e. the contradictions, inconsistencies, struggles and negotiations that it implies) means that there are many different intersecting knowledge frames – some more diffuse and frag-mented than others – that intersect in the construction of social arrangements and discursive practices. These 'multiple realities' may mean many things and entail different rationalities at the same time to the actors involved, but somehow they are contained and interact within the same social context or arena. It is these knowledge encounters and interactions that generate locally situated knowledge.

Knowledge as an encounter of horizons

By the late 1980s, researchers began to pinpoint certain critical limitations in the linkage approach, or what has been designated 'the transportational paradigm', to understanding knowledge processes. The model assumes that the process of knowledge dissemination/utilization involves the transfer of a body of knowledge from one individual or social unit to another, rather than adopting a more dynamic view that acknowledges the joint creation of knowledge by both disseminators and users. This latter interpretation depicts knowledge as arising from a fusion of horizons, since the processing and absorption of new items of information and new discursive or cognitive frames can only take place on the basis of already existing stocks of knowledge and evaluative modes, which are themselves reshaped by the communicative experience. Moreover, although knowledge dissemination/creation is in essence an interpretative and cognitive process, entailing the bridging of the gap between a familiar world and a less familiar (or even alien) set of meanings, knowledge is built upon the accumulated social experience, commitments and culturally acquired dispositions of the actors involved.

Hence,

> communicative action is not only a [cognitive] process of reaching understanding; in coming to an understanding about something in the world, actors are at the same time taking part in interactions through which they develop, confirm, and renew their memberships in social groups and their own identities. Communicative actions are not only processes of interpretation in which cultural knowledge is 'tested against the world'; they are at the same time processes of social integration and socialisation.
>
> (Habermas 1987: 139)

Processes of knowledge dissemination/creation simultaneously imply, therefore, several interconnected elements: actor strategies and capacities for drawing upon existing knowledge repertoires and absorbing new information; validation processes whereby newly introduced information and its sources are judged acceptable and useful or contested; and various transactions involving the exchanges of actors involved in the production, dissemination and utilization of knowledge.

Such cases lend support to the argument that so long as we conceptualize the issues of knowledge dissemination/utilization simply in terms of linkage concepts, without giving sufficient attention to human agency and the transformation of meaning at the point of intersection between different actors' life-worlds, and without analysing the social interactions involved, we will have missed the significance of knowledge itself. Our guiding notions, I suggest, must be *dissonance* not consonance, *discontinuity* not linkage, and *transformation* not transfer of meaning. Knowledge is also multi-layered (there always exists a multi-plicity of possible frames of meaning) and *fragmentary* and *diffuse* rather than unitary and systematized. Not only is it unlikely, therefore, that different parties (such as farmers, extensionists and researchers) would share the same priorities and parameters of knowledge, but one would also expect 'epistemic communi-ties' (i.e. those that share roughly the same sources and modes of knowledge) to be differentiated internally in terms of knowledge repertoires and application. Therefore engineering the creation of the conditions under which a single knowledge system (involving mutually beneficial exchanges and flows of infor-mation between the different actors) could emerge seems unattainable; and, if indeed one did succeed, this would be at the expense of innovativeness and adaptability to change, both of which depend upon the diversity and fluidity of knowledge rather than on integration and systematization.

Discontinuities and accommodations at knowledge interfaces

In order to explore these issues in more depth it is necessary to develop an analysis of interface situations. I define a social interface as a critical point of intersection between different social systems, fields or levels of social order where structural discontinuities, based upon differences of normative value and social interest, are most likely to be found. A similar idea is conveyed by Rörling (1988) when he suggests that interface is not simply a linkage mechanism but rather the 'force field' between two organizations. Interface studies are essentially concerned with the analysis of the *discontinuities* in social life. Such discontinuities are characterized by discrepancies in values, interests, knowledge and power. Interfaces typically occur at points where different, and often conflicting, life-worlds or social fields intersect. More concretely, they characterize social situations (what Giddens calls 'locales') wherein the interactions between actors become oriented around the problem of devising ways of bridging, accommo-dating to, or struggling against each other's different social and cognitive worlds. Interface analysis aims to elucidate the types of social discontinuities present in such situations and to characterize the different kinds of organizational and cultural forms that reproduce or transform them. Although the word 'interface' tends to convey the image of some kind of two-sided articulation or confronta-tion, interface situations are much more complex and multiple in nature.

In order to accomplish this, it becomes essential for actors to win the struggles that take place over the attribution of specific social meanings to particular events, actions and ideas. Looked at from this point of view, particular develop-ment intervention models (or ideologies) become strategic weapons in the hands of the agencies charged with promoting them (Long and van der Ploeg 1989).

This process is illustrated by van der Ploeg's (1989) analysis of how small-scale producers in the Andes succumb to 'scientific' definitions of agricultural development. He shows that, although peasants have devised perfectly good solutions to their own production problems (here he is concerned with potato cultivation), their local knowledge gradually becomes marginalized by the type of scientific knowledge introduced by extensionists. The former, that is, becomes superfluous to the model of 'modern' production methods promoted by 'the experts', and development projects become a kind of commodity monopolized and sold by experts who exert 'authority' over their subjects. In this way the rules, limits and procedures governing the negotiation between state agents and farmers and the resources made available are derived (in large part) from external interests and organizations. Hence, although it is possible to depict the relations between Andean peasants and outside experts or state officials in terms of a history of distrust and dependency, science and modern ideologies of development eventually come to command such a major influence on the outcomes of dealings with cultivators that they effectively prevent any exchange of knowledge and experience. This creates what van der Ploeg calls 'a sphere of ignorance' whereby cultivators are labelled 'invisible men' in contrast to the 'experts' who are visible and authoritative.

Such processes, however, are by no means mechanical impositions from the outside. They necessarily entail negotiation over concepts, meanings and projects that are internalized to varying degrees by the different parties involved. Thus the ability of extensionists to transform the nature of agricultural practice is premised on two elements: their skills in handling interface encounters with peasants; and the ways in which the wider set of power relations (or 'chain of agents') feeds into the context, giving legitimacy to their actions and conceptions, and defining certain critical 'rules of the game'. Counter-balancing this is the fact that cultivators, too, assimilate information from each other, as well as from 'external' sources, in an attempt to create knowledge that is in tune with the situations they face.

The final part of this chapter discusses the contradictions that arise over coca production in Bolivia, where the interests and discourses of development promoted by government and US aid severely conflict with the livelihoods, social priorities and development language of local producers.

Illegal crops in an age of global consumption: counter-development processes[3]

In Bolivia during the mid-1970s, a huge wave of people migrated to the Chapare region, following the collapse of the mining industry in which many thousands had been gainfully employed. This coincided with the increase in demand for coca leaves essential to the production of cocaine for illegal international consumption. It is no exaggeration to say that market-led development was extremely effective in generating the production of the crop in Bolivia. Coca leaves have now become the economic icon that links local producers, entrepreneurs and an ever-increasing market of consumers of illegal substances in the United States and Europe. It is now estimated that 80 per cent of the total of Bolivian coca production originates from the Chapare region, of which 90 per cent ends up as raw material for cocaine production (Lohman 1992).

From about 1985 onwards, the region became the target for a massively funded drug eradication programme aimed at persuading farmers to give up coca production in favour of what was called 'alternative development'. In this way, the Bolivian government, led by US military advisors, intervened in the region and declared 'a war against drugs'. With this came militarization, violation of human rights, and attempts to dictate the form of local development – a trilogy pitted against local coca farmers, who endeavour to resist this criminalization of their crop practices.

A further component of this language of 'alternative' development is the way it represents development primarily in terms of investment by outside private companies interested in promoting agro-industry based on tropical fruits. Thus Chapare farmers are relegated to being 'objects' of development instead of co-participants in a process of socio-economic change. In building this representation, the Bolivian Agency for Alternative Development and USAID (Rasnake and Painter 1989) have set about 'cleaning-up and legalizing' local markets through destroying illegal crops. They have also marketed the region to potential investors through the use of promotional films that picture how well equipped the area is for drinking water, electricity, roads, airports and a strong local culture that respects private property. It is paradoxical that much of this infrastructure, as well as the images of progress that it conjures up, is a direct and indirect outcome of the production of coca for the global drug trade.

Intersecting with this agro-export discourse are other alternatives to coca production. One advocates the transformation of the whole region into an area for tropical eco-tourism directed primarily at environmentalists and adventure tourists from the better-off northern countries. Another is more radical – the 'zero option'. This proposes that the Bolivian government should buy out all farmers in the area and turn the region into a national park for conservation purposes. Again, private investment is envisaged as providing the backbone for such measures.

Although some of these proposals try to deal with farmers' activities and commitments, their general tenor is rhetorical: that is, they represent political-cum-linguistic attempts to control the escalating influence of coca production, which remains number one on the Bolivian political agenda (see Leons and Sanabria 1997). They also make the assumption that Chapare farmers are either conservative or reactionary, and have no intention of legalizing their agro-production practices (Jones 1991). Hence, there is no acknowledgement that farmers have lived through the high financial and other costs of structural adjustment policies and have constantly been in search of new, economically viable crops. Farmers complain that in meetings with development experts officials outnumber them and local initiatives are always ignored. In one instance, this led to a group of farmers compiling their own database on the economic returns of alternative systems of production so that they might weigh up their own options. They simply did not trust the way these were being presented in the official language of development (Schoute 1994: 94).

Coca farmers reject the assumption that in itself eradication can contribute to local development; and they do not perceive themselves as accountable to, or dependent on, the drug barons of the cocaine industry. Instead they define themselves as the 'innocent' party, and see the narcotic problem as the responsibility of Western society and culture, and the result of the persisting global market for drugs. Thus, in local discourse, coca production is not synonymous with drug trafficking. Coca is a valuable commodity that allows them to sustain a diversified cropping system that also includes manioc, maize, fruits and animals. Although non-coca farming occupies a large amount of land and labour, it is the coca crop that provides them with the necessary income to meet their consumption requirements and to build up capital within the household.

These social and political contradictions in the Chapare region provide a somewhat different picture of the language and practices of development than the conventional model. Local farmers here have achieved a degree of economic progress and political voice through the production of an illegal crop, and in so doing have reshaped the ways in which the people of Chapare relate to global markets and the nation-state. Their views are also heard beyond the IMF, just as the Zapatistas of Chiapas, Mexico, and their voice clearly expresses a counter-development discourse. In their language and representations, the people of Chapare are negotiating their participation in the nation-state as citizens, as well as positioning themselves within global drug networks. This has been accomplished through the technological modernization of farming practices (of an illegal crop) coupled with new ways of using existing political and cultural discourses. From an orthodox development perspective, this situation is problematic, since the practices of local farmers have 'de-centred' the legitimacy and legality of the Western institutional language of development. In its place, they have constructed a discourse that combines the use of traditional 'idioms' with the 'need' to exploit the opportunities that are offered by the global market. Thus, local farmers seek political recognition and respect for their local translations of the signs and codes emanating from the global, neoliberal language of development.

In April 2001, the government of Bolivia and coca growers – after months of struggle – reached an agreement ending three weeks of protests that blocked the major highways and threatened the government's stability. The coca growers won concessions to improve working conditions and loan terms for small producers, peasant farmers and teachers (*New York Times* 2001). And by mid-2002, they were involved in supporting the leader of the *cocalero* campaign in a narrowly defeated bid for the Bolivian presidency.

This Bolivian case, then, highlights the need to explore the diverse discursive manifestations of modernity and how these legitimize various linkages that connect local knowledge, technology, nature, markets, violence, authority and power with newly emerging global modernities.

Conclusion

This chapter has explored the origins, powers and interests associated with specific policy ideas. The argument was developed in relation to two interconnected issues. The first concerned how ideas within the field of development policy and practice are given shape over time; and the second, with how the sociology of knowledge itself has struggled to come to grips with the complexities involved in these processes.

I started the discussion by indicating how the policy ideas and development discourses of multilateral organizations are shaped by those who have direct access to the policy arena – e.g. development policy practitioners, academics, national governments and multilateral administrative personnel. Yet it soon emerged that a much wider range of actors was implicated. These included a rapidly expanding body of 'lay' persons and civic organizations hell-bent on contesting the specific policy measures and decision making constituencies of multilateral organizations, as well as those locally 'targeted' or affected actors at the implementation end of the process. This was a theme that would reappear at central points in the argument. Indeed, I argued that the understanding of knowledge processes in general, as well as those associated with the generation of particular ideas and frameworks of thinking/acting, rested upon a close-up analysis of the dynamics of 'knowledge interfaces' made up of a multiplicity of actors and divergent (and often conflicting) interests, values and meanings. I also pointed to the usefulness of discourse analysis for highlighting the nature and significance of ongoing struggles between 'mainstream' development discourses and various forms of 'counter-development'.

These concerns led me in the last part of the chapter to provide an account of what, for many, may be regarded as an extremely atypical and ugly example of the kind of development promoted by Western aid donors and multilateral organizations. Yet, from another angle, the Chapare coca/cocaine production region of Bolivia may be considered as one of the most successful applications of the neoliberal idea of market-led development. By growing and processing this crop, the local population has found a way of generating enough income for its present and future needs, as well as for investing in local infrastructure and services. But, alas, this crop is earmarked as 'illegal' and so must be eliminated and substituted by 'alternative' forms of production that, actually, bring far fewer benefits. Also paradoxically, the combined efforts of the 'war on drugs' mounted by a Bolivian military force backed by US 'advisors', and the development aid package supplied by several international and multilateral organizations, has galvanized and disseminated 'counter-development' discourse and measures. Thus it has contributed to a countrywide movement against the Bolivian government aimed at extracting a number of critical social policy concessions. This process has now reached a peak, and we must wait and see how the government and its multilateral partners will attempt to resolve these issues. And we will have to see to what extent significant and longer-term changes take place in the thinking and practice of those multilaterals involved. Either way, the case clearly illustrates how discontinuities of interests, values and knowledge play a role in challenging existing power relations and generating new modes of political agency.

This chapter has also highlighted four further crucial points for analysing policy ideas:

1   the need to differentiate the process in terms of the types of struggle that take place in different arenas and at different levels of the political process;
2   the importance of the existence of multiple, but overlapping, discourses on development;
3   the significance of the interplay of 'expert' and 'lay' knowledge and the social relations that underpin them; and
4   the necessity of grounding understanding in terms of situated social practices rather than ideal-typical representations.

Notes

1   Building upon Foucault's perspective on discourse and knowledge/power, several works have explored the hegemonic nature of narratives, images and discourses of development organizations and ideologies. See for example Ferguson (1990), Hobart (1993b) and Escobar (1995b).
2   In a recent lecture presented at the Congreso Internacional de Latinoamericanistas en Europe (CEISAL) in Amsterdam, Escobar argues for the central importance of the notion of 'counter-development' for understanding multiple modernities. He draws upon Arce and Long (2000).
3   This section is derived from Chapters 2 and 10 in Arce and Long (2000).

4 The informal sector

Biography of an idea

Desmond McNeill

Year after year the Annual Report of the Uganda Protectorate has referred, under the heading of industry, to a few large undertakings directly sponsored by the Government. At the same time the multifarious development of furniture workshops, soap mills, tire retreading plants, bakeries and brickfields has gone on largely unnoticed. An official who was once asked about Kampala's industrial area said: '*There are no industries there – only a lot of furniture works, bakeries, maize mills and soda water factories.*'

(Elkan 1959, quoted in Livingstone 1974, italics by author)

Introduction

The term 'informal sector' entered the development vocabulary almost thirty years ago, to refer to the numerous and variegated activities engaged in by people in poor countries which fell outside the official categories of what counted as employment. The idea has had a long and productive life, leading to a much richer understanding of the daily productive lives of a substantial proportion of the world's urban population, and significantly modifying attitudes and policies towards them. In the early 1970s, the context, in terms of development research and policy, was a concern with the relationship between poverty and employment. The *conceptual* difficulty of understanding poverty – and especially urban poverty – in terms of existing categories and theories (modernization/dualism) was here closely related to the *policy* challenge of reducing poverty.

In this chapter I present a critical biography of this idea, which I hope will serve a more significant purpose than the mere chronicling of an important concept. For not only is the idea interesting in itself, but I suggest there are parallels between the fate of this and other more recent ideas which have influenced development policy – such as governance, or social capital – which are still in their infancy. By studying this particular one, in a structured and critical manner, we may learn something about others, and how best to deal with them. Furthermore, the history of this one idea gives us an insight into the history of development research and policy over this period, which may cast light on recent conceptual developments. The chapter falls into three sections: first, a brief 'biography' divided into historical periods; second, the presentation of a simple analytical schema; third, some brief reflections on trends in development research and policy which have both influenced, and been influenced by, the concept of the informal sector.

A great deal has already been written about the term 'the informal sector', and at least two annotated bibliographies have been prepared (Danesh 1991; Feldmann and Ferretti 1998). On the basis of these materials, supplemented by interviews with a few of the key actors, and my own experience in the early years, I have prepared the following 'biography'.

Biography

Creation, 1972–74

The term itself was coined at a conference on Urban Unemployment in Africa, held at the Institute of Development Studies (IDS), University of Sussex, 12–16 September 1971, at which Keith Hart, an anthropologist, delivered a paper entitled Informal Income Opportunities and Urban Employment in Ghana.[1] The concept fitted within an important contemporary debate on employment and growth and met a very specific need among some economists at IDS who were then involved in a collaborative series of studies with the International Labour Organization (ILO) under their World Employment Programme.

In the 1950s and 1960s the 'accelerated growth' model dominated development planning: industrial expansion would result in increased wage-sector employment, and the benefits would trickle down throughout society. In the process of modernization migrant workers from rural areas would gradually become absorbed into the city. But by the beginning of the 1970s it was apparent that the theory did not match the reality, for rapid economic growth had been of little or no benefit to perhaps a third of the population of underdeveloped countries. 'Although the average per capita income of the Third World has increased by 50% since 1960, this growth has been very unequally distributed among countries, regions within countries and socio-economic groups' (Chenery *et al.* 1974: xiii).

This quote is from the influential *Redistribution with Growth*, a joint study by the World Bank's Research Center and the Institute of Development Studies at the University of Sussex. These two, together with the International Labour Organization (ILO), through the World Employment Programme, played a central role in the creation and adoption of the informal sector idea. Applied researchers (who were mainly economists) here worked in collaboration with research-minded aid bureaucrats (also mainly economists). In the formulation of what came to be known as the *IBRD/IDS Redistribution with Growth* model, the earlier country missions in Colombia (1970), Sri Lanka (1971) and Kenya (1972), all headed by IDS personnel, was very influential.[2]

It was in the Kenya Report of the ILO that Keith Hart's term 'informal sector' was first officially used. The term replaced others, of which the most current seems to have been the 'working poor'. A few of the people on the (very large) visiting team undertaking the Kenya study made a visit to a poor neighbourhood of Nairobi. Here, with an American anthropologist as guide, they observed the large numbers of people and variegated types of activity which came to be called the 'informal sector'. Until then the focus of this and similar studies had been on what later became known as 'formal' employment, ignoring the activities of a large proportion of the working population.

The ILO played a particularly active role in this period in stimulating international debate on issues of poverty and employment. Their Employment Policy Convention, no. 122, 1964, had committed governments to adopt 'active full employment policies', and in 1969 the director-general of ILO launched the ILO World Employment Programme.[3] This set out to analyse employment problems and devise strategies, and to this end a series of country studies was undertaken, each with its own terms of reference, but within an overall brief to evolve employment-orientated strategies of development. Despite their limitations, these ILO country missions played a crucial role in the development of a new approach to the employment problem, with wide-ranging implications and repercussions for future research.

The ILO World Employment Programme also conducted a series of city studies, complementing the country studies, to identify the causes and extent of urban poverty. These studies contained recommended measures for increasing employment in major urban areas.

In the years that followed, there continued to be major disagreements in relation to both analysis and prescription (and indeed definition), which will be elaborated upon later in this chapter. The term itself – the 'informal sector' – was at the centre of this sometimes heated debate, but the very fact that the term was shared by all those concerned is evidence of the significant role that it played.

Adoption and proliferation, 1975–80

The late 1970s can, I suggest, be described as a period of adoption and proliferation of the idea, as a basis for both theoretical debate and policy formulation.[4] And these two arenas – of research and policy – interacted, with some people playing an active role in both. The ILO sponsored, or was in some way involved in, a long series of studies which are well summarized by Harold Lubell, one of the central actors, in his comprehensive review:

> Chapters on the informal sector were included in several of the urbanization and employment city monographs ... and a dozen special case studies were carried out in Africa, Asia and Latin America using, as a common element, a questionnaire designed by S.V. Sethuraman.
>
> (Lubell 1991: 22)

From 1974 to 1977, the ILO Urbanization and Employment Research Project undertook studies in Africa (five); in Asia (three); and in Latin America (three). In addition, Lubell refers to many other studies undertaken in Africa, Asian and Latin America extending over a longer period. Lubell makes some revealing comments on these surveys, referring not only to 'a variety of types of informal sector behaviour' but also 'a variety of perceptions of it by academic and other researchers'.

> Most of the field surveys have been carried out in Africa whereas most of the theorising has been done in Latin America. The approach in Africa has been largely pragmatic. The casual empiricism of the ILO Kenya Employment Mission has been reinforced and amplified by the considerable number of systematic field surveys cited above.
>
> (Lubell 1991: 64)

The point Lubell makes here about field surveys in Africa and theory in Latin America hints at a tension between the two to which I shall return below. He comments also on the 'remarkable resemblance' between informal sector activities across very different countries and continents, which also raises rather basic methodological questions. Does this similarity in findings arise because the concept is so loosely defined? (see below). On the basis of this overview, Lubell summarizes five similarities, including:

* informal sector activities absorb between 40 and 60 per cent of the urban labour force of many of the Third World cities studied;
* informal sector enterprise heads often earn more than the official minimum wage or the average wage in the formal sector; employees usually earn less than the official minimum wage;
* backward linkages to formal sector suppliers of inputs are strong; forward linkages are generally limited to households and other informal sector producers.

The second point dispels the common *a priori* assumption that 'informal' necessarily implies poor. It is also apparent that linkages with the formal sector are complex and varied. This issue was central in theoretical debate at this time, between what may be termed the reformists and the Marxists, a debate which drew partly on *a priori* and partly on empirical findings. In brief, were these links mutually beneficial or exploitative?

Lubell draws another contrast: between radical and critical researchers from academia, and more conventional and constructive researchers associated with aid agencies:

> Most of the studies sponsored by the international and bilateral aid agencies have focused on the potentially viable micro-enterprises that constitute George Nihan's 'modern informal sector'. Some of the university-generated studies, particularly those by the radical economists, have on occasion been more concerned with the ostensibly marginal activities such as garbage reprocessing and lottery ticket selling.
>
> (Lubell 1991: 64)

In parallel with these studies, and the policy debate associated with them, there was a lively debate also in academic circles, manifested in an increasing number of articles, and later books and doctoral theses. The former appeared both in multidisciplinary journals of development studies (such as *World Development*, e.g. Special Issue 1978), and development planning (such as *Regional Development Dialogue*), and also (though generally later) in mono-disciplinary journals, such as *Urban Anthropology* and the *Cambridge Journal of Economics*.

But the debate concerning the informal sector led also, from the mid-1970s, to both critique and resistance, primarily from two contrasting perspectives (this in addition to continuing debate concerning definitions – see below). First, among researchers, there was a radical political economy approach. Summarized as 'informal sector or petty commodity production?' this centred on the question of whether the relations between the formal and informal sector were exploitative or not.[5] A second, and very different critique, came from some policy makers in developing countries who were resistant to the implications of the debate, especially insofar as it was linked to the broader 'basic needs' approach.[6]

Although both the concept of basic needs and the informal sector were associated with the World Employment Programme (WEP) of ILO, the former was much more controversial. An interesting insight into this conflict may be gained from reading the account of Walter Galenson, who worked at the ILO and was critical both of the research undertaken, and of Louis Emmerij, Director of the ILO employment programme.

He is especially critical of the WEP conference in 1976. 'The US government representative objected to the implication that the conference ... was committing the ILO to support the New International Economic Order' (Galenson 1981: 181). 'A draft document designed to serve as the basis for discussion at the Conference was drawn up by the Office. ... A subtle shift of emphasis away from employment and towards the fulfilment of unspecified basic needs was (also) noted' (*ibid.*). US officials had a meeting at the Department of Labour to discuss the draft. 'The meeting was a heated affair, with the US participants denouncing the draft on many counts'. The last of the eight objections was: 'There was Marxist language in the draft that had no place in such a document' (*ibid.*: 182).

According to Galenson, the US view was in a minority at the 1976 conference, but a conference of foreign ministers in 1978 concluded that

> a basic needs approach at an international level would inevitably imply the imposition of global priorities on developing countries, thereby not only distorting the allocation of domestic resources of the latter but also perpetrating [sic] their technological dependence on the developed countries.
>
> (*ibid.*: 189)

A more measured assessment of the conference is to be found in Emmerij and Ghai (1976: 202).

But the concept of the informal sector was less controversial than basic needs, and it continued to have a significant and increasing impact on urban policy and programmes in developing countries in this period. Here, it is worth referring especially to the experience of the World Bank. In September 1973, the President of the World Bank, Robert McNamara, made a famous speech in Nairobi which signalled a major assault on poverty. But the emphasis was almost totally on rural poverty. Some in the World Bank were concerned that a major proportion of the world's poor lived in cities, like Calcutta, which were in danger of being forgotten. An Urban Poverty Task Force was established in 1974 to respond to this challenge, and a new Urban Development Division was set up. Missions were sent to a number of Third World cities to define urban projects to be funded by the World Bank, the first being in Dakar, Senegal. The main focus was on housing and infrastructure. The standard approach was to promote 'site-and-service housing', and later also 'slum and shanty upgrading'. Here they were much influenced by the ideas of the architect John Turner and others.

Although the concept of the informal sector was referred to in this work, employment was not a significant focus – at least in the early urban missions. An influential working paper – 'The Task Ahead for the Cities of the Developing Countries' – was published in 1975, and took up the issue of the urban labour market. It described the dualistic distinction between 'formal' and 'informal' sectors as simplistic (Beier *et al.* 1975: 51, 52). In this year also McNamara committed the Bank to an increased emphasis on urban development. The Bank was at this time collaborating closely with ILO, as noted above, and supported major efforts on urban research and policy, but it was only in the late 1970s that the Urban Division of the Bank incorporated its ideas on employment into urban programmes. On this topic, there was overlap with the responsibilities of the Industry Department. It is notable that the policies of this department towards small and medium enterprises (SMEs) changed substantially at this time, culminating in February 1978 with the publication of a policy paper entitled 'Employment and Development of Small Enterprises'. 'Following the new initiative, from July 1977 through June 1984, the World Bank lent US$1.97 billion in 63 projects to support SMEs' (Lewitsky 1985). It may be significant to add, however, that in the review by the Industry Department from which this quotation is taken, the term 'informal sector' is never used. It was used in the Bank for describing, and to some extent also analysing the urban economy, and thus had some influence on the choice and design of projects, but its impact was limited.

Mainstreaming, 1980s

In the 1980s the concept was very widely used, and by the end of the decade it is safe to say that the term 'informal sector' was fully within the mainstream in the worlds of academia and policy, appearing both in textbooks of development studies[7] and the plans of national and international agencies.

Within academia one can trace the debate, beyond development studies into different disciplines. The multidisciplinary journal *World Development* played a key role in this debate, as in many others. The *IDS Bulletin* also published extensively on the topic – understandably in view of the major role played by this institute. These were especially important in the early years, but others which were less policy-oriented also took up the term: such as the *Journal of Development Studies*, the *Journal of Modern African Studies* and *Economic Development and Cultural Change*.

Interest in this field generated further empirical data, and analytical and conceptual work, with a number of doctoral theses on the subject. The first doctoral dissertation concerning the informal sector (i.e. using the term) was completed in 1979. Thereafter, the number remained rather steady year by year. From 1979 to 1989, twenty-five such theses were written. In the 1990s, the figure was rather higher, thirty-nine. The peak period was 1994–97 (Data from Library of Congress, Washington).[8]

But strains were beginning to show. One source of tension was between different disciplines, with economists tending to use the term almost as synonymous with small-scale enterprises (Schmitz 1982), and even casting doubt on whether the concept had anything new to add to the understanding of employment (see for example Stark 1982). During this decade the term began increasingly to be used not only in interdisciplinary or policy-related journals, but also in mono-disciplinary journals. Researchers from several different disciplines used the term, ranging from sociologists and anthropologists (e.g. Moser, Rakowski) to economists (e.g. Adachi, Chandra and Khan, Gupta, Gibson and Kelley).[9] Another tension that was inherent from the start – between the reformist and radical approaches – continued. This was linked both to the theoretical analysis of the informal sector and to the policy implications.

In the policy arena, the term was widely used not only by the World Bank, as already noted, but also by other international agencies (e.g. UNCHS [United Nations Centre for Urban Settlements]), regional development banks (e.g. ADB), bilateral agencies (e.g. USAID and ODA) as well as national agencies (e.g. HUDCO [Housing and Urban Development Corporation], India).[10] It is certainly fair to claim that the concept helped to shape the urban agenda, and to ensure that the urban poor were not forgotten. Although it is not easy to demonstrate concretely how it influenced urban development policy, and the choice and design of projects, it is the case that the urban projects of the World Bank in the 1970s and 1980s were evaluated positively in terms of their overall performance, and were relatively successful in benefiting the poor, even though here, as so often, it proved difficult to reach the very poorest income groups.

Distortion/destruction, 1990s

In the 1990s, one might argue, the informal sector 'idea' became severely distorted, or even destroyed. Certainly it suffered the fate of many attractive ideas by being over–extended. This began to happen already in the 1980s, with the term 'informal' being applied to housing, transport, and later finance.

Another and more interesting development, was that the term was increasingly applied to cities in developed countries. This actually began earlier, and was initially applied mainly to studies of immigrant workers (e.g. in New York, Miami). But it was also extended to others (e.g. Italy, Spain, UK, Netherlands, Russia). There is now an extensive literature on this topic. The major bibliography (Feldmann and Ferretti 1998) contains far more references to studies of the USA – 118 – than the next largest, India, which in turn is followed by Britain.

But I would hesitate to characterize this extension of the concept as a distortion. Indeed, I would argue to the contrary that the split between developing and developed country discourses is unnecessarily wide, and that ideas can (indeed should) move in both directions. The use of the term 'informal sector' in developed countries is indicative, I suggest, not of a distortion of the term, but of significant changes in developed countries which make them more like developing ones: a shift in the nature of employment towards what is often called 'flexible labour,' which many see as regressive.

The adoption of the term in developed countries I therefore see as a legitimate extension. More controversial is the rebirth of the term in the writing of Hernando de Soto:

> The most significant recent change in emphasis has been the shift from the micro-enterprise as such to the regulatory framework that encourages informal micro-enterprises to stay small. Avoidance of government regulations and taxes was one of the characteristics of informality originally specified in the definition formulated by the ILO Kenya Employment Mission Report of 1972, but informality has taken on a new dimension since the publication of Hernando de Soto's *The Other Path* in 1986. The new wave of research on the informal sector may be described as an examination of the compatibility between regulations and growth of small and micro-scale enterprise activity, with a view to reforming the regulatory framework.
>
> (Lubell 1991: 64–65)

Lubell's presentation of the renaissance of the informal sector is neutral, but others see this as a clear distortion; its rebirth in a form which reflects what is seen as the neoliberal ideology of de Soto, and the Institute for Freedom and Democracy in Lima, Peru, which he established.

Finally, one might claim, on the basis of a very different – and rather formalistic – argument, that the informal sector idea is not simply distorted, but actually dead. It was born, as I have shown, out of an anomalous situation: the lack of fit between the categories of the 'developed countries' (as embodied most starkly in official statistics) and the 'reality' in developing countries. This led to a great deal of research, both empirical and conceptual, on the informal sector. But the statisticians were not entirely unmoved by this revolution, and during the late 1980s the ILO Bureau of Statistics launched a series of activities that culminated in the adoption of a resolution concerning statistics of employment in the informal sector by the Fifteenth International Conference of Labour Statisticians in 1993. What had previously escaped classification was now officially included.

Thus the development of the term finally turned full circle – in the formalistic sense of being defined out of existence. Central to the idea of the informal sector – at least initially, but also, I would argue, subsequently – is that it refers to activities that fall *outside* the scope of official statistics. Thus, to agree an internationally applicable definition of the informal sector is to make it disappear. It is government statisticians (and accountants) who are the ultimate arbiters of reality in the modern world. By finally granting official recognition to the informal sector they also issued its death certificate.

Whether this is the final word or whether further developments occur remains to be seen, but this completes my brief biography of the idea to date. In the remainder of this chapter I shall explore some aspects of it in more depth, and also reflect on what one may learn more generally from this analysis.

Analysis

A simple conceptual model

In this section I wish to suggest some hypotheses concerning the role of ideas in development assistance that may be of more general application, based on a simple schema in the form of a two-by-two matrix, distinguishing between the arenas of research and policy, and between the international (global) and the local. The development of 'the informal sector', and other ideas, can be traced in such a schema, to provide a sort of 'historical geography' of the spread of the idea. Thus the history related in the previous section could be crudely summarized as a flow through the matrix: how the idea started at the interface between policy and research, in the 'global' arena; then moved both into the policy arena (global and local) and into the academic arena (from development studies to mono-disciplines); and how – to a limited extent – there was feedback both from the academic world and from the 'field'. What is particularly revealing, also for comparative analysis of other ideas, are the interfaces between the four quadrants of the matrix, and I will briefly refer to each in turn.

The link between (international) research and policy

There is a close link between research and policy at the international scale. In the case of the informal sector a small group of people, working in key northern institutions at the interface between research and policy, played a crucial role – as noted above. Since then the number of people and institutions involved in development assistance has increased considerably, but some of the same patterns may be apparent. For the persons concerned there are shared benefits, but also, perhaps, costs. Both academics and bureaucrats are confronted with interesting challenges, but may as a result face problems *vis-à-vis* their respective peer groups. The writings of the academics involved may not measure up to the expectations of the research community, while those bureaucrats who become involved in conceptual and theoretical work may be criticized as impractical and irrelevant by their colleagues. It is worth again noting here the ideological dimension, which is relevant both in the arena of theory and policy, and which compounds the complexity surrounding a concept such as the informal sector. As already noted, there are major differences of viewpoint, both within academia and policy making, regarding the relationship between the formal and informal sectors, and the appropriate policy measures. It is, in principle, the intention of both researchers and policy makers to use neutral terms; with the 'informal sector' being just one example. In practice it is difficult, and by accident or design such terms are 'loaded'.

The link between international and national policies

When it comes to the link, or lack of it, between international and national policies, there is considerable variation by country and region. Two factors, which are closely related, are of determinate importance: both of which may be captured by the term ' autonomy'. First, to what extent does the country or region concerned have a stock of able and experienced bureaucrats? Second, to what extent is it reliant on grants and loans from the development assistance community? At one extreme are economically powerful countries such as Brazil and Malaysia that can both afford to resist the imposition of policies they disagree with, and have the competence to devise their own autonomous ideas and policies. At the other extreme, there are countries such as Tanzania and Nepal, which are in a much weaker position. In such countries the link between international and national policies may appear to be strong, but the policies may exist only on paper. It is beyond the scope of this exercise to assess whether and to what extent stated policies are actually carried out on the ground. In broad terms one might assert that while the link between international and national *policies* tends to be stronger in the case of less powerful nations, the link between national policies and national *practice* is weaker. But in the case of very heavily aid-dependent nations, national practice (as well as official policies) may be largely determined by donor agencies.

The link between international and national research

The relationship here is generally unequal. There is a clear hierarchy, with very few South countries (for example India, and some in Latin America) having high-status research institutes. Many individual researchers from the South, of course, enjoy high status, but they often move to the North, or at least associate themselves with academic institutions in the North for undertaking research studies. It is relevant in this context to refer to the studies undertaken by ILO and others, in Africa, Asia, and Latin America in the 1970s and 1980s. There is a significant variation in the extent to which the policy-related research studies were initiated and undertaken by the national government or by outside bodies; and to what extent local or foreign researchers were used for the work. It appears that Latin America and some Asian countries were far more 'autonomous' than the others.[11]

In the case of the informal sector idea, and, some would argue, in development research more generally, there is evidence also of an imbalance within the North: a dominance of the Anglo-Saxon world (perhaps even more narrowly focused on East Coast USA and England).

The (lack of a) link between national research and policy

The weakest link of all is often between national research and national policy, especially when aid dependence is high. The research world is relatively weak in many developing countries; and this may even be exacerbated by development assistance. At the risk of over-generalization, one may suggest that the link is weakest in most countries in Africa, very variable in Asia, and strongest in Latin America. The last of these is especially interesting, for this region, especially through the work of the Economic Commission for Latin America, played a major role in presenting an alternative paradigm in the 1970s.

In addition to studying the interfaces between the four quadrants of the matrix, it is also worth adding some brief comments on what goes on within the top and bottom halves of the matrix. First, the relationship between policy and practice in multilateral institutions and national agencies: in multilateral development agencies it is not uncommon to encounter an uneasy relationship between the research division and the operational divisions, and a gap between policy and practice.[12] Second, the relationship between disciplines: there is, as already noted, a tension within development studies between economics and other social sciences (Meier 1993). This manifests itself most strongly within academic institutions (especially universities), but also occurs within international agencies.

Policy consensus and definitional discord

The power of the informal sector 'idea' is, I suggest, that it may be capable of acting as a bridge, in several respects: a bridge between research and policy, between different disciplines, and – perhaps most important – between apparently conflicting positions (see also Chapter 8 on social capital). It holds out the prospect of a consensus; something which is crucially important for policy makers, though not necessarily for researchers. The danger is that such consensus is often gained at the expense of rigour.

Development institutions, such as the World Bank or the UNDP, are staffed by individuals who are subject to pressures which necessarily influence their behaviour. First, there is a desire to appear smart, or at least not to look foolish – in the eyes of the world – and especially those defined as peers. This pressure operates both at an individual level, and at the level of the agency, and 'relevant others' may be those in other agencies, the research community, NGOs, the media. This may foster originality, both because this is how one marks oneself out, and because new ideas may be better than the old ones they replace; but it also encourages caution.

Second, there is a desire not to criticize or confuse unnecessarily. In order to establish the validity and importance of a new idea, it would *a priori* seem to be necessary to point out the faults in those that are current, and thereby also criticize current policies – of one's own or other agencies. But this is an unwelcome activity in a bureaucracy.

Third, there is a desire for a common policy among donors, and between donors and recipient countries. There are very good arguments for donor co ordination regarding policies, and no doubt that policies which are fully endorsed by recipient countries are far more likely to be successful.

On balance, these forces create pressure for consensus, but at the risk that agreement is reached only by avoiding or concealing real differences of view. Prolonged discussions at international conferences end all too often with a compromise that is empty in analytical and policy terms. But in the case of the informal sector – and I suggest this is one reason that this concept was successful – it helped to create what I call substantive consensus.

A consensus is, ideally, achieved both in analytical terms (i.e. what the informal sector is) and in policy terms (what needs to be done). Certainly this consensus became strained, in the case of the informal sector, and the concept distorted. The focus of much of this discord was, of course, the definition of the term itself. What is an appropriate definition of the term, and who should decide? Here, the tension between researchers and policy makers is very marked: the latter need not just simple definitions, but also ones which enable action to be taken.[13] For a glimpse of some of these debates, see for example Khundker (1988) and Chandavarkar (1988).[14] I will not explore the details here, but simply make three comments. First, the question of definition was central in the discussion between radicals and reformists: whether the relation between formal and informal sectors is benign or malign – an issue which is necessarily very difficult to test empirically. Second, definitions varied between different disciplines: whether employment-focused or household/livelihood focused; whether generalizable or context-specific. Third, policy makers tended to be far less concerned with the niceties of definition than researchers. The lack of a clear definition opens the way both for poor quality research, and also for a policy consensus which is more apparent than real.

Relating to the wider debate

The idea of the informal sector had a significant impact on both development research and development policy – at least in the urban sector – over a ten and perhaps even twenty-year period. It was also, of course, itself shaped by all the other ideas and practice. We may learn a little more about both by reflecting on the changes over this period and how the informal sector related to them. To assist in the daunting task of summarizing development thinking over this period, I will draw on an excellent recent review by Lance Taylor in 'Development with a Human Face' (see Taylor *et al.* 1997).

In the 1950s and 1960s there was an important theoretical and empirical debate concerning the hypothesis that there was a necessary tradeoff between

equity and growth (Kuznets 1955; Kaldor 1957), which was challenged empirically (e.g. Adelman and Morris 1973). The important policy prescription that
resulted from all this information was that 'average per capita income growth
cannot be assumed to alleviate inequality and income-poverty automatically'
(Taylor *et al.* 1997).

The early 1970s was a period of rather radical theory (dependency theory,
unequal exchange, etc.) and radical expectations for change (the New
International Economic Order) (see for example Hettne 1995 for an overview).
In this context the informal sector appeared middle-of-the-road, reformist, and
was described as such – at least by its critics. This applied both to the analysis,
where the reformist concept of the informal sector was counterposed to the
more radical 'petty commodity production', and also to the policy prescriptions,
which consisted of projects and programmes as opposed to radical changes of
policy. This applies with even more force to the fate of 'basic needs', with which
the informal sector is linked.

In the late 1970s came reversal, and a downturn in many Third World
economies. The reasons for this downturn are complex (see Hobsbawm 1995)
but Taylor *et al.* believe that it explains why Chenery *et al.*'s *Redistribution with
Growth* (1974) not have the policy impact it could have had because the oil shock,
the ensuing international recession, and later the debt crisis soon reoriented the
priorities of countries and multilateral agencies' (Taylor *et al.* 1997: 438). As they
note, this was the time at which McNamara at the World Bank announced an
all-out attack on poverty.

The post-war golden age came to a close, and one consequence was a questioning of the role of the state and import-substitution industrialization policies.

> In the development literature, early examples are Little et al (1970) and
> Bhagwati (1971), while supply-side economics was a kindred trend in the
> industrialised world. … Since the early 1980s more and more countries have
> adopted market-friendly policies in the aftermath of the debt crisis. … With
> the first structural adjustment loans from around 1980, market-based
> reforms became tied to adjustment lending.
>
> (Taylor *et al.* 1997: 438)

During the second half of the 1980s, however, the positive impact of social
services (especially education) on growth was emphasized by a number of
neoclassical economists, and the human capital model was used in the new
Growth Theory. The 1980s was a period of recession, neoliberal ideas, and
neoliberal policies – most notably structural adjustment. Here the informal
sector did not feature prominently, until taken up again in a different guise (as
noted above).

In summary, the 'idea' of the informal sector was certainly much influenced
by the contemporary debates, and itself made a modest contribution to both
theory and policy. During the 1970s it appeared reformist – as did the publication that put it on the map: *Redistribution with Growth*. Marxists asserted that the

informal sector was exploited by the formal sector; and policies to promote it were seen as ignoring fundamental structural inequalities. By contrast, in the 1980s and early 1990s, such policies seemed almost radical; granting recognition and even support to groups who were at best on the margins, and at worst in conflict with state authorities.

In the new millennium we seem to be witnessing in development policy a sort of return to the middle ground of social democracy: 'structural adjustment with a human face' (following the efforts of UNICEF and others), 'participation with growth'. Certainly there is a return to poverty as the central focus, with civil society, governance and other catchwords, and the search for a complementary role of state and market. Whether the informal sector has a place in this debate remains to be seen. But it has both reflected and to a modest extent shaped the changes that have occurred – in both analysis and policy terms – in the previous twenty-five years. And an analysis of its history is, I suggest, revealing for the prospects of other ideas in development studies.

Notes

1 The paper was not published until 1973 (Hart 1973). As a result, the first and crucial reference to this paper (in ILO 1972) actually precedes it. This is a good example of a more general phenomenon which applies to the relation between research and policy: the time-lag in academic publication is often much longer.

2 Hollis Chenery, Vice-President of Development Policy at the World Bank, was formerly a Professor of Economics at Harvard and supervised Richard Jolly as a graduate student. Dudley Seers (Director, IDS) had some ten years earlier been a visiting professor at Yale, and had close contact with Chenery.

3 According to Emmerij (personal communication), it was very unclear what were the implications of these grand commitments; but there was enormous interest in the topic, and funding for the studies that followed was overflowing.

4 Some would argue that the leap from description to policy was too rapid. This is a common phenomenon in the interplay between research and policy, when the former is at what Portes might refer to as the 'pre-theoretical' stage.

5 For an excellent and concise review of the informal sector in historical perspective, see Gerry (1987).

6 The concept of the informal sector was, according to Emmerij (personal communication) not inextricably linked to basic needs. It is interesting that the latter (which might appear on the face of it to be as uncontroversial as apple pie and motherhood) should be the focus of such intense strife. But while the informal sector was more limited in scope and (relatively) more analytical, the term 'basic needs' was, in fact, very closely linked to a wide-ranging development strategy which was controversial.

7 A review of relevant textbooks over the twenty-five-year period reveals that use of the term began from the end of the 1970s, and continued quite steadily thereafter. But it is interesting to observe that it was increasingly taken for granted – in the sense that the definition of the term was not problematized – if it was defined at all; and references to Hart and/or ILO became less frequent as time went by.

8 By contrast, theses on social capital first appeared in 1989 and a total of sixty-two appeared in the following decade, the majority in the years 1996–98.

9 See for example *Annals of the American Academy of Political and Social Science* 1987.

10 For an overview see Harris (1992), which summarizes the experience of key figures from most of the agencies concerned.

11 The works referred to here are what might be called 'first generation' and more policy-related studies. A much longer list can be found in two recent bibliographies (Danesh 1991; Feldman and Ferretti 1998).

12 This is beyond the scope of this study, but the gap is clearly substantial. Examples from Indonesia and India are cited in Harris 1992. 'The recurrent gap between strategy and implementation was also a gap between two sets of people – those designing policy and those implementing programmes and projects' (44). The terms of reference of the Madras Metropolitan Development Authority included 'to alleviate the condition of the poor, pay special attention to the condition of the poor, and the improvement of the informal sector, etc. Did they do anything about it? Nothing at all' (75).

13 I have explored elsewhere (McNeill 2000) the criteria that need to be fulfilled for a good definition: e.g. value-free, not self-referential. In relation to the informal sector more specifically, I have argued the case for a 'polythetic classification'.

14 According to Ahwireng-Obeng (1996), studies in over seventy-five countries have generated more than fifty definitions.

5 Policy stories and knowledge-based regimes

The case of international population policy

Ole Jacob Sending

Introduction

The International Conference on Population and Development (ICPD), held in Cairo in 1994, produced a new consensus on international population policy. From the 1960s, an economic rationale for fertility control was embedded in the policy approach of 'family planning'. The ICPD placed a 'reproductive health approach' to population policy at the core of its Programme of Action (UN 1995). One close participant notes that the 'Cairo consensus'

> radically transformed the views and perceptions of thousands of policy makers and program managers ... moving away from top-down approaches and pre-planned demographic goals to those that would seek to respond to the needs of 'couples and individuals'.
>
> (Singh 1998: 1)[1]

In this chapter, I address two questions. First, what made for the relative stability of international population policy in the form of family planning for over thirty years, despite the constant controversies over whether and how to organize population policy? Second, what accounts for the change in international population policy from family planning to reproductive health that occurred through the ICPD process? It will be argued that a clue to answering both questions is found in the analysis of the knowledge-policy nexus. This is based on a reading of how the institution of science, because of its universally recognized cognitive authority, functions to stabilize international policy by legitimizing and validating certain facts, theories and concepts that create an internationally shared problem-definition of, and policy response to, a certain phenomenon. Changes in international policy will, in this perspective, have to be understood in relation to the changing content of that body of knowledge which underwrites an established policy approach, and which defines the cognitive-normative space in which political agency is performed. In an attempt to capture this dynamic, I will make use of two core concepts: *policy stories* and *knowledge-based regimes*. Before we proceed to discuss these two concepts, however, we need to reflect briefly on how the institution of science structures the modality of political deliberation and governance.

Science and politics

With the emergence of modern science in the seventeenth century, and its institutionalization during the next three centuries, the modality of political *discourse*
and *governance* undergoes a significant transformation. The metaphysical warrant
for the existence of society is partly replaced by the idea that man produces and
reproduces society through various actions (Touraine 1977). Central to this
process is the secularization and de-mystification of nature and society, and the
concomitant emergence of the belief that society must be known before it can be
governed (see Rose 1999). This makes for the establishment of distinct *modern*
forms of political discourse; although concerned with what 'ought' to be, political activity is intimately tied to, and grounded in, representations of how the
world 'is'. As an institution marked by cognitive authority, science is a crucial ally
for political actors who wish to persuade others that their problem-definition and
concomitant policy response are firmly grounded in facts (Barnes and Edge
1982).

Ezrahi (1990) has analysed the role of the institution of science in securing
democratic modes of political deliberation by making possible the reference to
facts independently produced and accessible to all. For Ezrahi, the significance of
the institution of science lies in the creation of a *horizontal* (as opposed to a hierarchical and self-referential) structure of accountability by which actors wishing
to persuade others must refer to and ground their arguments in relation to the
facts.[2] It can thus be said that there is an internal, constitutive relation between
the institution of science and modern forms of political discourse, in the sense
that reference to facts about the world is central for getting others to accept and
act upon a certain policy proposal. Various actors may thus be understood to
fund, interpret and use scientific knowledge in order both to try to convince
others of the validity and appropriateness of their preferred objectives, and for
making possible, as we shall see in a moment, the formulation and establishment
of policy practices.

Modern political *governance* is predicated on the existence of reliable, general
knowledge of the characteristics of the population to be governed (Foucault
1980; Wagner 1994; Rose 1999). Theories about the role of professions attest to
the intimate link between the production and use of scientific knowledge, and
the governance of society (Abbott 1988). As executors of a specific knowledge
base, professions occupy central roles within administrative structures as they,
through this knowledge base, define those categories, concepts and theories that
underwrite and legitimize those discourses that define the meaning of, and point
to solutions for, different phenomena to be addressed through policies.

Desrosières (1991; 1998) has specified the relation between a phenomenon's
conceptualization through statistical knowledge, and the forms of government
that this renders feasible. A central feature of statistics, Desrosières holds, is that
it serves to objectify and stabilize a specific meaning and significance of a
phenomenon, thus rendering certain policy options more feasible than others.
This position, informed by a scientific realist position, provides a fruitful

perspective for exploring the knowledge-policy nexus: a phenomenon, like fertility behaviour, may be categorized, explained and described through knowledge production in a variety of ways, and the resulting conceptualization will, because of the cognitive authority of the institution of science, structure the cognitive-normative space in which deliberations on policy take place and the range of policy options is rendered feasible. By building upon this perspective on the knowledge-policy nexus we may provide new insights about the role of knowledge in international policy making.[3]

Policy stories and knowledge regimes

Granted that the objectification and definition of a given phenomenon is open to a variety of normative and political considerations, it becomes interesting to explore how scientific knowledge constitutes a symbolic resource used by politically motivated actors. In order to justify and legitimize certain courses of action, and to render these possible and effective, scientific knowledge forms an important component both for efforts of persuading and mobilizing different groups, and for formulating and establishing policy practices. This can be grasped through the concept of *policy stories*. A policy story can be defined as follows:

> A set of factual, causal claims, normative principles and a desired objective, all of which are constructed as a more or less coherent argument – a story – which points to a problem to be addressed and the desirability and adequacy of adopting a specific policy approach to resolve it.

This conceptualization incorporates how politically motivated actors integrate scientifically produced knowledge in the form of facts, concepts or theories in order to

(i)   convince others *that* a certain phenomenon is a problem,
(ii) demonstrate that this problem is best understood in a certain way, as shown by the facts presented, and
(iii) link these factual claims to *normative* principles giving moral force to the argument that it should be resolved.

This perspective thus subjects the factual dimensions of political processes to the interests and normative commitments of actors, in the sense that knowledge is used to justify and legitimize calls for adopting certain policies to resolve what is seen to be a problem that 'ought' to be resolved.

The formulation is partly inspired by Rein and Schon (1991: 265), who refer to problem-setting stories that 'link causal accounts of policy problems to particular proposals for action and facilitate the normative leap from "is" to "ought"'. We depart from Rein and Schon's conception somewhat by emphasizing more strongly the *factual* claims (the characteristics of a phenomenon) and *normative principles* (the morally–grounded principles used to legitimize the policy formulation) invoked by actors as they define a problem and argue for a specific policy approach. The concept of policy stories seeks to capture how actors integrate knowledge claims into their politically charged arguments so as to 'frame' the issue under discussion. Because of the interlocking of the factual and normative dimension of policy making, a policy story can be seen to *create space for political agency*. That is: a policy story serves, by creating an argument grounded in a body of scientifically produced knowledge, to persuade and mobilize different groups as it represents a complete package: an authoritative problem-definition and a concomitant policy solution that is legitimized in both factual and normative terms.

A policy story that wins acceptance at the discursive level can be seen to define the terms of the debate for the establishment of policy and to de-legitimize competing conceptualizations and policy approaches. Through the political agency performed through a policy story, it may come to dominate the policy field as it forms the central *cognitive-normative organizing device* for specific formulation and establishment of policy within different organizations. In this way, the policy story may over time attain a 'taken for granted' char-acter as it comes to structure, and reflect, policy practice. This process of stabilization is best described as a process of *institutionalization*. Following Scott, we can define institutionalization as a 'process by which a given set of units and a pattern of activities come to be normatively and cognitively held in place, and practically taken for granted as lawful' (Scott *et al.* 1994: 10). This latter feature is critical to the argument presented here. In the change from an argument *for* a specific policy approach to the establishment of that policy in practice, the policy story comes to define the cognitive-normative outlook of a policy regime. This can be defined as an *interlock* between the knowledge which underwrites the policy story, and the establishment in practice of the policy advocated in a policy story. That is: the knowledge that once formed part of an argument for a policy is now an integral part of the very rationality and iden-tity of the organization involved with managing this policy in practice. As such it becomes part of the bundle of routines, rules, priorities and rationality of the organizations in the policy field (see Douglas 1986; March and Olsen 1989; Scott and Meyer. 1994).

Below, I employ the two concepts of policy story and knowledge-based regime to account both for policy change and policy stability in international population policy. I start off by tracing the formulation of the policy story of family planning, and proceed to discuss how this policy story, over time, formed the cognitive-normative identity of the emerging regime of population policy. Despite long-lasting and fierce political criticism from religious authorities, femi-nists and others, family planning defined the very identity of the policy field of population in the multilateral system. I then trace the process of formulating an alternative policy story of reproductive health. I conclude by reflecting on how the reception of the policy story of reproductive health was conditioned in its reception by the cognitive-normative content of the existing regime of family planning.

The making and institutionalization of the policy story of family planning

Establishing population policy to reduce population growth came about through the operations of a loosely coupled network of individuals that approximated a 'population movement' with its basis in the United States (Dixon-Mueller 1993; Hodgson and Wattkins 1997). For this reason, we shall focus specifically on developments in the United States in the post-World War II era, and trace how this network, advocating population control, built up a policy story that was exported internationally, with the aim of establishing family planning programmes in the developing world. Over time, the policy story of family planning effectuated the establishment of international population policy, and it thus came to form a regime that, in its cognitive-normative outlook, was based on an economic rationale for fertility regulation.

Creating a policy story

In the years immediately following World War II, the idea of governmental intervention to influence fertility levels was outside international political discourse. There was a general perception that governments had no business to intervene in something as private as reproduction (Sharpless 1997). All of this was to change in the next two decades, as the late 1960s saw a number of international and national organizations establish population policies in the form of family planning to reduce population growth (Dixon-Mueller 1993). Through the efforts of a neo-Malthusian movement consisting of businessmen, public advocates and researchers, the terms of this debate were recast through the strategic funding and interpretation of scientific knowledge, and through the linking of this knowledge to set of normative goals of securing and perpetuating (American) peace, stability and prosperity. The individuals involved in this effort were convinced that: 'To make the world safe for American democracy, global population needed to be controlled. American know-how and technology were needed to avert another war' (Critchlow 1999: 13).

The so-called 'theory of demographic transition' posited a causal relationship between economic growth and fertility levels. High population growth rates in the developing world were seen as an obstacle to economic growth. In its original formulation in 1945, the theory postulated the latter as a *dependent*, not an independent variable: socio-economic factors associated with development and modernization were used to explain changes in reproductive behaviour, not the other way around. The theory was based on historical data from Western Europe, where improved standards of living (socio-economic development) went together with reduced fertility levels. Initially, the driving forces behind reproductive decisions were embedded in social and cultural norms, which could not be easily changed and were subject to large-scale processes of modernization (Szreter 1993: 668). Later, in the early 1950s, Frank Notestein reformulated transition theory so as to identify fertility behaviour as an independent variable that could be manipulated to advance and speed up the process of development. In an address at an international conference in 1952 consisting of actors involved with economic planning, Notestein 'elaborated upon the apparently optimistic policy implications of the newly formulated possibility of reverse causation in demographic transition' (Szreter 1993: 679).

The strategic reformulation of the theory of demographic transition, in which the causal arrow was reversed, must be seen in light of the political motivation of Notestein and an emerging 'population movement'. There was a very grave concern that high population growth would lead to political instability, particularly in Asia and Africa, and that this would threaten vital American interests, particularly in light of the competition with communism.

This theoretical reformulation had significant implications, as it meant that a clear rationale for contraceptive delivery through family planning programmes was firmly grounded in the most authoritative theoretical formulation of the relation between fertility behaviour and economic growth.

John D. Rockefeller III had sought in the early 1950s to get the board of Rockefeller Foundation involved in the field of population. Due to the controversial character of the issue, the board refrained. Rockefeller instead established the Population Council in 1952, with the explicit goal of seeking to legitimize through research the claim that family planning programmes should be established so as to facilitate socio-economic development in the South. Established as a research institution, the Council was intended by Rockefeller also, over time, to get involved in action-programmes (Harr and Johnson 1991: 41). Together with the Office of Population Research at Princeton University under the leadership of Frank Notestein, a friend of Rockefeller, the Population Council served as a key producer of the knowledge which served to establish scientifically that there was indeed a direct relation between population dynamics and economic growth, and that it could and should be addressed through family planning programmes that would deliver contraceptive technology.

In short, the calls for family planning programmes were constructed as a policy story that established through science that there was indeed a relationship between population growth and economic development, and that this could be manipulated through family planning programmes. It linked this problem-definition and policy response to the evident goals of making developing countries more economically advanced and prosperous. The link between 'is' and 'ought' was particularly strong, as there was, in terms of research, no body of scientifically produced knowledge that seriously challenged the facts upon which this policy story was based. In an era where the idea of social engineering by technological fixes stood strong,[4] and the ideological contest with communism provided the normative framework to ground calls for action in the name of security,[5] family planning over time won acceptance, as the public was persuaded, and governmental officials came to perceive it as a cost-effective way of addressing a pressing problem.

The population question was controversial, however, as it challenged religious convictions and also raised questions of whether this was a proper concern for governments. On the question of whether the government should get involved in the regulation of reproductive behaviour, President Eisenhower declared, in 1959, that 'I cannot imagine anything more emphatically a subject that is not a political or governmental activity or function or responsibility' (*New York Times*, 3 December 1959, 1. Quoted in Dixon-Mueller 1993: 61). However, following successful lobbying by the population movement during the 1950s and 1960s, of political and public officials in the White House, State Department, USAID and the Ministry of Defense, the US government, as well as an increasing number of developing countries and international organizations, came to endorse family planning.

Thus, in 1965, President Johnson said in a speech at the twentieth anniversary of the establishment of the United Nations: 'Let us act on the *fact* that less than five dollars invested in population control is worth a hundred dollars invested in economic growth' (*ibid.*: 62. Emphasis added). Following an emerging support of family planning endorsement in the Kennedy administration, President Johnson took it further, as Congress enacted the Foreign Assistance Act in 1967, granting $35 million for family planning (Critchlow 1999: 78). The shift in policy orientation on the part of the US reflects a more general trend that can be found internationally during the same period (Sharpless 1997; Critchlow 1999). Starting from the mid-to-late 1960s, a range of international organizations became involved in population policy in the form of family planning. The year 1968 saw the World Bank become involved in family planning, and 1969 saw the establishment of the United Nations Fund for Population Activity (UNFPA). In 1965, USAID started to fund family planning programmes. In the same period 'the specialized agencies such as WHO, FAO, UNESCO, ILO and UNICEF were increasingly active' (Dixon-Mueller 1993: 63).

Stabilizing international population policy: the formation of a knowledge regime

Demographic research grew rapidly, precisely because demographic knowledge conformed to and was compatible with the goals of the increasingly well–funded field of population. Demographic research in this way became the scientific grounding or basis of a politically motivated movement; the latter being the major financer of the former. Critchlow notes that the decade between 1950 and 1960 saw an emerging *international* network of demographers:

> demography became not just a science but a policy science that viewed intervention in population growth as necessary. Professional demographers, academically trained at the leading universities, became members of professions that shared a core body of knowledge, a consistency in methodology, and a common discourse. Institutionalized through professionalized associations and supported by the philanthropic community. ... population experts accepted intervention in population with an almost evangelical fervor.
>
> (1999: 2. See also Hodgson 1988)

An interlocking of mutually reinforcing objectives in terms of promoting economic development, and countering the threat of communism served to identify family planning programmes as a necessary element in plans for socioeconomic development (see Demeny 1988; Hodgson and Watkins 1997; Presser 1997).

The UNFPA, the World Bank, USAID, and a range of non-governmental organizations such as the International Planned Parenthood Federation, as well as national organizations, were all, during the 1960s, involved in refining, establishing and administering family planning programmes. Through the training and hiring of personnel, the development of rules, organizational objectives and organizational units committed to family planning programmes, the policy story of family planning formed, over time, part of the institutional rationality and routine of these organizations.[6] Through this process of institutionalization, a regime was formed with its basis in the policy story of family planning. When the environmental movement came to force in the 1970s, it appropriated the already institutionalized idea that family planning programmes constituted a key policy tool to reduce population growth and thus preserve the globe's natural resources.

The profession of demography, although dependent on the expertise of health professionals in the field, did not allow for the integration of a clear health perspective in the effort to reduce population growth. This can be seen, for example, in the failure of the World Health Organization to establish its own population programmes in the 1960s, and in its continual conflicts over coordination of its primary health-care programmes with UNFPA's family planning programmes (Haas 1990: 139–40). Further, the UN Population Division, staffed with demographers, and the International Union for the Scientific Study of Population (IUSSP) co-organized the first two international conferences on population, in Rome in 1954 and in Belgrade in 1965. From its very infancy, then, the categories, facts and theories defining the cognitive-normative outlook of population policy were in the hands of demographers, all of whom promoted family planning. In the process, demography became a policy science (Hodgson 1983).

The regime defined by the policy story of family planning sustained attacks from an emerging women's movement and from health professionals, which called for a stronger emphasis on health as an end in itself (Dixon-Mueller 1993). In more theoretical terms, this knowledge-based regime served to stabilize the means and ends of population policy which enabled it to endure in the face of continued conflicts and criticism, especially from the Catholic church, precisely by virtue of providing a relatively stable 'background consensus', in terms of certain facts and theories that remained unchallenged.

Creating space for political mobilization: the making of the policy story of reproductive health

From the establishment of population policy at the international level in the late 1960s, until the ICPD in Cairo in 1994, family planning *was* population policy. Its longevity is remarkable, considering that the limitations and problems of the approach revealed themselves rather quickly. Indeed, as early as 1972, the president of the World Bank, Robert McNamara, told the Population Council's president Bernard Berelson that there was a growing concern that family planning was 'too simple, too narrow and too coercive' (Critchlow 1999: 178). Also, developing countries were starting to mount criticism against family planning for not addressing the root causes of population growth, namely poverty, economic injustice and the organization of world trade.

Just as the formulation of the policy story of family planning was a strategic effort on the part of a population movement concerned with the *economic* problems engendered by population growth, the emerging women's health movement was equally strategic in its efforts to advance a different policy approach focused on the health and rights of women. Their efforts took the form of strategically commissioning and using research to establish a different problem-definition of fertility behaviour, one that emphasized the importance of paying more attention to the socio-economic status, rights and health needs of women.

Creating space: formulating an alternative policy story

Interestingly, John D. Rockefeller III played a critical role in taking the first steps to re-direct population policy away from a sole focus on family planning. Already in 1974, at the first UN-organized inter-governmental population conference, Rockefeller argued that 'family planning programs that have been undertaken have proved inadequate when compared to the magnitude of the problems facing us', and continued by asserting that: 'Population planning programs must be placed within the context of economic and social development' (Critchlow 1999: 181).

The only detectable effects of this speech, besides the controversy it generated at the conference itself, were changes in the staff and research-orientation at the Population Council in the years that followed. Joan Dunlop was the person behind the scenes in these developments. Rockefeller had hired her in 1973 as his assistant on population matters. Bringing a feminist perspective to the thinking on population, she was instrumental both in writing Rockefeller's Bucharest speech and in selecting George Zeidenstein as the new head of the Population Council (Critchlow 1999: 179).[7] Gradually, the research focus of the Population Council changed towards addressing the health dimension of family planning programmes, and the causal significance of the quality of family planning services for increasing contraceptive use. This was significant, as the Population Council is arguably the most influential research institution in international population policy, through its close contacts with US foundations, USAID and foreign health and family planning administrators.[8]

Adrienne Germain came to the Population Council in 1985 from a position at the Ford Foundation's office in Bangladesh. Germain had for a long time advocated both the need for changing the research orientation in the field of population, and for re-organizing family planning programmes to respond to the health needs of women. In 1987, Zeidenstein asked Germain to write a paper for a conference in Nairobi entitled 'Better Health for Women and Children through Family Planning' and organized by the World Bank, WHO and UNFPA. Germain decided to use the paper to call for a 'reproductive health approach' to population policy. In this initial formulation, 'a reproductive health approach' meant integrating the already existing child survival programmes with family planning programmes to ensure a broader basis of service delivery that went beyond mere contraceptive delivery. At the time, none of these programmes were focusing on the broader health issues related to reproduction and addressing the concerns and rights of women.[9]

This conference paper marks the first steps towards the development of the policy story of a 'reproductive health approach'. Incidentally, Mahmoud Fathalla, Director of the WHO's Special Programme on Human Reproduction, wrote an article in 1988, published in *Human Reproduction*, a WHO journal, that called for the same kind of re-orientation of population policy that Germain was seeking to effect with her paper. These two papers by Germain and Fathalla reflect a convergence between feminist criticism of existing programmes, and a concern in the WHO and in the health profession more generally that family planning was too narrow and did not address the broader health issues involved in human reproduction. This convergence would later prove critical to the women's health movement, as it meant that their calls for re-orientation of population policy had an ally in the central international authority in the health field, the WHO.

Germain's paper did not go down well at the conference, as it challenged the cognitive-normative outlook and objectives of the knowledge regime of family planning, and was, in her words, 'heavily resisted'.[10] Later, when Germain came to work with Joan Dunlop at the International Women's Health Coalition (an advocacy NGO), they developed a strategy of seeking to reshape the population field from the inside.[11] This meant shying away from the more radical systemic criticism that certain elements of the women's movement had earlier launched against the population field (see Dixon-Mueller 1993). The strategy was quite explicitly to *document* and ground through scientific knowledge the health risks of Third World women related to reproduction, and to point towards a policy approach that would integrate the economic rationale for fertility regulation with its health aspects.

In 1987, the IWHC got involved in research on the issue of reproductive tract infections (RTIs) and sexually transmitted diseases (STDs) among women in the Third World. Prior to this, all research on these issues had focused on high-risk groups such as commercial sex workers, and was not included in discussions about family planning programmes (Dixon-Mueller and Wasserheit 1991; Wasserheit and Holmes 1992). The work culminated in the convening of a high-profile conference of health experts in 1991, out of which came a book, edited by Germain and three others, which not only documented the seriousness of the problem, but which also included a section with 'recommendations for action' (Germain *et al.* 1992). It was a strategic effort on the part of Germain and other like-minded actors to construct a policy story of reproductive health[12] grounded in scientifically produced knowledge, and so strengthen and make legitimate their calls for a re-orientation of population policy more attuned to the rights and needs of women.

At the Population Council, Beverly Winnikoff, Judith Bruce and Anrudh Jain in the late 1980s initiated a new research project focused on the 'quality of care' of family planning programmes. The objective was to highlight the importance of taking 'the user's perspective' and to assess the effectiveness of family planning services in the context of the quality of the services provided, which was assumed to have an impact on the degree to which people were using them. Their research revealed, for example, that the methods used to measure the effectiveness of family planning programmes, such as Contraceptive Prevalence Rates (CPR), and Couple Years of Protection (CYP), failed to examine the clearly important issue of whether the methods offered were in fact *used*. That issue can only be addressed, they argued, by assessing the perceived quality of the services provided, and by examining the social and cultural context of reproductive decision making and obstacles to contraceptive use (Jain and Bruce 1994). On this basis, they proposed a two-pronged strategy that integrated health concerns with the already established economic rationale for fertility regulation. It held that if you want to reduce population growth, the most effective and humane way of doing so is to

(i)   make family planning programmes 'responsible for reducing *unplanned* and *unwanted* childbearing and related morbidity', and

(ii) make 'Broader social and economic policies ... responsible for reducing levels of wanted fertility' (*ibid.*).

The significance of this research was partly that it documented serious shortcomings with the existing family planning approach; partly that it identified that this could be resolved through a focus on the health dimension of fertility. The policy story of 'reproductive health' in this sense invoked a different body of knowledge to undermine a series of assumptions that were contained in the institutionalized policy story of family planning.

Persuasion and mobilization

The effect of the work of the IWHC and the research produced at the Population Council can be seen by the impact it had on the new policy approach of the world's largest non-governmental family planning organization, the International Planned Parenthood Federation (IPPF). In the early 1990s, the IPPF was establishing a new strategy document. At the IPPF headquarters in London, Med Bouzidi was in charge of writing a draft of the strategic plan – Vision 2000. In formulating this new strategy document, Bouzidi made use of the arguments presented by Germain and Dunlop at the IWHC on 'reproductive health', and the research done by Bruce and Jain at the Population Council on the 'quality of care'.[13]

The policy story of a 'reproductive health approach' challenged and created space for a different policy approach to population policy. First, it held that family planning programmes are potentially coercive to women, referring to projects in China, India and elsewhere, where women's basic rights had been violated in the name of economic growth. Second, it challenged the idea that the mere delivery of contraceptive technology and services is enough to reduce population growth, let alone empower women and address their health needs and rights. Instead, it pointed to the centrality of providing women with education and jobs, and addressing gender relations and teenage sexuality to reduce fertility. Third, it challenged the narrowness of the focus of family planning, saying that it advanced a 'demographic imperative and a technological fix', and pointed to the need for addressing an emerging set of problems that were critical not only for reducing population growth, but also for the challenges posed by the HIV/AIDS pandemic, sexually transmitted diseases, reproductive tract infections, female genital mutilation, etc.

The IWHC was crucial in spreading the word and in mobilizing different groups around the policy story of reproductive health during the ICPD process. Together with organizations such as WEDO,[14] the IWHC brought together several constituencies under the policy story of reproductive health. Not only did IWHC, WEDO and other like-minded actors fund NGOs in the South, which enabled them to travel to meetings and conferences; they also helped fund and persuade the governments of the South to include these NGOs' representatives in national delegations. Importantly the IWHC and CEPIA convened, in February 1994, what the participants referred to as the 'feminist prep.com' that formulated the 'Rio Declaration', laying down a common vision and strategy for proceeding with the ICPD process.

These and other gatherings and networking processes served to mobilize several different groups and organizations around the policy story of reproductive health. The 'Rio Declaration' was sent to the ICPD secretariat and used frequently during the ICPD as a background document for persuading government officials and for suggesting specific wording in the draft ICPD document. Their advocacy, furthermore, came at an opportune time, as several governments used the preparations for the ICPD as an opportunity to evaluate their stance on population policy. In this context, the policy story of reproductive health, since it was grounded in scientific facts and legitimated through a discourse on human rights and health, proved persuasive. Over time, it gathered the support of a broad range of governmental and non-governmental organizations.

In February 1991, just prior to the start of the ICPD preparatory process, the IWHC and the Special Programme on Human Reproduction of the WHO held a joint conference in Geneva which resulted in a report entitled 'Creating Common Ground: Women's Perspectives on the Selection and Introduction of Fertility Regulation Technologies' (WHO 1991). Later, during the heated debates about the proper definition of reproductive health during the ICPD process, the WHO came to the rescue of the women's health advocates and issued a definition with the approval of the secretary-general of the WHO. This authoritative definition of reproductive health served to legitimize the policy story of a reproductive health approach to population policy.

The structuring effect of the existing knowledge regime

The policy story of reproductive health had, in order to be persuasive to several constituencies, to make reference to how it would in fact further those interests embedded in the organizations that, ever since the 1960s, had been in charge of formulating and administering family planning programmes. John Bongaarts at the Population Council had through his research documented that, although family planning services had been effective in reducing fertility levels in the developing world, they were not as effective as perceived, and would be less effective in the future. The argument, popularized in an article in *Science* in February 1994, was that of the three causes of population growth (unwanted fertility, high desired family size and population momentum), family planning programmes address only the first-mentioned cause, not the other two, which together had a greater influence on the total population growth than the first (Bongaarts 1994). Addressing the two other causes would mean: first, implementing programmes that sought to change the desired family size, which would mean addressing gender issues, promoting girls' education, and influencing the socio-cultural norms for family size; and second, educating teenagers on issues of sexuality and to delay early births by providing education, especially for women (Population Council 1994).

This argument further strengthened the policy story of reproductive health, in that it established that further reduction of population growth in the name of socio-economic development must move beyond family planning programmes and include a focus on general health issues, education (especially for women), teenage sexuality, and so on. In August 1994, Bongaarts was invited to brief US Secretary of State Warren Christopher and Vice-President Al Gore in preparation for the ICPD. Coming from an environmental background, Gore was mostly concerned with population growth, not women's issues in this context, and was only reluctantly supporting the right to abortion domestically.

Persuading Gore would mean establishing that a reproductive health approach would indeed be effective in reducing population growth. And Bongaarts' message came through. Just prior to the ICPD, Gore held a press conference in which he called for a more 'comprehensive and humane strategy' to reduce population growth that included a focus on girls' education, educating and empowering women, addressing unsafe abortions, and that generally 'fosters women's health'.[15] Bongaart's analysis proved essential because all the central organizations in the field of population – governmental, inter-governmental and non-governmental – jealous of their budgets and accustomed to think and act in terms of family planning with the aim of reducing population growth, had to be persuaded that a reproductive health approach would in fact be consistent with their long-term efforts and goals.

The impact of the policy story of a reproductive health approach on the ICPD Programme of Action notwithstanding, it remains to assess what effect it has had in actual policy formulation and implementation. As we will see, there has been a marked discursive shift in the field of population, in which reproductive health now forms a most crucial concept, partly replacing that of family planning.

The problems of implementation

Jain concludes, in a review of population policies, that: 'While governments of all developing countries have unanimously adopted the [ICPD] Programme of Action, an actual shift at the policy level and especially at the program level has not been swift' (Jain 1998: 16). An assessment of the implementation of the ICPD Programme of Action concludes that although some progress has been made, it is clear that:

> The reproductive health approach is still not widely understood, even within countries that have incorporated the approach into policy and strategic documents. This has led to concerns in some developing countries, such as Egypt and Indonesia, that the momentum gained through family planning programs in containing population growth will be lost if the reproductive health agenda is adopted. Vested interests and ideological positions also impede progress in implementing the reproductive health approach. Until facts and resources are mobilized in support of the reproductive health approach, it is likely to be an 'add on' to family planning programs rather than encompassing them.[16]

Our analysis above suggested that the reproductive health approach was effective as it undermined key assumptions of the existing knowledge regime and, on this basis, inserted new objectives (women's health and rights) that were defined as central to the advancement of the goal of reducing population growth. Yet, at this quote illustrates, the problems of implementation of the reproductive health approach suggest that the institutionalized policy practice of family planning, consisting of a network of population experts and programme managers, and of organizational routine and priority, heavily structures the motivation and ability to implement a reproductive health approach. This goes to show that once established as practice and over time consolidated and institutionalized, the cognitive-normative outlook of a policy field does have a strong structuring effect on the process of establishing new policy practices.

Conclusion

Several observers have noted that the outcome of the ICPD was due to the efforts of a globally organized women's health movement (see Finkle and McIntosh 1995; Johnson 1995; Hodgson and Wattkins 1997; Singh 1998). My interpretation, in drawing attention to the knowledge-policy nexus, is that this must be understood in the context of the way in which these actors strategically used knowledge to formulate an alternative policy story, one that made possible the establishment of a women's health perspective within the already established knowledge regime of family planning. The policy story of reproductive health opened up cognitive-normative space for the consideration of a new policy approach. This policy story served as the mobilizing platform for a range of women's organizations, both in the North and the South, and enabled the performance of effective political agency during the ICPD. In effectuating a change at the discursive level, the reproductive health approach has clearly inserted a clearer health rationale for population policy. The resistance to the new approach, and the slow process of concrete organizational change, attests to the hold of the already institutionalized goals and views contained in the policy story of family planning.

Notes

1   Singh was Deputy Secretary General to the Conference, and a close aide of the Secretary General of the Conference, Executive Director of UNFPA, Nafis Sadik. The Under-Secretary of Global Affairs for the United States, Timothy Wirth, declared on the last day of the conference that 'The World will never be the same after Cairo', while Nafis Sadik referred to the Programme of Action as a 'paradigm shift' (Singh 1998). For similar interpretations of the 'Cairo consensus' from less involved observers, see Johnson 1995; Finkle and McIntosh 1995; Hodgson and Wattkins 1997.

2   See Habermas 1998a, for an extensive treatment of the relation between facts and norms in his model of deliberative democracy.

3   For analyses of the role of knowledge in international policy making, see Haas 1990; Haas 1992; Litfin 1994.

4   For a good discussion of the notion of social engineering in the decades following World War II, see Wagner *et al.* 1991; Wagner 1994; Ezrahi 1990.

5   Kingsley Davis, the second main contributor to the theory of demographic transition, noted in an article in *Foreign Affairs* in 1958 that the US government should address population growth in the context of the fight against communism (Davis 1958: 296). When President Johnson sought support in Congress for international population assistance in 1966, Hodgson reports that he did so on the grounds that high population growth in the developing world 'challenges our own security' (Hodgson 1988: 549).

6   In the case of the World Bank and USAID, this relates to their offices of population.

7   Interview with Joan Dunlop, 10 May 2000.

8   Barbara Crane (1993) notes in her analysis of international population institutions: 'The Population Council ... has probably been the single most important supporter of policy and program research' (380).

9   Interview with Adrienne Germain, 10 August 2000.

10   *Ibid.*

11   Interview with Joan Dunlop, 10 May 2000.

12   Focusing on the efforts of Northern, primarily American, advocates does not imply that there were not similar networks of like-minded actors in Africa, Asia and Latin America. Germain had developed some of the basic ideas of proposing a reproductive health approach together with Sandra Kabir, who had set up in Kenya in the 1980s a health clinic that was sensitive to the demands of women in the region.

Similarly, the CEPIA network in Latin America played a crucial role in contributing to the formulation and advancement of the policy story of reproductive health, both in this period and through the ICPD. Interviews with A. Germain, 10 August 2000; J. Dunlop, 10 May 2000; A. Kabir, 30 August 2000.

13 Interview with Med Bouzidi, 5 April 2000.
14 Women's Environmental and Development Organization.
15 Transcript of remarks by Vice President Al Gore, National Press Club, Washington DC, 25 August 2000.
16 Executive summary of S. Forman and R. Gosh (1999) 'The Reproductive Health Approach to Population and Development', at http://www.nyu.edu/pages/cic/projects/pophealth/book_Publish.html#inter.

6 The World Bank and the environment

Robert Wade

Introduction

No other field of World Bank operations has grown as fast as its environmental activities. Starting with just five environmental specialists in the mid-1980s, the Bank employed three hundred a decade later, complete with a vice presidency for 'environmentally sustainable development' (World Bank 1994: 157).

On the surface, the history of the Bank's environmental activities appears to be a case of new insights leading an institution rapidly to integrate new objectives and criteria into its operational routines. According to the Bank, the change is the result of staff and management's 'increasing understanding of the relationship between environmental protection and development' (Shihata 1995: 184). But its many environmental critics say that the change has been driven largely by environmental non-governmental organizations (NGOs) mounting high-pressure campaigns to force the Bank to change its ways.

This chapter tells two stories. One is about the factors that led the Bank to pay attention to environmental criteria. The other is about the effects of its organizational structure and incentive system on what it has and has not done to advance environmental objectives.

Frontier economics with 'environment' added: the 1970s

When in the early 1970s, in response to burgeoning public concern with 'environment' in the West, the word entered into the Bank's lexicon, the staff was both sceptical and perplexed. They were sceptical because some environmental concerns seemed to be nothing new; perplexed because some sounded fuzzy, complex, and unquantifiable, and a threat to the familiar routine of project work.

In 1970 Robert McNamara took the occasion of his annual address to the United Nations Economic and Social Council to speak about the need to help developing countries mitigate environmental damage caused by economic growth. McNamara told his audience that the Bank had just created the post of environmental adviser to direct the Bank's environment work. This made the

Bank the first multilateral or bilateral agency to have an environmental adviser. Because the Bank was later to become the target of savage environmental criticism, its early leadership in this area deserves emphasis.

Why did McNamara take this initiative? The broader context provides some clues. The late 1960s was a time of growing concern about environmental issues in the West, especially in the United States. The number of articles on the environment in the *New York Times* rose from 150 in 1960, to 1,700 in 1970. Several schools of thought on the subject began to form and jostle for support, sharing an explicit regard for the value of 'the environment' and a disbelief that economic decisions based on market prices could safeguard that worth. They were reacting against what Kenneth Boulding usefully called 'frontier economics', the reigning assumption that economic growth and material prosperity were limitless, unconstrained by either 'sources' – the supply of natural resources – or 'sinks' – the waste-absorbing systems of the biosphere.[1] The most moderate reaction, beginning around the middle to late 1960s, came to be known as the 'environmental protection' approach. Threats to endangered species and the health effects of pollution and toxic wastes were considered the prime targets of public action, and legislation was sought to prevent unpriced environmental services from being overexploited. The US government, responding to pressures from US environmental groups, passed the National Environmental Policy Act in late 1969, which required US government agencies to undertake environmental assessments designed to mitigate or avoid the environmental damage caused by public investment projects.

As the recognized lead agency in the work on development issues, the Bank could not remain oblivious to this rising tide of concern, particularly because many in the new environmental movement were saying that economic growth should be stopped, an idea fundamentally opposed to the Bank's mission. In addition, the Bank had to consider what position it would take at the United Nations Conference on the Human Environment scheduled for 1972 in Stockholm. The prospect of having to stand up and explain what the Bank had been doing to protect the environment forced McNamara to think about what the Bank should be doing.

With the Stockholm conference in prospect, McNamara established the post of environmental adviser, to which he appointed James Lee. Lee was an American expert in public health and epidemiology, with earlier experience as a game warden in the United States. He remained the Bank's chief adviser on environmental matters until he retired in 1987.

The United Nations Conference on the Human Environment, 1972

The Stockholm conference put the 'environment' on the international agenda, and the World Bank did play an important role in this process. Late in 1971 it looked as though the whole conference might founder before it began (Prestre 1989). The developing-country representatives claimed that the conference was being strong-armed into adopting a rich-country view of environmental problems, seeking to impose on them mitigation measures that would only add to the costs of economic development and slow it down. As Lee recalled, the developing countries:

> threatened to pull out of it. ... So [Maurice Strong, chief organizer of the conference] called upon the World Bank and said, 'Well, after all, you are the closest to the developing countries. ... The developing countries will listen to you if you can make a case for us, that is, a case for the environment and its importance to the developing countries'. The Bank then assigned the responsibility for that to two of us. One was Mahbub ul Haq, who was going to look at it from the standpoint of the developing countries and economics. ... I was going to look at it ... from the point of view of identifying the environmental problems, the linkages, the relationship to people, and so on.[2]

The critical meeting was held in the village of Founex, Switzerland in 1971. This is where the first steps were taken toward the marriage between 'development' and 'environment'. In the event, Mahbub ul Haq persuaded the developing-country delegates that 'there really was good cause, both then and in the future, for them to be concerned about these matters'. And the Bank helped gain their support by agreeing to provide funds to cover any additional costs directly attributable to its environmental standards. The Founex report became the basis of the Declaration, Principles, and Recommendations issued by the Stockholm conference. It was largely drafted inside the World Bank, by Mahbub ul Haq and his team (Prestre 1989: 83).

At the conference itself, McNamara delivered a keynote address announcing the first formal commitment to environmental soundness in development from any of the multilateral development banks. This speech established the World Bank as the leading agency in dealing with the environmental problems of developing countries. In addition, the World Bank environmental adviser was a principal figure in the preparatory work, and senior World Bank official Mahbub ul Haq was the key person in persuading the developing countries not to withdraw.

Loss of momentum after 1972

All through the 1970s and into the 1980s the Bank was considered a leading advocate of environmental protection among those concerned with such issues. Yet having acquired the mantle of leadership, the Bank downplayed environmental issues in the years that followed, both to the outside world and still more to itself. Only three months after the Stockholm conference, McNamara made no mention of environmental issues in his annual report to the Board of Governors, neither in his review of Bank activities during the previous year nor in his outline of the programme for the next five years. Of the eleven annual reports between 1974 and 1985, only one had a separate section on the Bank's environmental work. Why? The answer has to do with McNamara's understanding, a change in the US role, and the wishes of borrowing countries, the inclinations of staff, and the nature of the environmental debate.

McNamara himself, though committed to minimizing the environmental damage caused by Bank projects, thought that the Bank could do what was needed with a minor initiative, worthy of no more than occasional advertising. He drew a contrast with the poverty work. 'We saw the direct attack on absolute poverty as very complex. We did not see the requirement of avoiding significant environmental damage as very complex. This reflected a lack of understanding on our part.'[3]

At the start of the 1970s the US government had taken a leadership role in multilateral environmental issues, but then it suddenly retreated. This move coincided with a wider sputtering-out of its leadership across the whole of the UN system as it became preoccupied with the 1973 oil crisis (Jacobson and Kay 1979).

Developing countries (especially big and important ones such as India and Brazil) reasserted their doubts about the Bank's role. This reflected their disagreement with the North's pressure for environmental protection measures at the expense, as they saw it, of economic growth.

Inside the Bank a large majority of the staff was also sceptical about McNamara's idea of subjecting Bank projects to scrutiny by self-styled 'environmentalist specialists' using different standards from their own 'good professional practice'. And like the developing countries, they equated 'environmental' problems largely with pollution (rather than, say, deforestation, desertification, or soil erosion), and saw pollution as a problem connected with affluence and therefore one that developing countries could afford to ignore.

In response to the burgeoning environmental movement, mainstream economists, political conservatives and industrialists in the West began to harbour *anti*-environmental sentiments. Some commentators portrayed the environmental movement as a Trojan horse for socialism. Much of what the World Bank said about the environment in the several years after Stockholm seemed intent on demolishing the idea of limits to growth. Little effort was made to set out a more positive agenda based on analysis of the environmental problems of developing countries (Haq 1972).

In short, the Bank's borrowers and most of its staff were sceptical about introducing explicit environmental considerations and self-styled environmental professionals. The Stockholm conference provided them with an excuse: it set up a new UN agency, the United Nations Environmental Programme (UNEP), to carry forward the Stockholm agenda. Its members could now say: let the Bank take care of development, let UNEP take care of environment.

Pressures for change: Polonoroeste, Brazil, 1979–89

The principal objective of the Polonoroeste ('northwest pole') project was to pave a 1,500-kilometre highway from Brazil's densely populated south-central region into the sparsely populated northwest Amazon. In addition, it was to construct feeder roads at the frontier end of the highway, rehabilitate existing agricultural settlements, establish new settlements, provide health-care, and create ecological and Amerindian reserves. The affected area was the size of Ecuador. Between 1981 and 1983, the Bank approved five loans in support of Polonoroeste, totalling US$457 million. Well over half went for the highway and feeder roads. The Bank was the only non-Brazilian source of finance (World Bank 1992).

Polonoroeste is important in the history of the Bank's environmental work for two reasons. First, it was conceived in the Bank as an innovation, which was to give unprecedented attention in the institution to mitigating the adverse effects of a development project on the environment and on indigenous peoples. In the Bank's eyes it was to be a model of comprehensive regional development planning.

Second, and ironically, Polonoroeste became the spearhead for the environmental NGOs' attack on the Bank. In a crescendo of articles, television documentaries and hearings before US congressional committees during 1983–87, the Bank's environmental critics held up Polonoroeste as the Bank's biggest and most disastrous involvement in forest colonization in the tropics; the quintessential example of its wider pursuit of misguided development strategies. Polonoroeste offered powerful images – of palls of smoke, bulldozed trees, blackened stumps – and a saga of victims (immiserized peasants and Amerindians) and villains (military governments, rapacious loggers, and multilateral banks). The *Ecologist* published a special issue called *The World Bank: Global Financing of Impoverishment and Famine*, with articles on Polonoroeste.[4] *Sixty Minutes*, the most widely watched US television newsweekly, featured Polonoroeste in a 1987 documentary that sharply criticized the World Bank for wasting US taxpayers' dollars.

Why did the World Bank become involved?

From the beginning some people in the Bank warned that the risks in this project were too high and that better alternatives for agricultural development existed elsewhere in the northern half of Brazil. But the Bank decided not to stay away for several reasons.

The Bank assumed that the Brazilian government would pave the highway, whether it helped or not. Migration would inevitably increase; the region could not be walled off. The Bank's help in financing what the Brazilians wanted – the highway – would give it leverage in promoting other components that the government was less interested in – agriculture, forest protection, Amerindian protection, and health – and thereby turn it into a model of integrated rural development.

The Bank presented Polonoroeste as a *poverty* programme. Sizeable numbers of settlers – would-be small farmers – were already in the area following earlier waves of migration, but they had been more or less abandoned since the government had failed to provide the expected infrastructure and services. Without the Bank (said the World Bank), the Brazilian government would continue its mistaken, geometrical-grid settlement practices and do little to make the small farmers viable. Therefore Bank involvement would help reduce poverty and reduce the environmental and Amerindian damage.

It was clearly also of importance that Brazil was a large, self-confident country, hailed as a 'miracle' grower in the 1970s. It had a competent bureaucracy at the top levels, and it was a big borrower from the Bank and therefore a most valued customer. The Bank wished to increase lending to an important borrower at a time when Brazil's foreign exchange requirements were rapidly increasing.

The force of these various reasons, especially those having to do with Polonoroeste as a model for the development of 'the world's last land frontier', came from the fact that they had a powerful champion in the Bank. This was Robert Skillings, who had become chief of the Brazil country programmes division in 1971 and stayed in that position until late 1982. Market exploitation of the Amazon was inevitable, he said, the only question was whether it happened wisely or in the free-for-all anarchy of the American West. The Bank could help ensure that this global asset was developed wisely.

Loan approval, 1981

In April 1981 the Loan Committee (of the operational vice-presidents) met to discuss the decision to proceed to negotiations with the Brazilians. This was the last point in the process that the project could, in practice, be turned back or modified. But by this time the project had too much momentum behind it for it to be redesigned. At the end of the meeting, the chairman concluded that 'this would remain a high-risk project, but one worth doing'.

The Bank did not go into Polonoroeste inadvertently, ignorant of the dangers. It was convinced that the dangers could be and would be offset by appropriate safeguards; and that come what may, the results would inevitably be worse if the Bank were not involved. Yet the Bank made no serious assessment of the probability that those 'adequate safeguards' would be carried out on the ground.

Performance on the ground

The roadwork raced ahead, whereas everything else lagged far behind. With most of the funds disbursed for the road building, the Bank had relatively little leverage left for getting the other things done.

The paved highway and the Bank's endorsement of the whole project brought a flood of migrants.[5] The population in the project-affected area surged from an estimated 620,000 in 1982 to 1.6 million in 1988 (World Bank 1992). The assumptions on which the Polonoroeste development strategy had been based turned out to be wildly inaccurate. Subsequently, neither the state government nor the national government did much to enforce the boundaries of the Amerindian reserves, or to limit the logging, or to provide the agricultural credit and the agricultural extension necessary to make the jungle settlements viable.

Deforestation and spontaneous settlement occurred outside the demarcated areas, helped by the feeder roads.

Brazil's fiscal crisis and inflation in excess of 100 per cent wreaked havoc on implementation planning. The problem was especially serious in the health component. Malaria raged like a monster out of control. Many thousands died.

Suspension of disbursements

At the working levels alarm bells continued to ring. A nine-member mid-term review mission went out in November 1984 and presented its report in late February 1985. The report documented at length the many failings.[6] Soon after the mid-term review was presented in March 1985, the decision was made to suspend disbursements until a 'Corrective Action Program' could be agreed upon and certain specific measures taken for Amerindian protection.

Then came two changes in the larger context. First, the Bank was hit with intense public criticism over what US and Brazilian environmental groups were calling the Polonoroeste 'debacle'. The NGOs were demanding suspension, and powerful figures in the US Congress were insisting that the United States cut its contributions to the Bank. Second, Brazil's first civilian government in twenty years had just taken office and accepted the suspension as an indictment of its predecessors rather than itself. Five months later, in August 1985, when the Brazilian government presented to the Bank an action plan to deal with the problems, and showed evidence that the settlers had been removed from the recently invaded Indian reserve, the Bank resumed disbursements.

After 1985

In the period from 1985 to the effective end of the Polonoroeste project in 1989, the Brazilian government somewhat strengthened the implementing capacities of the state agencies, roughly demarcated most of the reserves, and provided some of the infrastructure of the settlement projects. Gradually the government on the ground began to make some progress in doing some of the things it had agreed to do years before.

Yet the OED study found that 'Polonoroeste appears to have been largely unable to implement and/or sustain many of its environmental protection measures or to avoid the continuing invasion of reserve areas by loggers, prospectors, and spontaneous settlers' (World Bank 1992: 108). In retrospect, the outcome could hardly have been different. It was not just that the Bank and Brazil had few data on such fundamentals as soils and their distribution. It was, more basically still, that the Bank hardly addressed the question of the ability and willingness of the federal and territorial agencies to do what the plans required them to do. The Bank's desire to lend to Brazil and at the same time show the world how to conduct rain forest settlement well, coupled with its general avoidance of political analysis, led the relevant people to make assumptions about Polonoroeste that the Latin American vice-president described, looking back, as 'almost deliberately naive'.[7]

Pressures for change: the NGO campaign and the US Treasury's push for environmental reforms

In May 1987 the Bank's new president, Barber Conable, announced plans for a big expansion of environmental capacity, just what the Bank had been saying for years it did not need (Rich 1994: 125). Undoubtedly the campaign led by US environmental NGOs was a major factor in driving the Bank to change its ways. But there were other forces at play as well. The US Congress was one. It had to approve US contributions to IDA, and could be swayed by lobbyists. The US Treasury was another. The role of the Treasury helps to explain why the Bank held off the campaign for four long years.

The NGO campaign, 1983–87

Between 1983 and 1987 more than twenty hearings on the environmental and social performance of the multilateral banks were held before six sub-committees of the US Congress. The centre of attention was the World Bank. Congress had to approve US contributions to the Bank's lending resources, and decided at this time to base its approval on some new conditions. Among other conditions, the US executive director of the Bank would be required to press the Bank's management to undertake stipulated environmental reforms, the implication being that if the Bank's management did not act, Congress would look less favourably upon the next request.

The fact that there had been few actual reports of major environmental damage in its projects over the previous several decades made the Bank confident of its existing arrangements. In any case, it had no fora of consultation with NGOs.[8] Direct contact with NGOs seemed to contradict two of the Bank's constitutional principles: that it would deal with citizens and legislators of member governments through the designated representatives of those governments on the Board of the Bank; and that it would maintain a fiduciary relationship with member governments, a relationship of confidentiality in which the responsibility for releasing information pertaining to a borrower lay with the borrowing government.

First steps, 1983–84

Early in 1983 three NGOs (the Natural Resources Defence Council [NRDC], the Environmental Policy Institute, and the National Wildlife Federation [NWF]) began to consider the World Bank as a target for an international environment campaign.

The trio's basic strategy was to work with environmental and indigenous rights groups in the United States and in a few other countries having the largest share of voting rights in the Bank. They would publicize a small number of large projects against which it would be easy to mobilize opposition. Using these few projects as levers, they would build pressure on member governments to move the Bank, through the executive directors, to institute environmental reforms.

Then they persuaded the chairman of a House committee dealing with international development issues to hold hearings before going to legislation. The hearings would generate useful publicity. Referring to the Polonoroeste project in northwest Brazil, the witnesses argued that had the Bank not helped to finance the 1,500-kilometre highway, considerably fewer colonists would have come into the area and the environmental and social damage would have been much less. In the end, the House sub-committee issued nineteen recommendations, concentrating on actions that could be monitored by Congress and the public, in December 1984. The Treasury agreed with most of the recommendations, and assigned a full-time staff member in its Office of Multilateral Banks to monitor the environmental aspects of multilateral bank loan proposals.

Showdown over Polonoroeste, 1984–85

In October 1984, Bruce Rich of the Environmental Defence fund organized the sending of a letter to President Clausen about Polonoroeste. The letter called on the Bank to enforce its loan covenants with the Brazilian government by immediately suspending disbursements. It listed eight specific steps that the Brazilian government should carry out, and asked how the Bank would ensure that the steps were taken.

The letter was signed by thirty-two NGOs from eleven countries, including the presidents of the American and Brazilian anthropological associations; environmental groups in the United States, Europe and Brazil; and eleven members of the West German parliament.[9] It was accompanied by extensive research dossiers on Polonoroeste prepared by Bruce Rich and anthropologist Steve Schwartzman. The letter and accompanying dossier were featured in a *New York Times* article shortly afterward (Eckholm 1984: A17).

The Bank's letter of reply, cleared by Clausen and by the vice-president for Latin America but signed by the chief of the Brazil programmes division (the appropriate person to reply to an outside enquiry about the Bank's work in Brazil), was brief and formal. It said, in part:

> As you are aware, Polonoroeste is a carefully planned regional development program, which seeks to stabilize and maximize the economic development of the region, while minimizing the risks to the regional ecology and Amerindian populations. We very much share the concerns you have noted in your letter. We have discussed them in detail with the Brazilian authorities and are encouraged by those discussions to believe that effective action will be taken. We recognize, however, that close monitoring will be necessary and we will therefore continue to follow the situation very closely.[10]

Outraged, Rich showed the correspondence to Senator Robert W. Kasten Jr. Senator Kasten was chair of the key Senate Appropriations Sub-committee on Foreign Operations, and therefore had the power to set the sub-committee's agenda and to initiate legislation governing US participation in the Bank. His position made him, for the Bank, the most powerful senator of the most powerful member state. When Kasten and his staff saw the Bank's response to Rich's letter, they 'hit the roof'. [The Bank's reply] seemed to confirm their worst suspicions about the arrogance and lack of accountability of multilateral institutions' (Rich 1994: 123).

In January 1985, Senator Kasten sent a letter to Clausen, describing the Bank's letter to Rich as 'at best a brush-off, but frankly, more correctly described as an insult'.[11] Kasten also wrote a letter to Don Regan, Treasury Secretary, and sent copies of the correspondence to Regan's designated successor, James Baker.

After many draft replies had been discussed with the US Treasury and the US executive director, and after Kasten's office had angrily returned a reply that proposed a meeting between Kasten and the US executive director, Clausen invited Kasten to meet with him and his staff directly.[12]

The meeting, on 22 May 1985, was civil. It was more in the nature of a political ballet than a meeting; Kasten and the environmentalists already knew everything the Bank officials were about to tell them. But the symbolism was important: Senator Kasten had persuaded the president of the World Bank, as well as three other top managers whose attendance Kasten had requested, to meet with him and representatives of several knowledgeable NGOs and explain to them the current state of the Polonoroeste project. This, to Kasten and the environmentalists, looked like a breakthrough in accountability to a member government.

The US Treasury becomes serious and the NGO campaign intensifies, 1986–87

As 1986 approached, the campaign broadened and intensified. The change of stance at the Treasury helps to explain why the Bank changed its mind. What is striking about the first several years of the campaign is how little the Bank moved in response to all the pressure. For one thing, the top management was preoccupied with short-term issues of the debt crisis. And it considered that its Articles of Agreement precluded any direct bargaining-type dealings with NGOs or national legislatures.[13] In addition, the pressure was coming mainly from the Congress, not from the Treasury, and it was the Treasury, as the Bank's official interlocutor, to which the Bank had to give serious attention.

However, it began to be clear in 1986 that the Bank required a capital increase for it to be able to undertake the expanded role implied by the Baker Plan, and the Congress had to approve an increase in the US capital contribution to the IBRD. It was at this point that the Treasury had to take seriously what the Congress, and Senator Kasten in particular, had been saying about the Bank's environmental record. Hence the Treasury put weight behind the environmentalists' recommendations. It wanted the Bank to do what was necessary to diffuse the environmentalists' criticisms, and so remove the grounds on which Congress might hold up an IBRD capital increase.

In 1987 Congress was scheduled to approve both an increase in the US contribution to the IBRD's capital base and an IDA replenishment (IDA 8). The environmental NGOs recognized that 1987 would be 'a crucial year for the campaign to influence the MDBs', because 'considerable opportunity exists for organizations to influence the direction of foreign assistance'.[14]

In 1986 the Sierra Club published *Bankrolling Disasters*, a manual showing how ordinary citizens could link up with the campaign and influence the multilateral development banks.[15] Fifteen thousand copies were distributed to USAID missions, World Bank executive directors and staff, regional multilateral bank counterparts, government officials, and NGOs throughout the world.

The NGOs scored a significant if partial victory in June 1986, when Secretary Baker directed the US executive director of the Bank to vote against an Electric Power Sector Loan to Brazil. The loan was approved. But the US 'nay' represented the first time any member of the Bank had voted not to approve a loan on environmental grounds. By this time the executive directors of several major Part I countries, such as Canada, the Netherlands, Australia, the Nordic countries, and the United Kingdom, were also actively pressing for environmental reforms in the Bank similar to those that the US executive director had been urging for a long time. But they continued to do so more quietly than the United States, and were more inclined to accept the Bank's argument that its involvement in environmentally damaging projects would make the projects less bad. Indeed, several of them – and still more the executive directors from the borrowing countries – were critical of what they saw as the US government's double game, of criticizing the Bank on environmental grounds in order to play to the domestic environmental gallery, while doing little to hold up the flow of lending.

The World Bank responds, despite opposition

Former US Representative Barber Conable, veteran of twenty years in Congress, knew when he became president of the World Bank in 1986 that he had no choice but to defuse the environmental issue, the Bank's prickliest public relations problem at the time.

Many of the borrowing governments, however, especially the big and important ones like Brazil and India, remained strongly opposed to the Bank's assertion of environmental criteria, still considering that this infringed on their sovereignty over their own natural resources. They deeply resented the US pressure, regarding the US executive director as little more than the mouthpiece of US NGOs. To whom were those NGOs accountable, they kept asking. By what right could those US-based NGOs claim to speak for the citizens of their own countries, as though they had more legitimacy than the governments themselves?

To these questions the US NGOs admitted that they had no right to tell the governments of developing countries what to do. But they claimed every right to lobby the US government on what instructions should be given to the US executive director about how Bank lending resources, which included US tax dollars, should be used.

The Bank's shift on the environment, this account suggests, was largely tactical, a response to the need to reduce the threat to its lending resources. The circumstances that made it move were to shape the content of its environmental work.

Institutionalizing 'environmental protection', 1987–93

'The World Bank has been part of the [environmental] problem in the past', and it had 'stumbled' in Polonoroeste, declared Barber Conable to the World Resources Institute on 5 May 1987,[16] and he went on to promise significant organizational changes.

The new structure outlined by Conable was soon created. Having established a complex of in-house environmental champions, the Bank also had to design a set of procedures by which projects would be environmentally assessed. These two developments – environmental staffing and environmental assessment procedures – constituted the first serious attempt to move from 'environment as exception' to 'environment as routine'.

The first press statements announced '100 new environmental posts', but by the end of 1987 the figure was closer to fifty environmental posts (as compared with about five in 1986). In this structure the Environment Department was to be the flagship. Yet from the beginning the department malfunctioned for several years and was discredited in the rest of the Bank.

The division chiefs of the Environment Department could not agree among themselves on priorities and territory, and lacked the staff and budgets to implement both the serious policy work and the operational support being called for. All the while the NGOs barraged the department with criticism. In the meantime, the operational parts of the Bank were wracked by uncertainty over how to operate the new organizational structure, while being under great pressure to deliver lending programmes. The last thing they wanted to hear about was new environmental requirements.

The larger reorganization was partly about cutting staff numbers, and many people suddenly found themselves on the internal job market, their previous position gone. They scrambled for somewhere to go. Environment was the only expanding area. Some who had an environmental qualification or track record got positions there, as did several anthropologists (since 'social' issues of resettlement and tribal concerns were placed under environment, as before 1987). But a sizeable number of those who ended up in the environment complex had no training or experience in environmental issues; they went there on cascading cronyism networks, or in order to get onto other promotion ladders after their own had been blocked. Over the first two years the environmental complex experienced a staff shakeout; those who had gone there as a refuge left for jobs elsewhere, allowing the complex to recruit people with more environmental experience. At the same time, some of the best people also left, fed up with what they saw as the Bank's lack of seriousness.

Meanwhile, the operational departments steered clear to the extent they could. The department did 'nothing' for them, they complained. And when central staffs were made available for operational support, they tended – it was said – to be less than competent.[17] In short, the first several years after 1987 were a time of lost opportunity in the Bank's environment work.

Making environmental assessment procedures, 1988–91

The 1984 directive on environmental aspects of projects was vague on all the key questions of environmental assessments. After 1987 two forces – one external and one internal – combined to make the Bank establish environmental assessment procedures that matched the procedures already formulated for various bilateral aid agencies.

The external pressure arose from Bank and US Treasury negotiations regarding how much the United States would subscribe to the on-going IDA replenishment negotiations. The internal pressure came from the REDs (Regional Environment Directors). The 1987 reforms had given REDs review and clearance powers, but offered no clear guidelines on how those powers were to be used. Three of them had known each other for a long time and were almost the only people in the Bank with hands-on experience with environmental assessments as defined by the profession of environmental assessors. They started work in late 1988, to produce an Operational Manual Statement – by then rechristened Operational Directive (OD) – which would set out the procedures and conditions of use of EAs throughout the Bank. The OD format would make them as close to obligatory as any Bank procedures. The responses from the operating levels of the Bank were anything but enthusiastic.

The clauses that attracted the most criticism were those for consultation and project classification. The consultation clause in the May 1989 version said:

> If screening determines that an EA is required, a 'scoping session' is normally conducted to identify the key environmental issues to be analysed in the EA report. ... It is a forum of selected knowledgeable persons from national, municipal, and local governments; non-governmental organizations (NGOs); institutions of higher learning; and affected groups.
>
> (paragraph 14)

This caused a firestorm of criticism across the Bank. Many people said that it entered 'political' territory that the Bank had no business to be in.

When the EA draft reached the President's Council in late August 1989, another hot issue came up. When should the EA be released to the executive directors, and to others? Senior Vice-President Stern reported that US Treasury Secretary Nicholas F. Brady had recently sent a letter to the Bank asking for substantial advance notice – for the EA to be delivered to the US executive director well before the project came to the Board. Stern also reported that

NGOs were pressing hard for the EA to be disclosed long before the project design was set.

Some twenty-six drafts later, the final OD was ready by the time of the Annual Meetings of 1989.[18] The vice-president for central operations, the director of the Environment Department, and members of the writing team gave a presentation to an invited audience of some 300 government officials. They later did the same at a meeting of a hundred or more NGO representatives and others.

The NGOs were disgruntled, however, because they had not been consulted at any point in the drafting of the OD, and for reasons to do with the Narmada campaign (explained later in this chapter) were especially powerful at this time. In response, the Bank committed itself to an early revision to take account of NGO reactions. The revised version, OD 4.01, October 1991, said: 'The purpose of EA is to ensure that the development options under consideration are environmentally sound and sustainable.' This made clearer than had the earlier version that 'sustainability' was not a value to be traded off in an economic analysis. Rather, it implied that *all* the options under consideration should meet sustainability criteria.

By the late 1980s the Bank came under a second wave of attack for its environmental and social record, this time mounted by an international coalition of NGOs and eventually joined by several "rich countries" governments. What sparked this second attack were the Narmada projects in northwest India. This time the Bank was pressured to go further in integrating environmental and social criteria into its lending and advice, in the direction of the 'environmental management' paradigm.

Pressures for change: the Narmada project in India

The Narmada Valley Project constitutes a basin-wide, interstate development scheme to harness the Narmada River, one of India's last 'unexploited' resources, for hydropower and irrigation. The reservoir of the first of the big dams, Sardar Sarovar, would be 200 kilometres long and displace some 40,000 households. The canal, 100 metres across the water at the head, would be one of the biggest in the world. The canal network would extend for 75,000 kilometres and irrigate almost two million hectares of arid land. Its construction would remove some portion of the land of 68,000 households.

In response to years of concerted outside pressure, in 1993 the Bank and the government of India cancelled the Bank's disbursements for Sardar Sarovar. This was the first time the Bank had taken such a step anywhere in the world on environmental or social grounds (as distinct from financial or procurement grounds).

Resettlement and the environment

Not until 1983, as Sardar Sarovar was being appraised, did the Bank's sociologist and resettlement champion, Michael Cernea, discover that the appraisal mission's terms of reference contained no mention of resettlement. So he hired a well known resettlement expert, Thayer Scudder, to investigate the resettlement situation. Scudder was 'appalled' by what he found.[19] Nothing had been done to inform villagers about resettlement options and rehabilitation packages.

In 1987 a resettlement mission went out to see what progress had been made in the meantime. It found that those villagers who had already been moved to make way for the dam were still languishing in resettlement villages on sterile land without even rudimentary infrastructure. On its return the mission recommended that the Bank threaten India with cancellation for non-compliance with the resettlement agreement.[20]

At the Board approval meeting in 1985, only one executive director worried about potential environmental problems. The staff replied, 'although a full environmental impact assessment had not been completed, a *comprehensive first-stage assessment* had been conducted by the University of Baroda and then examined by members of the World Bank appraisal team'. This 'comprehensive first-stage assessment' was a short, general document dating from the early 1980s, which could not remotely qualify as an environmental assessment. By describing it as 'first-stage' the staff covered themselves; and by reporting only the finding that there were no endangered species in the area, the staff gave the impression that the environmental situation was better than it was.

By 1990 everyone was at everyone else's throat. The India Department blamed the Asia RED, the environment people blamed the project people, Bank staff blamed the Indians, the central government blamed the states, the states blamed the central government, and everyone blamed the Bank.

External pressure

Meanwhile, a local NGO had come to prominence in the Narmada Valley, later called the Narmada Bachao Andolan (NBA), translated as Save the Narmada Movement. The NBA by 1987 had linked up with the US-based Environmental Defence Fund (EDF). There, a new recruit, Lori Udall, took up the Narmada cause full-time, encouraged by EDF's seasoned Bank campaigner, Bruce Rich. Instead of pushing for better resettlement it launched a 'Stop the Dam' campaign. To many international NGOs, Stop the Dam was more attractive than Better Resettlement.

Udall coordinated the international campaign in the period from 1988 to 1992. First, she identified groups within the more important Part I countries that might support an anti-Narmada/anti-Bank campaign. Second, she prepared menus of actions they might take in the circumstances of their own countries: parliamentary or congressional hearings, public fora, press conferences, lobbying key officials, and letter-writing campaigns. She especially encouraged them to contact their country's executive director and to go to legislators. Third, she prepared information packs for them, drawing on materials sent by NBA and other Indian activists.

In 1989 the US-based NGOs in the campaign persuaded a congressional sub-committee to hold hearings specifically on Narmada. These hearings mark a watershed in the international criticism of the Bank. Thereafter the international anti-Narmada/anti-Bank campaign took off.

The independent review

World Bank President Conable, in the waning months of his presidency, was growing desperate; he needed someone fast. With support from Evelyn Herfkins (the Dutch executive director) and other interested executive directors, he approached his former congressional colleague, Bradford Morse, who since leaving the US Congress had been head of the United Nations Development Programme (UNDP). In June 1991 Conable announced that an independent review panel would be established and headed by Morse.

Ten months later, on 18 June 1992, the panel issued a 363-page report.[21] The report concluded, first, that the Bank had been seriously out of compliance with its own directives on resettlement and on environmental analysis of projects; second, that 'there is good reason to believe that the project will not perform as planned', that is, perform in the hydrological sense of getting the water to the expected areas; third, that adequate resettlement was unlikely to occur on the ground 'under prevailing circumstances', because 'a further application of the same [incremental] strategy, albeit in a more determined or aggressive fashion, would fail'. Finally, it recommended that the Bank 'step back' from the project. Essentially, it confirmed much of what the NGO campaign had been saying.

The decision to continue, and then to cancel

In July 1992 the Bank sent a large (fourteen-person) mission to review the status of the Sardar Sarovar project, with the implicit goal of assessing whether the review was right.[22] None of the mission members, including those resettlement experts who had not hesitated to criticize the Bank's performance, wanted cancellation, because they were convinced that without the Bank being involved, resettlement and environmental protection would be worse.

In September 1992 the Bank presented to the Board a document titled 'Sardar Sarovar Projects, Review of Current Status and Next Steps'.

In October the chairman and deputy chairman of the review, Bradford Morse and Thomas Berger, wrote to the president of the Bank saying that the Bank's reply, 'ignores or misrepresents the main findings of our Review. ... [W]e do want to ensure that the senior decision-makers at the Bank are not left with an account of our findings that is at variance with what we wrote.'[23] Review members subsequently flew to Washington to meet with the Board. Bank staff present at the meeting remember it for the sheer vindictiveness of the executive directors. The Dutch executive director, who had taken a coordinating role for the project within the Board and between the Board and the Bank, reminded the meeting that the Board had asked for an independent review because it felt it could not trust Bank management. The Austrian executive director criticized Bank management for its strong-arm lobbying of the executive directors to keep the project going. The US executive director, Patrick Coady, accused management of a 'cover-up', noting, 'what is at stake is the credibility of the Board' (Rich 1994: 301).

The Bank's management said: 'A decision by the Bank not to get involved could well mean that the project in question will still proceed but under much less favourable circumstances'.[24] It did not say, though this was in its mind, that cancellation would have severe consequences for the Bank's reputation as an infrastructure lender in India and elsewhere.

At the Board meeting a prominent Part I country executive director asked the key question: had the 'relevant authorities' agreed to the benchmarks (meaning, had the state governments agreed)? The management said yes. On the strength of this assurance, the executive director voted with the Part II countries, tipping the balance in favour of continuing subject to review against benchmarks six months later. The majority 'wished to give the benefit of the doubt to the new Government of India [at the federal level] and to acknowledge the recent efforts made by the Indian authorities'.[25]

At the end of March 1993, the Board was scheduled to decide whether to continue. The South Asia vice-president, Joseph Wood, who had resisted suspension or cancellation since taking charge in 1991, became persuaded there was no alternative to cancellation. The government of India and the government of Gujarat attitude was: 'Damn the NGOs, we are not going to submit to crybabies, we will continue to build the dam.' They did not wish to accommodate the Bank's attempts to respond to world outrage. In the end, President Preston informed the prime minister that Narmada was jeopardizing IDA, which would hurt India. The vice-president for South Asia told the Indian government: 'Either we cancel or you tell us you will not submit requests for disbursements.'

A few days before the Board meeting, the government of India announced that it would not ask the Bank for more disbursements. The central government was not unhappy to cancel. The project was generating too many headaches, and the benefits of Bank involvement went largely to Gujarat, not to the centre. In private, Indian officials said that what the Bank had been doing was 'not in keeping with the country's self-respect' (*National Herald* 1993). The NBA then succeeded in getting the Supreme Court to halt dam construction at the beginning of 1995, until resettlement was carried out in line with India's and the Bank's policies.

Why Narmada?

Narmada became a focal point for NGO activity because it had several characteristics that lent itself to the NGOs' general opposition to the World Bank: it involved the forced displacement of large numbers of people, many of whom could be presented as sympathy-deserving 'tribals'; forced relocation could support a radical campaign to stop the dam; local opposition was well organized, led by a charismatic figure (Patkar); the international campaign benefited from unusually energetic and tenacious organizers (in particular Udall and EDF); some Bank staff members and Bank consultants were severe critics of the way the project was being implemented, and could help the external critics with information; and the local opposition to Narmada began to reach a crescendo around 1986, just as Polonoroeste was losing its appeal to the NGOs. Finally, location in India also helped, because international NGOs had good access to English-language information and because India's democratic polity and free press allowed opposition.

What did make Narmada unusual was its timing, which put it in a set of 'hinge' projects. It was prepared, appraised, and approved at about the same time that the Bank introduced quite new directives on 'non-economic' criteria – resettlement and environment. The operational people, including South Asia Vice-President David Hopper, stoutly resisted these 'non-economic' criteria and directives inside the Bank. Their resistance, combined with ambiguity about the status of 'directives' (as analogous to national laws or as guidelines for what would be nice to achieve), allowed the project people to continue to prepare the project as they had prepared projects before the resettlement and environmental directives were introduced.

From 'environmental protection' to 'environmental management'

Around 1992 and 1993 the more comprehensive ideas of the 'environmental management' paradigm began to take hold at senior management and operational levels.

The Global Environmental Facility helped promote conversion. From 1989 to late 1990 the Bank was involved in negotiating a pilot phase, which was approved for a period of three years with funds of $1.3 billion, pledged by participating countries (Kjørven 1992; Sjöberg 1994). The preparations for the Rio Summit of 1992 also helped to 'seed' the environmental idea inside the Bank by providing it with the opportunity to demonstrate world leadership in environment–development matters and to refurbish its battered image. By this time, too, the environmental complex was well established and pushing to expand its mandate.

There is no doubt that 'the environment' now has greater legitimacy than it did in, say, 1991. As a prominent Ban k research economist put it: 'You can't write anything about development these days without mentioning the environment.'[26]

The publication of *Development and the Environment*, the title of the *World Development Report 1992*, was a milestone in this shift. The report helped move the process forward in several ways. First, it presented environmental issues in a language that economists (inside and outside the Bank) could understand, as economic problems entailing costs and benefits. Second, it imparted a strong bias toward thinking that the scope for policies that benefited growth, poverty reduction and environmental protection simultaneously was large, encouraging economists to hunt out such opportunities in their own particular countries. Third, it redirected attention toward the 'brown' agenda, i.e. much of the environment debate in the development context had been about green issues, in response to the dominant concerns of northern NGOs. Fourth, the report was written under the direction of a well–respected Bank economist, Andrew Steer.

He had no previous involvement with environmental issues, and his conversion helped other economists change their minds.

Integrating environmental sustainability in macro and sector work

By 1993 Bank economists sympathetic to an environmental agenda had come to agree that much greater environmental improvements could be achieved by integrating environmental criteria into the Bank's policy work at the country level (into 'economic and sector work', in Bank parlance) than by improving individual projects. Yet this integration, up to the mid-1990s, was noticeable by its absence.

It is true that National Environmental Action Plans (NEAPS) had been or were in the process of being prepared for Bank borrowers, initially for IDA countries as a condition of the IDA 9 negotiations of the late 1980s but continuing for non-IDA countries, too (World Bank 1990: 304). But at least up to the mid-1990s the plans were often 'ritualistic and second-rate', in the words of the director of the Environment Department.[27]

Even the many high-quality studies produced by the Bank on various aspects of development–environment integration mean less than they appear to. A high proportion of them are done not by staff members but by consultants, and therefore they expand the Bank's intellectual capital by less than would be the case if staff had written them.

In reviewing the Bank's efforts to integrate environmental considerations, one finds that the organization has handled them best when it has organized environment as a separate *sector*, alongside agriculture, energy, forestry, and so on – a sector bounded, moreover, by *national borders*. These are fully consistent with the Bank's long-established mode of organization: they can be given to a task manager located in a country department and handled just like any other project. But conflicts of interest and difficulties of budgeting arise when environment is organized *cross-sectorally*, as a perspective to be injected into all Bank work.

The governance reforms

In October 1992, just as the Board voted to continue Sardar Sarovar for another six months, negotiations for the tenth replenishment of IDA (for 1993–96) were entering their final phase. The NGOs that had been most active in opposing Narmada swung into a campaign to obtain two fundamental accountability reforms. They wanted a radical revision in the Bank's information policy so as to make information about projects more freely available. And they wanted an independent appeal panel that would give directly affected people access to a body empowered to investigate complaints that the Bank was violating its policy procedures and loan agreements. The NGOs announced that they would oppose pledges to IDA 10 by the United States and other governments unless these reforms were carried out. In testimony before the US Congress in spring 1993, they proposed that the Congress redirect its IDA money to other organizations that were more accountable and democratic than the Bank, should it not carry out the two reforms by June 1994 (Udall 1998).[28]

The accountability campaign focused on the sub-committee of the US Congress in charge of authorizing US contributions to IDA. The chairman of the sub-committee, Representative Barney Frank, informed Ernest Stern in private that the Bank had a simple choice: either it adopted an acceptable information policy and independent appeals panel, or it got no US money for IDA 10. The Bank took the threat seriously. It secretly sent drafts of the new information policy and a resolution creating an independent 'inspection panel' to Frank and his sub-committee for comments, before presenting them formally to the Board.

The new information policy approved by the Board in August 1993 fell short of what the NGOs and Frank were demanding, though it also represented a substantial change from the old policy.[29] The Board also approved a resolution creating an independent inspection panel in September 1993 (World Bank 1993; Shihata 1994). This, too, fell well short of what the NGOs had envisioned. Its basic principles of operation as approved by the Board gave it much less independence than had the independent review for Sardar Sarovar. Nevertheless, the creation of the inspection panel did represent a major departure from previous practice, and its existence owed much to the precedent of the independent review for Sardar Sarovar.

Critics of the panel, including many Bank managers, also said that the panel discouraged staff from seeking imaginative and risky solutions and caused management to steer away from projects that were inherently difficult to 'panel-proof', such as dams. It imparted a legalistic thrust to Bank work, eclipsing substance (as in the injunction: 'Make your projects panel-proof'), and strengthening an existing tendency toward 'OD absolutism', with ODs being interpreted by outsiders as legally binding, like the laws of nation-states. As the drive to codify procedures intensified in the late 1980s and early 1990s, task managers complained of being 'OD'ed [overdosed] on ODs'. A study of ODs covering Bank projects showed that as of 1992 they specified a total of about 200 separate tasks for task managers to carry out, and ODs then in the pipeline were expected to double that number.[30]

Conclusion

The history of the Bank's attempts to come to grips with the 'environment' can be read as a great battle over values, attitudes and images. As in religious wars, the (environmental) facts have often ended up as relatively unimportant details compared with the symbols and postures and the struggle for power. Yet there are no 'objective' standards of value and no consensus about causal relationships.

In principle, *all* Bank work should now be assessed for its effects on economic growth, poverty reduction and environmental sustainability. The change has consisted of a paradigmatic shift from 'frontier economics' before 1987, to 'environmental protection' up to the early 1990s, and on to the more comprehensive 'environmental management' thereafter. Throughout, it has been accompanied by changes in staffing, organization and procedures.

The process by which one paradigm shifted to another was anything but a deliberative response to new knowledge and new opportunities. It was more akin to the grinding of tectonic plates, as people of radically different worldviews were forced by the pressures of environmental disruption and the political responses to deal with one another again and again. Or perhaps it was more akin to learning through angst, as Bank task managers, Bank senior managers, Bank economists, Bank environmental specialists, borrowing-government officials, US NGO representatives, borrowing-country NGO representatives, villagers, and city dwellers tried in overlapping fora to find a common language and common ground, all calling upon powerful normative reasons for doing what they wished to do and not doing what others wished to do.

The new environmental values were championed by a spiralling international concert of environmental NGOs and agencies of some Part I governments. They were for the most part resisted by developing-country governments and by many economists and engineers working on development issues. The new environmental values, said the resisters, were based on criteria – such as 'ecosystem functioning', 'ecosystem damage', and (especially) 'environmental sustainability' – that had no clear empirical referents. Yet these kinds of fuzzy notions were being used to pose fundamental challenges to professional identities ('we only deal with hard numbers'), to question the role of 'experts' in relation to citizens, and to disparage the very concept of development as we know it.

The Bank moved to embrace the self-consciously named environment in 1987 in large part because the NGO campaign and the US Treasury made the costs of not moving too high. In this respect, what happened in the environment field is similar to what has happened elsewhere when the Bank has changed its mind: in most cases, the Bank has not moved without outside pressure from the major donors/owners of the Bank or from NGOs (Prestre 1989). No doubt the Bank would eventually have moved on the environment anyway because of the larger tide of ideas, despite the legacy of more than twenty years of internal resistance. But the fact that the other multilateral development banks made virtually no moves to integrate environmental considerations until well into the 1990s does support the argument that the NGO campaign was crucial. The NGOs paid much less attention to the other multilateral banks than to the World Bank, not because they thought it worse than the others but because it had a much higher political profile.

By 1992–93, however, the legitimacy of 'environment' inside the Bank began to turn strongly positive. Not only in *World Development Report 1992* but also in all its publications, it began to promote itself, evangelically, as a champion of environmental sustainability. In principle, 'environmental sustainability' imparts a still more distinctive and comprehensive set of objectives to the Bank's work. But the integration of these new concerns has been severely constrained by the Bank's established organization, incentives and knowledge.

A question should be raised concerning the Bank's environmental (and resettlement) standards. Do these standards create such a cost burden that they significantly impair the Bank's ability to compete against other sources of funds that are less stringent (the Japan Import–Export Bank or the regional multilateral banks, for example)? Should the standards be varied by country groupings rather than made uniform for all? The Bank's environmental critics have tended to forget that it is, at base, a lending institution; its ability to carry out its development-within-the-limits-of-sustainability function rests on its ability to lend, and hence on finding governments willing to pay its prices.

The Bank has moved from Old Testament harshness ('environment versus growth') to New Testament reconciliation ('environmentally sustainable development'). But it has yet to engage in an open internal debate about what it should be doing in the environment field, a debate in which the sort of questions raised in this chapter can be tackled – and disagreements honestly aired – with a view to finding answers that command some consensus and are operationally meaningful. This would be difficult, however, without reforming the command and control style of management and introducing ways to evaluate staff by the effectiveness of their projects more than by their reliability in moving them to the Board. Failing some change in the system of internal incentives, there is a danger that New Testament reconciliation may remain at the level of images and values and bring little improvement to what happens on the ground.

Notes

1 The following draws on Colby (1989).
2 Mahbub ul Haq had been secretary for planning in Pakistan. At this time he had just joined the Bank as a senior economic adviser, recruited directly by McNamara.
3 McNamara, interview with the author, 20 February 1995.
4 See *The Ecologist* 15 (1–2): 1995.
5 The World Bank did not make any estimates of the effects of the highway on migration, nor did it work out alternative scenarios based on different migration assumptions.
6 World Bank, mid-term review, internal memorandum of 25 February 1985, cited in World Bank (1992).
7 David Knox, who became vice-president for Latin America in time for the mid-term review of Polonoroeste, interview with the author, 15 May 1995.
8 This is not literally true. The Bank had long had contact with foundations such as Ford and Rockefeller, drawing on their expertise in policy making and in particular projects. It also established an NGO–World Bank Committee in 1982. It was window dressing, without significance, until the late 1980s, when it began to include southern NGOs and more radical northern ones (such as Development Gap).
9 The Green Party had been active in mobilizing opposition to Polonoroeste in Germany.
10 Robert Gonzalez Cofino, chief, Brazil Division, to Bruce Rich, NRDC, 7 November 1984.
11 Letter, Senator Robert Kasten to A.W. Clausen, 24 January 1985.
12 A.W. Clausen to Senator Robert Kasten, 1 March 1985.
13 IBRD, *Articles of Agreement*, Article III, Section 2.
14 See *Interaction Newsletter* (February 1986) published by the Global Tomorrow Coalition.
15 Written by Bruce Rich and Steve Swartzman.

16 His admission upset members of the Polonoroeste project team, who continued to think that the project was much better than it would have been without the Bank.

17 This was a common perception, yet operational staff would also agree that quite a number of individuals in the department, name by name, were exceptionally able.

18 'Environmental Assessments' is formally presented as 'Annex A' to OD 4.00; the OD itself was then unwritten.

19 Thayer Scudder, interview with the author, 3 November 1995.

20 Formally, the recommendation was for suspension followed by cancellation, since Bank procedures require that suspension precede cancellation.

21 This was four days *after* the World Bank rose from Rio as the key agency to implement 'Agenda 21', an informal intergovernmental agreement on global environmental priorities and actions. A draft had been discussed over two days in May by a group of eleven staff and three panel members.

22 Known as the Cox Mission, after its leader, Pamela Cox, a member of the India Department who had not previously worked on Narmada.

23 Bradford Morse and Thomas Berger to Lewis Preston, 13 October 1992.

24 The quotation comes from the first draft of the Bank's management's response to the independent review, dated 23 June 1992, p. 12.

25 Chairman's summary, 'India: Sardar Sarovar Projects', executive directors' meeting, 23 October 1992.

26 Lant Pritchett, interview with the author, 10 December 1996.

27 Andrew Steer, interview with the author, 28 October 1994.

28 See also the testimony of Barbara Bramble on behalf of the National Wildlife Federation, and the testimony of Lori Udall on behalf of Environmental Defence Fund, before the Sub-committee on International Development, Trade, Finance and Monetary Policy on 5 May 1993.

29 See 'Bank Procedures, Disclosure of Operational Information', BP 17.50, September 1993.

30 Critics of the panel also say that it is a vehicle for a small number of Washington-based NGOs to gain funding and prominence by initiating and preparing cases to go to the panel. The Centre for International Environmental Law, linked to the American University in Washington DC, has been especially active in this way.

7 Sustainable development and the World Trade Organization

Morten Bøås and Jonas Vevatne

Introduction

The World Trade Organization (WTO) was established on 1 January 1995, as part of the final agreements of the Uruguay Round negotiations. The establishment of the WTO is one of the most significant moments in the recent history of multilateral institutions, because 'its establishment provides a sister institution for the Bretton Woods pairing of the International Monetary Fund (IMF) and the World Bank some 50 years after their creation' (O'Brien *et al.* 2000: 68).[1] In the predecessor to WTO, the General Agreement on Tariffs and Trade (GATT), no explicit reference was made to the environment.[2] GATT's first experience with environmental issues came when the GATT Secretariat was asked to report to the *UN Conference on the Human Environment* (UNCHE) in Stockholm in 1972. GATT's report, *International Pollution Control and International Trade*, was a strong reflection of the dominant free-trade paradigm in GATT (Nordström and Vaughan 1999). The basis of GATT's approach to trade and environment was that trade had to be protected from environmental measures and not the other way around (Lund-Thomsen 1999: 51). As a follow-up to this report, it was decided that GATT should establish a *Working Group on Environmental Measures and International Trade* (EMIT). This group was supposed to review all kinds of trade-related aspects of measures for pollution abatement and preservation of the human environment (Nordström and Vaughan 1999). However, this group existed only on paper. The GATT did not adopt the notion of environment in its work and EMIT did not meet until November 1991. In fact, in almost all other comparable multilateral institutions, the idea of sustainable development was already firmly established by the time the idea was finally also taken up by GATT/WTO.

Already in the 1980s, the World Bank and other multilateral institutions were strongly challenged on environmental grounds by international environmental NGOs (see Chapter 6). GATT, however, did not receive much attention from these organizations. GATT was therefore able to continue the Uruguay Round without making any reference to sustainable development in the negotiations.[3] The reason for this, we suggest, was mainly the low level of public awareness of both GATT and the environmental impact of international trade. The low level of public attention and the non-existence of formal relations between GATT and civil society organizations left GATT out of the public eye, and, therefore, there was hardly any pressure at all on GATT to address environmental issues. The traditional, technical and juridical approach to international trade (law) could therefore prevail. However, in the early 1990s GATT's lack of concern for environmental issues came under fire from two sides. The European Free Trade Area (EFTA) countries, and in particular the Nordic countries, started a process at the Brussels Ministerial Meeting in December 1990 with the aim of bringing the work of the World Commission on Environment and Development (WCED) into GATT; and in the United States, the outcome of the Tuna–Dolphin Dispute between the United States and Mexico raised public awareness of both the trade–environment nexus in general, and in particular about the position and role of GATT within this nexus.[4]

The objective of this chapter is thus to explore GATT and WTO's encounter with the environment and sustainable development. More precisely, the major task is to explain why it took so long before GATT/WTO adopted the idea of sustainable development. In order to accomplish this task, we will build our exploration around a package of assumptions presented below. These will be analysed in the remaining parts of this chapter.

The argument

Our first assumption is that there are very few multilateral institutions in which the neoliberal orthodoxy is more dominant than in GATT/WTO. Our argument is that this has made it difficult for the organization to adjust to perspectives that potentially are different/diverging. The WTO Secretariat is not only strongly influenced by neoliberalism; it also adopts a highly technical approach to international trade. Our point is that new ideas do not enter an institutional vacuum. 'They are inserted into a political space already occupied by historically formed ideologies. Whether or not consolidation occurs often depends on the degree to which the new model fits with existing ideologies of important economic and social groups' (Sikkink 1991: 2).

This implies that the meaning of a new idea is derived largely from the political and ideological context of the institution it is absorbed by. We define the institutional identity of WTO staff members in terms of neoliberalism and technicality, and argue that staff members' institutional identity and loyalty was strengthened when they suddenly (and for them rather surprisingly) were confronted with strong criticism from the NGOs. The environmental criticism of the NGOs challenged the very foundation of WTO, namely its free trade theory; and when confronted with this criticism, staff members closed ranks around the WTO and its core ideas.

WTO inherited from GATT not only the dominance of neoliberalism and a technical approach to international trade, but also a tradition of secrecy and lack of transparency. GATT/WTO's organizational routines and procedures for formal relations with civil society are therefore not much developed, and staff members can isolate themselves from new impulses and competing worldviews and perspectives. This may help to explain the shock felt by WTO staff members when they witnessed the events in Seattle in 1999.

These three assumptions constitute the major basis for the following analysis of sustainable development and WTO. Before we turn to these tasks, it is necessary to briefly revisit the events that led to the inclusion of this idea in the Marrakech Declaration that established the WTO.

The road to Marrakech

Influenced by WCED's report, the EFTA countries worked hard to include sustainable development on the agenda at the GATT Ministerial Meeting in Brussels in December 1990. Their proposal was not enthusiastically received, and in particular, Brazil and India 'strenuously fought the GATT efforts to reinvigorate EMIT' (Esty 1994: 181). In the end, however, it was accepted that sustainable development was an issue for debate within the framework of GATT. The main reason for this was probably that the UN Conference on Environment and Development (UNCED) to be held in Rio in 1992 was already under preparation, and too outspoken opposition to sustainable development by GATT could entail considerable political costs. GATT had also been asked by the UN to report to UNCED on the trade–environment nexus (see GATT 1992). This task was delegated to EMIT, which then met for the first time ever in 1991. Nonetheless, EMIT had very little influence on the Uruguay Round.

This first attempt to place environmental issues and sustainable development on GATT's agenda was soon followed by much harder criticism from the environmental movement.

GATT's response to its critics in the environmental movement was perceived as arrogant and it led to a long-lasting hostile relationship between GATT and the NGOs. Instead of trying to deal with criticism in an open and transparent manner, GATT chose the approach of secrecy. Panel reports and other documents were stamped 'restricted' and relations between GATT staff and NGOs were generally actively discouraged (see Esty 1994). The consequence was that the majority in the environmental movement felt that it was impossible to have a fruitful dialogue, and the NGOs chose to make their criticism even more vocal. The increased strength of NGO criticism, however, seems only to have reinforced the institutional identity and loyalty of staff members to the organization's foundation: free trade theory. The hostile relationship that developed was also strengthened by the lack of organizational procedures for formal relations between GATT and civil society organizations. GATT, which traditionally had been a closed and secret institution with minimal contact with NGOs/non-members, was suddenly strongly criticized by radical environmentalists. This was a new and frightening experience for most staff members because originally GATT was organized in a manner that was supposed to insulate the organization and its staff from political pressure from particular interest groups (Esty 1994: 53). Until the 1990s GATT had been very successful in this respect, in fact so successful that the organization had ignored important changes that it should have observed and absorbed.

The environmental NGOs were instrumental in the last stages of the Uruguay Round. The United States in particular was pressured by strong national environmental NGOs. The result was that the United States demanded that a clear reference to sustainable development be made and that a committee on trade and environment be established. If not, the US argued that the strong domestic environmental opposition that the government was faced with would make it impossible for it to secure a majority in Congress for the ratification of the Uruguay Round Agreement. From the last negotiation meeting in December 1993 to April 1994, when the agreement was signed in Marrakech, the United States prepared the ground for a separate statement on trade and environment and for a direct reference to sustainable development in the preamble of the agreement that established the WTO. In the Final Act of the Uruguay Round (April 1994) sustainable development was therefore included in the rules of the international trade regime through the so-called Marrakech Ministerial Decision on Trade and Environment, and at the Marrakech Ministerial Meeting a reference to sustainable development was agreed upon and included in the preamble of the new organization:

> allowing for the optimal use of the world's resources in accordance with the objective of sustainable development, seeking both to protect and preserve the environment and to enhance the means for doing so consistent with [the parties'] respective needs and concerns at different levels of economic development.
>
> (WTO 1994)

Nonetheless, the concept 'sustainable development' remained undefined by the WTO, and the preamble contains only a vague formulation that refers to the Rio Declaration on Environment and Development. WTO's understanding of sustainable development differs significantly from WCED's definition and interpretation, which emphasized *solidarity* both within and between generations. This is an aspect that WTO documents are not concerned about. What these documents tend to underscore is rather that with the correct policies (neoliberal) the linkages between trade and environment can be mutually beneficial. 'The objectives of an open and fair multilateral trade system and sustainable development are not exclusionary' (St.prp. nr. 65 1993/94: attachment 738).[5] One interpretation of WTO's approach to the idea of sustainable development is therefore in accordance with what Jacobson (1995) calls 'consensual beliefs'. In WTO, sustainable development is implicitly defined as a consensual belief, used to shape the legitimate ends of economic activity.

WTO and neoliberalism

The creation of WTO can be seen as a conscious attempt to establish a strong global regulatory framework in support of increased trade liberalization. The architects of the post-World War II economic order interpreted international non-cooperation on trade as a function of domestic political pressures. GATT was therefore set up as a government-to-government contract anchored in support for freer trade (Esty 1994). By embedding the principles of liberal trade theory in an international regime, the individuals and governments behind the creation of GATT not only built an institutional mechanism for the supposed reduction of trade conflict among member states, they also heightened their commitment to liberal trade theory to almost a constitutional level. The consequence was a clear limitation on the power of governments to give in to the pleadings of various national interest groups and other social movements. In moving free trade principles to a higher place of authority, a buffer was constructed not only against protectionist pressures, but also against most other attempts at reform of the international trade regime. In order for new ideas to be incorporated into the existing trade regime as embodied by WTO, the idea in question must either be in accordance with liberal trade theory or it must be possible to adapt or distort the idea in question into accordance with liberal trade theory.

One way to approach the WTO is therefore to view it not only as a legal instrument for the promotion of free trade (O'Brien *et al.* 2000), but also as a bastion of a neoliberal worldview. According to the WTO, free trade and the abolishment of all kinds of trade barriers will promote economic growth, not only among the rich industrial countries, but worldwide. And according to the neoliberal economic paradigm, trade liberalization will encourage more efficient use of resources, the adoption and diffusion of cleaner technologies, higher productivity, and increased income levels: developments that the WTO see as a precondition for a cleaner environment. The WTO thesis is therefore that trade liberalization will enable less developed countries both to tackle the poverty problem and their widespread environmental degradation. This kind of reasoning makes it possible for liberal economists and free traders to see trade liberalization and environmental protection as compatible.

According to the neoliberal view of WTO, unsustainable economic growth is the consequence of market failure and the inability of governments to engage in adequate environmental pricing. This means that any trade-related environment measures (TREMs) will only make things worse because they will interfere with the free flow of goods, and thereby lead to less efficient (i.e. environmentally harmful) resource allocation. It is WTO's 'consensual belief' that restrictions on trade are not only inadequate but also positively dangerous, because under the cloak of sustainable development lies the troll of protectionism. The law of comparative advantage and the superiority of market-based solutions remain articles of faith in the WTO.

WTO and technicality

WTO is clearly biased towards a neoliberal agenda. However, in order to understand WTO's approach to sustainable development, it is equally important that we come to terms with the organization's distinct technical approach to international trade. Almost all multilateral institutions are defined in their agreements

and charters as functional and technical institutions.[6] However, lately several
multilateral institutions have adopted much broader agendas. With the broadening of their agenda, most of these institutions also had to rethink their
recruitment policies, and found that they also needed to employ people with
other kinds of background than law, economics and engineering. The same sort
of development has not taken place in the WTO. There are no statistics available on the employees' educational background,[7] but WTO's external relations
division confirms that lawyers and economists are predominant.[8] The result is an
institution with a highly technical approach to international trade (law) where
there is little room for other considerations, whether social or environmental.

The consequence was that sustainable development could only be incorporated
into WTO if the idea could be adapted and/or distorted in accordance with the
already existing problem definition of international trade in the organization. As
we have seen from the reference to sustainable development in the preamble to the
Ministerial Declaration, this was possible. Thus a real re-examination of
GATT/WTO's purpose was not necessary. The knowledge on which 'sustainable
development' was founded could be presented to the WTO in the same technocratic language as the old and familiar knowledge of neoliberal trade theory. This
meant that it was possible to keep the discussion on sustainable development in the
WTO within the frame of its 'standard operating procedures'. It is here that the
issue of knowledge and the assumed political neutrality of a certain type of
economics enters the picture, because the legitimacy of the WTO rests on the
claim that its economic advice reflects the best possible research, a justification
readily cited by member governments when imposing WTO policies on their often
unwilling populations.

The production of knowledge in the WTO is therefore produced within a
frame of reference that embeds certain cognitive interests, meaning that knowledge becomes an instrument, a tool, for the identification of manipulable
variables. The economics of the WTO is presented as an objective, value-free
scientific discourse. The laws of neoliberal economics, it is argued, are universal
and it is the task of the WTO to make certain that the member countries
conform to these laws. The various issues and questions concerning international
trade are presented as technical issues, because trade is seen as socially, politically
and environmentally neutral.

Secrecy and lack of transparency

The making of international trade policy has traditionally been the responsibility
of the state, or more precisely, an issue-area dealt with by a small group of trade
bureaucrats and politicians who conducted their policy making within a small
secure circle of like-minded persons, behind closed doors and under high levels
of secrecy.[9] Trade policy was rarely an item that was prominent on the public
agenda.

This may explain why the Secretariat was so stunned by the environmental
NGOs' reactions to the outcome of the Tuna–Dolphin Dispute in 1991. GATT

had no standing operating procedures for relations with civil society organizations, and the institution had little awareness of how important the
trade–environment nexus was becoming in the eyes of not only the NGOs, but
also large segments of the population in important member countries.

Thus, when the idea of a world trade organization was placed on the agenda
in the latter part of the Uruguay Round, the increased scope, permanence and
rule-making authority of the proposed organization alarmed environmentalists
and other civil society actors. The suggestion that authority over vital national
decisions was about to be transferred from the nation-state to a supranational
organization shrouded in secrecy was an idea many civil society organizations
found alarming (O'Brien *et al.* 2000: 136). Their main concern was precisely that
during GATT's history, the institution had failed completely to establish any
formal linkages with NGOs or other civil society organizations. Conditions for
consultations with NGOs had been clarified in article 87 (2) of the Havana
Charter. However, the failure to establish ITO made the preliminary GATT last
for forty-seven years, and the culture of secrecy in the multilateral trade negotiations that evolved effectively kept NGOs and civil society organizations outside.
The argument from the NGOs was that access to information and participation
was not only vital for democracy, but would also improve the policy outputs of
the WTO.

The WTO was forced to take some of these issues seriously. Article v.2 of the
Agreement establishing the WTO institutionalizes some standard operating
procedures for consultation with NGOs: 'the General Council may make appropriate arrangements for consultation and co-operation with non-governmental
organizations concerned with matters related to those of the WTO'. And it was
also suggested that NGOs could be consulted through the dispute settlement
mechanism (DSU). Article 13.2 of the DSU states that: 'Panels may seek information from any relevant source and may consult experts to obtain their opinion
on certain aspects of the matter.' In July 1996, the secretariat was also empowered to engage directly with NGOs (WTO 1996a). The Secretariat was therefore
now given the responsibility for liaison with NGOs. In the same year, the
General Council of WTO also agreed to declassify documents that previously
had been kept from the public (WTO 1996b).

The more reform-oriented of the NGOs are aware that the nature of trade
negotiations means that open-access for all civil society organizations is not
possible. However, they have argued strongly that membership of the WTO
Committee on Trade and Environment (CTE) should be enlarged to include
NGOs. They have criticized the DSU for not making more use of independent
experts. And on the issue of transparency they have focused on the existing
arrangements for declassification of WTO documents. In their view, the current
practice of keeping documents restricted until six months after being issued is
seriously handicapping civil society's ability to monitor the WTO. The WTO on
the other hand is mostly concerned with what the organization sees as the ever-
present threat of the forces of protectionism, and will therefore not encourage
the involvement of what it sees as potentially protectionist groups.

Institutional identity

Each multilateral institution has its own identity, and we will argue that the institutional identity of the WTO is formed around an organizational culture of neoliberal trade theory, a technical approach to trade issues and a culture of secrecy. There is clearly both an internal and an external side to an organization's identity, and for us it is clear that 'the response of the WTO to the environmentalist challenge has been shaped by its organizational ideology, organizational characteristic and the ability of environmental NGOs to threaten its core objective of trade liberalisation' (O'Brien *et al.* 2000: 141).

The way WTO met its critics in the NGO movement should be interpreted in light of the Secretariat's identification with the core of free trade theory. The lack of knowledge among WTO staff members about environmental issues and their links to international trade issues is one important reason why the environmental challenge was interpreted within a traditional free trade versus protectionism context. The environmental challenge was beyond their knowledge frame, and the response was therefore to treat it as a threat. The basic point is that 'knowledge is produced within a frame of reference that embeds certain cognitive interests' (Nustad and Sending 2000: 60), and the meeting between trade and environment was, if not a clash of paradigms and cultures, at least a clash between different types of knowledge. The vision, language, strategies, procedures and traditions of the environment movement are fundamentally different from those of the free traders of the WTO. The very different approach, measures and vision that the environmental NGOs promoted had few if any tangible points in common with the trade regime of the WTO.

WTO's approach to sustainable development: the work of the Committee on Trade and Environment

EMIT was established in 1971, but no meetings were held until the EFTA-initiative revived it in 1990. The working group therefore had only a few meetings before a more formal committee – CTE – was established by the Marrakech Ministerial decision on trade and environment in April 1994. CTE conducted its first meeting in February 1995. Since then the CTE has held thirty-five meetings, delivered annual reports to WTO's General Council, more elaborate studies to the Ministerial Meetings in Singapore in 1996 and in Seattle in 1999, and a paper for the *High-level Meetings on Trade and Environment* held in Geneva in March 1999.

The summaries of the CTE meetings are posted on WTO's website, but the committee is very much under the influence of WTO's general culture of secrecy. The meetings are held behind closed doors and NGOs are not allowed to participate in them. Even other multilateral institutions – such as the United Nations Conference on Trade and Development (UNCTAD), the United Nations Environment Programme (UNEP) and the Organization for Economic Cooperation and Development (OECD) – only have observer status and were allowed to make formal contributions only after the Singapore Ministerial in

1996 (Nordström and Vaughan 1999). The process in the CTE has primarily been driven by the member states, but the WTO Secretariat also has contributed to some reports and statements. According to Esty (1997: 15): 'The debates to date have been dominated by trade officials with little contribution from an environmental perspective.' The CTE is therefore perceived by the NGOs as being biased toward the protection of free trade and not towards environmental protection and sustainable development.

CTE's first report to the WTO Ministerial in Singapore in December 1996 was considered a disappointment by the NGOs: the CTE had not been able to clarify central issues such as the status of Multilateral Environmental Agreements (MEAs) in relation to international trade law and the issue of eco-labelling. A new attempt was made by the CTE to respond to environmental criticism prior to the Seattle Ministerial. This new report discussed the trade–environment nexus, and in particular it addressed the so-called 'race-to-the-bottom debate'. The general conclusion of the report was that trade liberalization reinforces the need for environmental cooperation. Apart from this conclusion, however, the report is more than anything a manifestation of the kinds of values that are embedded in the WTO. The study on which the conclusion is built is significantly influenced by the assumption that trade always leads to greater prosperity and improved environmental conditions. This assumption is arrived at via the environmental Kuznets curve hypothesis. The problem for the WTO with this kind of argument is that the environmental Kuznets curve is not only disputed among academics, but to most NGOs it also illustrates an econometric neoliberal worldview.

The argument from the majority of the NGO movement was therefore that not only has the CTE failed to make any progress on the trade–environment nexus, but it has also threatened the existing consensus by seeking to enlarge WTO's jurisdiction. In one interpretation of CTE's activities, it is suggested that trade measures agreed in multilateral environmental agreements could be taken before a WTO Dispute Panel. In other words, WTO members could try to use the dispute settlement mechanism in the WTO to undermine already existing agreements on trade and environment (O'Brien *et al.* 2000). This perception led the NGOs to shift their attention towards the WTO's dispute settlement system.

Sustainable development and WTO's dispute settlement system

The dispute settlement mechanism has become the new centre of attention for the NGOs. This alternative route of access to the policy making process of the WTO is, however, also full of barriers. The failure of the WTO to clarify the procedural rules for submitting amicus briefs to the Appellate Body is an important indicator in this respect. In October 1998, the Appellate Body did rule 'that dispute settlement panels could consider spontaneous submissions from non-governmental groups' (Bridges 2000a: 1). However, when the Appellate Body then established a procedural rule for the submissions of friend-of-the-court briefs, this was considered to violate the 'member's rights and the government-to-government nature of the WTO' (Bridges 2000a: 1, 4). One example is the important asbestos dispute, where strong opposition from member countries made the Appellate Body turn down all such briefs submitted for this case. This led most of the environmental NGOs involved in this case to condemn the Appellate Body for 'lack of procedural fairness' and for not clarifying which of the requirements their briefs failed to satisfy. Rémi Parmentier of Greenpeace International claimed in this respect that the WTO 'have not learned the lesson from Seattle' (Bridges 2000b: 1), and by dismissing the input from civil society, the WTO was 'fuelling the concerns about the secretive way in which it makes decisions that impact on human lives and the environment' (Bridges 2000b: 1).

We acknowledge that the outcomes of environmental dispute settlements are not a precise indicator of WTO's approach to sustainable development, but they do offer an indication of which values WTO favours in the settlement of disputes. However, there are other procedural issues that could explain these outcomes as well. The dispute resolution hearings are closed and highly secretive. Decisions are taken by trade lawyers and economists, who do not have much knowledge about environmental problems, and the Appellate Body that interprets and assesses the dispute panels' reports in accordance with international law, has changed the outcomes of several of the disputes.

Despite these institutional barriers, some moderate environmental NGOs have had a certain degree of influence on the handling of environmental disputes (see Vevatne 2000a). One example is the Shrimp–Turtle dispute. In this particular case, the World Wide Fund for Nature (WWF) and the Center for International Environmental Law (CIEL) submitted amicus briefs to the dispute panels. These briefs were rejected, but they re-appeared as an attachment to the statement paper of the United States. Here the NGOs did have quite substantial influence in the end, but this was much more due to their ability to lobby American policy makers in Washington DC than the openness and willingness of the WTO to hear their claims. In this case, the Appellate Body supported the United States, and thereby also the environmental NGOs on a number of issues. In particular, the NGOs welcomed the fact that the Appellate Body acknowledged that the sea turtle is a non-renewable natural resource close to extinction and thereby fulfilled the conditions of GATT article XX(g). And, even more important, for the first time the Appellate Body emphasized that WTO agreements had to be interpreted in light of the reference to sustainable development and environmental protection in WTO's preamble. The NGO community saw this as an important decision. However, their victory was only partial, because even though the Appellate Body did find that the US law in question in this case (Section 609 of ESA) was a legitimate attempt to protect the sea turtle, the implementation and design of the law was not. Even more important in this case, however, is the fact that the briefs from the NGOs were rejected by the WTO. The only reason they re-appeared was due to the ability of the WWF and CIEL to influence American decision makers.

WTO's relations to non-state actors: the post-Seattle trauma

The many people who voiced their opinion about the WTO on the streets of Seattle not only delayed the start of the meeting, but they also very successfully drew media attention to both the WTO in particular and international trade issues in general. The demonstrations had little direct impact on the negotiations, but they contributed to the strengthening of existing divergent interests and opinions within the WTO, and thereby also helped cause the failure of the Ministerial and the launching of the Millennium Round (Fitzpatrick 1999; Vevatne 2000b). The support the protesters gave the delegates from Africa, the Caribbean and the Pacific helped these delegates withstand the pressure from the leading OECD member countries (Ritchie 2000).

The actions of the NGOs and the collapse of the negotiations underscored several significant weaknesses both with respect to WTO's transparency policy and the procedures and practices of WTO negotiations. After Seattle, it became generally accepted that WTO had to address these issues. As Rémi Parmentier of Greenpeace International puts it: 'The WTO has two options. Either its next meeting is in Pyong-yang, North Korea, to avoid the protests from civil society or it changes its attitude toward public scrutiny and democracy' (quoted in Fitzpatrick 1999). In fact, for a long time, it was difficult to find someone willing to arrange the next Ministerial. In the end a candidate was finally found, but the choice of Doha, Qatar, as the host of the Ministerial of November 2001 was quite strange. To hold the next Ministerial in the middle of the desert in a country with limited rights to speak and demonstrate, illustrates in our view WTO's lack of understanding of the seriousness of the challenge from the Seattle events.

Conclusion

The WTO has adopted the concept of sustainable development, but only into its preamble, not into its trade rules. The main reasons for this are the WTO Secretariat's technical approach to international trade and the ideological hegemony of neoliberal free trade theory in the WTO. This has influenced its interpretation of non-trade concerns, such as sustainable development. In addition, we would draw attention to the fact that WTO employees' institutional identity was strengthened when confronted with the environmental NGOs' criticism because this criticism challenged the organization's foundation: free trade theory. Confronted with this external critique, the employees' loyalty to the WTO and its core idea increased. Related to this is the fact that the organization's lack of procedures for formal relations to civil society made WTO employees isolated from new impulses and competing views in the broader political economy.

An important insight to be gained from this case study is therefore that for an idea such as sustainable development to make a significant impact on an organization like the WTO, that idea and its promoters cannot be seen as contradicting the hegemonic knowledge system and the collective identity formed around this knowledge system. The main reason why the idea of sustainable development, which has had a lasting impact on other multilateral institutions, has failed to do so in the case of the WTO is precisely because the whole idea and its promoters were seen as in opposition to the *raison d'être* of the whole organization, namely to be the guardian of free trade.

Notes

1   The roots of the WTO can be traced back to December 1945 when the United States invited fourteen countries to begin negotiations on liberalizing world trade. The negotiations had two objectives: (1) to create an International Trade Organization (ITO) that would facilitate trading relations as the World Bank and the IMF facilitated monetary relations; (2) to implement as soon as possible an agreement to reduce tariff levels. The second exercise resulted in the GATT, which was signed on 30 October 1947. The idea was that once ITO was completed the GATT would be subsumed in the larger organization. However, the US Congress refused to give its agreement to the ITO. In fact, congressional opinion was so strong against the ITO that in December 1950 the US administration dropped the initiative and asked Congress to continue giving its support to the GATT.

2   The only reference to the environment in the GATT rules is GATT Article XX: general exception; (b) 'necessary to protect human, animal or plant life or health' and (g) 'relating to the conservation of exhaustible natural resources if such measures are made effective in conjunction with restrictions on domestic production or consumption'.

3   The agenda for the Uruguay Round was agreed upon in Punta del Este, Uruguay in December 1986. The report of the WCED was launched four months later. In the report of WCED both development and environment preservation are emphasized and the report tries to strike a balance between them. The concept of sustainable development was not new, but the WCED gave it a new and broader definition than the former more narrow environmental interpretation of the concept. The WCED underscored *solidarity* both within and between generations, by defining sustainable development as the ability 'to meet the needs of the present without compromising the ability of future generations to meet their own' (WCED 1987: 43).

4   The root of the Tuna–Dolphin Dispute is the US Marine Mammal Protection Act (P.L. 92–5222, 86 Stat. 1027), enacted in 1972. This law requires the US government to take steps to curtail the incidental killing of marine mammals by commercial fishermen, both domestic and foreign. Specifically, this law instructs the secretary of commerce to prohibit the importation of tuna products from countries whose dolphin kill ratio (dolphin deaths per net dropped) exceeds that of US fishermen beyond a certain margin. In 1988, Earth Island Institute, a California-based NGO, sued to enforce this law, and a federal judge agreed that the US government was failing to uphold the law and ordered Mexican tuna imports banned from the United States. Mexico then asked for a GATT dispute settlement panel to adjudicate the matter. In September 1991, the panel concluded that the United States was in violation of its GATT obligations. This decision provoked heated debate over the fairness of GATT resolutions of trade and environment conflicts. For further details see Esty (1994).

5   Authors' translation from the Norwegian.

6   The only important exception is the European Bank for Reconstruction and Development. This MDB was established after the end of the Cold War with the objective of transforming the former planned economies of Eastern Europe into market economies.

7   Personal interview with Risa Schwarz (WTO's Trade and Environment Division), 13 October 1999.
8   Personal correspondence with Bernard Kuiten (External Relations Officer, WTO), 27 April 2000.
9   It is only states that participate during the year-long negotiation rounds, with little or no participation from the parliaments and often with limited public debate, too. Only parties to the Convention (states) are allowed to submit objections/papers to the dispute settlement mechanism. WTO does not accept, as other international institutions do, that non-state actors file complaints or submit amicus briefs to denounce or allege a failure (ICTSD 1999). Despite the Appellate Body's opening for amicus briefs from non-state actors, the practice was again limited in the Asbestos Dispute (see Bridges 2000a: 1).

8 Social capital and the World Bank

Desmond McNeill

Introduction

The idea of social capital has been very actively promoted by the World Bank in recent years, and in this chapter I am concerned specifically with how and why this came about; and with the tensions, contradictions – and perhaps resolutions – that result from seeking to apply it in development policy. The concept, as presented by the political scientist Robert Putnam in his book *Making Democracy Work: Civic Traditions in Modern Italy* (Putnam 1993a), became astonishingly popular among academics and the wider reading public, at least in the United States, in the space of a very short time in the late 1990s.[1] Why this enormous appeal? One reason, which many have noted, is that the concept – and the main thesis of Putnam's book – appeals to a perhaps nostalgic view of community, and values which are in danger of being lost in the modern world. But Putnam also offers a hard-headed argument in favour of such values: that they actually encourage economic growth. The concept of social capital helps one to believe that community, trust and shared values are 'a good thing' – as demonstrated by Putnam's comparison between the very different economic fortunes of Northern and Southern Italy. And academics with widely differing perspectives find it appealing. As one reviewer puts it: 'He [Putnam] has interpreted his results in such catholic terms that students of cultural interpretation and public choice – who differ in so many ways – can find common ground in the outcome' (Tarrow 1996: 396).

Although it was the political scientist Putnam who hit the headlines, sociologists – notably Coleman and Bourdieu – played a major part in establishing the concept of social capital within their discipline.[2] It has in recent years been applied in a number of different fields, including the study of management. Within development studies, the concept and the argument fit very well with current debates among researchers and development assistance agencies concerning 'governance', 'democracy', 'civil society' and related issues: debates that badly need a strong empirical and theoretical base.

The first World Bank Working Paper on the subject refers to three alternative definitions, of which:

The most narrow concept of social capital is associated with Putnam (1993) who views it as a set of 'horizontal associations' between people: social capital consists of social networks ('networks of civic engagement') and associated norms that have an effect on the productivity of the community.

(World Bank 1998b: 1)

A second and broader concept of social capital was put forth by Coleman (1988) who defines social capital as 'a variety of different entities, with two elements in common: they all consist of some aspect of social structure, and they facilitate certain actions of actors – whether personal or corporate actors – within the structure'. In fact, this view of social capital captures social structure at large, as well as the ensemble of norms governing interpersonal behaviour. A third and most encompassing view of social capital includes the social and political environment that shapes social structure and enables norms to develop (World Bank 1998b: 1).

This third and broadest definition, I suggest, appears to include almost anything, and certainly extends social capital well into the domain of governance. This becomes clear in the World Bank Working Paper by Knack, 'Social Capital, Growth and Poverty: A Survey of Cross-country Evidence':

In keeping with the scope of the World Bank's Social Capital Initiative, it is defined broadly here to include features of both government and civil society that facilitate collective action for the mutual benefit of a group, where 'groups' may be as small as households or as large as a nation.

(Knack 1999: 1)

Knack here adopts Collier's (1998) terminology of 'government social capital and civil social capital'. The former, it is clear, overlaps with such concepts as civil liberty, political freedom and governance.

In this chapter I shall explore how the concept of social capital has been taken up in the World Bank, drawing largely on empirical material from a major conference on social capital organized by the World Bank in 1999, supplemented by material from an earlier and smaller World Bank workshop, from the *World Development Report 2000/2001*, and from some contacts with key individuals. Social capital is one of several 'ideas', which have the ability to or are expected to act, as 'bridging concepts', in one or more of three senses:

- a bridge between research and policy;
- a bridge between different disciplines;
- a compromise between competing policies.

The analysis in this chapter will be structured in relation to these three points. But I will preface this with a few words about the World Bank, which may help to explain its interest in the idea of social capital.

There has, in recent years, been an increasing recognition, in the World Bank – and more generally among development assistance agencies – of the importance of community participation. This is manifested in, or at least related to, an increasing involvement of 'civil society' – often, in practice, taken as synonymous with non-governmental organizations (NGOs) – both in the planning and implementation of projects in the field, and in consultation processes at headquarters. Also related is the increasing number of anthropologists and sociologists working for the Bank, and organizational changes, which have given greater prominence to social issues (Cernea 1994). There has also been a significant shift within the Bank towards the inclusion of political issues, notably through the Bank's work on 'governance'. These changes have given greater recognition to the need for insights from disciplines such as sociology and political science.

The World Bank has always had an ambition – one which it has generally been rather successful at achieving – to be at the forefront of ideas; if not initiating them, then at least rapidly taking them over (Ranis 1997; Stern and Ferreira 1997). The discipline and language, of economics has for many years been dominant within the World Bank, and especially in its Research Department. New ideas must, therefore, in order to be accepted, survive criticism by this particular discipline.[3] The reason why the concept of social capital is so attractive for the World Bank is that it allows the dominant economic perspective to take into account sociological and political considerations which have increasingly been recognized as important.[4] The concept fits well at the interface between economics and sociology – in the so-called 'new institutional economics'.[5] Thanks to the work of Putnam, Coleman, and others, staff in the World Bank could thus adopt a new term which was at the forefront of both academic and popular debate; not only within the disciplines of sociology and political science but – most important (for the Bank) – perhaps also in economics. It is therefore understandable that research-minded Bank staff had an *a priori* interest in the idea.[6] This was a necessary condition for its success, but hardly sufficient. The rapid progress of the idea required its being actively taken up by those that count.

Who decides what ideas are to be taken up in the Bank? This is a complex question to which I shall return below, which relates to the ethos of the Bank as a whole, and what constitutes the reference group or groups of individual staff members. As in any organization, certain key individuals play an important role, and in this case several seem to have played a part in giving the idea of social capital prominence in the Bank.[7] Edwards (1999: 2) gives the credit to the President, James Wolfensohn, and Joe Stiglitz, Chief Economist and Senior Vice-President. The former has certainly shown a special interest in participation and involvement of NGOs, which created a supportive context; while the latter, who has a very high reputation for his work on the economics of information and institutions, has also helped to legitimize the concept. But a very important role was undoubtedly played by Ismail Serageldin, formerly Vice-President, Sustainable Development, who has had a keen interest not only in the environment, but also in the social dimension of development – as evidenced from his writings on 'culture and development' and the 'ESD triangle' which combines the economic, the environmental and the social perspectives (Serageldin and Steer 1994).

External actors have also played a significant part – at the invitation of key individuals within the Bank. Mancur Olson was actively involved at an early stage, before his untimely death. Others participated in workshops and other events where World Bank staff and academia were in dialogue.[8] Putnam was brought in and participated in the Social Capital Initiative (SCI) of the Bank, including giving a high-profile public lecture at the 1999 conference. According to Collier, 'Putnam was the most important. ... You can get any old fad going, but to be sustainable it must have a core of rigour to it. That comes from the academic side' (personal communication, 1999). Neither Olson nor Putnam is an economist, but – in what may be seen as an important tactical move – a number of very prestigious economists, including Nobel Prize winners Arrow and Solow, were invited to informal meetings at the World Bank to discuss the concept.[9] It was of crucial importance that senior economists within or close to the World Bank should take it seriously. But opinions among influential figures in the Bank apparently differed. One regarded the empirical results claimed as 'terribly contrived'; while another felt that there was a 'pot of gold' here.

In addition to enlisting the interest, and in some cases support, of prestigious economists, Serageldin was also active in obtaining external funding – from Norway and Denmark – for the two research programmes on social capital described below.[10] Serageldin's definition of social capital is broad: 'the institutional and cultural basis for a society to function' (Serageldin 1996: 1888). Like others, he saw it as a natural addition to earlier types of capital – but in his case linked expressly to the concept of sustainable development. As he put it in the foreword to SCI Working Paper 1: 'The traditional composition of natural capital, physical or produced capital, and human capital needs to be broadened to include social capital' (World Bank 1998b: i).

In brief, a conjuncture of key individuals and structural factors may be said to have played their part in causing the concept of social capital to achieve such rapid prominence in the Bank. The two major research programmes on social capital which I shall describe may be seen as both a symptom and also a contributory factor.

The conference

The World Bank recently completed two major research programmes on social capital: one financed by Norway, the other by Denmark. Norway supported a set of three major studies – in Indonesia, Burkina Faso and Bolivia: the Local Level Institutions (LLI) Project.[11] The preliminary results from these three studies were presented at a small workshop in Bergen in May 1999 attended by about thirty participants, approximately one third of whom had been involved in the research itself. Denmark supported a larger number (twelve) of smaller studies –

with less ambition in terms of adopting a common methodology. The studies covered fifteen countries and a wide range of sectors. The conference at which the results were presented was held at the World Bank in Washington in 1999 and was attended by over 100 participants. In this chapter I draw mainly on experience from the latter conference, which not only included a far larger number of people, but was also broader in the range of types: from academics to operational staff. It is therefore more revealing in terms of gaps and tensions between different positions. I shall make extensive use of quotes (mainly from this conference), and in most cases attribute these to categories of people, as follows. (In some cases I shall [usually in addition] name the individual concerned.)[12]

- researcher – economist
- researcher – social scientist[13]
- policy staff – economist
- policy staff – social scientist
- operational staff

I have claimed that the concept of social capital may serve to bridge three different 'gaps', and I shall structure my discussion of the issues by focusing on these three in turn, offering in each case a brief analysis of the issue and some symptoms of the tensions. But first I will give a little more background information about the conference itself. Here I quote one of those who had been heavily involved in the research programmes:

> The Social Capital Initiative (SCI) was established three years ago at the initiative of Ismail Serageldin (then Vice-President, Environmentally and Socially Sustainable Development). The purpose was to understand it, measure it, and monitor its effect on development. There was much scepticism, in view of which he saw the need to set up a research programme ... to demonstrate [its importance] empirically in a rigorous way. Support was received from Denmark to finance 12 teams in 15 countries. The studies were multidisciplinary, involving economics, sociology, anthropology, political science and other disciplines. They ranged from quantitative to qualitative studies, and entered uncharted territory.
>
> (policy staff – economist)

Another staff member, also very closely involved, expressed support for the concept and the research:

> Social capital is precious. It is about human relations ... deeply embedded. What should be the meaning of these studies for development? I am convinced that institutions and relationships are important; this is the first time [we are studying them empirically].
>
> (policy staff – social scientist)

A similar point was made more forcefully by one of the commentators (researcher – social scientist) later in the conference: 'Social capital is the battering ram to get social issues into development'.[14] But perhaps the most revealing remark of all came in the introduction by Ian Johnson, Vice-President, Environmentally and Socially Sustainable Development Network.

> At long last, having used the word in numerous meetings, I can find out what it means. [There has been an] evolution of thinking in the Bank: from financial capital to physical capital, and then human capital. Now we need to add natural capital and social capital. I think it is a very profound concept and one that we absolutely have to come to grips with. ... Fascinating pieces of work, really at the cutting edge, which could have a profound impact on the way we do our work at the Bank.

This disarming blend of expectation and ignorance summarizes, I believe, the situation of many of those – of the policy and operational staff – attending the conference. Some were, no doubt, very sceptical. But many were eager to find out what this new 'idea' was, and how it might contribute to policy.[15]

The gap between researchers and policy makers

Complexity / simplicity

While policy makers and operational staff favour simple ('common sense') analysis and approaches, researchers revel in complexity. As I have argued elsewhere, this arises from the very nature of their differing tasks, and the imperatives that drive them.

> Policy-makers ... require that the world be simple and uniform. ... The researcher is, by training if not by nature, out to disagree: to find the exception to the rule, the subtle failing of logic, the anomalous case. ... Researchers thrive on complexity, variety and, indeed, on intellectual conflict. But this is no basis on which to establish general – let alone global – policy prescriptions; no way of building a consensus.
>
> (McNeill 2000: 327)

This gap was very evident at the conference, in the comments and discussion. For example, one of the comments on a paper was that it offered 'commonsensical conclusions'. The commentator (operational staff) asked whether 'all this wonderfully complex [analysis] was needed' (This evoked laughter from the audience).

In response it was claimed: 'The insights are commonsensical – but commonsense is not always evident in development thinking. Perhaps social capital can be a bridge between community needs and development theory. To bring commonsense into the mindset of development work' (researcher – social scientist).

Another researcher (economist) stated, 'I think I detect an underlying tension between academics on the one hand and practitioners on the other.' Another was clear as to the potential use of social capital: 'If social capital is to be valuable it should be of instrumental value. It should be an independent variable. ... The dependent variable is welfare.'

The importance of instrumentality, and 'operationalization' was made clear many times – not least in relation to the question of how to define the term social capital.[16]

Importance/non-importance of definitions

Academic social scientists, and perhaps especially economists, tend to be very concerned about definitions, and may devote enormous effort to competing alternatives. Policy makers often see this as a waste of time: 'academic' in the pejorative sense of the word. At the conference there was some reference to this issue. One of those presenting the findings of their research: 'We did not have a clear idea of what was meant by social capital, beyond a sense of cohesion leading to reduced transaction costs'. And another (policy staff – social scientist): 'Which definitions are most useful? – those which lead to what is fruitful in operational terms.' On the question of definition: 'It is all right if we [economists and sociologists] do not talk to each other' (researcher – economist). And: 'We need a refutable concept, relatively crisp.'

Here it is relevant to quote SCI Working Paper 1:

> The lack of conceptual clarity stands in the way of the measurement of social capital, and the variety of existing definitions makes it inherently difficult to propose a list of indicators. Instead, indicators will have to evolve as the conceptual and, *more important* [my stress], the operational definition of social capital, are developed.
>
> (World Bank 1988b: 7)

Concern/lack of concern with central methodological issues

The question of definition relates also to methodological issues, such as 'what is being measured?' and 'what is the direction of causality (when correlation is established between social capital and performance)?'.

At the conference, this issue arose only occasionally, for example when a World Bank staff member raised what he called 'the problem of endogeneity'. The response, from one who had conducted research, was: 'A great deal of fishing and data-mining went on' and 'I am not sure which way the arrows go [i.e. social capital to or from development outcomes]'. These issues were, however, taken up at greater length in the first workshop, perhaps because in that research programme more effort was made to ensure that the studies were undertaken on the basis of a common methodology – and there was more time to discuss detailed methodological questions.

These different manifestations of the gap between researchers and policy makers underline my central point that those concerned with determining and implementing policy do not have the time or the inclination for long-winded debate. This is well described by Michael Edwards, based on his experience as Civil Society Adviser in the World Bank:

> On a good day in my old job at the World Bank, I would be asked to define 'civil society' by any number of sceptical colleagues. ... On a bad day they would ask me ... 'what is social capital?' But worst of all was the inevitable sequel: in that case, what's the difference between social capital and civil society? Before I'd reached the end of my first paragraph of long-winded explanation, the questioner would have disappeared around the corner, back to the 'real work' of lending billions of dollars to recalcitrant governments. ... In the World Bank, as in all bureaucracies, this year's theory will be next year's policy.
>
> (Edwards 2000)

The gap between disciplines

The second major gap with which I am concerned is that between disciplines. In the case of social capital, and this conference, the relevant disciplines are economics, political science, sociology and anthropology. (Arguably, the first and last named define the extremes, in methodological terms.)

A researcher (economist) described the predicament he faced: 'This is pure smoke – not serious – this is what people say when I present this at economics departments.' He added: 'I have worked very little with social anthropologists. But quite a lot with political scientists. We find that it [the lack of communication] is mainly language, not substance.' A researcher (social scientist) was concerned that economics was dominant at the conference, as indicated by the order in which papers were given: 'I am struck that we have started from economic perspectives. We need to put others up front. We need a balance.'

The issue was also discussed at the earlier workshop, at which a social scientist researcher challenged what he referred to as the '*anthropologization* of political science and economics' and referred to the concept as 'anthropological wine in economic bottles'. A commentator defending the approach in Collier's paper, which had been described as too limited, argued for the necessity of starting with something 'tractable', and added: 'One comes with the disciplinary hat one has.'

It is beyond the scope of this paper to elaborate on the differences between disciplines.[17] I would, however, simply note the following contrasts between economics and anthropology, some of which were referred to during the conference: measurement vs. description, quantitative vs. qualitative analysis, specific vs. generalizable findings, rigour vs. richness.[18]

The last of these merits some elaboration, relating as it does to what might be described as varying degrees of risk-aversion in relation to one's peers (whether these are academics or policy makers). Insistence on rigour, sometimes equated with quantification, is a means to reduce risk.[19] But perhaps the very phenomenon which social capital seeks to grapple with eludes quantification – and even rigorous definition. This was the theme taken up by one of the key figures in the research programme and conference (policy staff – social scientist), at the very outset of the conference, who noted that social capital involves 'stories, myths, religion, proverbs, language', and that 'however able we are to box it and measure it' some of it remains impalpable. 'We are social creatures, living in social groups. [Social capital concerns] these values that hold us together.' Taking a considerable risk in relation both to the academic and the operational community, this presenter went so far as to quote from *The Little Prince* by Antoine de Saint-Exupéry in order to indicate what is the essence of social capital: 'I am a fox. ... I am not tamed. ... What does that mean? ... It is an act too often neglected. It means to establish ties.' Such views may be contrasted with those of Collier, Director of the Economic Research Group at the Bank, who sees the need to collaborate with other social scientists, but believes that economists have an important role in bringing greater rigour:

> Economists are trained to high standards of precision in thought, especially causal arguments. The mindset which gives you econometrics is the mental hygiene of disentangling causation. Putnam's work was interesting, but there was not absolute clarity on the causal structure. I felt it was right (but) what was missing was the analytical micro-foundations, the part economists are best able to get into is the notion of networks. That nests in neatly with costly information. This notion is the single most important revelation of economics in our lifetime.
>
> (Collier, personal communication, 1999)

The gap between alternative policies

As indicated at the outset, the attraction of Putnam's social capital is that it appears to promote both economic growth and community; giving the development policy maker the best of both worlds. The gap between competing policies is thus apparently bridged.[20]

Bowles sees social capital as the bridge between what may be an even broader ideological divide – state vs. market: 'The demise of the twin illusions of our century – laissez-faire and statism – [thus] cleared the intellectual and rhetorical stage for social capital's entry', and

> Once everyone realized that market failures are the rule rather than the exception and that governments are neither smart enough nor good enough to make things entirely right, the social capital rage was bound to happen. Conservatives love it. ... Those to the left of center are no less enchanted.
>
> (Bowles 1999)

When considering alternative policies at this level of generality, ends and means begin to become entangled. Certainly social capital relates to means as well as ends. Thus it appears also to provide a bridge between two usually contrasted approaches to development intervention: the participatory, bottom-up and the more technocratic, top-down approach (see Chambers, e.g. 1983).

Whether or not social capital will successfully provide a bridge in this regard is as yet uncertain, depending on how – if at all – the concept can be 'operationalized'. As already noted, this is an imperative in development agencies such as the World Bank, and this was, indeed, a major intention in the Social Capital Initiative, as indicated by Serageldin in his foreword to the SCI Working Papers: 'The challenge of development agencies such as the World Bank is to operationalize the concept of social capital and to demonstrate how and how much it affects development outcomes.'

It was clear at the conference that operational staff were of the same view. Two quotations will illustrate the point:

> For the concept to get a hold it has to be pushed out into the other sectors of the Bank and operationalized [with] indicators and measurement [leading to] mainstreaming in the World Bank, and other agencies.
>
> (operational staff)

> It is very difficult to get a grasp on social capital in an operational division of the Bank. [We are] too technocratic, too oriented to central government, supply side, changing the laws, supplying personal computers. One size fits all. [Perhaps we should try] not 'best practice' but 'good fit'.
>
> (operational staff)

The latter quotation indicates some reservations about developing a fully generalizable concept with direct applications for policy; a view which was shared by some others. In her introduction, Gloria Davis, Director, Social Development Department, noted that: 'Many people believe that large institutions like the World Bank should keep out.' In the final session (at both the conference and the workshop) others made somewhat similar remarks, for example 'Recommendation to the Bank: do no harm. ... History matters and politics matter' (researcher – social scientist). Another staff member said: 'This is more urgent than human capital. We may be doing harm now' (operational staff). But it was not clear for all whether taking account of social capital is necessarily at odds with a technocratic approach, or whether it offers a happy compromise between a top-down and a participatory approach.

Disagreement between participants related not so much to the merits of making the concept operational, but as to how best to do this: between those who leapt uncritically over the gap between research and policy, and those who paused to consider; between those who assumed that if social capital was a meaningful and useful concept of the Bank's operations, then the task must surely be to 'build social capital', to those who wondered whether the lesson might be very different – that an understanding of social capital should induce the Bank to restrict its activities – or at least to modify the form of its interventions. There was, in other words, a disagreement between those who sought to intervene or not intervene.

The three 'gaps' just described constitute a challenge both for the institution and each person within it. The actions of the World Bank are the outcome of many actions of many individuals. In determining what attitude to take to a new concept such as social capital, individuals within the World Bank ask themselves not only 'Will this concept lead to better policies?' but also 'Will this be good for my institution?', and further, perhaps, 'Will this be good for my department?'. And 'good for me?'. In asking the last of these questions, each person necessarily relates to a peer group, or perhaps more than one peer group – for example of other staff within the same division and of academic economists. Under normal circumstances, the boundaries and distinguishing features of the different peer groups are fairly clear, though a person's placement within them may be less so. Thus each individual has a rather clear map of the territory, but may either feel that they move within it, or are not entirely sure where they fit. This then raises the question of who defines the territory, who marks the boundaries, who guards the boundaries, etc. There is a considerable literature on this subject within the social sciences, though I shall not attempt to explore it further here. I do, however, suggest that the boundaries in the Bank have been challenged and perhaps redefined in the debate over the concept of social capital. But what has happened to the idea of social capital in the process?

It is apparent that it has been required to satisfy a wide range of largely conflicting purposes. It is my contention that this is both its strength and its weakness. To the extent that it provides a substantive bridge across these different gaps it is commendable. But if this bridge is illusory; if consensus is achieved only because the concept means all things to all people, then it has little value.

The term social capital featured quite significantly in the World Bank's controversial *World Development Report 2000/2001* on poverty, and before concluding this chapter it is worth commenting briefly on this document, which illustrates the continuing tensions, and to what extent these were reconciled in the World Bank's annual flagship document.

World Development Report 2000/2001

In the draft version of the report, made available for comment on the internet, the concept of social capital is referred to in several places, and used very extensively in chapter 4, 'Building Social Institutions and Removing Social Barriers'. In the final version of the report, social capital is used far less, and with more care.[21] The following is included (almost unchanged from the draft) as the introductory paragraph in chapter 7 (the earlier chapter 4):

Social institutions – kinship systems, community organizations, and informal networks – greatly affect poverty outcomes. They do so by affecting the productivity of economic assets, the strategies for coping with risk, the capacity to pursue new opportunities, and the extent to which particular voices are heard when important decisions are made.

(World Bank 2000b: 117)

This is so general as to be uncontentious. But it is interesting to note the mixture of agendas and 'languages': from 'productivity of economic assets' to 'voices being heard'. The following quotation from the draft version is more problematic:

The poor typically have a plentiful supply of bonding social capital, a modest endowment of bridging social capital, and almost no linking social capital.

(World Bank 2000a: 4.4)

This claim may be true by definition (depending on how you define 'bonding', 'bridging' and 'linking' social capital). But it has not been shown empirically, and its speculative nature is indicated by the give-away qualifier 'typically'. The final version is certainly more circumspect on this point (World Bank 2000b: 128). Turning from analysis and description to policy, it is interesting to contrast the following two quotations, again from the draft:

Development policy should thus seek to help marginalized groups build more diversified 'portfolios' of social assets. ... Responsibility for managing these assets should be transferred as soon as possible to the groups themselves.

(World Bank 2000a: 4.9)

To reduce poverty and empower the poor the key issue is to find ways of creating synergies between civic and state institutions and between formal and informal institutions.

(World Bank 2000a: 4.9)

The first is an economistic, and technocratic way of presenting the issue; indeed, a rather extreme example. The second is less so, but not particularly specific. A third quotation, by contrast, indicates the potential dangers of intervention, giving grounds for a cautious approach:

The National Federation of Herders in Central African Republic was 'contaminated' by donors giving it too much money.

(World Bank 2000a: 4.9)

This seems to reflect the more cautious, non-interventionist position of some of those at the conference, referred to above. What is interesting is that all three quotations are contained in the same chapter, indicating, I suggest, that there were markedly differing views as to what the World Bank should make of the concept. But in the final version the term itself is used far less, and the differences of view are barely apparent.[22]

Conclusion

It is not my purpose in this paper to prescribe, or even forecast, the fate of social capital in the World Bank, but this case study of an 'idea' and a development agency provides valuable insights into the inner workings of a single, powerful, multilateral institution. Between, and also within, development assistance agencies there is a degree of competition; but the contests are fought within a consensual arena, in that the explicit aim is common for all: namely better policies. Each institution (and perhaps especially the World Bank) seeks to lead the rest of the development community in 'the right direction'; to be *first* with the *good* ideas.[23] And social capital appeared to be such an idea. I suggest that the concept of social capital is potent. It is seen as having power in two respects: not only to steer policies in a good direction, but also the power to give authority – to an individual and/or an institution (or part of an institution).

This case study is interesting because the World Bank here took a leading, decisive role in promoting an idea which might, on the face of it, appear to be risky in both academic and policy terms. It was risky in academic terms because – at least within economics – it had yet to be tried and proved worthy. It was risky in policy terms because it drew the World Bank further into the morass of politics at the micro level. To push the point further, and develop the analogy of Collier, I suggest that the Bank *actively intervened in the marketplace of ideas* – in what turned out to be a hazardous venture.[24]

But then the question arises: who is the World Bank? Who was promoting the idea? I have named some of those involved – such as Stiglitz and Serageldin – and it seems that Wolfensohn himself was important; not perhaps in relation to the concept of social capital itself, but in creating a supportive environment for such ideas. And this helps to explain why others in the World Bank who might have been expected to be not simply sceptical but actively opposed have not been so; because the ethos of the World Bank is, perhaps, itself in flux – thanks in part to the efforts of its president. Staff of the World Bank also have – under normal circumstances – a fairly clear idea of what I might call the 'ethos' of the institution as a whole, and of the different groups that they feel they belong to; that is, their shared norms and values (whether explicit or implicit). But the World Bank has, in recent years, been in a state of uncertainty, and perhaps significant change. Under the leadership of Wolfensohn, it has presented itself not only as a 'leader in ideas' but also as a 'listening bank'. And it appears to be listening to some ideas which, for the World Bank, are quite novel. Does this imply a change of a very fundamental kind in the World Bank ethos, relating to what might be referred to as the deep ideology of the Bank?[25] Or are these merely surface changes? As I have sought to demonstrate, there are very diverse attitudes to the concept of social capital. It is accurate to state that the World

Bank is dominated by an economic perspective, and a technocratic perspective. There are perhaps some signs of change with regard to the first; the economic perspective is perhaps being modified to a limited degree. But the second can, perhaps, never be changed. The very nature of the World Bank – and other multilateral assistance agencies – is technocratic. And this surely limits the extent to which alien ideas can have a real impact. I quoted earlier the analogy of social capital as a 'battering ram'. To adopt another analogy in the same vein, some might portray social capital as a 'Trojan horse'. Now it has successfully been brought within the fortress – but are there any soldiers left alive inside?

Whether and how an idea such as social capital is taken up depends on a complex interaction between individuals and the institution as a whole. If, as I suggest, the institution itself is in a state of change, then individuals within it are less sure than usual about what counts. And the opportunities for policy entrepreneurs to take initiatives are greater.[26] What proves to be the fate of social capital will certainly depend in part on the merits of the concept in both the world of academia (especially economics) and the world of policy. But any inherent merit the term may have, in analytical and empirical terms, is not sufficient. Perhaps it is not even necessary. As I have suggested, the idea itself may be so unclear, so widely defined, as to mean almost anything. This, paradoxically, is what has enabled it to gain such wide acceptance. Whether it will prove to be potent in the longer term remains to be seen.

Notes

1 The study 'caused a sensation outside academic circles' (Tarrow 1996). The idea apparently even inspired a passage in Clinton's State of the Union address in 1995.
2 Not in collaboration; they adopt rather different approaches
3 Economists may not be in the majority in numerical terms, but the dominance of economic thinking is well established. The following comment by the Director of the Economics Research Group is very pertinent:

> The Research Department – which is mainly economists – generally sees itself as the guardian of rigorous standards of thought. [To] defend against unadulterated bullshit. There are flowery, flabby ends to everything – not just social capital. [The Research Department is] filtering the marketplace of ideas, which is full of charlatans. [It is] normal business to be testing to destruction ideas which may be good, or popular fads.
>
> (Collier, personal communication, 1999)

4 This view is implied, though not necessarily shared, by Grootaert (an economist) who states in SCI Working Paper 3:

> The term social capital has found its way into economic analysis only recently. Some social scientists claim that the term social capital has been coined only to make the underlying concepts acceptable to economics. Economists reply that institutions and other aspects of social capital have always been present in economic analysis. Economists have added the focus on the contribution of social capital to economic growth.
>
> (Grootaert 1998)

5 This is closely linked to rational choice theory in sociology (e.g. Coleman). Whether it fits the 'old' institutional economics of Polanyi (1944) and Veblen (1953 [1899]) is more doubtful.

6 By calling them 'research-minded' I deliberately blur the issue as to whether this refers to where they work in the organization (e.g. the Research Department), what are their current tasks (e.g. writing working papers), or what they are most interested in.

7 I have not included here those who have been most directly involved in the research programmes I shall describe – notably Gloria Davis (anthropologist), Deepa Narayan (sociologist) and Chris Grootaert (economist).

8 For example, the sociologist Norman Uphoff (Esman and Uphoff 1984), who was invited to a session at the rural development conference on George Washington campus in 1995, chaired by Ismail Serageldin; and later attended the 1997 workshop and the 1999 World Bank conference. The World Bank also maintained an email discussion group on social capital – 'Let's Talk' – for over two years (Deepa Narayan, Let's Talk posting no. 25, 10 Feb 2000, 07.12). Michael Woolcock acted as moderator for the year 1999.

9 This initiative led to the publication of a book by Dasgupta and Serageldin (2000) including contributions by several of the figures that I have referred to. Many are positive, but both Arrow and Solow express considerable doubts about the use of the term 'social capital' to refer to the phenomenon under study.

10 I was informed that these two programmes account for some 80 per cent of the work undertaken on social capital in the Bank.

11 This involved large-scale household surveys in the three countries, which provided strong empirical evidence, expressed in econometric terms, of the positive economic contribution of social capital. (The research was initially planned without the concept of social capital, as a study of local institutions.)

12 I have used the classification system partly to provide anonymity, but have named individuals where I believe their formal position warrants it.

13 It is a debatable point whether these should properly be classified as 'other social scientist'. As Collier noted in a revealing comment on the place of economics in the World Bank, there is a 'very interesting usage in the Bank. They use social scientists to mean non-economists. I was fazed by it!' (personal communication, 1999).

14 It is relevant to add another quote, this time from one of the local researchers on the Burkina Faso (LLI) study, at the earlier workshop in May 1999, who characterized the World Bank as 'a cumbersome, cold machine. ... Not qualified to work at the local level. ... Knows how to deal with big things, not little things', but added: 'We are delighted to have the concept of social capital.'

15 In a brief but interesting paper Edwards distinguishes three groups: 'the enthusiasts (mainly economists in the World Bank's research division). ... The tacticians (mostly other social scientists in various parts of the Bank) ... the sceptics (activists and academics outside the Bank and a few iconoclasts within)' (2000: 3).

16 An extreme (and perhaps intentionally provocative) example: 'Putnam had a neat idea, but it should not become a cult. If you cannot measure it, it is very unlikely anyone is going to do anything about it' (operational staff).

17 But see McNeill (1999b) and Becher (1989).

18 A World Bank Staff member suggested that with social capital one might achieve 'Integration of quantitative and qualitative. ... Precision vs. meaningfulness. ... Social capital as heuristic, not analytic'. Here may be an appropriate place to note that the study in Tanzania, 'Cents and Sociability' (Narayan and Pritchett 1997) which played a significant part in establishing the credibility of social capital within the World Bank, was written jointly by a sociologist and an economist. The latter's reputation as a reliable econometrician was apparently very important.

19 It is not unusual for economists (who favour quantification) to claim that they apply a greater degree of rigour than, say, anthropologists. But anthropologists might argue

that their discipline, although not employing quantitative methods, is more demanding in relation to the empirical basis of its research, and rigorous concern for context and local meanings.

20 There are similarities here with other earlier 'ideas'. The informal sector seemed to provide a bridge in the 'redistribution vs. growth' debate; and 'sustainable development' a bridge in the 'growth vs. sustainability' debate.

21 The term appears twice or more on every page from 4.2 to 4.10 in the draft. In the final version, it appears fewer times – and then mainly in 'boxes'.

22 The World Bank should, in my view, be highly commended for making the draft publicly available. It gives not only an opportunity for readers to comment, but also an invaluable insight into the debates as they unfold.

23 This has become even more apparent recently, notably with the World Bank's initiative to take a leading role in the 'Global Knowledge Network'.

24 See also e.g. Colander and Coats (1993).

25 This 'deep ideology' is difficult to describe, but an important aspect is an emphasis on results and a rejection of approaches which are 'soft'. (As the latter word exemplifies, the language of the World Bank is revealing. Other expressions which are commonly used include 'touchy-feely', 'gooey' and 'flabby'.)

26 I must here again stress the distance between the researchers and policy makers in Washington and the operational staff in the field. Even if major changes occur in relation to the former, these may not reach to the latter.

9 Hegemony, neoliberal 'good governance' and the International Monetary Fund

A Gramscian perspective

Ian Taylor

Introduction

The promotion of 'good governance', as advanced by international institutions such as the International Monetary Fund (IMF), is a powerful example of how certain ideas are constructed as common sense. In this analysis, good governance is seen as a hegemonic discourse pursued by the North in an attempt to define the South in its own image. A form of transformation, akin to a passive revolution, seeks to co-opt and assimilate elites within the South into a broader transnational historic bloc, sharing the assumptions and class interests of the dominant fractions centred in the core. Such ongoing impulses contribute to the reconfiguration of the South in an epoch of global restructuring. Crafting consent to such favoured solutions, this process is integral to a neo-Gramscian understanding of the role of international institutions in global politics. This being so, the promotion of 'good governance' reflects the potent role of ideas in international politics and the part played by multilateral institutions in such endeavours.

Currently, ideas surrounding the economic and political principles referred to as 'neoliberalism' are immensely powerful. Amongst a transnational elite class they have achieved hegemonic status on how best to restructure political and economic life. Although technological innovation and changes in production root much of this in the material realm, the importance of ideas is quite apparent when attempting to understand how neoliberalism is currently dominant. This is particularly so in trying to understand how these ideas are propagated by international financial institutions.

It is this chapter's contention that ideas centred around notions of what constitutes 'good governance' have been promoted by the IMF as an ultimate attempt to reconfigure territories in order to make them most attractive to international capital. Michel Camdessus, former head of the IMF, was quite open about this, asserting in 1998 that 'in a world in which private capital has become more mobile, there is mounting evidence that corruption undermines the confidence of the most serious investors and adversely affects private capital inflows'. He also made claims to a consensus over what such good governance was, saying that 'a broader consensus has emerged on the central importance of transparency and good governance in achieving economic success' (Camdessus 1998). Indeed, the

IMF's own prescriptions for designing 'good governance' structures draw upon what the body refers to as 'broadly agreed best international practices of economic management' (IMF 1997a).

Currently, many of those state elites perceived to stand in the way of restructuring and who flout the IMF's concept of good governance, stand to lose out, with loans from the body being withheld; the withholding of $53 million in aid to Zimbabwe by the IMF in August 1998, after Mugabe's government failed to meet the organization's demand for good governance, being a prime example. Obviously, in discussing such issues one is not siding with tyrants such as Mugabe, nor arguing for *poor* governance. However, it is important to make the link between the recent emphasis on good governance within the IMF and how this informs its lending policies, and the wider neoliberal agenda that 'good governance' advances. The theoretical insights provided by neo-Gramscian scholars, particularly *vis-à-vis* the role of ideas and the notion of hegemony, are utilized as a point of departure.

Hegemony and international relations

In Gramscian theorizing, hegemonic power is of a different type than that usually associated with pure material dominance, and is linked to 'intellectual and moral leadership' via ideology, which has the 'same energy as a material force' (Gramsci 1971: 377). Whilst it is true that the dominant economic class can (and does) exercise sheer coercive force, this factor does not solely account for its control: alliances are required with other fractions if this is to be achieved on a stable and lasting basis. Maintaining hegemony is dependent not only upon exercising coercive power, but also by attaining consent by acting as the 'moral' leaders of society and framing ideational terms of reference. As Robert Cox (1992a: 178–79) phrased it:

> Hegemony derives from the ways of doing and thinking of the dominant social strata of the dominant state or states insofar as these ways of doing and thinking have inspired emulation or acquired the acquiescence of the dominant social strata of other states. These social practices and the ideologies that explain and legitimize them constitute the foundation of the hegemonic order. Hegemony frames thought and thereby circumscribes action.

According to Cox, the essential function of international institutions is the justification and defence of a particular politico-economic project. In acting thus, they promote certain values as being comparatively fixed and appearing as natural:

> the rules and practices and ideologies of a hegemonic order conform to the interests of the dominant power while having the *appearance* [italics added] of a universal natural order of things which give at least a certain measure of satisfaction and security to lesser powers.

(Cox 1989: 825)

The achievement of the hegemony of a particular set of ideas is dependent upon their success on a broader ideological battleground, limiting the boundaries around which 'legitimate' and 'realistic' policies may be formulated. In this light, international institutions are the amalgamation of material and ideological impulses: 'the aggregations of influence on issue-areas which far overflow their own institutional boundaries' (Cox 1980: 393). This process is facilitated by international financial institutions (IFIs) (among others) who, whilst co-opting national elites in the periphery, also possess the strength to assimilate opposing (counter-hegemonic) positions.

This assimilation, in a Gramscian sense, takes on the form of a passive revolution whereby particular elites (in this case, those sympathetic to neoliberalism – money capital and outward-oriented fractions) attain power without rupturing the existent social fabric. This *trasformiso* ('transformism') serves to absorb possible counter-hegemonic elements into the dominant elites (in a globalized world, the transnational elites) through a process of compromise and amalgamation. Such passive revolution heads off counter-hegemonic impulses, integrating such elements into the broader consensus. 'Individual political figures ... are incorporated individually into the conservative-moderate "political class" (characterised by its aversion to any intervention of the popular masses in state life, to any organic reform which would substitute a "hegemony" for the crude, dictatorial "dominance")' (Gramsci 1971: 58). The agency of Southern elites in this process is quite apparent.

In his analysis of modern Africa, Bayart demonstrated that postcolonial Africa was marked by passive revolutions which co-opted potential opponents into the broader historic bloc (Bayart 1993: 274). This process of fusion in Bayart's concern is local: it can, however, be extended to the global, whereby a nascent historic bloc has formed. This has achieved a consciousness with a recognition of the mutual interests upholding the on-going system, and which allows certain elite fractions to prevail as ascendant. How this relates to the global power structures is captured by Cox (1999: 12):

> There is something that could be called a nascent historic bloc consisting of the most powerful corporate economic forces, their allies in government, and the variety of networks that evolve policy guidelines and propagate the ideology of globalisation. States now by and large play the role of agencies of the global political economy, with the task of adjusting national economic policies and practices to the perceived exigencies of global economic liberalism. This structure of power is sustained from outside the state through a global policy consensus and the influence of global finance over state policy, and from inside the state from those social forces that benefit from globalisation (the segment of society that is integrated into the world economy). ... Neo-liberalism is hegemonic ideologically and in terms of policy.

Following this, 'the precondition for the achievement of a hegemonic world order is the construction of strong international regimes', which is facilitated by the regulative effect of international organizations (Gale 1998: 274). The actors in this process are the dominant elites at the centre, who extend their conception of social and political order to the international and transnational level by exporting their preferred societal model through international institutions. These institutions then act as socializing agents of change, helping to draw in partners who share a particular worldview. Local elites come to share in the social values of the dominant core elite, as such interests consolidate their own class position at home.

In the current world order, with its shift from the Keynesian compromise to neoliberalism, there has been a

> transnational process of consensus formation among the official care-takers of the global economy. This process generates consensus guidelines, underpinned by an ideology of globalization, that are trans-mitted into the policy-making channels of national governments and big corporations.
>
> (Cox 1996: 301)

The active intervention by international institutions favourable – if not integral – to neoliberalism is profoundly important in this respect. A clear example of this was the role of the IMF in the aftermath of the crises in Asia, where, according to critics,

> many of the adjustment packages [of the IMF] are thought to have gone beyond traditional structural reform strategies, designed not only to restore stability to the regional financial markets and to reform banking sectors, but actually to contest the nature of the political process.
>
> (Higgott 2000: 259)

This activity was frequently portrayed as 'bailing out' or 'saving' whole nations from economic and social disaster. Immensely powerful multilateral bodies such as the IMF actively propagated particular ideas in a quest to restructure the developing world and defend sectional interests. How these activities have been centred around particular notions of what constitutes 'good governance' is what we turn to next.

The IMF and 'good governance'

It is via interventions, negotiations, conditionalities, the making of concessions and the arrival at 'consensus' that paramount sectional interests are able to be displayed as the common interest. Increasingly, the IFIs have advanced 'good governance' as a concept bound up with the normative framework of neoliber-alism. According to Keet, by pushing a particular vision of governance, the IMF and World Bank express a clear bias towards the assumption that it is free market governments with *sound macro-economic policies* which are *more reliable*. ... There is also a clear inclination to emphasise, or even equate good governance with the technical qualities of efficient management and the main accountability of client governments to funders/creditors and other external agencies.

(Keet 2000)

The International Monetary Fund (IMF), and the World Bank, were originally formed at Bretton Woods in 1945 as twin pillars in the post-war capitalist dispensation (see Helleiner 1994). The World Bank's role was to promote post-war reconstruction, whilst the IMF was conceived as the protector of the capitalist global economy, promoting international trade and regulating national exchange rates. The value of cooperating currencies was secured to the dollar whilst the American bank of issue promised to exchange dollars for gold. Concurrently, dealing in currencies was regulated by official exchange controls, thus fostering currency stability and allowing states to effectively plan their economies. In addition to this surveillance role, however, the IMF also took on providing short-term financing to states experiencing currency problems and/or failing to satisfy their trade obligations. It is important to note here that the institution's role then was to provide temporary liquidity to existing economies, rather than trying to restructure them.

A more limited role for the IMF was very much in line with the ideological underpinnings of the post-war capitalist world order, whereby various Keynesian welfare nationalist schemes established a tacit consensus by which the system was managed (Marglin and Schor 1990). During a period of unprecedented stability and growth, the ideas and institutions that fostered this order remained essentially harmonious and acted to bind together a strong working alliance between the elites in Washington, the NATO states, and Tokyo – a trilateral cooperation. This alliance emanated from the core state, the United States, and can be seen as an international historic bloc, which in turn cemented the post-war international economic order that became known as *Pax Americana* (Gill 1990a: 97).

However, dependent as it was on American largesse, this order began to unravel once Washington sought to stem the growing negative effects on its economy brought about by a decline in productivity growth and its competitiveness. Furthermore, an increasingly transnationalized capital began to see such restrictions as a dampening device on their profitability and 'freedom', and began pushing for a re-negotiation of the post-war consensus. Nixon's suspension of the convertibility of the dollar into gold and the setting of exchange rates based on market valuations, plus the imposition of import surcharges by Washington, rapidly forced an adaptation by the rest of the capitalist trading states. As a result, the world monetary system relied on a dollar (not gold) standard. An inflationary macro-economic policy served to share the costs of America's expensive adventurism in Vietnam, achieved through a devaluation of the dollar and a depreciation of external dollar-denominated holdings.

These policies brought on a profound recessionary wave throughout the capitalist world that lasted into the 1980s, and a crisis in the consensus that had characterized the global order. All previous assumptions about the organizing precepts of society were questioned. The post-war compromise was attacked in both senses of the term: the domestic compromise which tied in labour and welfare interests; and the international compromise of mediating between national interests and the global order.

For the IMF, these events were of profound importance. Indeed, it is true to say that in the early 1970s, with the demise of regulated exchange rates, the IMF 'lost' its main *raison d'être*. This has provoked a constant re-invention by the IMF – to find a new role, if not justify its very existence. This has increasingly stimulated the institution to involve itself in affairs that are beyond the remit of its original mandate – to indulge in 'mission creep'. According to one analysis:

> This has been done with grave consequences: the IMF, staffed with macro economists, does not have the expertise to provide the kind of advice that it is dispensing today. Nor is the IMF, which has no independent evaluation unit and has been labelled one of the most secretive public institutions in the world, held accountable for the policy advice that it gives.
>
> (Welch 1998)

This is of fundamental importance, for the IMF is one of the sites of a transnationalized ruling elite. Organizations such as the IMF have been at the forefront of an intense reappraisal of the role of the state and the suitable levels of public and private involvement in the economy. Essentially, this has been an attempt to contest the Keynesian project and, wherever feasible, to discard it. This project has been a struggle not only for pure power, but also for popular authority. In short, it has been a struggle for hegemony. Such a process has been conducted by a powerful phalanx of social forces, arrayed behind the agenda of intensified market-led globalization, who sought to actively promote the post-Keynesian counter-revolution.

For its part, the IMF began to emerge as a particularly important player in the propagation of ideas surrounding governance and in restructuring national economies, particularly in the South. This was facilitated first by the debt crisis of the 1980s, which saw the IMF emerge as the lender of last resort; and second by a resurgence of interest in the capitalist heartland in promoting liberal democracy in the developing world. At the same time, there was concern that the structural adjustment programmes that had attempted to reconfigure the South had been hampered, if not sabotaged, by 'poor governance'. As George and Sabelli (1994: 142) assert:

> If sustainable poverty reduction turn[ed] out to be just another mirage, institutional responsibility for failure must not be seen to be the fault of the [international financial institutions]. The only other possible culprits [were] the [IFIs'] partners. ...

Governance provide[d] a new tool-kit, an instrument of control, an additional conditionality for the time when the traditional blame-the-victim defence again becomes necessary. It further offer[ed] the opportunity both to instil Western political values in borrowing countries and to fault them if things go wrong.

Instead of questioning their own prescriptions, the IFIs instead sought to advance 'good governance' as a necessary precondition for neoliberal reforms to finally work. This in itself reflected the conviction amongst the institutions that neoliberalism was the only way forward, and that what was wrong, or had been going wrong, was not the ingredients of the adjustment programmes, but rather their implementation and wider institutional setting in the borrowing states. The World Bank took the lead in this new approach, with its report in 1989 entitled *Sub-Saharan Africa: From Crisis to Sustainable Growth* (World Bank 1989b). This report took a more holistic view than previous Bank documents, and argued that institutional change was necessary if reforms were to be effective. Not only did the Bank argue that governments should be rolled back, but also that what government remained had to be better administered along lines favoured by international capital. The report also argued that what was characterizing the economic crisis in Africa was not unequal trading relations with the North, or massive debt, or the negative effects of liberalization, etc., but rather a 'crisis of governance' (*ibid*.: 60).

A number of subsequent reports by the Bank continued with this theme, linking good governance and notions of liberal democracy with economic development (cf. World Bank 1991; 1997b). What was being advanced were particular ideas on how best to implement neoliberal restructuring, maintaining a core state apparatus to push through liberalization. This project combined coercion and consent as integral parts of the neoliberal push, wrapped up themselves within a broad liberal capitalist ethos (see Williams and Young 1994). Indeed, good governance was advanced as 'necessary for the creation of the consent for the new order which structural adjustment could not usher in; and, unsaid, is also needed to implement a sufficient quota of repression as the still unchanged policies of neo-liberalism are implemented' (Bernstein 1990: 23).

Although such ideas were outside of the IMF's actual remit, the Fund also began to take an increasing interest in good governance. In September 1996 a declaration entitled *Partnership for Sustainable Global Growth* was adopted by the IMF's Interim Committee, and in August 1997 a report, promulgated by the IMF's Executive Board, asserted that IMF must henceforth assist member countries in creating systems that 'limit the scope for *ad hoc* decision making, for rent seeking, for undesirable preferential treatment of individuals or organizations'. The IMF now boldly stated that it was 'legitimate to seek information about the political situation in member countries as an essential element in judging the prospects for policy implementation' (James 1998: 35).

The ability of the Fund to advance its new ideas on governance was considerably compounded by the structural features of the global economy. As one analysis asserts, the power of the IMF over developing countries 'was made all the more formidable since, in the aftermath of the debt crisis, all other potential sources of credit, bilateral or otherwise, required an IMF stamp of approval ... before any credit was extended' (Adams 1997: 162). Developing countries increasingly required the IMF's approval in order to secure new aid flows in order to help avoid defaulting on outstanding loans. Obviously, this gave the IMF an amount of influence over the economic policies of debt-ridden administrations. State administrations were repeatedly 'advised' that economic recovery was dependent upon what was vaguely termed 'business confidence', and that this in itself hung on a disciplined labour force and a state that pursued 'good governance'.

Such advice has been part and parcel of the Structural Adjustment Facility (SAF) and Enhanced Structural Adjustment Facility (ESAF) loan programmes of the institution. The conditions attached to such loans can include the dismantling of labour regulations, increasing foreign investment incentives, and privatization schemes. Yet such conditionalities and negotiations between the IMF and the host state frequently present what are essentially the interest of particular fractions, both national and international, as being in the interests of the wider populace. Concessions, such as the (limited) advancement of what are termed 'social issues' allow the IMF and the negotiating state parties to pass off conditionalities as being concerned with protecting the poorest. O'Brien *et al.* (2000: 178) remark that such interventions allow the IMF to cast general interests as paramount, thus strengthening the legitimacy of IMF prescriptions and maintaining political support for them. One such tactic is to stress 'ownership' of IMF prescriptions by implementing states and to portray IMF strictures as being voluntarily followed by administrations pursuing the general interest:

> [M]anagement and staff at the IMF have gone some way to accepting the importance of ownership, at least in so far as it may be an indispensable ingredient for successful policy implementation. ...
>
> That said, the change in rhetoric has not to date always translated into substantially different behaviour at the Fund. ... For the IMF, 'ownership' has tended to mean acceptance by the borrowing government and its citizens of Fund prescriptions. As one official has typically put it, 'we have to persuade the population that an adjustment package is legitimate'.
>
> (O'Brien *et al.* 2000: 187)

One way this has been done is for the IMF to move even further beyond its original mandate of facilitating short-term loans. Previously, it is true that the institution provided varying degrees of technical advice and assistance, often with conditionalities attached. However, traditionally the IMF's main focus was on encouraging administrations to 'correct' macroeconomic imbalances, reduce inflation, and embark on reforms amenable to the private sector. We can call this process 'first stage restructuring', referring to the package of measures adopted at the behest of the IFIs to open up domestic markets.

The IMF has increasingly promoted 'second stage restructuring' (centred around the ideas of 'good governance'), after it became apparent that much of the initial restructuring programmes were not working. Pinpointing exactly when this occurred is problematic, but according to one source,

> through 1982, less than 5 per cent of [IMF] upper tranche arrangements contained more than 11 or more performance criteria [i.e. conditionalities related to governance]. By the end of the decade, more than two thirds of such arrangements had 11 or more criteria.
>
> (Kapur and Webb 2000: 2)

Conceptually, poor governance has been blamed as a central problem. Current IMF policy is designed to lock-in administration to the liberalization process, whilst at the same time giving the reforms legitimacy based on liberal legal principles. As an IMF document asserts, 'the IMF has found that a much broader range of institutional reforms is needed if countries are to establish and maintain private sector confidence and thereby lay the basis for sustained growth' (IMF 1997b).

As mentioned above, in September 1996 a declaration entitled *Partnership for Sustainable Global Growth* was adopted by the IMF's Interim Committee in Washington. This identified 'promoting good governance in all its aspects, including ensuring the rule of law, improving the efficiency and accountability of the public sector, and tackling corruption' as a fundamental element of a restructuring framework. This process was rapidly followed by a 'Guidance Note', which was adopted by the Board in July 1997 (IMF 1997b). According to this Note, the IMF took on responsibility for two spheres:

- improving the management of public resources through reforms covering public sector institutions (e.g. the treasury, central bank, public enterprises, civil service, and the official statistics function), including administrative procedures (e.g. expenditure control, budget management, and revenue collection);
- supporting the development and maintenance of a transparent and stable economic and regulatory environment conducive to efficient private sector activities (e.g. price systems, exchange and trade regimes, and banking systems and their related regulations) (IMF 1997a).

It rapidly became apparent that the IMF saw good governance as a cornerstone in its new reconfigured mission, and that adherence to the ideas not promoted by the institution was not an option for administrations seeking IMF largesse. The IMF Director Michel Camdessus went so far as to warn state elites that 'every country that hopes to maintain market confidence must come to terms with the issues associated with good governance' (IMF 1997b).

Problematizing and explaining the rise of good governance ideas

There are four essential problems with the current emphasis on good governance: who is advocating it; how; what exactly constitutes good governance; and whose interests does it serve? Obviously, tackling issues of corruption, transparency and mismanagement is not a bad thing in itself and is a highly positive and lofty principle. However, conferring the IMF with the ability to determine what constitutes good governance, and the power to implement such prescriptions onto sovereign states is profoundly problematic. As one analyst writes, it further legitimizes the IMF's power grabs of the last several decades and entrenches the IMF in the position of giving development and stabilization advice even when its qualifications are highly dubious (Welch 1998). Collier comments that

> the extension of the practice of conditionality from the occasional circumstances of crisis management to the continuous process of general economic policy-making has implied a transfer of sovereignty which is not only unprecedented but is often dysfunctional, particularly as such conditionalities lacked moral legitimacy.
>
> (1999: 319–20)

Indeed, given the IMF's history, it is correct to be suspicious of the new-found principles supposedly governing the institution's lending operations. One need only remember that it was the IMF who advanced over US$1 billion to Mobutu Sese Seko in Zaire to realize that good governance has not always been high up on the list of concerns for the institution. Numerous countries, particularly in Africa, continued to receive IMF assistance long after the corrupt nature of their state polities was blatantly apparent. And then of course, the US$11 billion loan to Russia in July 1998 (over and above an already existing $10 billion loan) was approved in spite of the rotten nature and overtly corrupt practices of the Russian elites. Clearly, good governance principles, despite claims to the contrary in Washington, have never been a priority for the IMF, and in fact the institution has been complicit in many highly dubious activities and with many suspect administrations (Chossudovsky 1998).

What then explains this shift in ideas? Are such new ideas really new, or are they other means to help reconfigure the South? Central to any analysis is the ongoing process(es) of globalization and the hegemony of neoliberal ideas, whose

> architects require a universal vision, a picture of a globally conceived society, to join classes in different countries ... [in order] to institutionalise global capital accumulation by setting general rules of behaviour and disseminating a developmentalist ideology to facilitate the process.
>
> (Mittelman and Pasha 1997: 51)

These rules of behaviour reflect the second stage of capitalist restructuring that has already been mentioned, as state elites in the periphery are encouraged to lock-in the liberalization process by enacting good governance prescriptions that serve to isolate, and at the same time *legitimize*, economic reforms along neoliberal lines. This process is not simply a top-down activity that strips Southern elites of their agency. Indeed, circumstances may actually mean that liberalization and the selling-off of public enterprises may serve the interests of entrenched elites and their local and international class allies. In this sense, good governance rhetorically advances 'common sense' notions of governance by promoting sectional interests as the common interest and by appearing to be reasonable and beyond reproach, whilst actually covertly advancing liberalization. The good governance project is a highly effective strategy. As George and Sabelli remark, 'being against good governance is like being against motherhood and apple-pie', yet the IFIs' definition of governance 'nicely circumvents the issue of politics by focusing on ... the solely economic' (1994: 150).

According to Gill, the locking-in of reforms and the granting of legitimacy is at the heart of ideas surrounding new constitutionalism and good governance issues as propagated by disciplinary international institutions (Gill 1998). Good governance ideas can be seen as a means to 'reformulate and redefine the public sphere and rules for economic policy, according to orthodox market-monetarist postulates in macroeconomics (fiscal and monetary policy) and microeconomics (e.g. trade, labour market and industrial policy)' (*ibid*.: 30). They serve as the vanguard in the second stage of neoliberal restructuring, further acting to lock-in domestic elites, whilst at the same time bolstering the position of those fractions sympathetic to an increasingly cohesive transnational neoliberal power bloc. It is this which has been instrumental in efforts to create a mode of international economic policy coordination which is intended to ensure the coherence and stability of a new transnational accumulation regime.

Though there is, to be sure, a large degree of top-down coercion involved in this restructuring process, consensual elements are present, particularly on the part of the outwardly oriented fractions of capital in states in the periphery, as well as their elite allies within the state administrations. In this sense, the promotion of good governance can also be seen as an attempt to formulate and reformulate hegemony at the local level around neoliberal ideas, and is not a process devoid of agency on the part of Southern elites. Good governance ideas, as they are currently configured, may be seen as attempts to reconstruct hegemony through a reformulation of the mode of political rule: from the unstable and unpredictable to one that is most attractive to international investors.

Whilst the implementation of structural adjustment programmes may erode legitimacy in the eyes of some, the turn to 'clean government' does help ameliorate negative pressures. After all, the state is supposedly operating a tight ship and cannot be held accountable outright to dislocations that may occur – these are the 'natural' workings of the market! In addition, the involvement of institutions such as the IMF in promoting neoliberal ideas within borrowing states can also act as a useful alibi to be deployed in defence of administrations that intend to embark on neoliberal restructuring. As a Bank for International Settlements report put it, 'in many countries, explaining monetary policy decisions in terms of external constraints has been helpful in securing public acceptance' (Bank for International Settlements 1992: 124).

Furthermore, by holding administrations accountable to good governance strictures, institutions such as the IMF also avoid censure and can be actually seen as allies of the downtrodden citizen – even whilst the IMF's very policies contribute to the further erosion of citizens' livelihoods. Indeed, by advancing the classical liberal separation of the political from the economic, good governance strictures serve to obscure the real problems regarding social and economic power imbalances that characterize most states. By elevating good governance prescriptions into legally binding guidelines, and by predicating further funding on the compliance to such precepts, the IMF and other IFIs bolster the position of the neoliberal-inclined elites.

Equally important, by advocating good governance, the IMF and other intervening bodies help build up a considerable and influential support constituency in civil society. As one analysis framed it, 'local and foreign NGOs, the media, religious institutions, chambers of commerce and employers' organisations quickly mesh together as a local network of non-governmental bases of support to meet [the institution's] objectives' (Toissaint 1999: 149). This can be seen as part and parcel of 'a global strategy to promote *Western* values and institutionalise political regimes that arc likely to be non-belligerent and generally positive towards the realisation of the [neo-] liberal paradigm' (Hyden 1997: 236).

Conclusion

The promotion of certain ideas relating to good governance reflects developments within global capitalism in the era of globalization and where the ideology of neoliberalism is hegemonic. Good governance is part of a broader attempt to legitimize the political authority of liberalizing elite fractions in the South. These ideas have been advanced by international financial institutions such as the IMF as part and parcel of the neoliberal order. It is a reflection of the success of neoliberalism as a hegemonic project that particular ideas of 'good governance' now appear to be common sense, if not unquestionable. The incantations sounded by the organic intellectuals tied to this project whenever criticism is raised make its almost hallowed status quite clear. Williamson's remarks in defence of the consensus give a taste of such reflexes, claiming as he does, that neoliberalism is the 'spontaneous, automatic expression of economic facts':

> [T]he superior economic performance of countries that establish and maintain outward-oriented market economies subject to macro-economic discipline is essentially a positive question. The proof may not be quite as conclusive as the proof that the earth is not flat, but it is sufficiently well established as to give sensible people better things to do with their time than to challenge its veracity. ... I find it ironic that some critics have condemned the Washington consensus as a neo-conservative tract ... I regard it rather ... as an attempt to summarise the common core of wisdom embraced by all serious economists.
>
> (Williamson 1993: 1330, 1334)

Having said this, the promotion by the IMF of good governance ideas must be contextualized within a broader framework incorporating notions regarding the power of ideas within international politics. In fact, it is accurate to say that what the IMF and other disciplinary institutions are promoting is a form of 'passive revolution' that seeks to achieve the hegemony of neoliberalism. By appealing to the rule of law and emphasizing safeguards for market reforms, notions of governance more specifically related to liberalization, *alongside* issues such as corruption, can be covertly 'smuggled in' and entrenched at a constitutional and legal level, thereby locking-in administrations to the restructuring process (Cutler 1999).

In essence, good governance promotion can be seen as an expansion of the IMF's mandate into the realms of advocating constitutional and legal safeguards for transnational capital. In doing so, the harmonization of business practices is the ultimate aim, but so too is the defence and enlargement of a project in furtherance of a world-wide restructuring. In doing so, consent in supporting many of the prescriptions of good governance – a supposedly universal and 'neutral' set of values – is equally as important as the more coercive nature of institutions such as the IMF: 'Since the ideological formation of hegemony is necessary for the creation of *consent*, the reproduction of hegemony is dependent ... upon its ability to operate as a universal language' (Keyman 1997: 117), so that different interests belonging to different states are made compatible with one another. The extent and form of IMF interventions of course fluctuates over time and space, depending on the balance of class forces within each particular state. Nonetheless, good governance has become what development and modernization were two decades ago: a hegemonic discourse that seeks to allow the North to define the South in its own image. This is not to say that compliance with such governance strictures is automatic, and Southern elites have been at times quite successful in ducking such prescriptions. But questions over compliance or non-compliance to a degree miss the point. It is the legitimizing function that strictures on governance perform, attached as they are to liberalizing projects, that makes such projects incredibly powerful. Such prescriptions, even if ignored by the affected elites, serve to advance the idea that sectional interests are actually general interests and that restructuring, however unpalatable to many on the ground, 'at least' brings with it conditionalities that may rein in the corrupt rapacity of local elites, even if this actually does not happen. Good governance projects then serve at one level to obscure the actual implications of neoliberal programmes, whilst dressing them up as good common sense which may ameliorate the dire economic and political conditions of much of the South. They act as a means of legitimization and socialization. In this sense, the promotion of 'good governance' notions by bodies such as the IMF reflects the potent role of ideas in international politics, and the part played by multilateral institutions in such endeavours.

10 Balancing between East and West

The Asian Development Bank's policy on good governance

Janne Jokinen

Introduction

This chapter looks at the Asian Development Bank's (ADB) policy document on good governance, with the purpose of clarifying how its contents were influenced by the political and institutional environments within which it was created. The analysis begins with a discussion on the factors that led to its creation. The focus then shifts to the contents of the document: how do they reflect the ideological and political framework within which the Bank's management functioned in the early and mid-1990s when the policy document was drawn up? Two themes are highlighted: the definition of the proper role of the state in development, and the manner in which the policy on good governance is reconciled with the 'apolitical' role of the ADB.

The policy on good governance was adopted because the major Western donor countries wanted it. They were able to use the negotiations for the replenishment of the Bank's Ordinary Capital Resources (OCR) and the Asian Development Fund (ADF) to persuade the opponents of the policy to accept it. However, the policy was not just a product of the Western donors. Its contents were influenced by Japan, which was strengthening the policy aspect of its development cooperation in the late 1980s. The document was also modified to make it palatable to the Developing Member Countries (DMCs) and ease its integration to the ideological framework of the Bank. Consequently, the ADB policy on good governance differs in some important aspects from similar policies adopted by other development agencies in the 1990s.

Background of the policy document on good governance

In its introduction, the ADB policy document on good governance (ADB 1995) gives two main sources for the policy: the international development debate of the early 1990s, and the Bank's internal discussion concerning the approaches, priorities and objectives of its operational programmes. The international debate referred to was the exchange between the proponents of the so-called 'Washington Consensus' represented especially by the United States,[1] the World

Bank and the International Monetary Fund (IMF), and the East and Southeast Asian supporters of the 'Developmental State' model.[2] The intensity of the debate reached its peak at the same time as the policy document was under preparation.

The question of what good governance is and how it should be operationalized in developing countries became a key bone of contention in the debate, as it came to signify an extensive package of issues (see Bøås 1998). The Washington Consensus advocated a limited economic role for the state, while supporters of the Developmental State model argued for an active one. After the collapse of the Soviet Union, the linkage to human rights and democracy gained in emphasis. The relative merits of collective economic and individual political rights were widely debated, as were those of authoritarian political systems ('guided democracy') and liberal parliamentary democracy.

Japan's position in the post-Cold War development debate was particularly interesting because it was so ambivalent. Japan agreed with many of the arguments of the Washington Consensus, but also sympathized with its opponents. This was understandable, as it was Japan's own post-Second World War development strategy that had been refined into the Developmental State model. All the main contenders were members of the ADB, and the Bank thus became an important forum for the debate. Moreover, the ADB was at the time seeking to broaden its role from that of a project financier to what it called a 'broad-based development institution' (ADB 1998: 20–21). Whether or not the Bank should promote good governance, and by what means, was closely connected with what kind of an identity it was going to have in the future.

Contending visions: the Washington Consensus, the Asian Developing Countries, and Japan

Since the 1980s, the Washington Consensus had been offering to developing countries a policy package that consisted of privatization, liberalization and democratization. Its vision was an idealized version of American society: a minimalist state based on the establishment and enforcement of property rights, the rule of law, political democracy and individualistic economic transactions, as well as a selective social safety net (Black 1999; Standing 2000).

Economic growth was the paramount goal. It was believed to be impossible without the establishment of a free and open market economy that was based on the rule of law. The new urban middle classes that would emerge as a result of economic liberalization would not stand for any limitations on their personal freedom and would pursue an American-style political system. The globalization of the free market model would inevitably lead to the globalization of political systems, values and cultures.

Among the most vocal Asian critics of the Washington Consensus were the leaders of the People's Republic of China (PRC), Senior Minister Lee Kuan Yew of Singapore, and Prime Minister Mahathir Mohammad of Malaysia. According to them, its ideas were not based on 'scientific' but ideological grounds. Behind the campaign for good governance they tended to see a plot to keep Asian countries subservient to the West by undermining the strengths on which their success was based: an active dirigiste state, and the placing of collective economic rights before individual political rights. The critics referred to experiences from Africa and Latin America, where World Bank and IMF-enforced Structural Adjustment Programmes (SAPs) had been applied since the early 1980s with poor results. These programmes contained the same policy package that was now offered to Asians (Zakaria 1994; Yasutomo 1995; Root 1996; Gwynne and Kay 1999).

The supporters of the Developmental State model emphasized that the role of the state was crucial, especially in the initial phases of economic development. Technological adaptability and the accumulation of capital would be promoted by forceful policies, including protectionist ones. Public resources would be applied pragmatically to search for and implement market-augmenting and market-accelerating measures in cooperation with the private sector. Only after domestic corporations, and the society at large, were strong enough to withstand foreign competition in both home and international markets would the national economy be gradually opened up (Yasutomo 1995; Gore 1996). The rapid economic growth that first Japan and then several other East and Southeast Asian societies had experienced in the 1970s and 1980s was presented as evidence of the success of the Developmental State model.

Since the end of the 1970s, Japan had greatly increased its Official Development Assistance (ODA). It had also become the largest creditor in the world. At the end of the 1980s, Japan's Asia policy changed. It redirected its development aid to new recipients as a result of the 'economic miracles' that had taken place in several countries that it had assisted in the past. At the same time, Japan launched a campaign to match its political influence in international organizations with its financial contributions to them. A characteristically Japanese ODA philosophy had to be created to provide a substantive basis for a more prominent political role (Yasutomo 1995).

In the 1980s, humanitarianism and interdependence had been highlighted as the rationales for Japan's development assistance. In the post-Cold War era, the efforts of aid recipients to strengthen democracy, human rights and the market economy would be rewarded, while increasing military expenditures, development of weapons of mass destruction and arms exports would result in the reduction or discontinuation of assistance.[3] These principles, together with environmental concerns, were codified in the ODA Charter adopted in 1992 (Yasutomo 1995).[4]

Japan's position in the international development debate became more prominent at the beginning of the 1990s. At the same time, it moved closer to the opponents of the Washington Consensus. At the World Bank, Japan questioned the neoliberal approach to development operationalized in the SAPs, and sought the role of a mediator between the DMCs and the United States and other Western donors (Yasutomo 1995).[5]

The actors within the Asian Development Bank

The main contenders in the international debate were all members of the ADB. The proponents of the Washington Consensus wielded a great deal of influence over the Bank's thinking. Most of the economists working there had been educated in North American or British universities and adhered to the neoliberal school of economics. The authority of the IMF in the governance of the global economic system was largely unquestioned. The World Bank had close relations with its Asian sister, sharing information and staff, and the ADB tended to follow its lead in policy matters. The United States was the most powerful member country at the ADB, and it was not afraid to use its influence to promote its own interests (Kappagoda 1995).

At the end of the 1980s, opposition to the Washington Consensus gained in strength at the ADB. The PRC became a member in 1986 and got its own representative on the Board of Directors. It also soon became the largest borrower. The Chinese had little time for free market ideologues. Moreover, the first of the Asian 'tigers' – Singapore, Hongkong, Taiwan and South Korea – shed DMC status and became donors themselves. Also Indonesia and Malaysia made financial contributions to the Bank. The Southeast Asians matched their economic success with increasing assertiveness in international affairs (Kappagoda 1995).

Among the members of the ADB, Japan traditionally holds a special position. Its voting power equals that of the United States. Moreover, the Japanese Ministry of Finance (MOF) has provided the candidates for ADB presidency since the Bank's founding. Many other key positions in the ADB management are filled by MOF personnel as well, and positions at the ADB have long been considered almost an integral part of the career development of MOF's internationally oriented officials. By the 1980s, many top MOF officials had an ADB background and experience from the development of Asian societies, which they could put to use, for example at the World Bank and the IMF (Yasutomo 1995).

Until the late 1980s, Japan maintained a low profile at the ADB. The executive directors representing Japan focused on supporting the president and rarely disagreed with Bank management in public. Japan was also careful not to get involved in political disputes with the United States, because it wanted to maintain at least the appearance of a balance between its own position and that of the Americans to deflect accusations that the ADB was dominated by Japan. However, towards the end of the 1980s, this policy began to change. Japan could not hope to increase its influence in any other major multilateral development institution because these were all controlled by the Americans and/or the Europeans. Moreover, Japan was forced to adopt a higher profile at the ADB by the United States' open use of the Bank to implement its own political and ideological agenda, which the Japanese did not wholly share (Yasutomo 1995).

During the first years of the 1990s, the attitude of the United States towards the ADB changed. The post-Cold War Bush and Clinton administrations appeared to consider the Bank a relatively unimportant institution. Maintaining security alliances in Asia at any cost was no longer felt necessary, and the focus shifted to opening Asian economies for American exports and investments. There was less need to channel money to Asian allies through the ADB. The United States opposed the Fourth General Capital Increase of the Bank's OCR (GCI IV) and the Sixth Replenishment of the ADF (ADF VI), which were being negotiated in the beginning of the 1990s. Japan reacted by redirecting its efforts to keeping the Americans involved in the ADB, for example by serving as a mediator between the United States and its opponents the same way as it had done at the World Bank (Yasutomo 1995).

The ADB itself was undergoing deep-reaching changes in the early 1990s. Its management was seeking to change the Bank into a 'broad-based development institution', a move supported by many donors but opposed by some DMCs. The Bank needed new resources from the donors for the replenishment of its OCR and the ADF. Consequently, it had to adopt their agenda, in which good governance was a key theme at the time. At the same time, the ADB management had to make sure that its new identity would be acceptable to its powerful DMCs as well.

The debate on good governance within the Asian Development Bank

The opportunity for reforming the role of the ADB in the Asia-Pacific and for defining what good governance would mean in an Asian setting was provided by the negotiations leading to GCI IV and ADF VI. Several major donor countries argued that, as a result of the 'economic miracles' in East and Southeast Asia, a number of DMCs were no longer in need of ADB assistance – especially the 'soft' ADF loans – as they now had greater domestic resources and access to international financial markets. Consequently, a GCI would only be justified if the emphasis of the Bank's operations moved from supporting economic development as such to promoting institutional reforms and social development (Kappagoda 1995; Bøås 1998).

Despite strong opposition from DMCs, the ADB pledged to use more resources for social development and environmental protection programmes. It also promised to emphasize the development performance of borrowing DMCs as a criterion for the allocation of ADF resources, and to apply this criterion to operations financed from OCR as well, when appropriate (Bøås 1998). Good governance would be one element in measuring development performance (ADB 1995).

The DMCs had consistently opposed considering development performance in lending decisions. The use of good governance – including a democratic mode of government and respect for human rights as criteria for measuring this had been opposed even more vehemently (Kappagoda 1995). To assuage the DMCs, the ADB emphasized that progress in good governance would only be looked at in an economic context. Democratization and human rights were excluded by the Bank's charter (Bøås 1998).

The same theme was picked up in an important report drawn up by the Task Force on Improving Project Quality, which was completed in January 1994. The Task Force stressed the importance of increasing DMC capacity for policy analysis, formulation and management, as well as strengthening the 'ownership' of projects by executive agencies and potential beneficiaries. The Bank was to encourage DMC governments to give up tasks that could be handled better by the private sector (ADB 1994; 1995).

At the same time as the Task Force was winding up its work, the preparation of the policy document itself was underway. This process was led by Dr Hilton Root, who served as the Chief Adviser on Governance at the ADB from 1994 to 1997. He had previously worked as a consultant for the World Bank and the United States Agency for International Development (USAID). Root borrowed DMC and ADB staff, gathered the views of donors on governance, and prepared a draft policy document to serve as a basis for discussion (Root 1996).

In April 1995 the ADB organized the Governance and Development Workshop. It brought together experts who had been involved in drawing up the development strategies of Hong Kong, Indonesia, Japan, the Republic of Korea, Singapore and Taiwan. The workshop drew attention to the widespread impression in Asia that the existing definitions of governance reflected only the experience and interests of Western countries, and did not take into account Asian experiences. This despite the fact that in East and Southeast Asia, it had seemingly been possible to create rapid economic growth through interventionist industrial policies while maintaining equity and limiting the amount of bureaucratic corruption (Root 1996; Bøås 1998).

The participants of the workshop stressed that no standard measurement of good governance should be adopted because each country had its own political history, political system, institutional culture and level of development, none of which could be accredited with a comparative advantage. Many institutional alternatives permitted sound development management. The key issue was the capacity to successfully implement economic and social policies. This depended especially on the capability of state bureaucracy and the effectiveness of the state/society interface.

The conclusions made at the Governance and Development Workshop were taken into the policy document on good governance almost *ad verbatim*, which made it acceptable to the DMCs (ADB 1995; Root 1996). The document was brought to the ADB's board of directors as a Working Paper in May 1995 and formally adopted by the board the following October (ADB 1995).

The balancing act, part 1: the proper role of the state in development

The ADB policy document on good governance is a balancing act in several ways. It seeks to accommodate the interests of the donors with those of the DMCs, Asian viewpoints with the Washington Consensus, economics with politics, the role of the state and its citizens with that of private enterprise, the interests of domestic with those of foreign investors, and so on. The scales of this balancing act are not equally weighted, however.

The policy document was drawn up and adopted because the Western donors wanted it (ADB 1995; Bøås 1998). This is reflected in its contents, where standard arguments of the Washington Consensus are repeated. The document concentrates on the role and practices of public authorities. Most reforms either derive from, or aim at, increasing the role of domestic and foreign private enterprise in the national economy. Privatization and the integration of Asian economies to the global marketplace are important objectives (ADB 1995; Bøås 1998). The overall goal of the policy seems to be to facilitate the transformation of the institutions and practices of the borrowing DMCs so that they become compatible with the values and practices of the North American and European donors. The policy also seeks to make ADB investments in development projects in the DMCs more cost-effective – a traditional donor concern (ADB 1995).

The objectives of the policy on good governance are clothed in economic parlance to make it acceptable to DMCs and to reconcile it with the ADB Charter. It is repeatedly stressed that the ADB is only concerned with 'sound development management' – that is, the efficiency and effectiveness of the institutional environment within which citizens and corporations interact with their government agencies and individual officials – and not with governance as democratization or the strengthening of individual human rights. The document argues that the Bank is not interested in the specific sets of economic policies DMC governments are pursuing, let alone their political systems; the Bank's sole concern is that those policies have their desired effects (ADB 1995).

As its point of departure, the policy document takes the definition of the term 'governance' from *Webster's New Universal Unabridged Dictionary* of 1979: 'the manner in which power is exercised in the management of a country's economic and social resources and development' (ADB 1995).[6] Based on this definition and a World Bank discussion on the matter,[7] the ADB describes governance as being directly concerned with the management of the development process. It encompasses the functioning and capability of the public sector, as well as the rules and institutions that create the framework for the conduct of both public and private business. Accountability for economic and financial performance, and regulatory frameworks relating to companies, corporations and partnerships also fall under the term 'governance' (ADB 1995).

The policy document seeks to deflect DMC misgivings by stating that Asian experiences have shown that there is no direct correlation between the political environment and rapid economic and social development; democracies have fared no better than non-democracies in terms of good governance (ADB 1995). The ideological orthodoxy of the document is confirmed by the argument that, generally speaking, the market mechanism is to be preferred to state direction: markets allocate resources more efficiently than governments because the latter have limited access to information (ADB 1995).

The state can best carry out its tasks by concentrating on guaranteeing a 'level playing field' for private actors. Equity can be safeguarded by maintaining the mobility of factors of production, free flow of information regarding prices and technology, and competition among buyers and sellers. Taxation and public spending are also needed but should be applied in moderation. Cost recovery of public services should be increased by adopting user fees and discontinuing subsidies for low priority activities (ADB 1995).

The ADB policy document on good governance thus provides the model for the proper functions of the state. This conflicts with the claim made elsewhere in the document that the Bank will not identify specific criteria for government action because it would be impossible to choose the right ones – East Asian institutions, although different from Western ones, have proven to be just as effective in bringing about economic development. The Bank promises that it will not force the DMCs to change their institutions. This is done to deflect the accusation that it is attaching political conditions to its lending, which is forbidden by the charter. The promise is undermined, however, by the policy on good governance itself, and the commitments the Bank made to donors in connection with GCI IV and ADF VI (Wilson 1987; ADB 1995).

The principles of public administration

The main focus of the ADB policy document on good governance is on what constitutes proper public administration, or 'sound development management'. The document follows the categorization adopted by the World Bank: *accountability, participation, rule of law* – interestingly renamed in the ADB document as 'predictability' – and *transparency*. In short, accountability refers to making public officials answerable for government behaviour and responsive to the entity from which they derive their authority; participation implies that stakeholders – those affected – have access to public institutions that promote development, and are able to influence the design and implementation of their activities; predictability refers to the existence of laws, regulations and policies to regulate society, and to their fair and consistent application; and transparency refers to the availability of information to the general public and clarity about government rules, regulations and decisions (ADB 1995).

The policy document suggests ways for operationalizing the four elements. Improving accountability means strengthening government capacity for public sector management, public enterprise management and reform, and public financial management, as well as civil service reform. Increasing participation means making the public sector/private sector interface more efficient and decentralizing public and service delivery functions, as well as closer cooperation with NGOs. Enhancing predictability can be done by strengthening legal frameworks, especially for private sector development. Transparency can be improved by widening the disclosure of information (ADB 1995).

Although the policy document states that the primary responsibility for deciding on the direction and contents of public sector reforms is with the DMCs themselves, it does present a ready agenda for them to follow. The emphasis is on scaling down the state's involvement. The preconditions of success are government commitment to improving public sector operations, and movement towards a macroeconomic and sector policy framework that includes trade liberalization and exchange rate decontrol, as well as market-oriented interest rates and other basic prices in the economy (ADB 1995).

The policy document defends this approach by appealing to dispassionate reasoning: downsizing the public sector 'may not be an end in itself, but is likely to result from an unbiased examination of which goods and services are provided better by private institutions' (ADB 1995: 18). The document does allow some leeway in the privatization process, but argues that the autonomy from public authorities of those public enterprises deemed worth maintaining should be increased in the name of efficiency. At the same time, their accountability to these same authorities should be enhanced (ADB 1995).

Civil service reform is approached from the same perspective: the key issue is strengthening the confidence of the private sector in DMC economies. A professional and accountable civil service that can administer rules, maintain standards and competition, and respect property rights is necessary for this purpose. The policy document argues that market-friendly reforms are by nature likely to have a beneficial impact in this respect because decreasing the discretionary powers of officials leaves less space for corruption (ADB 1995).

In addressing the issue of participation, the focus is on the public sector/private sector interface and boosting the role of the latter in the economy. Market-friendly reforms are needed to release the energies and dynamism of the private sector. Consultative mechanisms are needed to provide a voice in public sector policy making, and to serve as safeguards against corruption. The policy document recognizes that involving all stakeholders – not just representatives of the private sector – in policy making will increase the effectiveness and accountability of development activities by providing governments with information concerning the needs of the people and different social groups with means for protecting their rights. Cooperation with NGOs, however, is considered to be potentially useful but risky because these may have political agendas, lack formal structures and accountability, have problems with continuity due to financial constraints, and want to maintain their independence by staying within the informal sector (ADB 1995).

The balance struck in the discussion on the proper role of the state in the development of a society is skewed. Recommendations correspond to the views of the Washington Consensus. The language used is that of (neoliberal) economics, although the issues dealt with are social, political, even cultural in nature. There is little in the document that would appeal to civil society activists or the proponents of the Developmental State model.

The balancing act, part 2: the Asian Development Bank as an 'apolitical' institution

Great efforts are expended to make the ADB policy document on good governance appear a 'technical' document. The political nature of its contents is made clear, however, by simply listing the topics that it deals with: the proper role of the government in society, the policies that flow from this role, the principles according to which state administration should be ordered, and the ADB's role in moulding DMC societies according to the model defined in the policy. Although the document maintains that it is only concerned with 'sound development management', which sounds 'scientific' and non-controversial, it is actually concerned with the way societies organize themselves. The use of economic parlance, and promises to act only at the request of the DMCs, appear already in the Bank's charter. The ADB was created in 1966 to change ('develop') Asian societies, but given the image of a bank, an institution that was considered to be apolitical by the founding fathers and thus acceptable even to the newly independent DMCs that were sensitive about their sovereignty.[8]

The point of departure adopted by the policy document on good governance is the definition of governance as the manner in which *power* is exercised in the management of a country's resources and development. However, the political aspects of governance are immediately discarded. The document does recognize, for example, that making participation more effective may have a positive impact on democratization or individual political and human rights, but promises that the Bank will not directly support such goals (ADB 1995). According to the policy document,

> the Bank will steer clear of overtly political goals, such as parliamentary democracy and human rights (however desirable these may be, for their own sake). That being said, however, it also needs stressing that, in many ways, the Bank's operations are conducive, albeit indirectly, to the pursuit of these goals (e.g. through wider participation in development activities, raising living standards, expanding access to public goods and services, women in development). Hence, though the charter provisions explicitly preclude any role for the Bank in the political aspects of governance, efforts to enhance the quality of economic governance in DMCs (i.e. management of resources for development) could well redound to the benefit of the former.
>
> (ADB 1995: 14)

The ADB policy document focuses on the role of the state, and says little on good governance practices in the private sector. The reason given is that the Bank has more experience of dealing with governments and thus more insights to offer to them than to private corporations (ADB 1995). However, one is tempted to see also another, ideological motivation for concentrating on the state. In the neoliberal economic development discourse of the 1980s and the 1990s, the state and public agencies were seen mainly as the problem, obstacles to development, while the market and private economic actors were believed to be the solution and agents of development. This view is repeated in the ADB policy document on several occasions, for example when the proper functions of the state are discussed (ADB 1995).

The economic-vs.-political debate goes to the very heart of what multilateral development institutions are and what they do. This debate intensified in the 1990s as their practical mandates expanded to new social and environmental fields. The ADB was no exception. It sought to move away from the old role of 'project financier' and towards the role of a 'broad-based development institution'. The adoption of the policy on good governance was one step in this process (ADB 1995).

The troublesome aspect in this shift was the fact that the ADB and other multilateral development banks (with the exception of the European Bank for Reconstruction and Development, which was set up in 1991 as a catalyst of both economic *and* political change in Central and Eastern Europe) were founded as 'apolitical' institutions. Their charters contain clauses which limit them to economic considerations and activities. In the case of the ADB, Article 36 of the *Agreement Establishing the Asian Development Bank* decrees that the Bank is to be free from ideological and political considerations and influences, should only pay heed to economic considerations, and engage only in economic activities (ADB 1966: art. 36).[9] The policy document on good governance makes great efforts to defend the broadening of the ADB agenda, and to dispel any impression that the policy might be in conflict with the charter.

In particular, the term 'economic considerations' has been widely interpreted by the Bank. A narrower definition of the term would exclude the Bank from engaging in the programming considered most important by some of its members, for example programmes that focus on the environment, education and the position of women. According to the ADB, while such programming may be viewed as *social*, the Bank finances it on the grounds that it has direct links to economic development. Therefore, while Article 36 prevents certain types of political activities, it does not prohibit the Bank from taking into account demonstrable and direct economic effects of non-economic factors as part of economic considerations (see ADB 1995).

These verbal gymnastics are necessary to allow the Bank to reconcile a document it cannot alter, its charter, to a changing operational environment. On the one hand, the ADB is forbidden to work towards anything but economic objectives – on the other, it is required to do so. It therefore needs to reinterpret the concept 'economic' in a way that satisfies the donors but does not threaten the ADB Charter or the sovereignty of the borrowing DMCs.

The real impact of the policy on good governance becomes clear when its application as a tool for measuring the success or failure of DMCs is taken into consideration. Donors have been keen on controlling the way the money they have contributed is used, and have been ready to punish or reward recipients according to their success in fulfilling the conditions placed on lending, whereas DMCs have generally opposed them (Kappagoda 1995; Bøås 1998).

In fact, political conditionalities – covert as well as overt – have never been absent from bilateral development cooperation, and many countries routinely use their assistance as a foreign policy tool. However, for multilateral development institutions such as the ADB the issue is more controversial. Although the

Bank has traditionally maintained that it does not subject its lending to political conditionalities, and has used this argument to ward off pressure from donors, this has never been strictly true even before the 1990s (Kappagoda 1995).

The concept of 'economic considerations' can be quite flexible, as the policy document on good governance shows. Moreover, the shift in the Bank's operational strategy from projects to programmes, sector activities and policy dialogue, together with the emphasis of its development ideology moving from the development of physical infrastructure towards social development, increased its policy making role in the DMCs. The use of development performance as a criterion for lending potentially made its influence even more tangible in the smaller DMCs who are dependent on external assistance.

Conclusion

The ADB was the first multilateral development bank to adopt a policy on good governance. There are several reasons for this. The Bank was a key forum where supporters of the Developmental State model and supporters of the Washington Consensus were present and able to argue their cases. At the beginning of the 1990s the ADB was in need of additional resources. This provided the opportunity for donors to call for the adoption of the policy in return for new contributions. The DMCs and the Bank's management were forced to give in but were able to influence the contents of the policy. In creating the consensus, the mediating role of Japan was important. The result was the balancing act that the ADB policy document on good governance represents: terminology borrowed from the Washington Consensus and neoliberal economics to give the Western donors what they wanted, but with a redefinition of key concepts, as well as an emphatic restatement of the 'apolitical' role of the Bank to protect the integrity of its charter.

The way in which the proper role and functions of the state in a developing country are defined provides an example of one of the balancing acts. The document does suggest a model that the DMCs are to apply if they wish to achieve development in the most effective way possible: the one promoted by the Washington Consensus. However, the document notes the value of Asian experiences and states that each society should find its own solutions to good governance. Furthermore, it is repeatedly promised that the ADB will not force reforms on the DMCs, but will act only if and when they want its advice.

This does not change the fact that the policy document provides only one set of solutions that the ADB is to promote. The real significance of the policy becomes clear when its role in lending decisions is considered. The DMCs will be rated according to their success in following the guidelines of the policy, and those who fail to meet the requirements will have difficulties in getting loans in the future. For those developing countries that depend on ADB assistance, this is a powerful inducement to conform.

What, then, is the role that the ADB is playing in the DMCs? The Bank has always treasured the self-image it has derived from its charter: an impartial, technical institution working objectively to assist its DMCs in their economic development. It lends money to worthy causes but it leaves the social and political effects of projects to the care of the borrowing governments.

However, as the ADB's operational environment has changed over the years, a rift has appeared between its self-image and actual activities. Especially in the 1990s, the Bank has moved to areas generally considered political. The ADB Charter cannot be changed and the self-image is too valuable to be relinquished. It has therefore been necessary for the Bank to reinterpret what the 'economic considerations' mentioned in the charter signify.

The ADB undeniably has an important role to play in helping make governance – both in public *and* private – sectors more efficient and effective in the DMCs. During its history, it has accumulated a great deal of experience and expertise on what development means in various Asian and Pacific contexts. Moreover, it has had access to talented individuals from both DMCs and donors, and considerable financial resources at its disposal. It should thus be well suited for this task. It can carry it out in an 'Asian' way, through non-confrontational consultation, as it has been wont to do in the past. This may be an inefficient way to do things, but it is still better than dictating ready-made solutions to countries in dire straits.

The fates of many of the Asian 'miracle economies' during the economic crisis that broke in 1997 highlights the importance of a constructive role. The crisis was dubbed by the dominant school of economic thought a crisis of governance: the Asian economies crashed because they were not practising accountability, participation, the rule of law and transparency in their public (and private) governance. The crisis was presented as proof that Asian experiences were, at best, misleading. The ADB was eclipsed by the IMF and the World Bank, which took the lead in providing both financial aid and a stringent package of reforms to the countries hit by the crisis. The practical effects of the ADB's policy on good governance were hidden by the impact of these reforms and the turmoil that engulfed some of the countries in question.

Critics of the Washington Consensus have seen the Asian economic crisis as a crisis of the very model of development advocated by Western institutions. If this is true, the IMF/World Bank-imposed reforms (providing that they have been implemented) have sown the seeds of future crises. The ADB as a regional institution has a special responsibility to seek good governance practices that are suited to local conditions in Asia and the Pacific. After all, it is Asians who should have ownership of their own development.

Notes

1 For a concise presentation of the ideas typical of the Washington Consensus, see Standing (2000).
2 For a presentation of the basic tenets of the Asian Development Model, as seen by the Japanese, see Yasutomo (1995). For an illuminating discussion of the Washington Consensus vs. Developmental State debate, see Gore (1996).

3   Interestingly in its 1992 *Asian Development Outlook*, the ADB presented the results of a study on the levels and growth of military expenditure in the DMCs. No conclusions were drawn from the results, however. See Kappagoda (1995: 150–51).

4   See also http://www.mofa.go.jp/policy/oda/summary/1999/refl html.

5   Some of these results were expressed in the 1991 *World Development Report* of the World Bank. However, the report itself was *The East Asian Miracle*, which the World Bank published in 1993. See also Gore (1996).

6   This definition is repeated in the 'Governance' section of the ADB Operations Manual. See http://www.adb.org/Documents/Manuals/operations/om54aps.

7   The policy document gives as the source for this section the World Bank paper *Managing Development: the Governance Dimension*, published in June 1991.

8   See e.g. Bøås' (1998: 120) comments on the impact that adopting good governance policies will have on the role of MDBs in the DMCs.

9   See also Article IV, Section 10 of the World Bank's charter.

11 'Good governance' and the Development Assistance Committee

Ideas and organizational constraints

Ken Masujima

Introduction: DAC and good governance

The concept of 'good governance', which came increasingly to be used in the development cooperation field in the 1990s, seems well entrenched at the dawn of the twenty-first century. 'Governance' is used at both international and national levels of analysis: governance of an international organization or governance of a country, not to speak of governance of a company (corporate governance) (UNESCO 1998). Although the analysis presented here is limited to the usage of governance in development policy discussion (hence governance of a developing country), the spread of the word governance in recent years seems to correspond to a certain reality in today's political and socio-economic life. Governance, in comparison with government, does not necessarily connote a moral tone. In addition, governance, as opposed to a government, does not imply crude power relations (the question of who rules whom). In short, governance seems to be adapted to the neoliberal mode of regulation of world affairs, which relegates politics to economics (see Chapter 9).

In the field of development, the appearance of the concept of governance is closely related to the dominance of the Bretton Woods institutions. As is well known, the International Monetary Fund (IMF) and the World Bank came to dominate the development field (in terms not only of financing but also of providing development ideas) during the 1980s with the spread of structural adjustment in most developing countries. The concept of governance, which was introduced in these institutions at the beginning of the 1990s, suited the particular circumstances in which they found themselves. On the one hand, these institutions came increasingly to recognize the importance of domestic political factors in realizing the economic policy reforms that they required in return for their structural adjustment loans. The first such statement was made in a World Bank report on Africa, which spoke about domestic bottlenecks (World Bank 1981). On the other hand, the Bretton Woods institutions are formally prohibited by their terms of reference from interfering in the domestic affairs of member countries. It was largely in order to escape from this dilemma that the World Bank began developing the notion of governance. Governance in the sense employed by the World Bank falls under 'administrative governance' as opposed to 'political governance', which is commonly used by bilateral donors (Leftwich 1993: 606).

DAC is particularly well suited to see the politics involved in a concept such as governance, which, it must be said, is more political in nature than most other 'ideas' in development policy – such as poverty or sustainable development. DAC is the donor forum of the OECD (Organization for Economic Cooperation and Development), and as such tends to reflect the thinking of bilateral agencies on development (Nunnenkamp 1995: 9). At the same time, the DAC clearly strives to establish itself as a multilateral organization with autonomous positions. The publication of the DAC Manual (OECD 1992), incorporating various DAC policy recommendations made over the years, should be taken as proof of such an endeavour on the part of DAC (especially of its secretariat). Thus DAC, as an organization, presents an interesting case where bilateral donors' perspectives interact closely with the secretariat's position. The history of how the recognition that domestic political factors matter came about at DAC, is therefore also largely a story about the discovery of 'the political' in DAC; and the concept of 'good governance' on which our analysis shall focus upon underwent a number of twists and turns.

It was argued at the time that DAC possessed 'comparative advantage' over other international organizations in discussing matters pertaining to good governance. The structure of representation at DAC (only OECD donor countries) was said to facilitate discussion on the subject. We shall see whether DAC found itself at ease in treating good governance issues, by tracing how this concept originated and evolved at DAC. More specifically, we shall argue how the organizational traits of DAC constrained its discussion of the issue.

DAC is a subsidiary body of OECD, among other OECD committees such as the Economic Policy Committee and the Trade Committee. Thus DAC, as part of OECD, shares the same characteristic as OECD: an intergovernmental and forum organization.[1] The OECD is organized around 'committees' which regroup member countries' representatives. The secretariat basically exists to render services to its committee. The role of the OECD is not to dispense money or services (there is a small exception regarding the provision of technical cooperation to less-developed member countries such as Greece and Turkey until 1994, and to the countries in transition from the beginning of the 1990s to this day). Its role is rather to provide a forum for discussion, based on analysis, among member countries. More specifically, DAC's purpose is to discuss ways of increasing the volume and efficiency of member countries' aid.

However, DAC is unique among subsidiary organs of OECD in that it has a more autonomous standing. The DAC Chair is entitled to express the opinions of DAC without gaining approval from the OECD Council. The relatively autonomous position of DAC within OECD originates from the following three factors. First, the fact that DAG (the Development Assistance Group) preceded OECD is important.[2] Second, the permanent DAC Chair, residing in Paris, the only such case among OECD committees, reinforces the autonomous character of DAC *vis-à-vis* OECD. Third, at DAC, delegates are usually high-level (deputy permanent representatives), which strengthens the standing of DAC among committees in OECD.

Officially, the highest level of decision making in DAC, as in other OECD committees, is the council, especially the council at the ministerial level, held in June of every year. The secretariat of DAC, Development Cooperation Directorate, is under the authority of the secretary-general of OECD. With a limited number of staff members (thirty in 2001), given the intergovernmental nature of the organization, the DAC Secretariat has only a limited role at least so far as initiating new ideas is concerned. For its part, DAC holds, besides regular meetings held at various intervals composed of DAC delegates, an annual high-level meeting (HLM) every December. This is attended by ministers and the heads of aid agencies and determines the priorities of DAC work. There is also a senior-level meeting (SLM) held every year attended by deputy-head-level civil servants in charge of aid policy. Although there is a potential risk that OECD's positions, as expressed by the council or the secretary-general, and DAC's positions diverge due to the relatively autonomous nature of DAC, such a divergence has in fact rarely materialized. Thus it can be assumed that HLM is the most important policy making body of DAC.

Framework of analysis: organizational constraints

There is a growing literature on the role of ideas in political science. Authors differ as to the place accorded to ideas: some take ideas to complement a rational-choice analysis based on interests; others emphasize the constitutive role of ideas, contending that perception of interests itself is formed by ideas. However, for our purposes it suffices to look at what the literature offers concerning ideas as dependent variables (what factors account for changes in ideas, and not how ideas affect policy outcomes).

From this perspective, a common framework of analysis can be detected in most of the existing literature. On the one hand, most authors point to the objective conditions which necessitate adaptation. On the other hand, the 'fit' between the idea and decision makers is pointed out. On the latter, Hall distinguishes between 'political viability' and 'administrative viability' in discussing the adoption of Keynesian ideas in different countries (Hall 1989a: 371). For our analysis of an international organization, 'political viability' can be subsumed under international and national explanations. Here the 'fit' is with international distribution of power (hegemony), or inter-organizational relationships,[3] or with the positions of (groups of) member countries.[4] In all of the cases, the roots of change are sought outside the organization itself.

Transnational-level analysis, and in particular an epistemic community approach, admits an autonomous role for the organization, but in a narrow sense. The communities of experts, who are supposed to play an influential role, are regrouped in the secretariat. Although the role of an international secretariat in policy making cannot be neglected (Barnett and Finnemore 1999; Hamlet 2000), the structure of the organization itself needs to be taken into account to evaluate more precisely the power of the secretariat, as it operates under the constraints of the organization. Among scholars who underline the role of organizational structure, Sikkink (1991) distinguished a difference between organizations charged with development in Argentina and in Brazil. However, such authors basically compare organizations across nations. It is necessary to adapt these previous approaches for an analysis of an international organization. For that purpose, one should speak of 'organizational constraints', which derive from the characteristic of the organization, and which hinge upon the choices available to policy makers.

We can distinguish the following three organizational constraints:

1   *Internal structure*: In the case of DAC, we can discern three points. First, the fact that DAC is not engaged in any operations (technical cooperation, etc.) is important. The contrast with the World Bank and UN agencies such as UNDP (United Nations Development Programme) could not be clearer. Second, the relatively weak role of the secretariat should be underlined. The intergovernmental structure, with the committee at its centre, clearly limits any multilateral ambition of the secretariat. Third, the composition and size of the secretariat need to be emphasized. The relatively small size of the staff and its composition (mostly economists) has an impact on how ideas are treated in the DAC.

2   *Representation (extra-unit, unit and sub-unit)*: For an organization with an intergovernmental character, the question of representation is crucial. For DAC, the problem was posed at the following three levels of representation: extra-unit level, unit level and sub-unit level.

    Extra-unit level representation refers to the relationships with other international organizations. DAC, like any other international organization, is engaged in a permanent competition with other international organizations. Thus rivalry with other international organizations in the same field (the World Bank, etc.) is an important constraint on DAC.

    Unit level or national representation refers to the membership of the organization. Thus in the case of DAC, the fact that it is composed solely of donors has a significant impact. Sub-unit level representation refers to which ministries are in charge of DAC within each member government. Many members are represented by aid agencies (or ministries), but some are represented by the foreign ministry, and still others by the finance ministry. Most importantly, the fact that the US is represented by USAID (and not by the US State Department) has had an extremely important impact on the positions taken by the US and hence on the positions taken by DAC as a whole.

3   *Culture*: The question of structure and representation is important, in its own right, in constraining directly the choices of agents. However, it is also important in bringing about certain forms of organizational culture. Kier (1996) defines organizational culture as 'the set of basic assumptions, values, norms, beliefs, and formal knowledge that shapes collective understandings'. It should be noted that factors other than internal ones relative to the orga-

nization in question could also shape its culture. Especially important are the international norms prevalent at at any given time (human rights, democracy, self-determination, etc.).

Such organizational cultures are important because choices are constrained not only by objective conditions but also by cognitive factors. In the case of DAC, one can point to a certain attitude of the organization as a whole, evident since the time of its creation, as regards its mandate. There is a certain hesitancy on the part of DAC to talk about the internal structure of developing countries. The fact that these countries are not represented on the committee has not made it easier to discuss their internal affairs. Another example of the organizational cultures at work in DAC is related to the sub-unit level representation. The fact that aid agencies, which typically hold particular views on development, different from those of the treasury, are dominant representatives at DAC, reinforces its ideational outlook. The neoliberal economic doctrine, which swayed the Bretton Woods institutions, has never predominated at DAC.

In what follows, four periods in the adoption of a good governance agenda are examined, based on the analytical framework presented here. The relatively short time-frame chosen is justified in view of the dramatic transformation that the world was undergoing during that period.

Growth and equity (1987–89): broad-based growth

The recognition that developing countries' internal policy and structure is vital to the success (and hence the efficiency) of development aid was apparent in DAC circles by the end of the 1980s. The first manifestation of such recognition can be found at the twenty-sixth HLM of 1–2 December 1987. Although in the press release this received only a small mention ('Support for policies which promote widely shared growth and, in particular, foster the creation of productive employment'), DAC members debated at length administrative problems in developing countries. The HLM decided to initiate a mid-term study to elaborate a strategy for the 1990s, taking stock of the experiences of the 1980s (OECD 1988).

The most vocal public pronouncement on the question was made at the twenty-seventh HLM held on 5 –6 December 1988. It was decided to call the on-going DAC work on the strategy for the 1990s 'Working with Developing Countries towards Equitable and Sustainable Growth and Development' (OECD 1988). The title is revealing in several respects: 'working with developing countries' shows DAC's intention not to appear as trying to impose its own ideas on developing countries. And the adoption of the notion of sustainable development reflects a consensus among DAC members for incorporating environmental concerns. The concept of 'sustainability' was going to become a key word for the 1990s without raising a major debate from the outset at the DAC. However, it was not without some tension and debate that the two notions, 'growth' and 'equity', came to coexist in the text.

The debate on growth and equity goes back to the beginning of the 1970s when the idea of 'basic human needs' came to the fore of the development agenda, but it surfaced again at the end of the 1980s. It was the US which took a position in favour of a growth-oriented approach, insisting in particular on the force of the market economy. It argued in fact that the DAC work on development strategies for the 1990s be entitled 'Broad-based Economic Growth'. Although the US side took note of the vulnerable groups who do not benefit from the market economy, it basically emphasized the crucially important role of market-oriented policies. Some countries showed more interest in the social cost of the adjustment process, and they argued that DAC should put more emphasis on equity.

It is, thus, in large measure a compromise between the two camps that lies behind the coexistence of 'growth' and 'equity' in the press release of the HLM of December 1988. Following the HLM, Joseph Wheeler, chairperson of DAC, explained that 'equity' is shorthand for a variety of concepts such as 'broad-based development', a 'participatory approach', 'basic human needs', 'human resources development', 'common drive to eliminate the worst aspects of poverty', and 'investing in people' (OECD 1988: 27).

However, the transition from 'equity' to 'participatory development', which occurred in 1989, is not very clear. Although in the press release of the 1988 HLM the term 'participatory development' was used for the first time, it occupied rather small place in the text. It was used in a paragraph enumerating major developmental challenges in the years ahead: 'A need to ensure broad-based growth and participatory development' (OECD 1988). The notion of participatory development was put forward especially by UNRISD in 1985, and therefore was in circulation at the end of the 1980s in the development community.[5] We have merely to note that 'participatory development' in DAC discussions came gradually to replace the notion of 'equity'.

Up until 1989, discussion of the internal political factors of developing countries was confined to three considerations regarding economic development. First, the neoliberal economic doctrine was important in raising an issue of political nature which had been judged too sensitive up till then. At the HLM in December 1988, the most influential presentation was made by the US, which argued for 'broad-based economic growth'. The US emphasized the positive role of a free market economy. It was argued that some measure had to be taken to ensure access of the broad mass of people to the fruits of growth, to enable them to participate in the productive process. This US position thus opened the way for discussion of equity, participation, human rights, and the political structure of developing countries.[6] Second, concerns with the social impact of structural adjustment programmes were raised at the HLM. They were voiced especially by countries such as Canada, Norway and Sweden, but other countries also expressed concern. Although no country was opposed to growth as such, there were differences as to what kind of growth should be sought. This debate on the relationship between growth and equity continues to this day. Third, the HLM's press release spoke of 'political bottlenecks' as a cause of debt problems, and of 'institutional weaknesses' in many developing countries. This corresponds to the World Bank's discovery of governance issues in its 1989 report on Sub-Saharan Africa (World Bank 1989b), though it did not employ that word. Thus the mention in the press release of 'a need to ensure broad-based growth and participatory development' can be said to be the origins of the 'participatory development' approach that DAC was to embrace later as a lead theme of development cooperation in the 1990s.

How can we explain the process by which the three origins of the 'political' found their way into the formulation 'working with developing countries towards equitable and sustainable growth and development'?

International explanations cannot account for the outcome, as the US position (adoption of 'broad-based economic growth' as the leading theme of the DAC strategy for the 1990s), did not predominate. In addition, there was no established idea prevalent on the international scene. Therefore explanations must be found at the national level. The outcome in terms of the final formulation of the press release can be seen as the result of a compromise between the US and those calling for more equity. The structure of DAC acted to constrain the outcome. The ways in which DAC resolves differences of opinion among its members typically put the two opinions together without analysing relationships and contradictions between them. This was facilitated by the fact that DAC is not engaged in any operational activities. The contrast with the World Bank could not be clearer. Whereas the World Bank needed to develop the notion of governance to give guidance to its operational staff, DAC could rest content with formulating ideas largely to please its member countries. The sub-national character of representation was important too, in the sense that the US position seemed well calculated to appeal to the domestic constituency which wanted to preserve USAID's policy. Another point regarding the organizational constraints at work concerns the culture of DAC. Although some members raised the issue of human rights and democracy, it was judged better not to put this forward in public pronouncements as in the past. This act of self-restraint can be said to form an organizational culture of DAC.

Participatory development (1989–90): recognition of the linkage between economics and politics

Following the discussion on the elaboration of the DAC strategy for the 1990s, the approach taken by the DAC was that of 'participatory development'. It was asserted that:

> participatory development implies more democracy, a greater role for local organizations and self-government, respect of human rights including effective and accessible legal systems, competitive markets, and dynamic private enterprise.

(OECD 1989)

The notion of participatory development, which originally was used as a catch-word for equity, now came to mean such political concepts as democracy and human rights. It is of course true that participatory development, which signifies access by people to decision making in development, ultimately implies all these things. However, in 1988 no such explicit linkage with politics was made. Further, participatory development, which was just one of the three headings in the DAC strategy, came to be elevated to the principal theme in 1990. The title of the press release at the conclusion of the DAC's HLM of 4 December 1990 was: 'Participatory Development: A Lead Theme for Development Cooperation in the 1990s'. Closer to the content of what is referred to elsewhere as good governance was a call, in the same document, for a strong role for governments: 'New emphasis on participatory development does not imply bypassing governments. Indeed, effective development requires strong and competent governments and public services' (OECD 1990). Here the issue of governance is clearly stated, but without employing that term. In the press release of 1990 cited above, the word 'good government' (not 'governance') was used for the first time, designating the need for strong and effective governments. Thus DAC came to recognize the problem more or less at the same time as the World Bank within the framework of participatory development. It was partly for these reasons that DAC initially tried to comprehend the problem in terms of participatory development.

At the HLM of 1989, when the DAC strategy for the 1990s was finally adopted, explicit mention of such political factors as democracy and human rights was made. However, this was contained within the limit of relevance to economic development, even if DAC was said to possess 'comparative advantage' in dealing with this kind of issue.

How can we explain this? International explanations can offer us clues as to why this sudden surge of 'politics' came about. The wave of democracy which surged through the countries of Eastern Europe and many developing countries was putting the idea of democracy at the forefront of the international agenda. In addition, the US was for the first time stating at DAC that support for democracy had become an official objective of US aid policy. But the call for working to support democracy, as part of DAC aid strategy, was not heeded. Thus the US was not able to dominate the discussion. Here national explanations can help understand the outcome. While some countries, like the US, had already taken up democracy support as part of their aid policy, many members were still grappling with the issue. Under the circumstances, it was conceivable that the outcome should be a middle way.

It was, as pointed out earlier, the structure of DAC itself which was responsible for the compromise character of the outcome at DAC. The fact that the DAC secretariat was mostly composed of economists helped to confine the problem to the traditional field of economic development. As to the representation of DAC, it is also relevant to point out the sub-national character of the US position. In a way, the US had been engaged in political assistance since 1961 when the Foreign Assistance Act was passed, and more particularly since the 1980s. It is interesting to note that, as DAC was itself struggling with the newly emerging idea of political aid, USAID, which represents the US government on the DAC, was also trying hard to contain the political dimension of aid within the US (the executive and the legislative). USAID, as an institution, is also mostly composed of economists and was from the beginning uncomfortable with political aid. It is thus ironic that USAID was calling for the adoption of democracy assistance as a main agenda item at DAC. However, once USAID decided to adopt democracy support,[7] the US tried to move DAC in a direction that it had not favoured in the first instance.

The PD/GG approach (1991–93)

DAC began to take a more explicitly political position once it had adopted the terminology of good governance. The turning point in DAC's approach to the question came at the DAC HLM of December 1991. Although at the previous HLM of December 1990 the question of the relationship between aid and the emerging trend of democratization in developing countries was debated at length, it was treated within the framework of participatory development. At the OECD ministerial council, the highest policy making echelon of the organization, held on 4–5 June 1991, the question of the relationship with non-member countries was extensively discussed as the first item of the agenda. The press release referred to 'good governance' for the first time in major OECD policy documents, though in a timid way:

> Ministers emphasize the need for participatory development, including broad-based economic growth and equity, protection of human rights and improvement of governmental effectiveness. An optimal public resources allocation can only be achieved through good governance.
>
> (OECD 1991)

However, the question was still treated under the umbrella of PD. Thus at the SLM of 17–18 June 1991 it was agreed to launch a survey of DAC members' policies and practices on PD. The emphasis was put on gaining information on 'good government, democratization, and respect of human rights'. In the field of 'good government', the DAC distinguished between, on the one hand, 'more traditional' aspects, which had been treated in 'Principles for New Orientations in Technical Cooperation' (OECD 1992: 51–64) under the heading 'institutional development', and on the other hand, 'more political' aspects, in the context of strengthening transparency and accountability, and assuring broader participation in decision making processes.

Following the decision at the HLM of 1990, DAC continued its work on the question, and the interim result of its reflection was published in the 1991 edition of the DAC chairperson's report, written around September 1991. It noted:

> In the short time since the High-Level Meeting of last December, the dialogue has moved markedly to expand discussion beyond traditional

concepts and perceptions of participatory development. The concept of 'governance' has assumed a more central focus as an area of key attention by both bilateral and multilateral donors. The World Bank, in particular, has moved to better define the concepts and programmatic aspects of assisting the Bank's clients toward improved governance.

(OECD 1991: 33)

This recognition of the importance of the concept of governance found its way into the discussion at the HLM of December 1991. There, one of the two items of the agenda was entitled 'Participatory development, democratisation, human rights, and good governance'. Based on a donor survey made for the meeting, DAC identified the following areas for discussion under that item;

- economic reform and democratization
- strengthening the human resources base
- contributing to improved functioning of governments and civil services at central and local level
- encouraging democratization
- working towards reduced military expenditures
- attacking corruption
- implications for policy dialogue and coordination

The DAC's HLM of 1991 is remembered for announcing the link between the allocation of aid and progress in this area. It also led the way toward an approach on the issue, which came to be referred to as the 'PD/GG' approach (Robinson 1999). It was thus important in marking the transition from 'participatory development' to 'PD/GG' at DAC. It should be noted, however, that good governance is employed here still in the sense of 'administrative governance' *à la* World Bank. In the HLM's press release, mention was made of 'good governance within the framework of law', which was preceded by a reference to 'representative government'.

For explaining the adoption of the PD/GG agenda, international explanations apply. The continuing democratization on the world scene contributed to the consolidation of the agenda at DAC. However, the existence among DAC members of divergent views on the question was largely to account for the outcome. Some countries did not want DAC to tackle the issue of good governance, which was considered more political than participatory development. These countries were cautious, not wishing to be seen as interfering in the domestic affairs of sovereign nations, for various reasons. But the US, supported by several other countries, proposed the creation of a new permanent structure within DAC to tackle the issue of PD/GG. The US government even offered a voluntary contribution toward that goal. However, the US was only partially successful, for as we shall see, only an ad hoc working group was created, and for a short, fixed term. It was evident that as long as there were countries opposed to the modification of the work programme (France was most vocal in its opposition), the result had to be a compromise. Thus DAC's institutional timidity toward the question can be attributed to national causes.

Organizational constraints were also at work. One such constraint was DAC's relatively early grasp of the problem under the heading of participatory development. It was the 'DAC approach'. The fact that the World Bank was pushing for 'governance' was, at least initially, not considered reason to adopt the same terminology. However, once it was recognized that good governance was making headway on the international scene, DAC changed its initial attitudes and adopted this term (although in parallel with participatory development).

However, the most relevant explanation seems to be the secretariat's economist bias. The head of the secretariat of the time confided to the author of this chapter that aid people mostly trained in economics confronted for the first time the question of politics at the beginning of the 1990s and revealed themselves to be unequipped to deal with it.[8] Indeed, within the secretariat only one staff member was charged with the PD/GG issue at that time.

Whither the PD/GG approach? (1993–)

At the HLM of 1991, it was decided to convene a special DAC meeting on PD/GG issues, and to entrust the DAC Expert Group on Evaluation to pursue analysis on the issue. The discussion at the DAC PD/GG meeting of 12–13 May 1992 was important in illuminating where DAC members agreed and disagreed. It was evident that there were some countries, such as the US, Germany and Sweden, who were already experimenting with assistance in the area now defined by DAC as PD/GG, and that there were others who were not engaged in this activity. Thus, although there was consensus in recognizing the link between economics and politics, there was divergence as to how far to go. Countries such as Australia, New Zealand, Finland, and to a certain extent Japan and France, seemed rather cautious at the discussion. Although the secretariat now affirmed that DAC need not be confined any longer to the timid and concealed way of discussing the matter ('participatory development'), some countries still hesitated to overtly discuss the domestic political affairs of developing countries at DAC. Their hesitant attitude was in marked contrast to that of the US and others, for whom democracy and governance are goals in themselves to be pursued with the means of development aid.

Another point of discord concerned the definition of the problem, which stems from the above-mentioned difference of basic attitudes on the issue. For some countries, it was still desirable to confine discussion at DAC to participatory development, and hence within the classical context of economic development. Some other countries (notably the UK), for different reasons, preferred to focus on GG, which in their view encompassed PD. For still other countries (the Netherlands, Sweden and Canada), it was not desirable to limit the discussion within the PD/GG framework; the human rights issue was for them in itself important. Thus DAC was not able to agree on definitional problems, and had to be content with listing various concepts without analysing the linkages among them. It was not clear, for example, whether democracy fell under PD or GG, or was to be treated separately under its own heading. This was true of 'DAC Orientations on Participatory Development and Good Governance' (OECD 1993), a kind of good practice/guidelines document endorsed by the HLM in December 1993.

The 1993 HLM set up, for a three-year term, an Ad Hoc Working Group on Participatory Development and Good Governance. This submitted, at the end of its three-year term, a final report. At the same time, the DAC Expert Group on Aid Evaluation published a thick synthesis report in 1997. The term of the Ad Hoc Working Group was not renewed, and instead an informal network on PD/GG was established to continue work on PD/GG issues. This informal network concentrated on 'pilot studies', involving donors and partner countries, and produced findings for Benin, Bolivia, Burkina Faso, Malawi, Mauritania and Uganda. It was decided that the informal network on PD/GG be merged with DAC's nformal network on institutional and capacity development (I/CD) in February 2001 (called GOVNET – Governance and Capacity Development Network). It remains to be seen how much of DAC's activities on good governance will continue after the fusion with I/CD, which regroups officials in charge of traditional technical cooperation activities in the capitals.

In explaining why DAC ceased to treat the problem of PD/GG as a principal item after it had become the lead theme in 1992, national explanations, which highlight the lack of consensus among its member countries (notably the opposition of certain countries toward the idea of a permanent structure in charge of PD/GG at DAC), are valid. However, transnational explanations also seem to account well for the outcome. The fact that a distinct network of aid agency officials in charge of PD/GG in the capitals did not materialize (in contrast to the issue of gender, which saw the institutional establishment of sections in charge of the issue, and which led to the establishment of the Working Party on Gender Equality) was important in limiting the eventual creation of a permanent PD/GG organ at DAC.

However, with the passing of time, the limits of DAC as an institution became apparent. To put it bluntly, DAC does not have much to say about PD/GG beyond carrying out surveys of donor practices. Above all, as discussions on PD/GG, especially GG, became more and more sophisticated, the DAC secretariat was not sufficiently equipped for dealing with the technical matters in depth. Besides, competition with the World Bank played a role. DAC, under the leadership of a new director of the secretariat, turned increasingly to the question of conflict (peace-building) to show its distinctiveness. It is revealing to note that the question of conflict and development came before PD/GG in the 1997 edition of the report of the secretary-general which referred to the activities of OECD in 1996. Further, when it came to questions of more political nature, DAC was not a favourite place for bilateral donors either. It should be noted that important diplomatic questions have always been discussed outside DAC. On the most politically sensitive issues of political conditionality, i.e. democracy and human rights, member governments did not find it useful to come to DAC. The question of representation is important here. These matters are not always within the competence of an aid agency.

Notes

1   The distinction between forum organizations and service organizations was made by Robert W. Cox and Harold K. Jacobson (Cox and Jacobson 1973).
2   The Development Assistance Group (DAG) was created at the meeting of representatives from twenty governments on 14 January 1960. The OECD came formally into being on 30 September 1961. The relationship with the DAG was one of the issues of the negotiations leading to the creation of the OECD (Masujima 1999).
3   For an overview of the work on inter-organizational perspectives, see Finnemore (1996b).
4   Miles Kahler distinguishes between 'multilateralism with large numbers' and 'multilateralism with small numbers', referring to patterns of coalitions in multilateral organizations in the post-war period (Kahler 1992).
5   UNRISD's study on popular participation was published in 1985.
6   It should be noted that USAID's new policy on democracy promotion also originated partly from the neo-conservative economic doctrine. It is also probable that USAID intentionally adopted the neo-conservative tone in its discourse to justify its development agendas (Carothers 1999).
7   USAID issued a series of four initiatives in December 1990 to help shape its programme for the crucial issues of the 1990s. One of these was the 'Democracy Initiative'. Following this paper, USAID published its policy statement on democracy in November 1991 (USAID 1991).
8   Interview with Mr Helmut Führer, Director of the Development Cooperation Directorate of the OECD from 1975 to 1993, 26 August 1996.

The evolution of the concept of poverty in multilateral financial institutions

The case of the World Bank

Alice Sindzingre

Introduction: the conceptual framework

An analysis of the determinants of the birth and evolution of new ideas within development institutions can be made from the angle of different disciplines: political science, economics, development studies. This chapter will examine the role of poverty as an idea in one specific multilateral institution, the World Bank, and the exchanges between ideas and institutional forms, between institutional forms and politics, and between the inside and outside of the institution. The trajectory of the concept of poverty in academic research and the World Bank is presented first. The political economy of knowledge and the meanings of poverty are then examined, as the outcome of complex processes involving ideas and power, reflected and simultaneously created by the Bank, inside and outside the institution.

The concept of poverty in the academic world

The evolution of ideas in development economics and external aid agencies has influenced the concept of poverty both within the agencies and the Bank. This evolution includes the two ideas of inequality and multidimensionality.

In academia, ideas relating to poverty and inequality have changed profoundly during the nineties (see Sen 1998; 1999; Kanbur and Squire 1999). A series of academic papers has shown that a high degree of inequality may be detrimental to growth (Kanbur and Lustig 1999; Rodriguez 2000). Increased inequality between countries and within certain industrialized countries like the US has led to many reflections on its determinants (Krugman 1992). These debates are intensively developed in international economics, labour economics and international political economy. Another debate has focused on poverty in rich countries, demonstrating that there is no 'evolutionary force' towards better standards of living (Hoff and Stiglitz 1999).

The Nobel Prize awarded to Amartya Sen was an important milestone, adding weight to the concept of poverty in economics. Poverty is no longer solely defined as income or consumption poverty. Health, education, dignity and democratic participation have become intrinsic components, in line with Sen's concepts of 'capabilities' and 'functionings'. The concept of relative poverty has gone beyond the notion of human needs expressed solely in terms of subsistence. Poverty may thus be conceived as asset poverty – land, education, health, social claims. This multidimensionality is dynamic, health and education being simultaneously assets, dimensions, causes and effects, and it incorporates risk and lack of security as dimensions of poverty. This has led to new questions of measurement, controversies on the relevance of poverty lines, and quantitative vs. qualitative approaches. Debates over definitions are reflected in policies, in particular on the role of the state in alleviating poverty, with delicate political tradeoffs relating to the priority of dimensions (income poverty, social services or the reduction of inequality) and of instruments (direct ones via public redistribution, or indirect ones via the increase of opportunities). These extensions of the definition have entailed new ambiguities due to the expanding notions of empowerment and participation (Vieira *et al.* 1997).

The meanings of the concept of poverty within the World Bank

There is a genealogy of concepts of poverty, starting from the idea of basic needs (Lipton and Ravallion 1995). Since the 1960s, the concept of poverty has changed in meaning and has followed different trajectories depending on the development agency concerned, spreading progressively as a major mission (Sindzingre 1997): the ILO which is more focused on employment and labour-intensive policies, the FAO with priority on food security and production, the United Nations, in particular the UNDP, and later the OECD. As for the World Bank, the concept has been at the heart of its lending policies since the 1950s (Kapur *et al.* 1997). After the 'trickle-down' approach relying on growth, the McNamara years were the era of 'waging war on poverty', before the structural adjustment paradigm. The theme of poverty tended to fade away in the 1980s, during the era of structural adjustment. The criticism that adjustment programmes lacked a 'human face' was an opportunity for UNDP to become the advocate for more social and comprehensive policies rather than purely macro-financial objectives, and to push to the forefront the popular concept of human development, resulting in the Human Development Index, with the intellectual support of Amartya Sen, although some scholars refuted the scientific foundation of this index.[1] In the late nineties, a wide consensus emerged within the global 'development community' of donors, giving priority to poverty reduction as a key issue on the development agenda.

Changes and mechanisms in the evolution of ideas

Several determining factors affect the nature of the changes and evolution of ideas within the Bank. Given the organization, large staff, and periodic reforms of incentives, changes are only at the margin, and have also been very slow in being implemented. The Bank feels challenged by its external critics, and it has a strong capacity to absorb them by hiring these individuals as staff members and, in this way, to absorb their ideas too. Changes are also introduced as a result of developments in the domestic policies of member countries. Thus the evolution and differences in the 'messages' emitted by the Bank can only be noticed over a significant time-span.

The Bank is, first and foremost, a bank and not a research institution. It continues to be dominated by economists and financiers (and also engineers). Proof based on econometrics and cross-country regressions is the fast track towards validation. Among the mechanisms constraining the evolution of ideas, the literature of the Bank is deeply self-referential (making extensive use of grey literature from inside the institution). Another mechanism is the phenomenon of amnesia *vis-à-vis* previous work. This is not peculiar to the Bank but characterizes the development discourse and agencies in general. Furthermore, the Bank has become increasingly a producer of knowledge about development, perceiving it as a global public good, and of economic analysis.[2] Research has been in an expansionary mode, and the sizeable financial and logistical resources of the Bank, compared to academic research centres or bilateral agencies, facilitates the construction of vast original databases, the conducting of surveys, and the collection of information from national institutes, which few can afford.[3] The Bank has the capacity to attract and hire the best scholars and experts on the international market, as well as former ministers and other high-profile personalities. It also pursues a policy of high visibility through journals, a number of publications about development, networking and training, addressed to scholars and officials in developing countries.

The evolution of ideas: the Washington Consensus and its aftermath

After the 'Washington Consensus'– a term coined in 1990 by John Williamson referring to macroeconomic instruments and objectives of stabilization and adjustment – the idea of a 'post-Washington Consensus' focused on the role of institutions and on a broad concept of development – a 'transformation of society' – was circulated in the late 1990s, especially in view of the widely differing outcomes of reform in transition economies.[4] Owing to his position as Vice-President and Chief Economist, Joseph Stiglitz was able to introduce some of his ideas into the research activities of the Bank. In the writings of Joseph Stiglitz, the state has been rehabilitated, market failures recognized, and the key role of institutions confirmed. Some of the permanent intellectual attitudes within the Bank include the importance of market reform, liberalization and openness. The Asian economic crisis accentuated the traditional antagonism between partisans of market reform and analysts of institutions (states and firms), which became a subject of disagreement between the IMF and the Bank during Stiglitz's tenure.

World Development Reports are simultaneously an expression of the evolution of ideas inside the Bank, and a contribution to it. They play an important role as a platform for debate within the Bank, but also constitute important sources of data for researchers and policy makers on a global scale. Presented in the World Development Report of 1990, following the WDR of 1980, the key ideas relative to poverty were economic growth based on rapid market liberalization, the provision of basic health, social services, and safety nets. The *WDR 2000/1* on poverty (World Bank 2000b) is a balanced and heterogeneous mixture of internal and external influences. A kind of 'third way' is being advocated, reflecting the notion developed by centrist political parties in the United Kingdom and the US in the nineties, and its alternative policies to free marketism and active state interventionism. It refers to market forces but is accompanied by redistributive policies and institutions of social support (Kapstein 1998–99; Sachs 1999), and it is a rather consensual notion. Yet the ideas surrounding the *WDR 2000/1* are still the consequences of fierce debates originated by the staff – operations, research – and member countries. Growth is still considered to be the best instrument for poverty reduction, as well as opportunities created by the private sector, but policies must address social inequalities within and between countries and the possible short-term negative consequences of liberalization.[5]

The political economy inside the Bank: the political economy of knowledge

Within the Bank, two levels contribute to the elaboration of ideas: the staff, and the Board composed of twenty-four executive directors representing the 184 member countries. The proportion of their shares in the capital of the Bank reflects their economic weight. The Board is responsible for conducting general operations under powers delegated by the board of governors, and it is the executive entity. Within the Board, relations between the executive directors' offices reflect the power countries exert 'outside' the Bank.

The economics paradigm

The cognitive tools favoured by an institution determine the production of knowledge and the norms associated with it. The last decade has witnessed a movement within economics towards a greater penetration of mathematics, as well as recognition of economists by their community, founded on an increasing formalization and the use of econometrics as an instrument of proof (McCloskey 1983). This leads to specific types of arguments of authority, based on the latest and most sophisticated statistical and econometric techniques. The use of econometrics and cross-country regressions is sometimes criticized within the economics community (Srinivasan 2000), but it is presented to laypersons as scientific certainty.

This product of the internal research department is widely used to confirm the results contained in reports, but makes it difficult for laymen to evaluate and criticize such reports. The problem of validating conclusions pertaining to economics is reinforced by a tendency within the Bank to use the grey literature it produces. The Bank has implemented an intensive dissemination and publications policy.

This has the dual advantage of offering better conditions for external validation, and exerting a stronger influence on the discipline of development economics.

Political scientists or sociologists have been hired, but in terms of decision making their power is weak. These disciplines are confined to specific topics, e.g. 'social' topics, gender, education, health, refugees, community participation, in the case of sociologists; and the public sector, decentralization and corruption in the case of political scientists. This prevents new approaches to problems, particularly those that are considered to be of a purely economic nature and, therefore, within the strict competence of economists, such as macroeconomic shocks, trade relations, financial crises, and so on.

The status of research within the Bank: ambiguities and debates

As already mentioned, the World Bank is a development bank and not a research institution. It is a Bretton Woods multilateral institution, defined by precise mandates. In principle, once the Board has given its approval at the different stages of an operation, staff members have the flexibility to choose its appropriate design and technical aspects. Even if not linked directly to it, the choices of the staff are backed by the existence of a research department. The research department bases its legitimacy on both sides: on the one hand, an internal level of validation, i.e. the Bank's higher organizational bodies, the Board and other members of staff, and on the other, an external level of validation, i.e. the international market of research and academic journals. The Bank's researchers must publish according to the rules of this market if they are to be considered as researchers belonging to the scientific community and not just as officials of a development bank.

This produces a wide range of research topics and conclusions. Many of the papers and reports contain conclusions full of nuances on strategic and ideological issues. A significant number of these papers do not reflect the homogeneous orthodoxy that is perceived outside the Bank as the 'party line'. They cover, for instance, the necessary role of the state, or the impact of globalization on inequality. Some even suggest that structural adjustment has had no effect on poverty reduction (Easterly 2000a). Disagreements exist among researchers on certain issues, or with operational staff, for example, on the effects of public spending on education, health, growth and poverty, or on the relationship between income poverty and social indicators. Some studies allocate the responsibility of poor performance to external shocks much more than to national policies (Easterly *et al.* 1999; Easterly 2000b). Financial deregulation may be clearly criticized, as well as the retreat of the state, and here research functions as a support for more political positions, for instance the politics of the Asian crisis and the competition between the two Bretton Woods institutions.

Debates over the research results produced by the Bank reflect analogous disagreements in the academic world. The debate on the relationship between inequality and growth, as well as on the relationship between growth and poverty, may be taken as examples. With respect to inequality and growth, the position put forward in several papers is somewhat to the left by US political standards and in the classical discussion within welfare economics on the tradeoff between efficiency and equity.[6] Putting forward arguments about growth but with a redistributive position, some papers demonstrate the negative role of inequality and argue in favour of active public social policies and transfers.[7] Parallel to the raging controversies in academic economics, other studies within the Bank have provided contrary evidence.

The policies recommended in the *WDR 2000/1* encountered explicit disagreement. The report stated that growth can reduce poverty, but to a lesser extent in unequal societies than in egalitarian ones, and that since poverty implies powerlessness, it recommended reducing social inequalities and empowering poor people. The resistance to this view stems not only from political circles but also from academics, inside and outside the Bank, who have shown growth to be the best instrument of poverty reduction.[8]

From the nineties onwards, many studies favoured democracy and political participation. Corruption, discrimination and exclusion have become important topics of research. The lack of empowerment of the poor was a major pillar of the analysis of poverty presented in the *WDR 2000/1*. Stiglitz, who defends democracy as an intrinsic good, in line with Amartya Sen's position, backs this approach. He refuses to be trapped in a technical debate on whether democracy is good or bad for growth and its economic efficiency (Stiglitz 2000a), which may have contributed to the hostility of more orthodox economists inside the Bank. In some studies undertaken by the Bank, institutions are included as essential determinants of growth, which must exhibit a certain level of 'quality'. However, these consensual themes have led to strong debates among the Bank's researchers. Although the theme of 'quality' is put forward by recognized scholars (e.g. Rodrik 2000), such disagreements have also occurred outside the Bank, where the analysis has been described as trivial, unscientific or 'muddled',[9] and claims about inequality, institutions or democracy as unproven assertions.[10]

On the other side of the coin, these ventures outside traditional economics are not even welcomed by the other social sciences. This good intention to include qualitative concepts, or concepts situated at the borders of economics, is easily exposed to their criticisms. The importance of institutions is often seen as a vague concept, quantified by approximate measures. The recourse to external influential scholars is instrumental in these debates.[11] However, their studies remain sources of disagreement among the Bank's researchers.[12]

Political economy of the Bank: the member countries

The diversity of positions on poverty

First of all, the different member countries have divergent positions on development and poverty within the Board. These different positions obviously entail a variety of policy recommendations. They show clearly the limits of common international priorities and joint policies on poverty. The US position traditionally favours growth, the openness of markets, particularly open capital markets, liberalization, free trade, privatization, and a minimal state role. Growth and market-oriented policies are perceived as serving national security, foreign policy and economic interests (Bergsten 1998). In line with its domestic policies, the US does not have a strong interest in poverty reduction *per se* in its development policies. This is visible, for example, in the traditional policies advocated by USAID, and in the treatment of poverty within the US, where growth is a more urgent priority than poverty reduction. This approach has been supported by the decrease in poverty that has accompanied the exceptional period of continuous growth in the nineties. In this particular instance, by putting poverty at the forefront, the Bank cannot be criticized for reflecting slavishly the economic views of the US government, and it can even claim to be independent of its influence.

As revealed in the WTO summit at Seattle in 1999, the US defends the idea of core labour standards and the interdiction of child labour supported by unions. These views imply policies against poverty that are opposed to others advocating export-led growth, the openness of developed countries to products from poor countries, or observations that child labour is, in the present context, one of the means for the poor to escape poverty (Basu 1998). The latter views are backed by some developing countries, and such issues continue to be the subject of fierce controversy.

Other rich countries have different ideas and try to voice them inside the Board. For instance, Japan would give the state in developing countries a more interventionist role than would the US.[13] The UK, like the Netherlands, has become active in aid for poverty, both on a bilateral basis as well as through the multilateral system, with an emphasis on human rights.[14] Scandinavian countries take into consideration recipient countries and their poverty the most seriously. Being major bilateral donors, whose funds are welcomed by the Bank, there is a certain rivalry between these countries over the leadership of European countries in terms of models of poverty policies (Cox *et al* 2000). Generally, European countries tend to be more cautious about a minimized role for the state and the intrinsic virtues of market policies and growth. Yet all the rich countries of OECD participate in the Development Aid Committee, which has elaborated common objectives on poverty reduction, the International Development Targets. Likewise, the framework of the Poverty Reduction Strategy Papers (PRSPs) initiated in 1999 has been designed by the Bank with the objective of being a common basis of poverty reduction strategies for all donors as well as recipient countries.

There are differences in the concepts of poverty adopted by each country. For instance, the quantitative poverty criteria used in the US are not accepted by other countries that follow relative poverty criteria and consequently place more emphasis on inequality and exclusion (Atkinson and Bourguignon 1999). Similar problems affect the themes of safety nets, taxation and social protection. Moreover, poverty as a concept may not belong to a country's intellectual tradition, as in France where social protection is more relevant. Second, institutional arrangements and decision making procedures differ between member countries and influence their stand on particular issues. The influence of the ministries (finance, foreign affairs, cooperation) in charge of relations with the Bretton Woods institutions can vary. Third, member countries may use their own national research institutions in order to have at their disposal possible alternative analyses to those of the Bank, or they may prefer to use the Bank's research. Furthermore, the influence of domestic public opinion on the positions of member countries in the Board differs, reflecting their different forms of democracy, lobbying, role of NGOs and citizen's voicing (see Bøås and McNeill 2003).

Power relationships between member countries

Power relationships within the Board reflect power relationships between member countries and the political preferences of their governments in the outside world. However, the political games are complex and constrained by a number of factors. In the first place, the foundation of a multilateral institution such as the Bank is built on efforts to achieve a certain degree of consensus. Consensus is obtained when an operation is presented at the Board. It is easy to achieve when the geo-strategic stakes are evaluated as weak, when its impact is negligible (for instance, in view of the size or income level of the recipient), or when agreement results from previous bargaining. In these cases, the arguments produced by the Bank's management, and supported by its research, may play a role in convincing Board members. In other instances, consensus is negotiated before the meetings by informal means. Consensus therefore depends on the evaluation of a particular situation. If the latter is deemed to be strategic (for example, in the case of big emerging borrowers, in terms of geopolitics or debts outstanding), compromises will reflect power relations and coalitions, as formed in other bilateral and multilateral settings. Consensus depends on the importance of the use of Bretton Woods institutions in a country's foreign policy. Consensus also depends on the issue in question, whose major themes and pillars will always be the subject of intense controversy between officials representing member countries, especially such subjects as the role of growth and its priority compared to other economic objectives, inequality, the effects of liberalization and trade openness, the role of institutions, the struggle against corruption, and the political economy of aid.

Second, the Bretton Woods institutions are constrained by legal limitations, i.e. their articles of agreement. The Bank has an explicit mandate to fulfil objectives of economic development, and it is prohibited from taking political considerations into account in its lending operations (Bøås and McNeill 2003). This has caused constant tension whenever the Bank has ventured increasingly into fields that are peripheral to the traditional economic and engineering sectors, such as governance, corruption, core labour standards; or when Joseph Stiglitz advocated explicitly that international financial institutions should support democratic processes (Stiglitz 2000b). But at the same time, the Bretton Woods institutions are under heavy political pressure, and non-economic considerations influence the process of approving programmes and projects. The Bank is trapped in a paradox: it is a political institution, it cannot avoid getting involved in politics, its projects are the outcome of political bargaining, but its legitimacy stems from political neutrality and technical competence (Sindzingre 2000).

The Bretton Woods institutions follow *de facto* the US influence since it is the lead shareholder, and weighted voting gives it the biggest share of the voting power. In 2002, the voting power of the US accounted for 16.4 per cent of the total votes for IBRD and 14.49 per cent for IDA; Japan accounted for 7.87 per cent and 11.06 per cent respectively, while Germany, France and the UK each held about 4.3–4.5 per cent of the voting power. In addition, the distribution of seats reflects the hegemony of rich countries, with for instance one seat each being allocated to the US, Japan, Germany, the UK and France, and only two seats to the entire continent of Sub-Saharan Africa.

Since the mandate of the Bank focuses on the promotion of development, on which conceptions may diverge and evolve with time, the relative influences of member countries interact in a complex manner within the Bank. The US Treasury has a strong influence over some dimensions, since it is the major shareholder and considers the Bank as an instrument of its foreign policy. But this influence is not absolute and is limited by the understanding on the part of the US that the Bank must be seen as an independent and non-politicized institution (Gwin 1997; Bøås and McNeill 2003). It played a strategic role in the handling by the IMF of the 1997 Asian crisis. The US Treasury insisted on the resignation of Joseph Stiglitz, following his open disagreement with it on how to deal with the Asian crisis and other issues. Yet the game is complex and at the same time involves different levels: the two Bretton Woods institutions, regional blocs, and individual countries, forming variable coalitions and putting forward certain ideas in response to specific situations. International core labour standards, for example, have been strongly defended by the US government, but the Bank is more cautious on this issue, due to its rules prohibiting political elements in its loans.

The struggle against poverty in developing countries was not a traditional goal of US foreign aid during the Cold War (rather it was promoting security, trade and democracy). However, since 1989, tackling environmental crises and epidemic diseases, as a way of improving the quality of life of the poorest, has become a feature of the new diplomacy. Although a common 'European model' is expressed in the discourses of member countries, no European model can be detected in reality. Added together, European countries represent more weight than the US. But within the Board there is no joint position of European countries on development, nor has any attempt been made to establish structured coalitions on a specific topic. The European Commission's directorate in charge of development explicitly aligns itself with the conceptual framework of the Bank, for example the Poverty Reduction Strategy Papers (PRSPs).

Member countries can put forward their preferred themes and research centres by funding some of the Bank's initiatives (e.g. through the 'trust funds'). And in this particular instance, they can influence a multilateral institution like the Bank, which always needs additional resources and has been subjected to several streamlining schemes in the past. But bilateral institutions are unable to compete with the vast resources of the Bank when it is a question of hiring the best experts and producing data and studies. Some agencies consider this to be unnecessary, and choose instead to adopt the conceptual framework proposed by the Bank.

All countries accept the policy frameworks of the Bretton Woods institutions because they are members. A number of countries impose the signature of an agreement with the Bretton Woods institutions as a condition for their own bilateral loans and grants. But it can happen that at the level of their bilateral policies within a developing country, in the field, even within this common framework and apparent acceptance, donor countries give only weak support to IMF and Bank policies. Donor countries also give themselves room for manoeuvre in their bilateral relations with developing countries (e.g. the aid-dependent sub-Saharan Africa), where their political and economic interests can be expressed clearly, using bilateral aid as a more direct dimension of their foreign policy.

Political and economic evolution of the concept of the role of the Bretton Woods institutions

There is an increasing amount of criticism of globalization and the role of multilateral institutions from the expanding 'global civil society', the paradox being that the latter is typically an outcome of this globalization. Since the 1990s, the Bretton Woods institutions have been widely criticized, for different reasons, by NGOs, governments, academia and the private sector. The private sector was not willing to bear the financial burden of the Asian crisis, as was recommended by the Bretton Woods institutions in their reflections on the new financial architecture (Eichengreen 1999). Criticism has spread in the US (especially in the Congress),[15] and a consensus emerged on a division of labour between the IMF and the World Bank. Many observers recommend that the IMF should return to its original mandate and refocus on short-term financing. The Bank has a comparative advantage in development issues, long-term financing and poverty reduction. This situation was precipitated by the Asian crisis, followed by the others (Russia, Brazil). The controversy between Stiglitz and the IMF was widely covered by the press, and forced the Bretton Woods institutions to open their doors. The increasing attention paid to safety nets may perhaps be an expression of guilt, and an attempt to moderate public criticism of 'globalization without a human face' (Stiglitz 2000a: 1).

There are also critics in the academic community, who constantly attack the ineffective bureaucracy of international organizations and their inefficient and badly designed programmes. A number of facts have fed these criticisms, such as the failed reform in Sub-Saharan Africa. The explanation put forward by the Bank – that reforms are beneficial but that countries failed to implement them correctly – is not perceived as satisfactory. This has led to an erosion in the credibility and legitimacy of the action taken by the Bretton Woods institutions (Sindzingre 2000). The Bank seeks to distinguish itself from the IMF, in the context of a rivalry between the IMF and the Bank over the best development model, despite the official division of labour.

The Bank has reacted to its critics by pushing poverty to the top of its agenda, and poverty reduction has now become a major component in its programmes and projects. But for poor countries, programmes and conditionalities are drawn up jointly with the IMF (following the ESAFs, the PRSPs). In this way, the IMF has also extended its brief to poverty. NGOs, religious representatives and trade unions are invited to participate in the process. The objective of poverty reduction has to be included wherever possible, and the Bank has increased its lending for Human Development (from 5.1 per cent of total lending in 1980 to 21.8 per cent in 2000) (World Bank 2000b).

Policies and reactions of the recipients: the poor countries

Research and operations may function as parallel worlds. Policies do not necessarily follow directly from the conclusions of research, or from previous studies or surveys. Both domains imply different cognitive mechanisms. Their validation processes differ, with 'efficiency' as the norm for operations, and 'truth' or knowledge as the norm for research.

The first reason for this is that some findings from research studies on poverty are difficult to put into operation. Moreover, operationalization is made more difficult if the Bank extends its interest more and more beyond the traditional domains of infrastructure and economics, and the same difficulties ensue from a broad definition of poverty. For instance, although economic growth is a familiar theme for the Bank, which has the appropriate toolkit to deal with it, this applies less to a more political topic like income inequality, now considered to be an important factor in influencing poverty. Another illustration is the reform of local institutions, since they are, by definition, the outcome of endogenous processes. Donors cannot impose institutions from the outside, yet they can have an important impact on them through the design of reforms, throu،ؤ‎ا conditionalities or financial support. The Bank – and the recipient governments – are aware that given the nature of states and institutions in developing countries, civil groups are rarely isolated from local politics, and at worst their representative character can be questionable. Projects with a greater emphasis on social or political issues are thus more difficult to implement. Projects are tied to criteria of feasibility, and project officers are evaluated accordingly. Relevant indicators of effectiveness and progress are also difficult to design.

A second reason is that the operational level has its own rationality and works within the frameworks provided by the projects. For example, an anti-poverty project may be a social fund project. But social fund projects, like any other type of project, form a class of their own. As such, they are relatively standardized, and include other components than those strictly focused on poverty reduction (e.g. 'community development initiatives', public works programmes, institutional development). Other projects may include public works or labour-intensive schemes concentrated on employment; while they reduce poverty, this is not their primary objective (Sindzingre 1997).

Adjustment programmes follow a relatively standard framework, and their design is indirectly inspired by macroeconomic research and by models. Likewise, projects follow from the internal rationale of disbursements and management of a portfolio, and cover standard sectors, for example the public sector or the banking sector. They are accompanied by a series of reports relating to the project cycle, but not necessarily by research. In the nineties, the move towards poverty as a visible objective acted as a driving force to launch new programmes, poverty reduction being the key theme. These involved the PRSPs designed with the IMF, the replacement of the ESAF facility by one on Poverty Reduction and Growth (PRGF). Yet there is a risk that although the word 'poverty' may be included in project documents, many projects are not in reality focused on poverty.

The recipient countries

The new ideas and programmes of international financial institutions insist on participation, one of the pivotal leitmotivs. However, it is still a matter of debate whether the concepts of poverty elaborated by the poor countries are seriously taken into account. Local studies and research, when they exist, are often considered to be irrelevant, like the approaches of non-economic social scientists when these are not validated by donor funding or publication in Western journals.

Many factors are involved here. One reason is the difficulty of how to ask the poor. Furthermore, the poor are by definition a totally heterogeneous group, merely defined by a series of heterogeneous properties: low income, bad health, illiteracy, and so on. This raises the difficult question of the criteria for representation, and the groups who are able to represent them and express their opinion. Participation is often reduced to meetings with an established group of NGOS. Experts and scholars from developing countries are likewise often the same people belonging to the networks known by the Bank, and who are regularly invited to consultations. It is therefore difficult for them to criticize the Bank too strongly. Diversification of viewpoints is insufficient because the Bank has few contacts with scholars outside this network. As the latter do not benefit from the facilities given to the Bank's regular experts (information, conferences), these scholars are not always as effective. This creates a vicious circle in the collection of homogeneous opinions from developing countries.

Moreover, until recently, the Bank by mandate dealt directly with governments – governments which in Africa, for instance, built their power on indifference towards their poorer citizens. As for the intellectual elite of the developing countries, they tend to be channelled into the donor agencies or offered better jobs in developed countries, with improved prospects and salaries. The political economy of local politics interacts with the mistrust of leaders *vis-à-vis* the Bank, for example in sub-Saharan Africa. Given the current political economy of aid, African governments are frequently indifferent to new trends in reform. Under constant financial pressure, and primarily concerned with domestic politics and retaining their power – preoccupations that are much more relevant to them than 'development' – they tend to accept anything from the donors, as long as it means the release of fresh financing.

Another dimension of the reactions of recipient countries is dependence on aid: some of them have no other alternative than to adhere to the policies of poverty reduction established by the Bank, and its recommendation that the processes be participatory. The relationship with the Bank and its policies is much more asymmetrical in the case of poorer countries. The richer developing countries, which borrow on non-concessional terms, have greater powers of negotiation and more room to propose their own ideas to the Bank when it recommends a particular policy of poverty reduction.

Conclusion: different meanings, different ideas of poverty

The World Bank's emphasis on poverty is a strategic response, and may be a sign of the guilt of rich countries or an implicit admission of the failure of past policies. It can be perceived as a short-term political answer. To speak of poverty is to postpone speaking of development, marking a shift in the temporality – shorter time-frames – of ideas as well as policies. Simultaneously, it is a concept built by the life span of other concepts: poverty has re-emerged because of the failure of previous beliefs – the benefits of structural adjustment and the automatic virtues of reforms, among others. It corresponds to the emergence of new types of growth and crises, and to increases in world inequality between countries even more than within countries (Bourguignon and Morrisson 1999; Milanovic 1999).

The evolution of the concept is also determined by the features and cognitive routines of the institution applying it. The World Bank has a remarkable capacity to adapt to external circumstances, always at the margin. Change takes years to occur, due to the Bank's size as well as its internal constraints. Among the conceptual changes, which usually occur long after their appearance in the outside world, there is the multidimensional nature of poverty; the key role of the state; and participatory processes with civil society. The Bank's capacity to adapt is also due to its major shareholders, which push it towards change because of their intellectual traditions and their political stakes.

There remains an intrinsic flaw in the actual concept of poverty as used by a bank. The World Bank tends to continue to base its definition on income or consumption, even if it claims that this definition is multidimensional. Income is an easier instrument for analytical studies and surveys. But the conceptual difficulty arises from the fact that income can still be considered as a more relevant dimension than all the others, such as health, education and participation, and that multidimensionality does not address the question of a possible hierarchy of dimensions (Ravallion 1994; 1997). Another flaw lies in the extensive use of the term itself, which qualifies a concept, a dimension, observations, outcomes, objectives, or policies, and refers to causes as well as to effects. Poverty is thus a more ambiguous concept than others in development research.

Finally, the concept of poverty exhibits a plurality of meanings, which allow for a plurality of policies. Not only does it emerge as a response to hegemonic processes and as a dimension of the transformation of an idea, but the fact that there are at present multiple meanings of poverty is the outcome of power relationships within countries and within a multilateral institution like the Bank: for example, meanings based on the American vs. the Nordic tradition. Some meanings may also emerge as opposed to others, for example a hypothetical European concept of poverty compared to the US one. At the same time, this multilateral arena produces a consensus and a temporary stability for the concept of poverty despite, or because of, this plurality.

Notes

1 A tough critique has been made by Srinivasan (1994).
2 Squire (2000: 111) shows that Economic and Sector Work (ESW) has accounted in the early 1990s for around 30 per cent of the operational budget.
3 In 1996, expenditure on development research amounted to $25 million, or about 2.5 per cent of operating expenditure.
4 See the influential Prebisch Lecture (Stiglitz 1998).
5 As summarized in Kanbur and Vines (2000); see Wade (2001a) on the politics of the *WDR 2000/1*.
6 Keefer and Knack (2000); outside the Bank, among a growing literature, for instance Perotti (1996); Rodrik (1998)
7 This is analysed in several papers by Martin Ravallion; see the review of the literature by Kanbur and Lustig (1999).
8 See the controversial paper of Dollar and Kraay (2000).
9 The *WDR 2000/1* and *The Quality of Growth* (2000) have been described as 'harmful muddle' in the *Economist* (30 September 2000: 108).
10 For instance by Jagdish Bhagwati or T.N. Srinivasan; Naim (2000: 508) concludes that the so-called Washington Consensus is much more a 'Washington confusion'.
11 For instance Amartya Sen, Dani Rodrik (Rodrik 1998; 1999), Jeffrey Sachs, or Alan Winters (Winters 2000a; 2000b).
12 For instance over Joseph Stiglitz's arguments that development is a transformation of society entailing not only the creation of market institutions but also of political institutions (Stiglitz 1998; 1999).
13 As shown by the tensions surrounding the World Bank's study on the East Asian Miracle in 1993; see Amsden (1994). Japan's efforts to put forward the lessons of its own experience of development are examined in Gyohten (1997).
14 See the White Paper issued in 1997, 'Eliminating World Poverty'.
15 See the 'Meltzer' report, set up by the US Congress in 1999.

13 The role of ideas in the United Nations Development Programme[1]

Asuncion Lera St Clair

Introduction

The United Nations Development Programme (UNDP) was created to function as the specialized agency that coordinates all the development assistance and technical cooperation of the United Nations (UN). Since its creation in 1965, UNDP has evolved from an agency giving technical and scientific assistance to less developed countries (LDCs) to become a post-project agency, a policy agency whose role is to provide advice, advocacy and resources to empower the poor. Ideas in UNDP have changed significantly over time, particularly when we look at the changes in values embedded in this organization's view of development and poverty. In the 1960s poverty and lack of development were conceptualized by UNDP as income and consumption problems, supposedly solved by increases in economic growth and external aid. Since the 1990s UNDP has promoted 'human development', in part based on Amartya Sen's 'capability approach', and has lately reformulated this development perspective in terms of human rights and freedoms. Such conceptualizations of development and poverty explicitly look at the ends and means of the process of development in terms of intrinsic values and what these mean for people's lives. In short, UNDP has moved – at the conceptual level – from endorsing an *economic view* of poverty and development to increasingly include an *ethically formulated perspective* that conceptualizes and evaluates the role of development in terms of securing the freedom, well-being and dignity of all people, and framing these goals in terms of social justice.

This explicit concern for ethical issues has evolved unevenly, but has eventually emerged in UNDP's official statements and documents as a means to respond either to crises in the world or to weaknesses in the theories used to conceptualize development and poverty. This has helped to draw attention to the fact that development theories have important ethical components. Although some use the term 'development' in a descriptive sense, meaning a process of economic growth, modernization or industrialization, there is also a normative sense of the term. Most would argue that development *per se* is a value-laden term that tacitly entails that certain types of economies and societies are better than others (Dower 1983). Some moral principles are relevant to the relations of richer countries and international agencies with poorer countries; and we may ask questions such as: What is good development? How is good development related to human well-being or a good life? Who is or should be responsible for bringing about good development? What are the most important obstacles to good development? The value dimensions of development – as well as the moral costs of development and poverty eradication policies – have been the subject of study by a heterogeneous – and in many cases disconnected – group of researchers since the early 1970s (Crocker 1991; 1998; Dower 1998; Gasper 1986; Goulet 1971; 1995). These authors have promoted ethically explicit conceptualizations as alternatives to dominant notions, as more appropriate options precisely because of their moral content. But it is not only moral values that have an important role to play in accounting for the evolution of ideas in UNDP.[2] This chapter focuses on the role of some cognitive values, such as measurability, coherence, or simplicity. Like scientific theories, policies have not only moral or ethical but also non-moral normative constraints. They must be able to satisfy certain criteria in order to be considered successful, such as testability, quantification, or simplicity.[3] Changes in values are ways to respond to failures of theories or to crises in the world. Values change at the same time as theories evolve or are replaced by other theories. Theories – sets of doctrines and assumptions – in the social sciences, need to offer coherent and adequate solutions to the problems they aim to solve. Alterations of these theories are a response to their inadequacies or flaws as much as a response to real problems in the world (Wolin 1980). Cognitive values are a source of power for ideas. For example, whether a concept is suited for quantification and therefore easily measurable has been an important reason for the rapid or slow institutionalization of that idea. Furthermore, each science has an ordering of cognitive values; thus the identification of the roles of such non-moral norms also helps to account for the predominance (or lack of it) of certain disciplines in the thinking of UNDP.

The focus on both cognitive and moral values implies blurring the distinction between facts and values, given that all values — coherence or measurability as much as goodness – arguably derive their authority from ideas of human flourishing and ideas of reason.[4] In an important sense, we take as rational what helps us achieve what we conceive as good for us as human beings. That is, conceptions of rationality are always guided by our idea of the good. Ideas can be powerful for many different reasons, including their moral and cognitive content. Thus the moral and cognitive values implicit in many ideas used by UNDP endow them with power: the power of morality and the power of rationality.[5]

This chapter begins its analysis with the origins of UNDP, deals rather briefly with the next twenty-year period, which saw increasing concerns for distribution and basic needs approaches, and mostly focuses on the new values and goals brought about by the idea of 'human development' in the 1990s. The last section of this chapter elaborates on what may be characterized as a learning process in UNDP; how the organization, although unevenly and in a non-linear way, has not only increasingly accepted more explicitly ethical values as the basis for its conceptualizations, but has also been forced to keep its conceptualizations open to public discussion and democratic deliberation.

The early years: first goals and values

UNDP was created in 1965 through the merger of two UN agencies, the Expanded Programme of Technical Assistance for Economic Development of Underdeveloped Countries (EPTA) and the United Nations Special Fund (SP).[6] Since its creation, UNDP has taken on the task of promoting one of the most important goals stated in the UN Charter:

> To achieve international co-operation in solving international problems of an economic, social, cultural or humanitarian character, and to promote higher standards of living, full employment and conditions of economic and social progress and development.
>
> (UN Charter 1948)

Yet the values put forward by the UN Charter – freedom from want, human dignity, human rights, equality, etc. – were not taken as integral elements of the actual conceptualizations and practices of these agencies. UNDP assimilated the practical goals of the agencies it replaced and thus continued that trend; and sharing of technical and scientific expertise, political neutrality, and respect for self-determination and national sovereignty are principles still embraced by UNDP today. UNDP also inherited from EPTA its *modus operandi*. EPTA made deals only with governments of underdeveloped countries; put its emphasis on the poorest of those developing countries; gave its funds in the form of grants, and distributed its funds to other UN specialist agencies according to sectoral projects. EPTA also started the process of establishing connections in each recipient country through country offices, thereby laying the foundation of the current UNDP's field offices network. Last, EPTA operated through collaboration with other specialized agencies, distributing its funds in a sectoral manner. Health grants were channelled through the World Health Organization (WHO), support for employment programmes through the International Labour Organization (ILO), and so forth. The Special Fund, created in 1958, had as its main goal to provide for pre-investment opportunities for poor countries, and was headed by Paul Hoffman, former manager of the Marshall Plan. Neither of the two earlier UN agencies operated under a particular theoretical framework, nor did they make contact with scholars or use the results of think-tanks working on the subject of development.[7] Economist W. Arthur Lewis, Hoffman's deputy, 'gave the Fund an intellectual initiative, drive, and dynamism in the face of agency opposition and vested interests, but many of his initiatives were dissipated after he left' (Mendez 2002).

Although Lewis never thought that economic growth was an end in itself (Streeten 1993), UNDP seems to have followed the international consensus on the faith in the powers of industrial progress and the capacity of a strong economy to solve all problems as the dominant paradigm of development economics. According to Hoffman, the main goal of development was 'to help the people of the low-income countries become more productive and, hence, able to purchase more, consume more, and contribute more to expanding the whole world's economy' (Hoffman 1970). Finally, Hoffman ordered a study of the UN system's capacity for development from one of the leading figures of development cooperation at the time, Sir Robert Jackson. The Jackson Report stated that UNDP lacked a think-tank that could work out ideas and launch them as directives for policy. The report emphasized the need to transform UNDP into an effective operational organization; it supported the country approach as a means to assure that national goals were the starting point of all UNDP assistance; it endorsed the role of UNDP as endowing the LDCs with the conditions of pre-investment; last, it asserted that the most important goal of development was the transfer of knowledge – scientific and technological – in order to raise people's living standards. The Jackson Report emphasized that UNDP could only provide training and well-being to people if the needs of the LDCs, not some other view of aid, were the starting point of UNDP's programme design (UNDP 1969).

UNDP officially accepted many suggestions of the Jackson Report, particularly a strong emphasis on the values of science and technology and the ratification of country programming as its operational strategy. These views coincided with the principles being put forward at the time by the Second Development Decade (UN 1970). In short, UNDP embraced an economic conception of development and its default view of poverty as income poverty (usually measured using the one-dimensional indicator of individual income). By the end of Hoffman's term, UNDP was the coordinating agency of the UN for development and technical cooperation, it had been endowed with more funds than ever before, it had started creating its own think-tank, and had accepted the position of a morally concerned and even obligated international actor; but it did not include this ethical concern in its conceptual tools.

From poor countries to poor people: distribution and basic needs

The intellectual contributions of UNDP during this period were very limited. Following the recommendations of the Jackson Report as well as its own mandate, UNDP allowed recipient countries to formulate their own priorities and was not concerned with conceptualizations of development. But to a modest extent, as part of its mandate to coordinate the development work of the UN, UNDP provided some funding to studies that were influential in development thinking. It was, for example, a minor financial contributor to the influential studies on employment in the early 1970s, which led to the important concepts of the informal sector and basic needs (see Chapter 4), and to an increased focus on the issue of distribution, notably through *Redistribution with Growth*, the landmark publication co-authored by Hollis Chenery, the chief economist of the World Bank at the time, which stated very clearly, first, that growth policies cannot solve poverty by themselves; and second, that poverty-oriented development strategies cannot be achieved with the traditional conceptual tools of development theory (Chenery *et al.* 1974).

The inclusion of concerns for distribution required the re-orientation of development policies, but the primary role of growth was not questioned, nor did the authors address the question of whether there were different kinds of growth.[8] The appropriate balance between growth and redistributive mechanisms is still highly debated in the field.[9]

ILO's *Employment, Growth and Basic Needs: A One-World Problem* (ILO 1976) was, conceptually, a highly advanced document that integrated all the new ideas analysed above: employment, inequality, the economic role of the poor, and the focus on the least advantaged sectors of the population, as well as adding a new concern for participation. The identification of a set of human needs, which aimed to constitute an account of what is a minimum standard of living, was used to identify the poor and to provide analytical tools to target development aid. However, the identification of human needs, although allegedly only an economic exercise (UNDP 1977), adds an important ethical dimension: the conceptualization of what it is to be a human being, and the most important aspects of a fully developed human life.

The picture of poor people that emerges from the inclusion of basic needs, distribution of income and the surveys of the informal sector, however, is an expanded version of the traditional account of humans in the science of economics, the *homo economicus*. Such a being is moved by self-interest and acts on behalf of individual concerns. The surveys used to measure the informal economy and its agents – the poor – as well as the measurements of basic needs, did not take into account, for example, people's social and political environment, nor their relations with the natural environment.

Part of the struggle we see in the use of revolutionary ideas by UNDP and other multilaterals, then, is due to the strong position that certain disciplines have and the prevalence of their cognitive tools. Although political scientists, social anthropologists, sociologists and others started joining development research teams in the 1970s, when it came to actually recommending changes these disciplines seemed to lack the tools to compete with those in the economist's toolbox and the economic data available on which to work (which, of course, reflects earlier perceptions of problems and the sort of data which would illuminate them). We would have to wait until the 1990s for the emergence of broader conceptions of poverty such as capability approaches, human rights, or sustainable livelihoods strategies, and the inclusion of the idea of social capital, in order to see considerable challenges to the idea of *homo economicus*.[10]

The inclusion of the new ideas discussed above – the informal sector, distribution, and basic needs – led to minor adjustments in other elements of the toolbox or knowledge system of UNDP and the UN. The ideas were 'added' to the dominant position of economic growth, but did not succeed in undermining such prevalence or in offering an alternative paradigm. For example, a follow-up document from the Commission on the Second Development Decade maintains the goal of growth, the endorsement of the policy norms of measurability and quantification, and the allegation that all these knowledge systems are value-free and politically neutral (UN 1973). Poverty-oriented development, however, challenged the growth paradigm in very substantial ways and set an agenda for development that was people-oriented.[11] It also challenged the predominant role of the science of economics. In closing the analysis of UNDP since its inception until the end of the 1970s, I will argue that UNDP shared most of its ideas with the rest of the development community, while it struggled to identify its area of action in relation to other UN agencies and the Bretton Woods institutions. These ideas, however, were the beginning of a process of cognitive and empirical learning – as to how development ought to be conceptualized and how poverty may be alleviated – which continues today.

Institutionally, UNDP initiated another set of reforms in order to recognize all these practical goals. UNDP had not only to acknowledge the analytical limitations of development economic models pointed out by Chenery's team and the ILO reports, but also to restructure itself as an institution. Among the most important reforms, UNDP changed the evaluation system from a focus on inputs (amount and types of expertise and grants transferred to the LDCs), to a focus on outputs, evaluating which projects had worked, and drawing lessons from experience. This emphasis on outputs has allowed UNDP to gain elasticity in its operations, to decentralize, and to strengthen its presence and partnerships with recipient countries.[12] Some of these reform objectives were set up through a proposal called New Dimensions in Technical Cooperation (UNDP 1975). Such reforms pointed, however, to an important issue that marks much of the later reforms of UNDP, the successful implementation of policies.

From poor people to the 'infrastructure' for their self-realization: human development, social capital, governance, and rights

During the 1980s, UNDP had to struggle with the consequences of including social objectives: how to make this coherent with the pursuit of economic growth, and with economic approaches and their inbuilt cognitive values. It also had to adjust its goals to the changing international context. In the 1970s, Third World countries increasingly gained influence in the UN and were very critical of basic needs approaches. They demanded a New International Economic Order (NIEO), which besides economic claims, argued for the inclusion of self-reliance and respect for the dignity of the poor. The 1980s, by contrast, were characterized by the neoliberal agenda and dominance of the Bretton Woods institutions and their structural adjustment policies. While some other UN agencies, particularly UNICEF, were criticizing the negative consequences of such policies on the poor, UNDP published several documents endorsing structural adjustment that became the guide for official policy.[13]

But UNDP also harvested some concepts that would lead this institution to become an active actor in the intellectual conceptualization of ethically explicit ideas. The 'human factor' became a subject inside UNDP under the leadership of Bradford Morse,[14] through the inclusion of concern for the interests of women, and the elaboration of ways to promote self-reliance (an idea which originated in the dependency school of the late 1960s and 1970s).[15] The former led to the establishment of UNIFEM as an independent part of UNDP in 1985. The latter idea led the institution to strengthen its operational system, and made the figure of the Resident Representative a key actor, as UNDP sought to place emphasis on country offices, which were mandated to deal exclusively with governments; and to help the LDCs to achieve more self-reliance, UNDP was required to respond to the needs of central governments, but also to evaluate and assess the needs of local communities, and all with minimal resources. Even in such a difficult economic, political and conceptual environment, Bradford Morse succeeded in shifting UNDP goals towards building self-reliance, strategies that would later be called capacity development (UNDP 1984). Building self-reliance, in turn, led UNDP to focus on grassroots groups, in particular minorities (such as women), and to start building up contacts with non-governmental organizations (NGOs) (UNDP 1985).

The focus on self-reliance through the establishment of relations with NGOs was not only a response to political pressures, but ended up also as a conceptual step in order to accomplish the task posed by the inclusion of social objectives: to know the context of poverty. The emphasis on self-reliance and NGOs may thus be seen as linked to the focus on the informal sector, as a continuity of values: the values and ways of life that come from the particularities of the environment where the poor live. Contacts with NGOs and a focus on the informal sector relate to the sociological aspects of poverty; that is, they bring concerns about the values of social life. What is a society? What are the relations between individuals and their social environment? What is the role of social foundations in poverty reduction or creation? The 1980s mark a transition in which UNDP advances from the position of apparently placing almost no value on the poor, to one where it conceives of poor people as agents of their own destinies, taking them at least as informants for – if not designers and implementers of – any poverty strategy.

It is in 1986, during the Islamabad North–South Roundtable, that the idea of human development first breaks to the surface (Haq and Kirdar 1986). As early as 1985, Bradford Morse claimed: 'In the past, development policies tended to favour the build-up of physical capacities over human capabilities. More attention must be given to these latter resources as the true agents and sole objects of development' (UNDP 1985). The institution was ripe to take on the challenge posed by Mahbub ul Haq (1976; 1995), who since the late 1960s had defended human-centred views of development: to conceptualize and espouse the ideas of human development and human poverty, developed with the help of Paul Streeten and Amartya Sen. UNDP created the arena where these conceptions developed – the Human Development Report Office, although this was an independent think-tank not officially reflective of UNDP policy. This independence was intended to avoid possible distortions of the idea brought about by the usual consensus process that UN agencies go through. Although the HDRs did not express the official views of UNDP, they were extremely influential, and the ideas and strategies developed in these publications became accepted by the mid-1990s by UNDP. Human development has influenced the choice of many other goals in UNDP, such as governance. Arguably, some of the values of the UN Charter were finally incorporated into the actual conceptual tools of the main institution coordinating the UN's development work.

The ideal of human development evolved during the 1990s as a response to structural adjustment policies, mostly embraced by the Bretton Woods institutions, and as an attempt to integrate other concerns, such as the environment and the promotion of democratic ideals. Armed with the idea of human development, UNDP could also respond to the demands posed by the NGOs of shifting from top-down approaches to bottom-up strategies, thereby giving local communities and local government a role to play in poverty reduction strategies.

In the words of its architect, Haq, human development aims to be a 'judicious mix of market efficiency and social compassion. ... [At the time it offered] a candid, uninhibited development dialogue that would serve the interests of the global community' (Haq 1995: 28). At the core of human development and its accompanying indices is Sen's capability approach. This is an alternative conception of development economics and poverty that expands the informational basis of development to include concerns for the quality of life, social justice, entitlements, and rights. Sen's approach to development originates from a critique of the reductionism and hegemony of a particular conception of moral philosophy, utilitarianism, and of social justice, that of Rawls (1971). His approach represents a social and political ethics based on pluralism that locates its main normative force in the ideas of public deliberation and freedom.[16]

The multidimensional view of well-being and poverty flowing from human development, a conception explicitly stated in ethical terms, places the emphasis not on goods and consumption, nor on preference satisfaction or happiness, but rather on facilitating people's opportunities to live productive and creative lives according to their needs and interests; or as Sen often says, those lives that people have reason to value (Sen 1997; 1999; UNDP 1990). Human development offers an explicit and thorough analysis of the ends and the means of development, thereby challenging – this time in a rather substantial way – the traditional view of growth and consumption as ends in themselves. Most importantly, Sen's conceptualization is a new analysis for public policy, given that his approach directs attention not only to the poor as an end, but rather to their supporting infrastructures or 'social arrangements' as means that are provided by society. In an important sense, it is arguable that although Sen's approach is focused on the individual, he indeed introduces the idea of social capital (Douglas and Ney 1998). The *Human Development Report* series, following Sen's lead, shows that the link between economic growth and progress is not automatic. 'For once, an international body dares to speak of a number of cases of high human development at modest income levels, and poor levels of human development at fairly high income levels' (Rist 1997: 206).

The rapid acceptance of human development within UNDP – including the increasingly widespread production of country *Human Development Reports* after the mid-1990s – and the spread of the idea to other multilaterals and bilateral donors – with the exception until very recently of the World Bank, which has been very slow in assimilating the lessons from the UNDP – is due, no doubt, to the analytical power of this idea as well as to the moral content of its message.[17] Haq 'took on the leadership of large armies of discontent that were gunning, somewhat sporadically, at the single-minded concentration on the GNP' (Sen 2000a). Haq's personality and qualifications made him a respected partner in the South, given that he was representative of their views, as well as a respected and recognized economist. Haq was capable of producing an idea that offered an alternative view able to accommodate a plurality of concerns, thereby coordinating discontent (Sen 2000a).

There is, however, another reason for such rapid acceptance: human development gradually evolved several indices, such as the Human Development Index (HDI) and the Human Poverty Index (HPI). This showed that at least some aspects of human well-being can be measured – although indirectly – and UNDP is therefore not departing from the same cognitive values of mainstream approaches. It is clear, however, that human development and capability poverty have more elements than those expressed in the main HDR indices.

The rapid acceptance of human development has had a domino effect within this institution, leading to very substantial changes in many other ideas and in the operational structure of UNDP. The effort to conceptualize the implementation of human development has forced the UNDP to re-assess the means used until now for this purpose. Many of the means now proposed by UNDP are also viewed as having intrinsic as well as instrumental value. In 1995, UNDP made poverty reduction one of its main objectives and created a division – the Social Development and Poverty Elimination Division (SDPED) – to work out ideas and strategies with enough holistic capacity to integrate the different dimensions of development and poverty. Capacity building, sustainable livelihoods, and the Civil Society and Participation Programme (CSPP), among others, are the result of UNDP's attempt to reach an understanding of the lives of the poor, and implement sustainable human development. All these strategies share the common denominator of looking at the contextual factors of poverty. They broaden their arena of action to the whole society, to incorporate concerns for informal patterns of behaviour (social as well as personal), and to look at poverty as an issue with multiple dimensions as well as changing needs (UNDP/SL 2000a; 2000b; UNDP/CSOPP 2000a; 2000b). The effort of implementing human development principles leads UNDP to concentrate on the ways in which the infrastructure of society can be transformed so as to help promote and respect people's choices.

The current focus on human rights and governance are, then, further consequences of UNDP's attempt to deepen the idea of, and implement, human development. Yet UNDP re-conceptualizes them, as well as human development, by focusing on the double added-value they generate together. There is also an important connection between human rights concerns and governance: both ideas depart from the assumption that democracy is the most appropriate environment for progress, and consider that it does not directly or by itself entail the protection of people's choices. For UNDP, democracy – especially just voting – is no vaccination against poverty (UNDP 2000a).

Human rights, for example, are conceptualized in terms of freedoms, a strategy that conceptually links rights with the notions of capabilities and entitlements at the core of human development. The *Human Development Report 2000* (UNDP 2000b) talks about freedom *from* discrimination, want, fear, and injustice; freedom *for* the realization of people's human potential and decent work; and freedom *of* participation, expression and association. If human development shifts the conceptualization of development and poverty from a matter of charity to a matter of justice, then human rights approaches add analytical force to the implementation of human development, since rights place claims on others (individuals or institutions) to satisfy them. Rights entail duties, and duties bring with them responsibility, accountability, and culpability; all these concepts point to an agency-based approach to development and poverty. Given that human development, as we have seen above, focuses on the social arrangements or infrastructures provided by society to enable people to live fulfilling lives, rights approaches bring possible tools to locate accountability for failures in the social system and responsibilities for present and future tasks (Sen 2000b). In short, among other issues, human rights analysis involves assessments of the extent to which institutions and social norms are or should be in place to provide security to the human development achievements within society (UNDP 2000b). Last, UNDP rightly points out that the fulfilment of rights must be distinguished from their mere existence. Indeed, many rights go unfulfilled precisely because of the failures of duty-bearers to perform their duties. There is nothing rhetorical about endorsing rights, even if those do not have clear duty-bearers. In the absence of a world citizenship or an institutionalized legal order, human rights provide the sole legitimation for the politics of the international community (Habermas 1998b). Human rights expand the scope of human development as well, as they have expanded UNDP's measuring indices to the point of using the cognitive tools of simplicity and measurability as a power for advocacy and accountability of the freedoms named above.

Ideas as tools for a learning process

The conceptual evolution of UNDP from focusing on poor countries to focusing on the enabling environment that encourages and allows – or does not encourage or allow – for the self-realization of people's ways of life, is an ambitious project that has become more and more explicitly normative. This project has increasingly included ethical concerns, which some claim are the product of

Western values. Also, some may see UNDP's ideas as technocratic, grounded only in Northern knowledge and science. UNDP's evolution may thus be marked by a tension provoked by the many possible ways to answer the question: Who, and for what reasons, decides what is best for the poor? Many of the technocratic and market-based values espoused in the 1960s remain on UNDP's agenda, thereby creating a conflict of values. The strategy of taking the particularities of the lives of the poor as a point of departure for poverty reduction policies, the goals of opening people's choices and respect for the natural environment, or the emphasis on human rights, may sit uneasily with technocratic rationality – and the aim of continuous economic growth, and the market-driven diversification of human wants brought about by the apparently inevitable consumerist side of development.[18, 19]

It has been argued that UNDP's increased normativity is not the result of an effort to include more worthy goals based on the assumption that the poor are moral agents, but rather a 'default' strategy – a way to justify its existence given its lack of practical power. It is true that there is a discrepancy between UNDP mandates and principles, and its economic capacity. But to claim that UNDP is normative by default undercuts the importance of normative justification, especially when such justification has some power to appeal to people's reason and commitment – as is the case, I argue, with human development. Aspiring to normative ideals can and should lead UNDP and other multilaterals to seek more effective power precisely to protect people from exploitation and repression.

It is also relevant to note that unlike the World Bank, for example, UNDP has a democratic voting system that assures, to a certain degree, the presence in its ideas of various values and worldviews as well as universal membership. Indeed, the UN as well as the Economic and Social Council (ECOSOC) are normative institutions: their role is to promote norms and principles, many of them stated in the UN Charter, which are the result of deliberation among, and the non-weighted consensus of, member countries. The egalitarian voting system of the UN and the economically weighted system of the Bretton Woods institutions have created a substantial philosophical gap between these two types of multilateral institution. The latter have accepted the defence of the principles of the market economy above any other type of principle, including ethical ones. If the power of ideas were exclusively derived from their economic support, the UNDP's would have close to none, and that is simply not the case. Indeed, the World Bank is now increasingly following the path marked by UNDP in its conceptualization of development and poverty (World Bank 2000b). The prevalence of UNDP, in this case, can be partly explained by a real moral and cognitive power in some of this organization's ideas. Ideas are more important in development than the public is led to believe. Governments around the world have a stake in the HDR rankings, and moral blame is starting to be significant where countries lag behind in certain rankings, even if full responsibility is not assigned. And that is one of the first steps towards changes in social values and eventually in policies.

I suggest that in order to characterize the evolution of ideas in UNDP, it is more accurate to avoid the dichotomy of seeing UNDP as either a body of knowledge that defends narrow interests or as defending universalistic knowledge; one that explains the role of ideas in this agency beyond a standoff between political and economic reasons. UNDP's use of ideas in its policy documents is not independent of politics, but neither is it reducible to politics. In an important sense, UNDP's conceptual evolution is an instance of continuity: a continuity of ethical values – to some extent suggested by critiques of past failures – that revamps the role of development aid in terms of social justice at the same time as it keeps the particularities of many of its ideas open-ended. The changes brought about by the ideas of self-reliance and later human development have shifted the focus of this multilateral from a universalistic and algorithmic top-down approach, aiming at changing the way of life of poor countries, to a learning experience aiming at utilizing poor people's values and knowledge as a valuable input for policy design. This process is not, let me emphasize, unique to UNDP. The United Nations Fund for Population Activity, for example, has also moved from traditional targets of family planning to broad issues such as reproductive rights or women's freedom to choose (see Chapter 5). Even the academic field of development economics itself has undergone many changes, which in some formulations now includes concerns for the human beings behind variables and structural adjustments, as well as for the ethical values embedded in development projects and planning. UNDP has not only borrowed from the new approaches of scholars such as Streeten, Sen and others, it has participated in the process of learning to understand and identify the many dimensions of poverty and of well-being that ought to be taken into consideration when making development and poverty policies. That is, it has moved to a different development paradigm that transfers the social values of freedom, rights, and justice to development studies.[20] The values of social justice and democracy are not exclusive to the North. Sen offers compelling arguments for the idea that most of their elements are also found in many non-Western cultures. In addition, although it is true that UNDP emphasizes the role of the market, this institution is viewed as a means that must be corrected and balanced with other means (such as state regulations).

Earlier sections of this chapter have shown that once UNDP began questioning some of the ethical implications of the goals and means of development, it set into motion a process that had (perhaps unintended, but) far reaching consequences. By questioning the ethical meanings of its goals, UNDP has shifted its focus from poor countries and macroeconomic concerns to poor people and their ways of living, and later to the infrastructures of society that prevent or enable people to flourish. Indeed, once UNDP began conceptualizing the poor as moral agents, it had no rational alternative to moving towards development policies of greater social justice and democracy. First, the problematization of development goals in ethical terms demanded the questioning of the means to achieve such goals. Second, questioning the ethical content of means demanded the reconsideration of the goals they had to serve. The continuous re-evaluation of the means to achieve human development is an instance of such dynamic processes. Human rights and good governance are used by UNDP as means to achieve, and in turn re-define, the goal of human development.

However, UNDP must add to this process of open-ended re-evaluation of goals and means a renegotiation of ideas, as the social settings of developing countries change and the shared understandings between aid donors and aid recipients evolve, which entails that the objectivity of the ideas that form UNDP's policies on poverty and development can only be such when seen from multiple points of view (Hacking 1999; Putnam 1994). In other words, UNDP's evolution of ideas is a learning process, as long as we can reconstruct this evolution of ideas as a move from scientifically proven concepts rooted in the experience of the North, to broad, open-ended, and pluralistic ideas for continuous re-evaluation and public discussion. As long as UNDP concentrates on a continuous renegotiation of knowing and valuing, this organization will not be imposing a particular rationality or a particular set of allegedly exclusively Western values. In fact, the ethical norms underlying many UNDP documents since the 1990s are not based on a particular theory of value, but rather on a theory of valuation. For example, the main normative emphasis of human development is on a particular formulation of freedom based on Sen's philosophical work. And Sen argues at length that the freedom he refers to must be conceived as something whose 'real' essence is unknown, because in practice the idea of freedom refers not to one freedom but many. Furthermore, as long as the poor are viewed as moral agents with their own particular social settings, freedoms must be posed in the context of choice situations. The challenge for UNDP, therefore, is to keep its ideas open to both academic and popular deliberation. Such emphasis on public deliberation and its connection to justice are at the core of Sen's conception of development as freedom (Sen 1999). Mahbub ul Haq must certainly have been aware of this when he referred to human development:

> Here we have a broad framework; if you want something to be included in this list, which may deserve a table in the *Human Development Report* (and with incredible luck it may even be considered for inclusion in one of the indices like the Human Development Index, or the Human Poverty Index), tell us *what*, and explain *why* it must figure in this accounting. We *will* listen.
>
> (quoted in Sen 2000a)

Haq and Sen have raised the stakes high for UNDP. This multilateral agency must keep its formulations of the good life open to democratic deliberation, and this entails that the only *reasonable* way to proceed is by guaranteeing every party's participation, including the poor.

Notes

1 The research necessary for writing this chapter was funded by Norwegian Research Council grant no. 141147/730. Thanks to Desmond McNeill, Morten Bøås, David Crocker, Desmond Gasper, Nils Gilje, Inmaculada de Melo-Martin, Sanjeev Prakash and Stephen Turner, for useful comments on an early version. Special thanks to Richard Jolly for valuable empirical information.

2 Hoksbergen (1986) makes a similar point.

3 The *Human Development Report 2000*, for example, also links the moral and the non-moral together, given it argues that there is an ethical duty to quantify the success and failure of the goals posed by development.

4 Putnam (1990) makes a similar point.

5 The editors of this volume claim that the best theoretical framework to analyse the role of ideas in multilaterals is a middle path between two theories of international relations, constructivism and realism. Philosophically, constructivism refers to the contingency of knowledge and realism and is related to the acceptance that objects and facts are independent. As much as I acknowledge that knowledge is constitutively a social product, it is important to distinguish between the 'idea of x' and x.

> For example the idea of a woman refugee, which is but a classification of certain type of woman, and the reality of women refugees. Certain social conditions in certain countries force people into flight (or to flee for their lives), but we cannot talk about social construction in that context. We must therefore distinguish between ideas themselves and the matrix of that idea. The matrix in which the idea of a woman refugee is formed, is a complex of institutions, advocates, newspaper articles, lawyers, court decisions, [or] immigration proceedings.
>
> (Hacking 1999: 11)

6 The merger was ratified by Resolution 2029 (XX) on 22 November 1965, and UNDP started functioning in 1966.

7 A UNDP document claims that technical assistance was 'an inexpensive means of assisting and uplifting the world's poor. A few skills imparted, some techniques transferred, key people trained, some basic equipment provided and the developing countries would move in unison into the thriving tumult of the world industrial economy' (UNDP 1985).

8 Chenery *et al.* (1974) argued in that direction and aimed to demonstrate that the right type of distribution would benefit everyone.

9 The World Bank was also instrumental in the spread of this new idea about development and poverty. In his address to the Board of Governors in 1973, McNamara pledged the reorientation of development policies towards the achievement of basic needs for all (McNamara 1981).

10 It is important to notice that there were substantial differences between the use of basic needs by multilaterals and the conceptualizations of their creators, Mahbub ul Haq and Paul Streeten. The move from academia to policy distorted this approach in a considerable way. For important contributions to the understanding of basic needs, see Doyal and Gough 1991; Stewart 1985; Streeten *et al.* 1981; Streeten 1984.

11 I am assuming here that UNDP policies since the 1970s have become more poverty-oriented. But in an important sense that is not so straightforward as UNDP seems to believe.

12 This shift from inputs to outputs is very important. Bureaucratic structures usually concentrate on measuring inputs. A focus on outputs requires an elasticity that bureaucratic structures usually do not have. This points to a peculiar characteristic of UNDP: its capacity to decentralize more easily than other multilaterals, to be more elastic and therefore to tune in easily with the recipients of aid.

13 See Cornia *et al.* 1987–88.
14 UNDP administrator from 1976 to 1986.
15 See Desai 1979; Nyerere 1968; Prebisch 1971.
16 For an analysis of the ethical foundations of Sen's capability approach and its differences with philosopher Martha Nussbaum's formulation of capability, see Crocker 1995; Gasper 1997.
17 See World Bank 2000b.
18 For a substantial discussion on these conflicts, see Wolfe 1996.
19 For substantial postmodern criticism of the discourse of development, see Cowen and Shenton 1996; Escobar 1995b; Rist 1997; Sachs 1995.
20 It is important to notice here that although some of these later conceptualizations take social justice as the thrust of development aid, there are many reasons to believe that charity will still have an important role to play. For a substantial discussion of the role of charity in development aid, see Gasper 1999.

14 The power of ideas

Across the constructivist/realist divide

James J. Hentz

Introduction

Unquestionably, the West, and in particular the United States, controls the key multilaterals (Woods 1999: 9). The US dominates the weighted voting in the IMF, and the primary producer clause of the WTO codifies the West's leading role in shaping the international trading order. However, international institutions also increasingly play an autonomous role. In fact, it was the relative decline of the US that pushed multilateral institutions into a prominent role.[1] As Escobar argues, albeit in a different context, 'from these institutional sites' (Escobar 1995b: 41) flows the 'process of institutionalisation and professionalisation' (*ibid.*: 45) of dominant forms of knowledge, or in the context of this volume – ideas. This, nonetheless, is not a tale of metropolises and peripheries because it describes:

> not epistemological centers and peripheries but a decentralized network of nodes in and through which theorists, theories, and multiple users move and meet, sharing and contesting the socioepistemological space.
>
> (*ibid.*: 224)

In fact, powerful factions within developing countries can be convinced through a discourse with multilaterals that certain developmental ideas are in their interests. As such, interests are often treated as distinct from ideas, when in fact ideas help shape interests. But this can only happen if configurations of power at the domestic level can sustain such policies. This demands bringing the state back in, not necessarily as an actor, but as an arena (or node) and as an active agent in the production and reproduction of a structure of dominant knowledge. In Ferguson's words:

> The 'state' in this conception, is not the name of an actor, it is the name of a way of tying together, multiplying, and coordinating power relations, a kind of knotting or congealing of power.
>
> (Ferguson 1990: 273)

How do ideas trigger new policies and transform institutional arrangements? What makes an idea attractive? The answer rests in the interstices of the persuasive power of an idea, 'knowledge politics', and the material power of that idea. In international politics, the former is often explained by the diffusion of successful policies that act as avatars of a particular idea. But ideas do not exist in isolation from the broader political context. Ideas are part of a larger competition pitting the relative power of different 'civilizations' against one another, and this competition has interlocking international and domestic dimensions. In the context of this volume, ideas are part of the developmental discourse, which has marginalized and disqualified non-Western knowledge systems (Escobar 1995b). These ideas, nonetheless, become locked in at the domestic level, which is an essential part of the agent/structure dynamic. This is part of what Ferguson calls the 'instrument-effects' (Ferguson 1990). Ideas are marketed as technical solutions to developmental problems (Ferguson 1990; Escobar 1995b), but they come packaged as political solutions favoured by powerful domestic actors.

The power of ideas, therefore, rests not just in their innate logic or even their essential correctness, but also in how they are embedded in material forces for change (or inertia), including structural transformations (from a bi-polar to a multi-polar or to a loose hegemonic international system), the actions of transnational actors and the rational behaviour of domestic agents. To answer the questions posed at the start of this chapter we need a framework that explains how the ideational and material power of certain policy choices lead states down specific pathways of development. A constructivist approach does the first, and reintroducing a realist approach does the second. Certain 'ideas' contribute to both the development of new policy approaches and to institutional innovation and change.

Constructivism provides the essential analytical tools for understanding ideational influences in international politics. The spread of new ideas is not merely due, for instance, to the financial power of the International Financial Institutions (IFIs), or other international organizations. It is also because individual governments develop ownership of those ideas (Hanson and Hentz 1999). The ability of multilateral institutions to establish a global consensus around certain 'ideas' is conditioned by an intersubjective process of learning. But this process can neither be understood outside its structural context, itself contested, nor abstracted from domestic political contests (Bøås 2001b). In both cases power matters.

Constructivism argues that not only is it important to explain the intersubjective nature of interests, but that structures and agents reconstitute each other in a dynamic process of iteration (Klotz 1995). The agent/structure model acknowledges that structure alone explains only the possibilities of action (Wendt 1987). In Dessler's words: 'A complete explanation must also appeal not only to the material [structural] but also the efficient causes of action, which can be located only within a theory of agents' (1989: 445). This is why an agency complement to the systemic elegance of constructivism is necessary. Its ontology of mutual constitution means that the process of interests formation and the institutionalization of interests flow from agent to structure as well as vice-versa. To unlock the analytical power of the agent/structure approach the rationalist/constructivist dichotomy must be bridged.

Although constructivism has opened the door to a better understanding of ideational influences in international politics, this chapter argues that without a realist complement it falls short of its ambition. The argument is made in three parts. First, I look at the constructivist critique and why its analytical power falls short of its purpose. Second, I look specifically at ideational explanations in international relations. Third, I offer a realist complement, which draws on, in particular, classical realism but includes elements of neorealism and postclassical realism.

The constructivist critique

The role of ideas in international relations theory has been the province of constructivism. As Katzenstein argues: 'State interests do not exist to be discovered by self-interested rational actors. Interests are constructed through a process of social interactions' (1996: 2). Economic liberalism, for instance, as Wendt might expect, has been the catalyst for new interest formation (1992). However, while constructivists assert a state's interest formation is global (Klotz 1995), as March and Olsen relate, '[H]istory is created by a complicated ecology of local events and locally adaptive actions' (1998: 968). The inability of rationalist approaches in international relations, both neorealist and neoliberalist variants, to explain how interests are formed, is well covered in the literature and will not be canvassed here.[2] The most often-repeated challenge to rationalist approaches, as Bukovansky reiterates, is that 'interests may be reconstituted in the political process' (1997: 211). Rationalist approaches treat interests as exogenous, when in fact they are an endogenous part of the political process. This, of course, includes the role of ideas and the construction of social knowledge within and across national boundaries.

There is, however, a second problem with rationalist approaches that is most prominent in constructivism's favourite sparring partner – neorealism; that is, the role of reason in international relations is ignored. But it goes largely unchallenged in the constructivist critique because, I would argue, constructivism conflates the positivism of neorealism with the rationality of the rational actor assumption it shares with classical realism (and rational choice). Constructivism thereby ignores not only classical realism's nuanced appreciation of power, but also the implicit role of reason in some positivist approaches. Also, while both neorealism and rational choice are positivist theories (or approaches), their respective understanding of the link between reason and rational action is distinct, and not only because they largely operate at different levels of analysis. Neorealism explains the reasons for actions, or as Ikenberry and Doyle argue, 'neorealism is preoccupied with the consequence rather than the cause of structure' (1997: 271); rational choice is concerned with the reasoning behind actions. This also distinguishes neorealism from classical realism. For instance, for

Thucydides the actions of states are grounded in the decisions of individuals (Bagby 1994). Forde (1995) has argued that the simplifying assumptions of neorealism, in particular the assumption that states are unitary actors, ignores the rich analysis of, among other non-systemic forces, domestic politics. If, as argued here, the agency side of the agent/structure process is under-examined, we must look at the reasoned behaviour of domestic actors. In an approach focusing on ideas flowing within, and concurrently constituting, the agent/structure process, the reasoning behind behaviour is as important as the consequence of structure on that behaviour.

Constructivism is a self-conscious challenge to the positivist ontology of both realism and rational choice. It is only natural that in carving out its own analytical space in international relations theory, it focused on the differences between its own approach and positivist theories. However, in the process, constructivism misses the opportunity to form synergies that will shape IR theory, if not (unfortunately for those that enjoy this game) ferment the next meta-debate in IR (e.g. Katzenstein *et al.* 1998). Elements of realism, particularly classical realism, as well as of rational choice, complete the analytical power of constructivism.

While the constructivist critique is essential for understanding the role of ideas, it is, therefore, incomplete. First, it lacks an appreciation of power. Classical realism, and even neorealism, can complement the ideational focus of constructivism. For instance, the importance of diffusion in constructivism's explanation of the spread of ideas is similar to the 'sameness effect' of neorealism (Brooks 1997). The hegemony, in a Gramscian sense, of certain developmental discourses, is partially a product of solidified Western hegemony in the immediate post-Cold War era, and in the ability of the multilaterals that anchor that hegemony to shape and spread those discourses. Among and within these multilaterals there is a competition to produce 'good' ideas.[3] Second, constructivism lacks a theory of agency. In fact, both neorealism and constructivism are agent/structure theories, with weak theories of agency. As Jervis, citing Waltz, explains: 'Waltz's conception of the relations between the units and the system is not so different from theirs [constructivist]':

> B's attributes and actions are affected by A, and vice-versa. Each is not only influencing the other, both are being influenced by the situation their interaction creates. ... The behavior of [a pair of units in a system] cannot ... be resolved into a set of two-way relations because each element of behavior that contributes to the interaction is itself shaped by their being a pair.
>
> (Jervis 1998: 978)

While neorealism cannot explain how interests are formed, constructivism cannot explain how those interests become institutionalized. As Biersteker argues: 'The reception of ideas in a particular national context is rarely identical from country to country' (1995: 175). We must understand how they are embedded in, and shape domestic political institutions where actors deploy whatever means necessary to further their interests. As Legro states: 'This oversight has led scholars to ignore significant subsystemic social understandings that can contradict and overwhelm international prescriptions' (1997: 32). An instrumental complement to the intersubjective ontology of constructivism is necessary; a theory or model of agency is therefore essential, to complement a constructivist explanation of interest formation.

Ideas as 'materials for action' is the central explanatory variable. Ideas, specifically learning, can account for new interest formation. But, as Hall states: 'Ideas have real power in the political world, [but] they do not acquire political force independently of the constellation of institutions and interests already present there' (1989a: 390). Part of that constellation is a web of multilaterals and academics promoting certain ideas. That is, ideas inform policy not only because they are vested in interest, but also because they become embedded in institutions (Sikkink 1991; Biersteker 1995).

Constructivism's anti-positivist ontology led it to mimic neorealism's systemic bias and to largely ignore the dynamics of domestic politics. In fact, much of constructivism was more forgiving of neorealism's unitary actor assumption than of neoliberalism's individualism (for which it claimed greater affinity). It has also ignored the central place of power in politics.

The structural power of ideas

Stein states, '[C]hanges in the nature of human understanding about how the world works, knowledge, can also transform state interests' (1993: 49). In Maynard Keynes' famous words: 'The power of vested interests is vastly exaggerated compared with the gradual encroachment of ideas' (cited in Odell 1982: 12), and as Jervis states, 'actors who believe the theory of mercantilism will behave very differently from those who have been schooled in neoclassical economics' (1998: 976).

The central conundrum in most of the ideas literature remains, nonetheless, how to prove causality (Goldstein and Keohane 1993; Garrett and Weingast 1993; Yee 1996), or how to show that ideas are more than mere hooks that competing elites use to legitimize and promote their interests. In fact, this is what distinguishes constructivism from the classical realism of E.H. Carr. Carr well understood that laissez-faire economics was 'a cloak for the vested interests of the privileged' (cited in Burchill 1996: 69). His notion that the *harmony of interest*, which was at the centre of Woodrow Wilson's idealism, was a fallacy, was based, ironically, on an implicit acceptance of the Marxist dictum that *the ruling ideas are the ruling-class ideas*.

Unfortunately, the literature on ideas often conflates ideas and ideology.[4] Getting past the chicken and egg problem and imputing causal significance to ideas demands separating independent and dependent variables, and thereby more clearly explaining cause and effect. If ideas are merely one way, among others, to promote interests, which are already given, they do, indeed belong to the rationalist paradigm. Institutionalist explanations of interest formation, for instance, typically treat ideas as epiphenomenal, or use them as post-hoc explanations (see

Blyth 1997). Ideas are treated either as weapons used by competing elites, or one set of interests among others that powerful groups are promoting. But ideas are this and more. The causal power of ideas rests in their ability to redefine state interests. As Ernst Haas stated: 'learning is but one other word for reinterpreting one's interest' (1980: 370). Learning is stimulated by the introduction of new ideas, but not just any kind of idea will suffice.

An argument using the spread of neoliberalism to demonstrate the power of ideas demands confronting powerful materialist counterfactuals,[5] such as the structural power of international capital and the hierarchical ordering within multilaterals. But which ideas are promoted cannot be explained by purely material factors, nor why some gain traction and others do not. Finally, as Blyth cautions, 'Attributing a change in behaviour to a change in ideas is tenable only if it is counterfactually demonstrated that the change could not have occurred without the ideas' (1997: 236). This does not imply that ideas must be proven sufficient for change, but only that they be shown to be necessary for change.

Political actors competing to promote policies favouring their interests are the intermediaries through which a state's interest is defined, or redefined. Ideas have causal power; that is, they ferment policies, precisely because of their advocacy by powerful groups. If, returning to Haas' dictum, 'learning is but one other word for reinterpreting one's interest', what we want to know is what ideas triggered such learning and how (if) those ideas have defined or redefined a state's interests – its broad objectives of policy. As Nau argues, the policy process is more than interest (society) and institutions (state). There is a competition within what he calls a 'cocoon of non-governmental actors' (1990: 44). That competition plays out on the ideational plane as well as the political, and each influences the other.

Finally, this volume's historical perspective highlights the ebb and flow of ideas within Nau's 'cocoon of non-governmental actors'. At different times particular ideas seem to capture the attention of multilaterals: the informal sector in the 1970s, sustainable development in the 1980s, and governance and social capital into the twenty-first century. In remains to be seen how ideas become locked in, and this reminds us to examine how states gain ownership of those ideas.

Bringing realism back in

The strength of constructivism rests in its agent/structure framework. The international system and its constituent parts interact to constitute and reconstitute each other. Part of this process is the creation and dissemination of ideas that shape states' identities and interests. Multilaterals, such as the World Bank, United Nations Development Programme, the International Labour Organization, the Asian Development Bank, the African Development Bank and the Inter-American Development Bank, in partnership with academic institutions such as the Institute for Development Studies in Sussex and the Harvard Institute for International Development, powerfully influence the formation of those meanings and identities.

However, until recently, constructivism has focused on historical transformations (Klotz 1995), and on a debate over competing ontologies for understanding systemic change (Bukovansky 1997). There are good reasons for this; Checkel (1998) points out that constructivism's core criticism of international relations theory was the latter's materialism and methodological individualism. But, as with an earlier challenge to structural realism, constructivism has done battle, almost exclusively, on the systemic plane,[6] and ignored domestic politics (Keohane 1989; Ferguson and Mansbach 1991). Thus, while recent work in the constructivist mode has begun to focus on policy choices (Klotz 1995; Risse-Kappen 1995; Bukovansky 1997), their analytical frameworks tend to have under-specified theories of domestic behaviour.[7] Klotz, for instance, acknowledges the lack of determinism in her explanation (1995). Kowert and Legro state:

> the relationship of normative to material structures is rarely examined or explicitly theorized, despite the likelihood that the influence of norms may be related to the characteristics of the material structures in which they are imbedded or the qualities of the actors that adopt or promote them.
>
> (1996: 490)

Constructivism, nonetheless, has left room for a theory of agency. First, as Wendt has argued, there is a natural affinity between constructivism and neoliberalism, because the latter is about process, including interaction and learning and about institutions (1992). Recent constructivist explanations of empirical events at least implicitly acknowledge that the domestic side of the agent/structure framing of their analysis is important. The recursive nature of the intersubjective meanings, or learning, depends on the institutionalization of those meanings (or ideas) at the state level.[8] But, because constructivism lacks an explanation of power, it also must call on realism.

Realism has been called the dominant international relations theory of post-World War II America. As such, it has become a favourite straw man of competing theories, such as neoliberal institutionalism and constructivism. But in the process, it has become almost a caricature in IR. As is increasingly being noticed, there are competing realisms: neorealism; postclassical realism and classical realism. Each offers important insights, but classical realism offers the best complement to constructivism.

Following World War II, American neorealism moved away from its European roots (Deudney 1997: 97). The positivist agenda of neorealism, exemplified by Waltz, replaced rationalism, and reason, with sparse economic assumptions of utility maximization and *homo economicus*. Elster (1984, cited in Kahler 1998: 924) argues that pure structuralists deny the importance of rational choice in favour of structural constraints. Waltz, in fact, purposefully challenged the anti-scientific traditional approach originally promoted by modern classical realists such as Hans Morgenthau and E.H. Carr. The result, as Kahler nicely summarizes, is:

The realm of reason within neorealism remains ambiguous. Under tight structural constraints of international competition and selection, the rationality of agents seems superfluous.

(1998: 925)

Waltz's systemic theory has its own mirror weaknesses to constructivism. Waltz states: 'In a systems theory, some part of the explanation of behaviours and outcomes is found in the system's structure' (1979: 73). Structure, for Waltz, is defined by how the units stand in relation to one another (*ibid.*: 80). And for Waltz, like most realists, states are the units that define the structure. Most importantly, however, unlike systemic constructivism, Waltz argues that '[S]truc-ture is sharply distinguished from actions and interactions' (*ibid.*). Neorealism not only could not explain system change, such as from the Medieval system to the Westphalia system (Ruggie 1972), but the structural change from the bi-polar world of the Cold War to the multi-polar (or loose hegemonic) world of the post-Cold War era (Lebow and Risse-Kappen 1995).

Brooks has introduced what he calls postclassical realism (1997). He looks at the work of a number of contemporary realists, such as Robert Gilpin, John Mearsheimer and Stephen Walt, and notes that collectively they, and others, have introduced three new material factors to neorealism: technology; geography; and international economic pressures. However, he also claims that postclassical realism 'focuses on international-level factors and does not examine domestic political variables' (1997: 469). Postclassical realism is an improvement over neorealism because it brings back in essential players and processes, such as multilaterals and international economic pressures, but it is inadequate for building a realist agent/structure model.

Within classical realism there are significant differences, such as between the classical realism of Thucydides and Machiavelli and the post-World War II realism of Carr and Morgenthau. But unlike neorealism, or postclassical realism, traditional realism neither ignored nonmaterial influences, nor the importance of the second level of analysis. Carr and Hans Morgenthau are the central figures in post-World War II traditional realism. Carr, a historian, sought to build a scientific study of world politics that accepted the realities of power. Morgenthau sought to create a 'science of international politics' by adopting a positivist methodology, such as that advanced by the hard sciences after World War II, to international relations (Burchill 1996). He can be considered, along with system theorists such as Morton Kaplan, as a transitional figure between classical realism (brought over from Europe) and neorealism.

Both Carr and Morgenthau, as representatives of the classical tradition, have a fuller understanding of the use of power. For instance, Morgenthau argued that the political, cultural and strategic environment would largely determine the forms of power a state will use (Burchill 1996). In his list of the 'elements of power', he includes: 'national morale': an 'intangible factor without whose support no government ... is able to pursue its policies' (Morgenthau 1949: ch. 4). Carr's multisectoral approach, as well, expands realism's reach. Most importantly,

Carr understood the idea of language as power, and that discourse helps shape politics (Buzan 1996). In fact, as Buzan (1996) notes, even post-structuralists such as Der Derian and Robert Ashley have found classical realism useful.

Waltz argued that classical realism was limited by its behaviourist methodology, which explains political outcomes by studying the constituent parts of a political system (Burchill 1996). This led to the curious anomaly, from a neorealist perspective, of what is a rational institutional design, from a rational choice perspective, being irrational from the perspective of a state trying to survive in the international system. Classical realists understood this dilemma. Thucydides noted that states do not always act in a way that maximizes self-preservation (Bagby 1994). Neither was Machiavelli wedded to the principle of the rationality of international actors (Forde 1995). The individualist ontology of rational choice is apparently in direct conflict with structural realism because it does not necessarily lead to optimal state behaviour. States often act irrationally. Conversely, state behaviour in the face of structural constraints may conflict with what rational choice might expect at the domestic level. Rational choice and neorealism can offer different and conflicting predictions of 'rational' state behaviour because what is rational is defined by the *a priori* choice of your level of analysis.

The agent/structure model can square the circle. Examining systemic or domestic logics in isolation cannot solve the riddle of rationality in international politics, particularly in times of change. The dynamic interaction of agent and structure creates its own logic. As Ikenberry and Doyle explain:

> The key to a middle position ... lies in relaxing the ontological primacy of either states (self-interested states) or international institutions and in introducing interactive processes into the relation.
>
> (1997: 273)

The end of the Cold War, of course, changed how the units stand in relation to each other – a structural change. But Waltz's omitted variables are key for explaining this. One constructivist explanation of how the international structure was changed through the actions and interactions of transnational actors illustrates the weakness of neorealism. Stein argues that the Soviet Union's reaction under Gorbachev to economic decline is partially explained by the influence of *new thinkers*, whose 'international contacts facilitated the exchange of ideas between transnational communities and the development of mutually understandable vocabularies and concepts' (1995: 241). Transnational relations influenced the dynamic interplay of domestic political forces in the Soviet Union, which led to a redefinition of its security interest (Deudney and Ikenberry 1991/92). The Soviet Union 'learned' that it had to make a tradeoff between immediate security (a continuing emphasis on heavy industry and defence spending) and economic reform. The difference, as Brooks points out, is concern for short-term military security versus long-term military security (1997). Neorealism argues that states heavily discount the future and thus would not make such a decision. The Soviet Union should not have allowed its vassal states to become independent nor loosened its grip on Eastern Europe. Ultimately, embedded in a reconstitution of its own interests that was strongly influenced by transnational activity, the Soviet Union's decisions led to a reconstitution of the international system (Koslowski and Kratochwil 1994).

An agent/structure model of realism that incorporates non-state actors is necessary. In this volume, multilaterals are the medium through which transnational ideas influence the development policies of individual states. But without incorporating how power affects relationships you end up with indeterminate explanations for how transnationalism affects policy. For example, the literature on epistemic communities suffers from this problem, because it fails to specify the conditions under which specific ideas are selected (Garrett and Weingast 1993; Risse-Kappen 1995).[9] Epistemic communities built around specific ideas can compete with each other, something academics should surely understand. Epistemic communities do not operate in vacuums. A vignette from the post-World War II era can illustrate this point. This concerns the broader globalization process of neoliberal economics and describes an epistemic victory and defeat. The dominant economic idea of the post-World War II era was Keynesianism, as reified in the Keynesian Welfare State (KWS). The strength of this idea cannot be understood outside the context of the Cold War. In Hall's words:

> By articulating an image of the managerial state that endorsed a measure of state intervention but preserved the capitalist organization of production, Keynes reinforced the belief that a middle way could be found between the complete socialization of the means of production and the excess of unbridled capitalism. ... They [Keynesian ideas] contributed to a change in the very terms of political discourse after the Second World War. They provided a new language that diverse groups of political actors could use to forge a common purpose, and conception of the state's role in the economy that appealed to forward-looking conservatives and Social Democrats alike.
>
> (1989a: 366)

The KWS was an essential tool in the West's defence against the spread of communism, which had intuitive appeal to the war-torn societies of Western Europe. Without the Cold War, the structural imperative of the KWS is lost. But it also had facilitated domestic political coalitions necessary to support the edifice of the KWS.

Constructivism must account for domestic political power struggles, and the nature of state institutions. A realist agent/structure model would expect that these would be reconstituted and constitute the international system. Carr understood this relationship:

> The predominance of the manufacturer and the merchant was so overwhelming that there was a sense in which an identity between their prosperity and British prosperity as a whole could be correctly asserted.
>
> (1964: 81)

And as Jervis argues, rational choice has something to add here:

> Game theory rests on assumptions about each actor's expectations about how the other will behave, expectations that form socially, both through establishing conventions about the meaning of behavior and by actors trying to convince others to accept their explanations.
>
> (1988: 978)

Reason, taken out of the neorealist mix, needs to be thrown back in. And ideas, or 'knowledge politics', play out within and shape domestic political contests, which are strongly influenced by and embedded in transnational activity. Constructivists understand this, but the ability of ideas to penetrate states can vary. As Risse-Kappen argues, state characteristics may facilitate or inhibit the flow of external ideas (1995). But Risse-Kappen treats state characteristics as given, and little attention is paid to the fact that states themselves adopt institutional arrangements deemed necessary to adapt to a changing international environment. The Parliamentary Reform Act of 1832 in Great Britain, for instance, revised the system of representation, reducing the power of the landed elites. Without this institutional change, the Corn Laws could not have been repealed. It was, thus, a reflection of, and an institutionalization of, the growing power of the industrial class. Eichengreen, for example, argues that the coalition of specific agricultural and industrial interests that supported the Smoot-Hawley Tariff was successful because of reforms in Congressional procedures (Eichengreen 1989).

The literature on globalization acknowledges the central role state institutions play in either promoting or inhibiting that process.[10] Maxfield argues that economic policy is likely to reflect bankers' preferences under three conditions: an independent central bank, if the finance ministry is allied with the central bank and exercises hegemony over other ministries, and if state industrialization or planning authorities have little ability to control the flow of investment funds (1990). Other scholars argue that globalization occurs more easily where there is a concentration of state power (Pantich 1997). But how particular institutional configurations come about, or how they might change, is not addressed. The causal arrows actually flow both ways. As Bradshaw and Zwelakhe argue, the penetration of foreign capital influences state characteristics (1990). Globalization strengthens certain ministries, typically including finance (Cox 1992a),[11] and these ministries gain strength because, as Haggard and Lee (1993) argue, a concentration of banking/industrial economic power reinforces the power of groups in favour of economic liberalism. In South Africa, for instance, Kornegay and Landsberg argue that a Keynesian economic strategy would demand a central role for the Ministry of Public Works, 'which curiously seems to have adopted a low profile' (1998: 9). The point is, of course, that a monetarist economic strategy privileges other departments, such as finance and the reserve bank. Interests and states are typically treated as separate analytical entities, but they are better appreciated as being mutually constituted.

In the case studies, the idea of 'good governance' is an example of ideas translated through multilateral bargaining shaping state institutions. The idea of good governance is closely linked to the state-market debate, and in the African context to structural adjustment programmes. As such, it is about creating strong Weberian states out of the wreckage of patrimonial states.

Conclusion

International relations should now build on constructivism's contributions. This will entail, however, not further ontological and epistemological entrenchment where rationalist and reflectivist continue to take shots at each other across the metatheoretical battlefield, but rather an exploration of the *terra incognita* in between. This can include post-structuralist analysis of development.

In fact, although this contribution does not take a post-structuralist position, it is consistent with Nustad and Long's chapters. Both focus on the development discourse from below, claiming that a technocratic discourse from above ignored the importance of human agency from below. From a critical perspective, a positivist/technical discourse of development dominated by the West and its multilateral surrogates entrenches power relations between North and South. As Nustad points out, Truman's faith in scientific and expert knowledge was part of his anti-communist crusade. Similarly, Waltz's neorealism has often been labelled conservative. To use Ferguson's phrase, 'the anti-politics machine' is cloaked in positivist rhetoric and discourses obscuring political processes and their underlying power relationships. Whether the current international system is most accurately characterized as multi-polar or loose hegemonic, the power of multilaterals in international politics is still hierarchically arranged (Woods 1999). Nonetheless, because agents can affect the structure, the participation of developing countries in the larger developmental discourse can abrade the strict hierarchical arrangement of international politics.

The case studies presented provide a rich vein for testing the framework of analysis offered here. The varied pace and impact of different 'ideas' across time can be explained by a realist agent/structure model. This chapter has therefore avoided framing the latest dichotomy in international relations as being positivist vs. interpretive,[12] because as constructivism can demonstrate, societal interests and state institutions are continually reconstituted within a process of reconstituted interests, where the web of multinationals imbued with the power of ideas operates.

Notes

1 Hegemonic Stability Theory predicted a decline of the international economic system as the US slid off its hegemonic perch. However, the international institutions created during the early post-World War II years sustained relative stability. For a complete discussion of the central role of international institutions, see the writings of G. John Ikenberry (1993; 1996).

2 For discussions of this problem see Sandholtz (1993), Wendt (1992) and Cohen (1990).

3 Although not covered in this chapter, this competition includes alliance-building between multilaterals and academia, as well as between multilaterals and specific domestic interests within certain developing countries.

4 For instance, Emanuel Adler (1997) in his seminal study on 'power of ideology' never seems to untangle the two. He considers ideologies as a 'specific type of idea', but uses ideas and ideology as seemingly mutually reinforcing by repeatedly pairing them together.

5 For a similar agrument see Biersteker (1995).

6 Robert Keohane and Joseph Nye (1987) acknowledged the importance of linking a process-oriented version of systemic theory with an analysis of domestic politics, but purposefully limited their analysis to the level of the international system. The subsequent literature, as they later pointed out, followed their lead.

7 Two possible exceptions are Risse-Kappen (1995) and Legro (1997). The former uses different state structures to explain the power of ideas. This might be considered a reification of the state, since state structures are given. The latter uses the cultures of national military organizations to specify which norms matter.

8 Kratochwil (1989) and Keohane (1989) both acknowledge the importance of institutionalizing norms, but do not go far enough in explaining the robustness of those institutions.

9 Blyth (1997) argues that the two main schools of institutionalist theory that focus on ideas, historical institutionalism and rational institutionalism, suffer from this problem. The examples he uses for the former are the works of Peter Hall and Kathryn Sikkink, and for the latter Judith Goldstein and Robert Keohane's edited volume, *Ideas and Foreign Policy* (1993).

10 For an example of the former see Garrett (1995).

11 Weeks (1996) has claimed the same for countries in Southern Africa adopting structural adjustment programmes.

12 See Keohane (1988) and Adler and Haas (1992).

15 Ideas and institutions

Who is framing what?

Morten Bøås and Desmond McNeill

'The question is', said Alice, 'whether you can make words mean so many different things'. 'The question is', said Humpty Dumpty, 'which is to be master – that's all'.

(Lewis Carroll, *Alice's Adventures in Wonderland*)

Introduction: power and ideas

The role of ideas in the making of multilateral development policy is the main concern of this book. In drawing conclusions from the various case studies presented here, we seek to avoid two extreme positions, which may be briefly summarized – or even caricatured – as follows.

Alternative 1 Multilateral development policy is determined by institutions driven by the common good. New ideas are welcomed, and those which are well founded empirically and analytically are adopted as the basis for decision making.

Alternative 2 Development policy is determined by neoliberal forces, epitomized by the US Treasury, which use multilateral institutions to further their own agenda. Ideas that run counter to this agenda are either suppressed or distorted.

The former is politically naive, ignoring the fact that there are powerful interests at stake – both internationally and also within and between different multilateral institutions. The latter is simplistic, ignoring both the power of ideas and institutionalization, and the complexity of power relationships within multilateral institutions. For us, the challenge lies not in simply rejecting these two extremes, but in establishing a coherent intermediate position which is theoretically rigorous and supported by the empirical experience of recent years.

Our central theme – the relationship between power and ideas – is not new to the social sciences; it has been debated since humankind started to reflect on the world and our place in it. But this book has been concerned with the power of ideas in a very particular setting, namely the system of multilateral development institutions. Such a system, and the institutions which constitute it, must be anchored in some sort of perception about what kind of collective good one would like to achieve, and more broadly in a 'shared' set of ideas. An important question is, therefore, how shared sets of ideas come into being, and change over time.

We believe that ideas cannot be separated completely from their context or relationship to various political interests. Even when a potentially challenging idea is introduced, its power can be weakened, destroyed or redirected to other purposes than those originally intended. Here, we clearly see the relevance and the wisdom of the quotation at the head of this chapter, because the question is not necessarily 'whether one can make words (ideas) mean so many things', but rather, 'which is to be master'. The role of ideas cannot be separated or analysed in isolation from considerations about the power relations of the social system that we wish to study.

The social system that this book explores is a new and different arena for the literature on the role of ideas, and we hope that by focusing on this particular social system we may not only enhance our understanding of development policy, but also make some contribution to theory in general.

Realism, constructivism and neogramscianism

The aim of this volume is thus not only to study a matrix of ideas and institutions, and thereby learn more about the multilateral system in general, but also to be innovative in theoretical terms. We did not wish to impose a predetermined theoretical apparatus, but rather allowed the empirical data to guide the methodology – adopting an eclectic approach which benefits from insights from several disciplines. However, it is apparent that the authors of the various chapters in this book share considerable common ground, and we therefore feel some confidence in formulating a common framework for the relationship between power and ideas in multilateral institutions, and drawing some general conclusions. Our theoretical approach may be briefly summarized.

It is widely acknowledged that the most important implication of political realism for the study of politics is that outcomes cannot be studied in disregard of the distribution of power. A political realist will understand the institutionalization of the multilateral system as resting upon specific forms of power relations. Nevertheless, very few realist scholars think that ideas do not matter, and likewise few constructivists maintain that political activity is solely about ideas and identities. The question is rather the relationship between power and ideas in specific circumstances. Ideas give material power direction and cause by defining priorities, whereas material capabilities may cause actors to change their ideas and priorities by affecting their ability to control their external and internal affairs (see Wohlforth 2000).[1]

We argue that power relations in the multilateral system are used to promote some ideas and some specific interpretations of ideas over other possible ideas and interpretations of ideas. There are two related, but different kinds of power involved in all types of social interaction. One is relational, the other is structural. Conceptually they are different, but an actor can exercise both simultaneously, and the use of them is dependent upon both material and ideational factors (Strange 1997). Relational power – as the power of A to get B to do something they would not otherwise do – does not have to be legitimate in any sense. Its use, however, is still dependent upon the interplay of material conditions, interests and ideas; for without ideas there will be no interests, and the wielding of relational power is built upon interests. Similarly, without interests there are no meaningful material conditions upon which to enforce one's relational power. And, finally, without the material conditions there is no framework of reality in which to act at all. Structural power is power over the 'order of things' and the beliefs sustaining the 'order of things'. The structural power of the institutions within the multilateral system is legitimate to the extent that states, firms, NGOs and people accept it. This way of reasoning suggests that it may be possible to form a bridge between material and ideational explanations.

To continue further we need to draw on the constructivist perspective. This perspective implies that the structures of the multilateral system are determined by shared ideas to a larger degree than by material conditions, and, equally important, that the identities and interests of the actors within this system are constructed by social interaction around competing interpretations of different ideas. However, the relationship between ideas and power in the multilateral system is not only a question of shared ideas, but equally of opposed and contested ideas; we must still come to grips with the realities of power. Any framework for understanding the relationship between power and ideas in the multilateral system must also take seriously the basic premise of political realism: outcomes cannot be properly analysed in disregard of the distribution of power. Equally important, since we here are talking about ideas as collective images, we need to establish a clear connection between ideas and institutionalization. This bridge we find in the neogramscian approach and Gramsci's understanding of hegemony as a *structure of dominance*.[2] Here, the question of whether the dominant power is a state, a group of states or some other combination of public and private power is left open. What is of greater importance to this interpretation is that the position of hegemonic power is sustained not merely by force, but by broadly based consent through the acceptance of an ideology and of institutions consistent with this structure. In other words, a hegemonic structure of world order is one in which power primarily takes a consensual form. We reserve the term hegemony for a consensual order, whereas dominance refers to a preponderance of material power.

In such a consensual order, institutions and an institutionalized multilateral system play an important role because they provide ways of dealing with conflict so as to minimize the use of force. There is, of course, enforcement potential in the power relations that underlie any social structure, in the sense that the strong can discipline the weak if they think it is necessary to protect their interests. However, also more nuanced mechanisms can be used for that purpose. The strong may make concessions that will secure the acquiescence of the weak in their leadership. One way of achieving this is for the strong to express their leadership in terms of a constructed 'global good', rather than overtly serving their own particular interests. It is precisely here that the institutions in the multilateral system may become the locus for such a hegemonic strategy, because through the ideas and policies they embody they lend themselves both to the representation of diverse interests and to the universalization of those ideas and policies. The current struggle over the hegemonic interpretation of governance is but one example of such processes.

In short, our argument is that a neogramscian perspective has much to offer for an understanding of the relationship between power and ideas in multilateral institutions, not least because of its emphasis on the consensual aspect of hegemony. However, for a framework that seeks to interpret the relationship between power and ideas in multilateral institutions, it is but one part of the larger equation. If we accept the central premise that both ideas (shared and contested) and the distribution of power (ideational and material) matter, then we need in addition to study the interplay between actors and structures in the various power games that take place in relation to these material and ideational struggles in multilateral institutions.

One possible approach to this issue is to apply elements of structuration theory, which opens the way for conceptualizing agents (actors) and structures as mutually constituted or co-determined entities (Giddens 1979; 1984). Social agents are seen as reflexive and able to gather and accumulate knowledge. They have an advanced view of the world, and they are able to evaluate their actions in light of their knowledge and experience. Social agents are therefore constantly performing actions – often intentionally, but also sometimes unintentionally – which ensure that social structures are reproduced. 'Structure', in this sense, is rules and resources, recursively implicated in the reproduction of social systems. Structures exist as memory traces, the organic basis of human knowledge, and as instantiated in action. 'A structure constitutes a structure only because of the behaviour of the agent, which in turn is intimately bound up with knowledge of the structure' (Buzan *et al.* 1993: 107).

Within multilateral institutions there are complex sets of social structures, sometimes unobservable, that shape the behaviour of the various agents (state and non-state) involved in the power games that take place in these institutions concerning the use of ideas. Such structural constraints are observed, not necessarily because of the sanctions imposed on deviants, but because of the reflexive capacity of the agents concerned to see what would happen in a context of interaction where such structures did not exist. Structural constraints are effective only as long as they are reproduced by the action of agents. The circumstances of social constraint where individuals have few or no alternative paths of action should not be equated with the dissolution of action as such, because social constraints do not operate like forces of nature. To have no choice is not quite the same as being driven irresistibly and uncomprehendingly by mechanical forces. Rather, within all social systems (multilateral institutions included) power creates regularized relations of autonomy and dependence between agents in contexts of social interaction. Nonetheless, in all dependent relationships, and especially hegemonic relationships, those who are subordinate can influence the activities of their superiors. Power will always be expressed in the duality of structure, where resources are structured properties of social systems, drawn upon and reproduced by knowledgeable agents during the course of social interaction.[3]

The multilateral system: a diversity of institutions

In order to understand the relationship between power and ideas in multilateral institutions, we must recognize that the multilateral system is composed of many different institutions, established for various purposes at different points in time. The articles of agreement of the IMF and of the World Bank were drafted and signed by representatives of forty-four nations at Bretton Woods, in July 1944. The major regional development banks were established in the period between the late 1950s and the mid-1960s.[4] The UNDP was created in 1965 through the merger of two already established development agencies, and the WTO was established on 1 January 1995 as a result of the decisions taken by the contracting parties to the GATT at the conclusion of the Uruguay Round.

We must also recognize that there have been substantial changes in their problem definitions. For instance, let us consider the World Bank. After the Second World War, the main task of the World Bank and the other Bretton Woods institutions was to contribute to the reconstruction of Western Europe (and thereby to prevent these societies from falling into the sphere of influence of the Soviet Union). Some years later, the problem definition of these institutions had been completely redefined to creating industrial growth in what were termed, after the process of decolonialization, developing countries. In the 1970s, another change took place, and the main goal was no longer supposed to be industrialization in itself, but poverty alleviation, and in its footsteps followed an emphasis on employment, the basic needs approach (and the related concept of the informal sector). The 1980s were marked by the increasing influence of the World Bank and other Bretton Woods institutions (Emmerij *et al.* 2001). The approaches of these institutions were substantially redefined in accordance with the emergence of neoliberalism as the dominant economic paradigm. One important, though unintended, outcome was the increased importance of NGOs within the international development debate. The consequence was renewed criticism of the development approaches of multilateral institutions, and a search for new solutions to development, which both made these institutions more aware of issue-areas like sustainable development, governance and social capital, and diminished their ability to stick to their formula of political neutrality (Bøås and McNeill 2003). As several of the chapters of this volume have shown, the limits to the technocratic consensus preferred by multilateral institutions became more and more evident towards the end of the previous millennium.

The institutions that make up what is known as the multilateral system do not only vary in terms of age, but also with respect to what kind of functions they are supposed to perform (development, finance, trade, etc.), geographical area, location of headquarters, membership structure (global or regional) and organization of their ownership. Some are organized as MDBs (e.g. the World Bank and the regional development banks) with a specific type of ownership structure in which votes are allocated on the basis of paid-in and guaranteed capital. In the IMF also, votes are allocated on the basis of financial contribution, but here the sum contributed by each member country also serves as the basis for determining how much the contributing member can borrow from the IMF or receive from the IMF in period allocations of special assets known as Special Drawing Rights (SDRs). The WTO as the successor to the GATT provides the legal and institutional foundation of the global trading system. Thus, as an institution, the WTO has three main dimensions:

(i)   the legal and institutional foundation of the world trading system;
(ii) a forum for multilateral trade negotiations;
(iii) a centre for the settlement of disputes.

The UNDP as a UN agency, on the other hand, operates, in principle, on the basis of one-country one-vote, but *de facto* its operating procedures are not that different from those we find in the MDBs. The Executive Board of UNDP is elected by the Economic and Social Council of the UN (one-country, one-vote). In the Board, although consensus is the norm, it is hard to imagine that the consensus that emerges from discussion is unrelated to each Board member's financial contribution both to the UN at large and UNDP in particular (i.e. power on the basis of contribution).

Thus there is wide variation between institutions not only with respect to their governance (for instance, the extent to which they are formally controlled by the donor or recipient countries) but also the extent to which they have power and resources. There is also variation in the degree to which they promote neoliberal views, and are dominated by economics – as discussed below. Thus, as summarized in Table 15.1, one might compare the various multilateral institutions in terms of these four factors:[5]

• the level of direct control by donor countries/the G-7 countries;
• the extent of their power;[6]
• the extent to which they promote neoliberal views;
• the extent to which their activities are dominated by the discipline of economics.

These factors are inter-related – some almost by definition. For example, in order to promote neoliberal views it is necessary that an institution adopts an economic perspective (although the latter does not necessarily imply the former). Donor control tends to be positively linked with resources available. Referring to Table 15.1, we should also note that the combination 'high' for 'neoliberal' and 'economics' tends to be positively correlated with 'high' on the other two factors ('control' and 'resources').

Table 15.1 Classification of multilateral institutions

	Donor control	*Power*	*Neoliberal*	*Economics*
WTO	High	High	High	High
IMF	High	High	High	High
World Bank	High	High	High–medium	High
UNDP	Low	Low	Medium–low	Medium–low
ILO	Low	Low	Low	Medium–low
UNFPA	Low	Low	Low	Low

The summary table gives some support to our general hypothesis. Our interest is especially in what might be called 'the economic–technocratic nexus'. All multilateral institutions are, of necessity, technocratic. In order for ideas to be used in such organizations they must be translated into terms which can be operationalized. This, we suggest, (together with the importance of achieving consensus), tends to involve a process of 'depoliticization', and a tendency for economics to become the dominant discipline. In short, we suggest that ideas that challenge the conventional wisdom become distorted as a result of a series of related pressures; depoliticization and 'economization', which may be, but are not necessarily, linked to neoliberal ideology and the material interests of those countries with most power in the system.

A strong claim is thus that the most powerful multilateral institutions, in terms of the resources at their command, are controlled by the donor countries (and most particularly the USA), promote neoliberal ideas, and are dominated by an economic perspective. Any challenging ideas that arise, if not directly refuted, are distorted, in keeping with this worldview (and world interest). A weak claim is that multilateral institutions are necessarily consensual and technocratic; and that new ideas are diluted and distorted in the process of gaining broad acceptance for them, and putting them into operation. The contributors to this volume occupy varying positions along this range. To present and support our own position, we need first to elaborate further on key components of the argument: the role of USA, and the meaning of neoliberalism; the place of economics and its relationship to a technocratic approach.

The United States – even though its powers vary from one institutional context to another (e.g. the World Bank vs. the ADB) – is, without doubt the hegemonic power within this system. It might be argued, with respect to the role of the United States, that multilateralism under the control of a hegemonic power is not much different from disguised bilateralism (see Ascher 1992). However, this would in our view represent a huge simplification of the complex power structures and relationships that multilateral institutions represent. And none of the contributions to this volume suggest such an approach. What does seem to be the case is that strong member countries (and even NGOs with the right kind of connections) can sometimes use multilateral institutions to send messages that it would have been awkward to send through bilateral channels. The consensus produced by multilateral institutions around controversial ideas such as governance can be a sophisticated way of making a particular viewpoint less offensive and more generally accepted. This is clearly what has happened at some point in time to many of the ideas discussed in this volume.[7]

We need to identify more clearly what we mean by neoliberalism. Every society has a set of rules, which governs access to resources, and one can argue that the contemporary world political economy operates on an allocation system based on neoliberal ideas. In the 1980s, most multilateral institutions were strongly influenced by the economic ideas advocated by world leaders such as Ronald Reagan and Margaret Thatcher. This advocacy, in combination with the breakdown of the communist bloc, led to the universalization of a particular view of development by some of the most powerful multilateral institutions (especially the IMF and the World Bank). The basic wisdom became that the market, rather than the state, should be the main vehicle for development. The post-war era of *embedded liberalism* was therefore seen as a thing of the past,[8] and in its place came the so-called *Washington Consensus*.[9]

It is no coincidence that this term refers to the capital of the USA. To think that it does not matter where a multilateral institution is located is to us naive. The institutions that we have dealt with in this volume are international institutions, but they are clearly also embedded in local, national and regional power structures and contexts. As Janne Jokinen's contribution indicates, it is of vital importance that the ADB's headquarters are located within its region and not elsewhere. Similarly, it is for us quite clear that the fact that the World Bank and IMF are located in Washington DC, only a few blocks from the White House and the US Treasury, gives the Treasury many subtle ways to control and influence these institutions that other important member countries do not have.

US support for the World Bank has been guided by the view that promoting economic growth and acceptance of market liberalism in other parts of the world is in the national interest, and that multilateral institutions are an effective way of achieving these objectives (Gwin 1994). The latter is the case precisely due to the potential connection between ideas, international norms and domestic change. If the US through multilateral institutions can persuade powerful segments of national elites to embrace these objectives, it can achieve its foreign economic policy objectives more effectively and at less cost than through bilateral negotiation or coercion. Thus the United States would like multilateral institutions such as the World Bank to push as hard as possible for market reforms in borrowing countries (as a condition for aid) and to ensure that the appointment procedure to these institutions yields people who support and actively promote this objective. However, for such a strategy to be effective it is of crucial importance that multilateral institutions appear to be acting in accordance with a common collective good agreed upon in general by all member states, rather than by US Treasury diktat. If not, the legitimizing benefit of a multilateral strategy may easily be lost (Wade 2002).

It is here that the issue of knowledge and the political neutrality of a certain type of economics enters the frame, because the World Bank's 'legitimacy rests on the claim that its development advice reflects the best possible technical research, a justification readily cited by borrowing governments when imposing Bank policies on their unwilling populations' (Wade 2001b: 128). The production of knowledge in multilateral institutions is therefore produced within a frame of reference that embeds certain cognitive interests, meaning that knowledge becomes an instrument, a tool, for the identification of manipulative variables (Nustad and Sending 2000).

There is clearly an enforcement potential in the power relations that lie under the social structure of multilateral institutions, but most often this enforcement potential takes the form of more nuanced mechanisms than simply an open disciplining of the weak by the strong. Even though nearly all the contributions to this volume in one way or another point towards the strong role played by the United States in multilateral institutions and the importance of understanding the hegemonic position of neoliberalism in the policy debates in multilateral institutions, we find little evidence for a conspiracy approach to the 'who is framing what?' question. Neoliberalism as the current dominant economic paradigm certainly is important with respect to how the debates around specific ideas are framed in multilateral institutions. To that extent, we agree with Taylor's contribution. The main contention of his chapter is precisely that ideas centred on notions of 'good governance' have been promoted by the IMF as part and parcel of the neoliberal order and are attempts to reconfigurate territories in order to make them more attractive to international capital.[10] The United States through the US Treasury is the most important player in most of the multilateral institutions that we have dealt with in this volume, but to suggest that the power of a specific idea or interpretation of an idea is simply a matter of whether or not it is supported by the US is by far too simple an explanation. As is apparent both from Taylor's contribution and others in this volume, neoliberalism seems to have become some sort of common sense during the two most recent decades. Theories opposed to the wisdom of neoliberalism have often been treated during this period 'with the bemused condescension usually reserved for astrological charts and flat-earth manifestos' (Cardoso and Helwege 1992: 8). This implies that the role of neoliberalism as the dominant economic paradigm in most multilateral institutions should be approached as what Pierre Bourdieu (1977: 164) entitles *doxa*:

> [S]chemes of thought and perception can produce the objectivity that they produce only by producing misrecognition of the limits of the cognition that they make possible, thereby founding immediate adherence in the doxic mode, to the world of tradition experienced as a natural world and taken for granted.

This concept of doxa can be equally applied not only to neoliberal economics, but perhaps to economics in general. The dominant liberal approach to the study of economics assumes that it is an objective, 'value-free' scientific discourse. The laws of economics, it is argued, are universal and it is the task of economic theory to discover these laws (Williams 1993).

Several of the chapters indicate that in order to understand the relationship between knowledge, ideas and the power of multilateral institutions, we have to come to terms with the role of the hegemonic position of economics in multilateral institutions. In the analysis and prescriptions from these institutions, economics is presented as an objective discipline that provides a value-free and correct picture of the world. Presenting the problem definition in this way means that development becomes a technical question and not a political one: an issue concerning sustainable development or governance that appears to be a matter of making the correct choice based on data and analysis, rather than a political decision. Such an approach fits 'hand in glove' with the overall mandate of these institutions, which is built on a functional and technical approach to development. The only valid evaluations are those built on economics, because this is assumed to be an objective science. Undoubtedly this understanding of economics has contributed immensely to the dominant position of this discipline in multilateral institutions. The consequence is ,therefore, that these institutions in their approach to ideas such as the informal sector, governance, social capital and sustainable development are operating 'within an empiricist/positivist epistemology, whose hallmark is an ontological distinction between subject and object which in turn produces the possibility of objective knowledge' (Abrahamsen 2000: 13).

Clearly, structural adjustment has been imposed on a number of countries, but when it comes to the ideas studied here, we would not claim that these have been imposed by USA and associated neoliberal forces. They may well be modified, and even distorted by these, but more importantly by the economic–technocratic nexus. Material interest alone does not provide a sufficient explanation of how and why ideas are adopted or transformed. The norms of institutions, and groups within them, are of great importance.

The ideas discussed in this volume have been introduced to various multilateral institutions over a fairly wide time-span: from the idea of development in Truman's inaugural speech in 1949 (see Chapter 2), to that of social capital, which entered into World Bank discussion in 1996 (see Chapter 8). Of particular interest is the way in which ideas travel between the institutions within the multilateral system. All the ideas discussed in this volume were first adopted by one or two institutions, and only after becoming manifest there through policy papers and statements were they taken up by other multilateral institutions; sometimes voluntarily, but just as often because they had come under strong pressure from NGOs to do so. In this volume we find several examples of agenda-pushing. One example is the story of WTO and sustainable development (see Chapter 7). Another, rather different, case – and perhaps the clearest example in this volume of an agenda being single-mindedly altered by the initiative of a group of like-minded actors – is the story told in Chapter 5 concerning international population policy.

However, when we look at the late–comers to an idea, we often find that they have learned little from the experiences of those institutions that have been concerned with the idea for some time. This observation becomes strikingly apparent if we compare the experience of sustainable development in the World Bank and the WTO (see Chapters 6 and 7 respectively). Wade's analysis is a history several decades long that takes us through three paradigmatic shifts from 'frontier economics' (prior to 1987), 'environmental protection' (up to early 1990s) and 'environmental management' thereafter. However, as we can see from Bøås and Vevatne's contribution, there is very little evidence that the WTO has learnt from the World Bank experience. Rather, it seems that the WTO, when finally forced to confront the issue of environment and sustainable development in 1995, adopted an approach quite similar to that of the World Bank prior to 1987 (i.e. 'frontier economics'). Both the internal debate in the WTO and the external debate with its critics in the NGO community bear a striking similarity to those in and around the World Bank over a decade before. It was thus only rather a general notion of the idea of sustainable development that 'travelled', not the whole debate surrounding it. Yet in other cases communication between multilateral organizations can be rapid and effective. There is considerable contact between different and potentially competing parties, not only through commissions, conferences and regular meetings, but also through staff members changing their position from one institution to another. But the extent of this varies considerably. For instance, there seems to be much more movement of people between the World Bank and the regional development banks than between UN agencies and institutions like the IMF and the WTO. The latter two seem to have had a much greater ability to insulate themselves from on-going policy debates elsewhere in the multilateral system than the other institutions that have been discussed in this volume. Indeed, one can speak of the different cultures of multilateral organizations – varying even within one family (e.g. the IBRD, the IFC and the IMF), and to a greater extent between them (e.g. ILO and WTO). Each has its own identity, socially constructed through the practice of specific multilateral institutions (an obvious example is the WTO secretariat: see Chapter 7). These are also manifest in the publications of these institutions, for example the *Human Development Report*, the *World Development Report* and the annual reports of institutions like the ADB. These are flagship publications, presenting an image of independence and conclusions based on empirical evidence and the best technical research available. They define the ideas the institutions are most eager to project in the near future.

Each of the multilateral institutions has its own identity – even if it does change over time, and is perceived differently from inside and outside. As some of the chapters have suggested, those working within these organizations are seeking to fulfil perhaps conflicting roles – in keeping with the identities of the organization for which they work and their own sense of professional purpose. And multilateral institutions are not static institutions; they do change, and so do the collective identities which they embody; and ideas play an important role in these processes of change.

However, for an idea to be of importance to a multilateral institution in the first place, that idea cannot represent total opposition to the hegemonic knowledge-system and the collective identity formed around this knowledge-system. In fact, an important insight to be gained from this volume is that for an idea to make an impact in a multilateral institution it must be possible to adapt or distort that idea in accordance with the dominant knowledge-system, the collective institutional identity formed around this knowledge system, and the power relationships in the world political economy that maintain them.

If we then accept one of the central assumptions behind this book, namely that the power of ideas is tied up with the institutionalization of social action and the material capabilities that such kind of institutionalization is built upon, the question still remains: what is the nature of this relationship? To what extent do ideas change institutions; or do institutions change ideas?

Power and ideas in multilateral institutions: an interpretative framework

Our suggestion is that the economic, technocratic (and in some cases also neoliberal) nexus provides a two-way link between the ideas and institutions studied in this volume. The idea of poverty (see Chapters 12 and 13) is an example of both the interplay between ideas and institutions, and the dynamic component of these processes. From the late 1980s, a more political (or at least ethical) concept of poverty favoured by the UNDP counterposed a more economic, technocratic concept favoured by the World Bank. The UNDP (or perhaps more accurately, the *Human Development Report*) initially sought actively to be distinct from the established position, associated with the World Bank; but over the subsequent years the World Bank and UNDP seem to have moved closer to a common position. What forces lie behind such processes? How – more broadly – can one explain the interplay between ideas and institutions in the making of multilateral development policy?

In seeking answers to these questions, we have found inspiration in a neogramscian approach, for two main reasons. First, it provides an ontological and epistemological foundation for the construction of non-deterministic yet structurally grounded interpretations of social change. With its emphasis on the transformative capacity of human agents it offers a path between the pre-determined units of neorealism (i.e. states) and the unexplored domestic foundations of world-systems theory. We see the relevance of such an approach in almost all chapters in this book, for instance in Jokinen's analysis of the ADB's policy on good governance and Sindzingre's account of the idea of poverty in the World Bank. In particular, we see this in Jokinen's embedding of the ADB's governance debate within the context of the larger exchange that took place between the proponents of the Washington Consensus, represented by the United States, the World Bank and the IMF, and the East and Southeast Asian supporters of its challenger, the Developmental State model; and in Sindzingre's examination of the various dimensions of the trajectory of poverty in the World Bank, which she links with an on-going production of a political economy of knowledge.

Second, the approach provides a flexible and ultimately historicist reading of institutions and the power of ideas; in particular, it offers us insight into the basis for hegemony, its construction as a social artefact and its inherent moments of contradiction. By viewing hegemony in itself as a product of leadership, we can more easily see both its contestability and the impossibility of reducing it to a preponderance of material resources. It is, for instance, obvious that the position of the United States within a multilateral institution like the World Bank is not built solely on its financial contribution to this institution; equally important is the way in which American premises structure the very mindset of World Bank staff, management and Executive Directors' offices (see Wade 2001b).

What we find more problematic is the neogramscian claim that at the apex of an emerging global class structure sits a transnational managerial class. We do not necessarily reject the existence of a kind of transnational managerial class. The international bureaucracies of multilateral institutions share several traits, whether we are talking about the international bureaucrats of the World Bank, the ADB or the UNDP. However, as is evident from the case studies presented here, there is also much that separates these institutions and thereby also the staff within them. Socialization is clearly an important aspect of multilateral institutions, but again, as the case studies have shown, the processes of socialization in multilateral institutions are diverse. This is evident in the chapters in this book that deal with the World Bank and the ADB respectively (see the contributions from Jokinen, McNeill, Sindzingre and Wade).

A second problem with the neogramscian approach is that hegemony appears to be total. There is no way to measure the strength of its power, or to assess countervailing tendencies. It gives us an inadequate understanding of the nature of agency in policy making and agenda setting (see Germain and Kenny 1998). One example is the assumed dominance of the neoliberal paradigm. Some neogramscian approaches see the hegemonic position of this paradigm as the product of a transnational managerial elite who are at the forefront of globalization trends worldwide, and who have established a convincing set of intellectual arguments to underpin their fortunate material position within a global political economy (e.g. Gill 1990a; Pijl 1998). By doing so, neogramscians perhaps unwillingly come to understand hegemony as a one-directional power relationship; it is fashioned by this transnational elite class on its own terms and then forced or imposed on subaltern classes/masses/states. The consequence, as we see it, is that the actual discursive battles that take place over ideas, both as intersubjective meanings and as collective images, vanish from the analysis. Everything can be explained by reference to the hegemonic position of neoliberalism and the dominant position of the transnational managerial class. This tends to make neogramscian analyses less relevant than they potentially could have been, both in empirical and theoretical terms.[11]

Nevertheless, and in the light of the various contributions to this volume, we feel that we need the neogramscian perspective because it draws our attention to some very important matters, (among them the consensual aspect of hegemony).

However, for a framework that seeks to interpret the role of ideas in multilateral institutions, it must be combined with perspectives that enable us to design more precisely defined actor-oriented studies.

This point takes us back to the issue of the relationship between realism, constructivism and neogramscianism raised in our introduction to this collection. Our major point in this regard is that in all social systems (multilateral institutions included) power creates regularized relations of autonomy and dependence between agents in contexts of social interaction. However, those who are subordinate can still influence the activities of their superiors. It is here that we see the need to revisit the arguments made by James Hentz in Chapter 14. Here Hentz draws our attention to several theoretical points of importance. First, by utilizing Escobar (1995b) and Ferguson (1990) he draws our attention to how ideas are marketed as technical solutions to developmental problems. Constructivism, with its emphasis on the social construction of politics, can help us understand the construction of political issues as technical solutions (i.e. the economic–technocratic nexus), whereas realism helps us to expose the political interests and power relationships that underwrite such constructions. The basic point, as Hentz argues, is that while the constructivist critique is essential for understanding the role of ideas, it lacks a clear appreciation of power. Realism can therefore complement the ideational focus of constructivism. The importance of understanding the 'lock-in' process is evident in several of the contributions to this volume, but perhaps most strikingly in Taylor's analysis of IMF and 'good governance': the political implications of locking into the liberalization process as legitimate reforms aimed at normalizing the national political economy. He interrogates the idea of good governance as promoted by the IMF as a value-free and correct picture of the world. In this argument, the three main theoretical propositions highlighted in the introduction come to the forefront and speak to each other: constructivism helps us understand the process of social construction of governance; realism exposes the power relations not only beneath this process of social construction, but also how this interpretation of governance becomes locked in at the country level; and neogramscianism elucidates the larger macrosocio-economic environment in which these processes take place.

In summary, we favour an intermediate, and somewhat eclectic approach, which may be contrasted with two others:

Alternative 1 is an extreme version of the constructivist/ideational model: the policies of multilateral institutions are determined by ideas derived from shared norms – of rational behaviour and the common good; institutions embody these norms and adopt policies consistent with them.

Alternative 2 is an extreme version of the realist/material model: the policies of multilateral institutions are determined by the material interests of those that control them; ideas – to the extent that they play a part – are also a reflection of these same material interests.

Alternative 3   is the more complex, mixed approach which we favour. Policies are the outcome of interplay between institutions and ideas; and each of these is influenced both by material interests and norms.

This implies that one must take account of several different interconnections – between interests and norms on the one hand, and institutions and ideas on the other. In brief:

Link 1   Material interests shape the nature and behaviour of institutions: different ownership structures (by states) have a major impact on the outcome.

Link 2   Material interests shape ideas: what is agreed – indeed even what is thought – is strongly influenced by the interests of powerful actors.

Link 3   Norms shape institutions: concepts of the common good and consensus, as well as bureaucratic rationality, objectivity, neutrality, strongly influence how institutions are organized and operate.

Link 4   Norms shape ideas: both bureaucratic norms (as above) and also academic norms (rigour, complexity – perhaps also originality) influence what ideas emerge and what form they take.

These, then, underpin the relationship with which we are primarily concerned in this book – between ideas and institutions. To the question: 'Who frames what in the making of policy?', we give no simple answer. It is apparent that ideas can indeed bring about change in an institution's policy, but also that institutions modify and distort ideas.

Central to our argument is the concept of framing – and more broadly the exercise of hegemonic power. We suggest that powerful states (notably the USA), powerful organizations (such as the IMF) and even, perhaps, powerful disciplines (economics) exercise their power largely by 'framing': which serves to limit the power of potentially radical ideas to achieve change. The exercise of framing is composed of two parts: one, drawing attention to a specific issue (such as the environment or urban unemployment); two, determining how such an issue is viewed. A successful framing exercise will both cause an issue to be seen by those who matter, and ensure that they see it in a specific way. And this is achieved with the minimum of conflict or pressure. For the ideas appear to be 'natural' and 'common sense'.

Our argument is that neogramscian approaches offer some potential in helping us to deconstruct such doxas and thereby give them their proper place within the wider political economy. In this book this is explicitly argued in relation to governance and structural adjustment in Taylor's contribution (see Chapter 9). As George and Sabelli (1994: 150) put it: 'Being against good governance is rather like being against motherhood and apple-pie'. An effective 'frame' is one which makes favoured ideas seem like common sense, and unfavoured ideas appear unthinkable. We suggest that a similar argument can be applied also to the other ideas, because as Cox (1992a: 179) argues, 'hegemony frames thought and thereby circumscribes action'.

Readers may be critical of our eclecticism and pragmatism towards issues deeply entrenched in decades of epistemological and ontological debate within international relations theory and international political economy literature. We would, however, claim that even within political realism there is no single tradition, 'but rather a knot of historically constituted tensions and contradictions' (Walker 1987: 80). This implies that the tradition of political realism is in itself a social construction, and although constructivism constitutes a challenge to positivist ontology and rational choice theory, there is more to realism than just these two tenets. As vividly described by Hentz, both in classical realism and in post-classical realism we can identify several 'meeting spaces' between these two broad strands of theory. Supported by the findings from the case studies, we choose to leave the metatheoretical battlefield, preferring to study how processes of policy making are actually carried out, and move into the *terra incognita* between the three positions highlighted here. This is for us the only way to make progress in understanding the complexities of the role of ideas in multilateral institutions.

Conclusion

In earlier days, a simplistic model of the development arena had capitalism pitted against communism: the US on one side and the USSR on the other. More recently the dividing lines have changed: first 'state versus market', and more recently, perhaps, 'globalization versus local civil society'. Some would claim that the conflict is – and has always been – between right and left, and that this is manifest both in relation to multilateral institutions (the extent to which they are dominated by the US) and in relation to ideas (the extent to which neoliberal ideas are dominant). We would support only a much modified version of this argument. Clearly, a policy such as structural adjustment can be seen as favouring the material interests of the US; and it can plausibly be argued that it has been promoted by some (e.g. the IMF) and opposed by others (e.g. UNDP). But such an argument can hardly be applied to all the ideas discussed here. With the exception of governance, most of the ideas can only to a limited extent be directly linked to a neoliberal agenda. Rather, one can postulate a continuum of ideas, according to the extent to which they can be mapped onto a 'right–left' axis. Governance would be at one end; poverty, the informal sector and perhaps sustainable development in the middle; and social capital and reproductive health at the other.

We suggest that political interests such as those represented by the US Treasury do indeed exercise considerable influence, but there are two major limitations with this account. One is, as just noted, that with regard to most of the ideas that we have discussed, there is not one clear neoliberal position as such. The second point is that when ideas are contested, at least in the arena of multilateral institutions, neoliberal and other forces do not generally exercise their power over ideas directly – by simply rejecting those that they oppose or enforcing those that they favour. The power of new ideas to change the policy of multilateral institutions is typically limited not by direct opposition from such forces, but by a more complex process in which ideas are distorted. The debate in multilateral institutions is, we argue, 'framed'; that is to say that it is constrained in certain ways, which are largely implicit and even unintentional. And this is the result not only of the forces of neoliberalism but to a much more substantial degree what we have identified as the 'economic–technocratic' nexus.

To illustrate, let us briefly contrast the 'ideas' of governance, on the one hand, and sustainable development and social capital on the other. In the case of governance, neoliberal interests are directly associated with the emergence of the idea in multilateral institutions; but this is not so for the other two. In all three cases, a new issue was successfully placed on the agenda, and the way in which it was discussed was strongly determined. (For example, not only did the environment become central for most multilateral institutions; the concept of 'sustainability' became central to the way in which people thought about it.)

These were thus most effective framing exercises. The ideas have been diluted and distorted in various ways; but it is evidence of their potency that they have seldom been rejected outright. One could claim that in the case of governance, material interests were of significant importance, but what emerges from the case studies is that the distortions that have occurred – also in the case of governance – have been predominantly technocratic/economic.

There are thus two distinct, but partly related, forces at work: one is neoliberal ideology, the other what we call the economic–technocratic nexus. Whether and to what extent a specific idea is distorted as a result of the former depends on the type of idea; but all, we suggest, are subject to the latter. What is common to both is depoliticization: ideas are drained of any overt political content, even if they are not wholly drained of their power. This perhaps helps to explain the frustration of those who seek to oppose multilateral institutions and the policies they explicitly stand for; and why opposition to these institutions is increasingly taking an anarchistic form.

In seeking to understand the political forces underlying the processes under study, we have found inspiration in the works of Cox and others, in what may be broadly described as a neogramscian approach. But, as we have also come to discover, this approach has its limitations, because the final policy outcome seems more to be the resolution of competing forces, none of which is completely dominant, than a well–defined and clearly intentional strategy on the part of one or a few dominant actors and interests. We therefore found it necessary to take account of the institutionalization of social action, and the material capabilities that such institutionalization is built upon. Our argument was that in order to understand the nature of this relationship we had to draw not only on neogramscianism, but also on a combination of constructivism and realism. This necessarily follows from one of the central premises of this book, that both ideas (shared and contested) and the distribution of power (ideational and material) matter. The triangular relationship between constructivism, realism and neogramscianism is clearly problematic both in epistemological and ontological terms, but the findings from the case studies all seem to indicate that answers to the generic question – to what extent do ideas change institutions or do institutions change ideas – can be obtained from pragmatic and eclectic approaches to this triangular relationship. We therefore choose to end on the optimistic note that both we and other researchers (perhaps inspired by this collection) will be able to build on the initial research that this volume represents, and penetrate deeper into this *problematique* in forthcoming publications.

Notes

1 Or in the words of Wendt (1999: 96–97):

> The proposition that the nature of international politics is shaped by power relations invariably is listed as one of the defining characteristics of Realism. This cannot be a *uniquely* Realist claim, however, since then every student of international politics would be a Realist. Neoliberals think power is important, Marxists think power is important; postmodernists even think it is everywhere. ... Better instead to differentiate theories according to how power is constituted.

2 Gramsci's main application of the concept of hegemony was to relations among social classes, and in Gramsci's work the term is mainly related to debates in the international communist movement over revolutionary strategies. The basic logic of the concept is, however, closely related to Gramsci's interpretation of Machiavelli's ideas to his own time. For Gramsci, as for Machiavelli, and also for most of those in the contemporary debate that have put the concept to use once more (such as Robert Cox, Timothy Sinclair, Stephen Gill and Craig Murphy), the general question involved in hegemony is the nature of power (i.e. power springing out of a combination of force and consent).

3 This understanding of power is in accordance with Lukes' (1974) three-dimensional view of power.

4 The only exception is the European Bank for Reconstruction and Development (EBRD), which was established in 1990 as part of the transition package for Eastern Europe after the end of the Cold War.

5 In each case the assessments are relative, e.g. the extent of donor control in UNDP is low by comparison with IMF, but it is still considerable.

6 Power is largely, but not solely, a matter of financial resources.

7 See also Casaburi *et al.* (2000: 496), who argue that 'despite the complexities, these multilateral institutions have wholeheartedly incorporated the concept of governance into their thinking and even into their lending programs. Good governance has become desirable in and of itself, for the benefits of the subjects that are governed'. For a discussion of various multilateral approaches to good governance, see Weiss (2000). For inquiries into the broadening of the governance agenda see Nelson 2000; Santiso 2001.

8 By 'embedded liberalism' is meant a practice wherein states worked towards reducing trade barriers, but simultaneously recognized the importance of state intervention in national markets. See Ruggie (1982). Ruggie's analysis draws on Polanyi (1944), which introduced the terms 'embedded' and 'disembedded' economic orders, referring to situations where the economy is merely a function of the social in which it is contained, and situations where a separate economic system emerges with an idea of a distinctive economic motive. In the latter case, economic relations are taken to be

autonomous and responsive only to their own endogenous laws of motion (Ruggie 1983). For an excellent review of Ruggie's work, both with respect to embedded liberalism and in general, see Wæver (1997).

9 The term 'Washington Consensus' was coined by Williamson (1993) and refers to the neoliberal economic thinking which shaped development policy in the 1980s and 1990s. Paul Krugman (1995: 28) later elaborated on Williamson's concept in the following manner:

> By 'Washington' Williamson meant not only the US government, but also all those institutions and networks of opinion leaders centred in the world's de facto capital – the IMF, World Bank, think tanks, politically sophisticated investment bankers, and worldly finance ministers, all those who meet each other in Washington and collectively define the conventional wisdom of the moment.

To some observers the Washington Consensus is as strong as ever – see Thomas (2000: 51) who argues that: 'As we enter the twenty-first century, the dominant approach to development and therefore to promoting human security is more deeply rooted in neoliberal values than ever before' – whereas other scholars have argued that we are in the process of entering the era of the post-Washington Consensus: see Braathen (2000). In his analysis based on a discursive approach to the *World Development Report 2000/1: Attacking Poverty*, Braathen argues that the World Bank seems to be moving in the direction of a new type of social corporatism: it tries to counter-balance the mechanisms of social exclusion inherent in modernizing and industrializing societies, and hence construct collective arrangements that include individuals in a caring community.

10 See also Stiglitz (2002: 196), who argues 'market fundamentalists dominate the IMF: they believe that markets by and large work well and that governments by and large work badly'.

11 To a certain degree, several neogramscians seem to have forgotten one of Gramsci's central messages, namely that dominant and subaltern classes engage in a number of material and ideational struggles which potentially change the whole socio-economic fabric of their relationship. See Germain and Kenny (1998).

Bibliography

Abbott, A. (1988) *The System of Professions: An Essay on the Division of Expert Labor*, Chicago: University of Chicago Press.

Abrahamsen, R. (2000) *Disciplining Democracy: Development Discourse and Good Governance in Africa*, London: Zed Books.

Adachi, H. (1984) 'On the Economic Implications of the Growth of the Non-market Sector', *Oxford Economic Papers* 36: 418–37.

Adams, N. (1997) *Worlds Apart: The North-South Divide and the International System*, London: Zed Books.

ADB (1966) *Agreement Establishing the Asian Development Bank*, Manila: ADB.

——(1994) *Report of the Task Force on Improving Project Quality*, January, Manila: ADB.

——(1995) *Governance: Sound Development Management*, August, Manila: ADB.

——(1998) 'From Project Financier to Broad-based Development Institution – Effecting Change through Technical Assistance', in *Asian Development Bank Annual Report 1997*, Manila: ADB, 19–39.

Adelman, I. and C.T. Morris (1973) *Economic Growth and Social Equity in Developing Countries*, Stanford: Stanford University Press.

Adler, E. (1987) *The Power of Ideology*, Berkeley: University of California Press.

——(1997) 'Seizing the Middle Ground: Constructivism', *European Journal of International Relations* 3 (3): 319–63.

Adler, E. and P. Haas (1992) 'Conclusion: Epistemic Communities, World Order, and the Creation of a Reflectivist Research Program', *International Organization* 46: 367–90.

AfDB (1964) *Agreement Establishing the African Development Bank*, Abidjan: AfDB.

Ahwireng-Obeng, F. (1996) 'The Impact of Informal Sector Interpretations on Policy', *Scandinavian Journal of Development Alternatives and Area Studies* 15 (2): 103–11.

Amin, S. (1976) [1973] *Unequal Development: An Essay on the Social Formations of Peripheral Capitalism*, Hassocks: Harvester Press.

Amsden, A.H. (1994) 'Why Isn't the Whole World Experimenting with the East Asian Model to Develop? Review of the East Asian Miracle', *World Development* 22 (4): 627–33.

Annals of the American Academy of Political and Social Science (1987) 'Special Edition: The Informal Economy' (September).

Apfel-Marglin, F. and S. Marglin (eds) (1996) *Decolonizing Knowledge: From Development to Dialogue*, Oxford: Clarendon Press.

Appel, H. (2000) 'The Ideological Determinants of Liberal Economic Reform: The Case of Privatization', *World Politics* 52: 526–29.

Appleton, S. and L. Song (1999) 'Income and Human Development at the Household Level: Evidence from Six Countries', commissioned paper for *World Development Report 2000/2001*, University of Bath and Washington DC: World Bank.

Arce, A. and N. Long (1987) 'The Dynamics of Knowledge Interfaces between Mexican Agricultural Bureaucrats and Peasants: A Case from Jalisco', *Boletin de Estudios Latinoamericanos y del Caribe.* CEDLA 43, December: 5–30.

——(2000) 'Reconfiguring Modernity and Development from an Anthropologial Perspective', in A. Arce and N. Long (eds) *Anthropology, Development and Modernities*, London: Routledge, 1–31.

Ascher, W. (1992) 'The World Bank and U.S. Control', in M.P. Karns and K.A. Mingst (eds) *The United States and Multilateral Institutions: Patterns of Changing Instrumentality and Influence*, London: Routledge, 115–39.

Atkinson, A.B. (1998) 'Equity Issues in a Globalizing World: The Experience of OECD Countries', paper presented at the Conference on Economic Policy and Equity, 8–9 June, Washington DC: International Monetary Fund.

Atkinson, A.B. and F. Bourguignon (1999) 'Poverty and Inclusion from a World Perspective', paper presented at the Annual World Bank Conference on Development Economics, Paris, June.

Augelli, E. and C. Murphy (1988) *America's Quest for Supremacy and the Third World: An Essay in Gramscian Analysis*, London: Pinter Publishers.

Bagby, L.M.J. (1994) 'The Use and Abuse of Thucydides', *International Organization* 48: 131–53.

Bairoch, P. (1973) *Urban Employment in Developing Countries: The Nature of the Problem and Proposals for its Solution*, Geneva: ILO.

Bank for International Settlements (1992) *Annual Report, 1992*, Basle: Bank for International Settlements.

Barnes, B. and D. Edge (eds) (1982) *Science in Context: Readings in the Sociology of Science*, Milton Keynes: Open University Press.

Barnett, M.N. and M. Finnemore (1999) 'The Politics, Power, and Pathologies of International Organizations', *International Organization* 53 (4): 699–732.

Barr, A.M. (1996) 'Entrepreneurial Networks and Economic Growth', D.Phil. dissertation, University of Oxford.

Basu, K. (1998) 'Child Labor: Cause, Consequence and Cure, with Remarks on International Labor Standards', Policy Research Working Paper no. 2027, Washington DC: World Bank.

Bayart, J.F. (1993) *The State in Africa: The Politics of the Belly*, London: Longman.

Becher, T. (1989) *Academic Tribes and Territories: Intellectual Enquiry and Cultures of Disciplines*, London: The Open University Press.

Beier, G., A. Churchill, M. Cohen and B. Renaud (1975) 'The Task Ahead for the Cities of the Developing Countries', World Bank Staff Working Paper, no. 209, Washington DC: World Bank.

Berger, D. (1997) 'Kausachum Coca! The Case of Coca Farmers in Bolivia: Livelihood and Resistance in the Shadow of Illegality', unpublished M.Sc. thesis, Wageningen University.

Bergsten, C.F. (1998) *The International Monetary Fund and the National Interests of the United States*, Washington DC: Institute for International Economics (IIE website).

Bergsten, C.F. and R. Henning (1996) *Global Economic Leadership and the Group of Seven*, Washington DC: Institute for International Economics.

Berman, M. (1992) 'Why Modernism Still Matters', in S. Lash and J. Friedman (eds) *Modernity and Identity*, Oxford: Blackwell, 33–58.

Bernstein, H. (1990) 'Agricultural Modernisation and the Era of Structural Adjustment: Observations on Sub-Saharan Africa', *Journal of Peasant Studies* 18 (1): 3–36.

Biersteker, T. (1995) 'The "Triumph" of Liberal Economic Ideas in the Developing World', in B. Stallings (ed.) *Global Change, Regional Response: The New International Context of Development*, New York: Cambridge University Press, 174–98.

Black, J.K. (1999) *Development in Theory and Practice: Paradigms and Paradoxes*, Boulder: West-view Press.

Blyth, A. (1997) 'Any More Bright Ideas? The Ideational Turn of Comparative Political Economy', *Comparative Politics* 29: 229–50.

Bøås, M. (1998) 'Governance as Multilateral Development Bank Policy: The Cases of the African Development Bank and the Asian Development Bank', *The European Journal of Development Research* 10 (2): 117–34.

——(2000) 'Ideas in the Multilateral System: Master or Servant? Thinking About Studying the Role of Ideas in the Multilateral System', paper presented at the 41st Annual Convention of the International Studies Association, Los Angeles.

——(2001a) 'Multilateral Development Banks, Environmental Impact Assessments, and Nongovernmental Organizations in U.S. Foreign Policy', in Paul G. Harris (ed.) *The Environment, International Relations, and U.S. Foreign Policy*, Washington DC: Georgetown University Press, 178–96.

——(2001b) 'Governance, Leadership and Ownership: The Case of the African Development Bank and the Asian Development Bank 1979–1996', doctoral dissertation, Oslo: Centre for Development and the Environment/Department of Political Science.

Bøås, M. and D. McNeill (2003) *Multilateral Institutions: A Critical Introduction*, London: Pluto Press.

Bongaarts, J. (1994) 'Population Policy Options in the Developing World', *Science* 11 (February): 771–76.

Bourdieu, P. (1977) *Outline of a Theory of Practice*. Cambridge: Cambridge University Press.

——(1986) 'The Forms of Capital', in J. Richardson (ed.) *Handbook of Theory and Research for the Sociology of Education*, Westport CT: Greenwood Press, 241–58.

Bourguignon, F. and C. Morrisson (1999) 'The Size Distribution of Income Among World Citizens: 1820–1990', Paris: Delta and University of Paris, 1 (mimeo).

Bowles, S. (1999) 'Social Capital and Community Governance', *Focus* 20 (3): 6–10.

Boyer, R. (1999) 'Le Paradoxe des Sciences Sociales: Les Vues d'un Economiste Dissi-dent', *Current Sociology* 47 (4): 19–45.

Braathen, E. (2000) 'New Social Corporatism: A Discursive–Critical Review of the WDR 2000/1, Attacking Poverty', *Forum for Development Studies* 27 (2): 331–50.

Bradshaw, Y. and T. Zwelakhe (1990) 'Foreign Capital Penetration, State Intervention and Development in Sub-Saharan Africa', *International Studies Quarterly* 34: 229–51.

Braudel, F. (1969) *Ecrits sur l'Histoire*, Paris: Flammarion.

Bridges (2000a) *The Appellate Body of the WTO*, Geneva: ICTSD.

——(2000b) *WTO and Civil Society*, Geneva: ICTSD.

Bromley, R. and C. Gerry (eds) (1980) *Casual Work and Poverty in Third World Cities*, London: Macmillan.

Brooks, S. (1997) 'Dueling Realism', *International Organization* 51: 443–77.

Brown, M.M. (1999) *The Way Forward: The Administrator's Business Plans, 2000–2003*, New York: UNDP.

——(2000) 'Profits or Human Rights? The Development Answer is Both', *International Herald Tribune*, 21 July.

Bruce, J. (1990) 'Fundamental Elements of the Quality of Care: A Simple Framework', *Studies in Family Planning* 21 (2): 61–91.

Bukovansky, M. (1997) 'Early U.S. Identity and Neutral Rights from Independence to the War of 1812', *International Organization* 5: 209–44.

Burchill, S. (1996) 'Realism and Neorealism', in S. Burchill and A. Linklater (eds) *Theories of International Relations*, New York: St Martin's Press, 67–117.

Burchill, S. and A. Linklater (eds) (1996) *Theories of International Relations*, New York: St Martin's Press.

Buzan, B. (1996) 'The Timeless Wisdom of Realism', in S. Smith, K. Booth and M. Zalewski (eds) *International Theory: Positivism and Beyond*, New York: Cambridge University Press, 47–65.

Buzan, B., C. Jones and R. Little (1993) *The Logic of Anarchy: Neorealism to Structural Realism*, New York: Columbia University Press.

Camdessus, M. (1998) 'The IMF and Good Governance', address by Managing Director of the International Monetary Fund at Transparency International (France), Paris, January 21, 1998, http://www.imf.org/external/np/speeches/1998/012198.htm.

Caporaso, J.A. (1993) 'International Relations Theory and Multilateralism: The Search for Foundations', in J.G. Ruggie (ed.) *Multilateralism Matters: The Theory and Praxis of an Institutional Form*, New York: Columbia University Press, 31–90.

Cardoso, E. and A. Helwege (1992) *Latin America's Economy: Diversity, Trends and Conflicts*, Cambridge MA: MIT Press.

Carothers, T. (1991) *In the Name of Democracy: U.S. Policy Toward Latin America in the Reagan Years*, Berkeley: University of California Press.

——(1999) *Aiding Democracy Abroad: The Learning Curve*, Washington DC: Carnegie Endowment for International Peace.

Carr, E.H. (1964) *The Twenty Years Crisis*, New York: Harper & Row.

Carroll, L. (1865) *Alice's Adventures under Ground (Alice's Adventures in Wonderland)*, London: Macmillan.

Casaburi, G., M.P. Riggirozzi, M.F. Tuozzo and D. Tussie (2000) 'Multilateral Development Banks, Governments, and Civil Society: Chiaroscuros in a Triangular Relationship', *Global Governance* 6 (4): 493–517.

Caufield, C. (1996) *Masters of Illusion: The World Bank and the Poverty of Nations*, New York: Henry Holt.

Center for International Environmental Law (1997) *Center for International Environmental Law Annual Report 1996–1997*, Washington DC: CIEL.

Cernea, M. (1994) *Sociology, Anthropology and Development: An Annotated Bibliography of World Bank Publications 1975–1993*, Washington DC: World Bank (ESSD monograph no. 3).

Chambers, R. (1983) *Rural Development: Putting the Last First*, London and New York: Longman.

——(1995) 'Paradigm Shifts and the Practice of Participatory Research and Development', in N. Nelson and S. Wright (eds) *Power and Participatory Development: Theory and Practice*, London: Intermediate Technology Publications, 30–42.

Chandavarkar, A. (1988) 'The Informal Sector: Empty Box or Portmanteau Concept? (A Comment)', *World Development* 16 (10): 1259–61.

Chandra, H. and M. Ali Khan (1993) 'Foreign Investment in the Presence of an Informal Sector', *Economica* 60 (February): 79–103.

Checkel, J.T. (1998) 'The Constructivist Turn in International Relations Theory', *World Politics* 50 (2): 324–48.

——(1999) 'Why Comply? Constructivism, Social Norms and the Study of International Institutions', *Arena Working Paper* 24.

Chenery, H., M.S. Ahluwalia, C.L.G. Bell, J.H. Duloy and R. Jolly (eds) (1974) *Redistribution with Growth*, Oxford: Oxford University Press.

Chossudovsky, M. (1998) *The Globalisation of Poverty: Impacts of IMF and World Bank Reforms*, London: Zed Press.

Cohen, B. (1990) 'The Political Economy of International Trade', *International Organization* 44: 261–81.

Colander, D.C. and A.W. Coats (eds) (1993) *The Spread of Economic Ideas*, Cambridge: Cambridge University Press.

Colby, M.E. (1989) 'The Evolution of Paradigms of Environmental Management in Development', PPR Working Paper WPS 313, Washington DC: World Bank.

Coleman, J. (1988) 'Social Capital in the Creation of Human Capital', *American Journal of Sociology* 94 (supplement): S95–120.

Collier, P. (1998) 'Social Capital and Poverty', SCI Working Paper 4, Washington DC: World Bank.

——(1999) 'Learning from Failure: International Financial Institutions as Agencies of Restraint in Africa', in A. Schedler, L. Diamond and M. Plattner (eds) *The Self-Restraining State: Power and Accountability in New Democracies*, Boulder: Lynne Rienner, 313–30.

Commander, S., H. Davoodi and U.J. Lee (1997) 'The Causes of Government and the Consequences for Growth and Well-being', Policy Research Working Paper 1785, Washington DC: World Bank.

Cornia, G.A., R. Jolly and F. Steward (1987) *Adjustment with a Human Face*, 2 vols, Oxford: Oxford University Press.

Cowen, M. and R.W. Shenton (1995) 'The Invention of Development', in J. Crush (ed.) *Power of Development*, London: Routledge, 27–43.

——(1996) *Doctrines of Development*, London: Routledge.

Cox, A. and J. Healey, with P. Hoebink and T. Voipio (2000) *European Development Cooperation and the Poor*, London: Macmillan.

Cox, R.W. (1980) 'The Crisis of World Order and the Problem of International Organization in the 1980s', *International Journal* 35 (2): 370–95.

——(1981) 'Social Forces, States, and World Orders', *Millennium: Journal of International Studies* 10 (2): 162–75.

——(1986) 'Social Forces, States, and World Orders: Beyond International Relations Theory', in R.O. Keohane (ed.) *Neorealism and its Critics*, New York: Columbia University Press, 204–54.

——(1989) 'Middlepowermanship, Japan and Future World Order', *International Journal* 44 (4): 823–62.

——(1991) 'The Global Political Economy and Social Choice', in D. Drache and M.S. Gertler (eds) *The New Era of Global Competition: State Policy and Market Power*, Montreal: McGill-Queen's University Press, 335–50.

——(1992a) 'Multilateralism and World Order', *Review of International Studies* 18 (2): 161–80.

——(1992b) 'Global Perestroika', in R. Miliband and L. Pantich (eds) *New World Order? The Socialist Register*, London: Merlin, 26–43.

——(1994) 'Global Restructuring: Making Sense of the Changing International Political Economy', in R. Stubbs and G. Underhill (eds) *Political Economy and the Changing Global Order*, London: Macmillan, 45–59.

——(1996) 'Global Perestroika', in R. Cox with T.J. Sinclair, *Approaches to World Order*, Cambridge: Cambridge University Press, 296–313.

——(1999) 'Civil Society at the Turn of the Millennium: Prospects for an Alternative World Order', *Review of International Studies* 25 (1): 3–28.

Cox, R.W. (ed.) (1997) *The New Realism: Perspectives on Multilateralism and World Order*, New York: Macmillan and United Nations University Press.

Cox, R.W. and H.K. Jacobson (1973) *The Anatomy of Influence: Decision Making in International Organisation*, New Haven: Yale University Press.

Cox, R.W. with T.J. Sinclair (1996) *Approaches to World Order*, Cambridge: Cambridge University Press.

Crane, B. (1993) 'International Population Institutions: Adaption to a Changing World Order', in P. Haas, R.O. Keohane and M.A. Levy (eds) *Institutions for the Earth: Sources of Effective International Environmental Protection*, Cambridge MA: MIT Press, 351–93.

Critchlow, D.T. (1999) *Intended Consequences: Birth Control, Abortion and The Federal Government in Modern America*, Oxford: Oxford University Press.

Critchlow, D.T. (ed.) (1996) *The Politics of Abortion and Birth Control in Historical Perspective*, Pennsylvania: Pennsylvania State University Press.

Crocker, D. (1991) 'Toward Development Ethics', *World Development* 19 (5): 457–83.

——(1995) 'Functioning and Capability: The Foundations of Sen's and Nussbaum's Development Ethic', in M. Nussbaum and J. Glover (eds) *Women, Culture, and Development: A Study of Human Capabilities*, Oxford: Clarendon Press, 153–98.

——(1998) 'Development Ethics', in E. Craig (ed.) *Routledge Encyclopedia of Philosophy*, vol. 3, London: Routledge, 39–44.

Crush, J. (ed.) (1995) *Power of Development*, London: Routledge.

Culpeper, R. (1997) *Titans or Behemoths?*, Boulder: Lynne Rienner.

Cutler, C. (1999) 'Locating "Authority" in the Global Political Economy', *International Studies Quarterly* 43 (1): 59–81.

Danesh, A. (1991) *The Informal Economy: A Research Guide*, New York: Garland Publishing.

Dasgupta, P. and I. Serageldin (eds) (2000) *Social Capital: A Multifaceted Perspective*, Washington DC: World Bank.

Davis, K. (1958) 'The Political Impact of New Population Trends', *Foreign Affairs Quarterly* (January): 293–301.

Demeny P. (1988) 'Social Science and Population Policy', *Population and Development Review* 14 (3): 451–78.

Desai, M. (1979) *Marxian Economics*, Oxford: Blackwell.

Desrosières, A. (1991) 'How to Make Things Which Hold Together: Social Science, Statistics and the State', in P. Wagner *et al.* (eds) *Discourses on Society: The Shaping of the Social Science Disciplines*, Dordrecht: Kluwer Academic Publishers, 195–218.

——(1998) *The Politics of Large Numbers: A History of Statistical Reasoning*, Cambridge MA: Harvard University Press.

Dessler, D. (1989) 'What's at Stake in the Agent-Structure Debate', *International Organization* 43: 441–73.

Deudney, D. (1997) 'Geopolitics and Change', in G.J. Ikenberry and M. Doyle (eds) *New Thinking in International Relations Theory*, Boulder: Westview Press, 91–123.

Deudney, D. and G.J. Ikenberry (1991/92) 'The International Sources of Soviet Change', *International Security* 16: 74–118.

Dixon-Mueller, R. (1993) *Population Policy and Women's Rights: Transforming Reproductive Choice*, London: Praeger Publishers.

Dixon-Mueller, R. and A. Germain (1993) *Four Essays on Birth Control: Needs and Risks*, New York: International Women's Health Coalition.

Dixon-Mueller, R. and J. Wasserheit (1991) *The Culture of Silence: Reproductive Tract Infections Among Women in the Third World*, New York: International Women's Health Coaltion.

Dollar, D. and A. Kraay (2000) *Growth is Good for the Poor*, Washington DC: World Bank.

Douglas, M. (1986) *How Institutions Think*, Syracuse NY: Syracuse University Press.

Douglas, M. and S. Ney (1998) *Missing Persons: A Critique of Personhood in the Social Sciences*, Berkeley: University of California Press.

Dower, N. (1983) *World Poverty: Challenge and Response*, York: The Elbor Press.

——(1998) *World Ethics: The New Agenda*, Edinburgh: Edinburgh University Press.

Doyal, L. and I. Gough (1991) *A Theory of Human Need*, New York: The Guilford Press.

East African Standard (Nairobi) (2000) 31 July, August.

Easterly, W. (2000a) 'The Effect of IMF and World Bank Programs on Poverty', Washington DC: World Bank (mimeo).

——(2000b) 'The Lost Decades ... and the Coming Boom? Policies, Shocks, and Developing Countries' Stagnation, 1980–1998', Washington DC: World Bank (mimeo).

Easterly, W., R. Islam and J. Stiglitz (1999) 'Shaken and Stirred: Explaining Growth and Volatility', Washington DC: World Bank (mimeo).

Eckholm, E. (1984) 'World Bank Urged to Halt Aid to Brazil for Amazon Development', *New York Times*, 17 October, p. A17.

Ecologist, The 15 (1–2): 1995

Economist, The 108 *The Quality of Growth* 30 September 2000

Edwards, M. (1999) 'The Irrelevance of Development Studies', *Third World Quarterly* 11 (1): 116–35.

——(2000) 'Enthusiasts, Tacticians and Sceptics: The World Bank, Civil Society and Social Capital', http://www.worldbank.org/wbp/scapital/library/edwards.htm.

Egeberg, M. (2000) 'What Organisation Tells us About Preference and Identity Formation: EU Committees and National Officials', paper presented at the ARENA/IDNET Workshop, 16–17 June.

Eichengreen, B. (1989) 'The Political Economy of the Smoot-Hawley Tariff', *Research in Economic History* 12: 1–43.

——(1999) *Toward a New International Financial Architecture: A Practical Post-Asia Agenda*, Washington DC: Institute for International Economics.

Elster, J. (1984) *Ulysses and the Sirens: Studies in Rationality and Irrationality*, Cambridge: Cambridge University Press.

Emmerij, L. (1972) 'Research Priorities of the World Employment Programme', *International Labour Review* 105 (5): 411–23.

Emmerij, L. and D. Ghai (1976) 'The World Employment Conference: A Preliminary Assessment', *International Labour Review* 114 (5): 289–99.

Emmerij, L., R. Jolly and T.G. Weiss (2001) *Ahead of the Curve? UN Ideas and Global Challenges*, Indianapolis: Indiana University Press.

Escobar, A. (1984) 'Discourse and Power in Development: Michel Foucault and the Relevance of His Work to the Third World', *Alternatives* 10 (3): 377–400.

——(1991) 'Anthropology and the Development Encounter: The Making and Marketing of Development Anthropology', *American Ethnologist* 18 (4): 658–82.

——(1995a) 'Imagining a Post-development Era', in J. Crush (ed.) *Power of Development*, London: Routledge, 211–27.

——(1995b) *Encountering Development: The Making and Unmaking of the Third World,* Princeton: Princeton University Press.

Esman, M.J. and N.T. Uphoff (1984) *Local Organizations: Intermediaries in Local Development,* Ithaca NY: Cornell University Press.

Esteva, G. (1995) 'Development', in W. Sachs (ed.) *The Development Dictionary: A Guide to Knowledge as Power,* London: Zed Books, 6–25.

Esty, D. (1994) *Greening the GATT: Trade, Environment and the Future,* Washington DC: Institute for International Economics.

——(1997) 'Why the World Trade Organisation Needs Environmental NGOs', *Bridges Series on Public Participation no. 1,* Geneva: ICTSD.

Evans, P. (1996) 'Government Action, Social Capital and Development: Reviewing the Evidence on Synergy', *World Development* 24 (6): 1119–32.

Everett, M. (1997) 'The Ghost in the Machine: Agency in "Post-structural" Critiques of Development', *Anthropological Quarterly* 70 (3): 137–51.

Ezrahi, Y. (1990) *The Descent of Icarus: Science and the Transformation of Contemporary Democracy,* Cambridge MA: Harvard University Press.

Fals-Borda, F. (1981) *Sciencia Propria y Colonialismo Intelectual,* Bogotá: Carlos Valencia Eds.

Feldman, S. and E. Ferretti (eds) (1998) *Informal Work and Social Change: A Bibliographic Survey,* Ithaca NY: Cornell University Press.

Feldstein, M. (1998) 'Refocusing the IMF', *Foreign Affairs* 77 (2): 20–33.

Ferguson, J. (1990) *The Anti-politics Machine: 'Development', Depoliticization, and Bureaucratic Power in Lesotho,* Cambridge: Cambridge University Press.

——(1997) 'Anthropology and its Evil Twin: "Development" in the Constitution of a Discipline', in F. Cooper and R. Packard (eds) *International Development and the Social Sciences: Essays on the History and Politics of Knowledge,* Berkeley: University of California Press, 150–75.

Ferguson, Y. and R. Mansbach (1991) 'Between Celebration and Despair: Constructive Suggestions for Future International Theory', *International Studies Quarterly* 35: 363–86.

Fine, B. (2000) *Social Capital versus Social Theory: Political Economy and Social Science at the Turn of the Millennium,* London: Routledge.

Finkle, J.L. and C.A. McIntosh (1995) 'The Cairo Conference on Population and Development: A New Paradigm?', *Population and Development Review* 21 (2): 223–60.

Finnemore, M. (1996a) *National Interests in International Society,* Ithaca NY: Cornell University Press.

——(1996b) 'Norms, Culture, and World Politics: Insights from Sociology's Institutionalism', *International Organization* 50 (2): 325–47.

——(1997) 'Redefining Development at the World Bank', in F. Cooper and R. Packard (eds) *International Development and the Social Sciences: Essays on the History and Politics of Knowledge,* Berkeley: University of California Press, 203–27.

Fischer, F. and J. Forrester (eds) (1993) *The Argumentative Turn in Policy Analysis and Planning,* Durham NC: Duke University Press.

Fitzpatrick, M. (1999) 'Protesters Claim WTO Failure as Victory', http://biz.yahoo.com /rf/991204/bj.html.

Fogel, R.W. (2000) *The Fourth Great Awakening and the Future of Egalitarianism,* Chicago: University of Chicago Press.

Forde, S. (1995) 'International Realism and the Science of Politics', *International Studies Quarterly* 39: 141–60.

Forman, S. and R. Gosh (2000) *Promoting Reproductive Health: Promoting Health for Development,* Boulder: Lynne Rienner.

Foster, G.M. (1962) *Traditional Cultures: And the Impact of Technological Change*, New York: Harper & Row.

Foucault, M. (1965) *Madness and Civilization: A History of Insanity in the Age of Reason*, New York: Pantheon Books.

——(1972) *The Archaeology of Knowledge*, trans. A.M. Sheridan Smith, London: Tavistock.

——(1976) [1990] *The History of Sexuality, Volume 1*, London: Penguin.

——(1980) 'On Popular Justice: A Discussion with Maoists', in C. Gordon (ed.) *Power/Knowledge: Selected Interviews and Writings, 1972–1977*, New York: Pantheon Books, 1–36.

——(1991) *Remarks on Marx: Conversations with Duccio Trombadori*, New York: Semiotext(e).

Frank, A.G. (1967) *Capitalism and Underdevelopment in Latin America*, New York: Monthly Review Press.

——(1978) *Dependent Accumulation and Underdevelopment*, London: Macmillan.

Freire, P. (1970) *The Pedagogy of the Oppressed*, New York: Herder and Herder.

Friedmann, J. (1992) *Empowerment: the Politics of Alternative Development*, Cambridge MA: Blackwell.

Gale, F. (1998) ' "Cave! Hic Dragones": A Neo-Gramscian Deconstruction and Reconstruction of International Regime Theory', *Review of International Political Economy* 5 (2): 252–83.

Galenson, W. (1981) *The International Labor Organization: An American View*, Madison: University of Wisconsin Press.

Galjart, B. (1980) 'Counterdevelopment', *Community Development Journal* XVI: 88–96.

Gardner, K. and D. Lewis (1996) *Anthropology, Development and the Post-modern Challenge*, London: Pluto Press.

Garrett, G. (1995) 'Capital Mobility, Trade and the Domestic Politics of Economic Policy', *International Organization* 49: 657–89.

Garrett, G. and B. Weingast (1993) 'Ideas, Interests, and Institutions: Constructing the European Community's Internal Market', in J. Goldstein and R.O. Keohane (eds) *Ideas and Foreign Policy: Beliefs, Institutions and Political Change*, Ithaca NY: Cornell University Press, 173–206.

Gasper, D. (1986) 'Distribution and Development Ethnics: A Tour', in R. Apthorpe and A. Krähl (eds) *Development Studies: Critique and Renewal*, Leiden: E.J. Brill, 136–203.

——(1997) 'Sen's Capability Approach and Nussbaum's Capability Ethic', *Journal of International Development* 9 (2): 281–302.

——(1999) 'Ethics and the Conduct of International Development Aid: Charity and Obligation', *Forum for Development Studies* 1: 23–58.

GATT (1992) *Trade and Environment Report*, Geneva: GATT.

Geertz, C. (1963) *Peddlers and Princes: Social Change and Economic Modernisation in Two Indonesian Towns*, Chicago: University of Chicago Press.

George, S. and F. Sabelli (1994) *Faith and Credit: The World Bank's Secular Empire*, Harmondsworth: Penguin.

Germain, R. and M. Kenny (1998) 'Engaging Gramsci: International Relations Theory and the New Gramscians', *Review of International Studies* 24 (1): 3–21.

Gerry, C. (1987) 'Developing Economies and the Informal Sector in Historical Perspective', *Annals of the American Academy of Political and Social Science – Special Edition: The Informal Economy* 493 (September): 100–19.

Gibson, B. and B. Kelly (1994) 'A Classical Theory of the Informal Sector', *The Manchester School of Economic and Social Studies* LXII: 81–96.

Giddens, A. (1979) *Central Problems in Social Theory*, London: Macmillan.

——(1984) *The Constitution of Society*, Cambridge: Cambridge University Press.

Gill, S. (1990a) *American Hegemony and the Trilateral Commission*, Cambridge: Cambridge University Press.

——(1990b) 'Two Concepts of International Political Economy', *Review of International Studies* 16: 369–81.

——(1998) 'New Constitutionalism, Democratisation and Global Political Economy', *Pacifica Review* 10 (1): 23–38.

Goetz, A.M. and R. O'Brien (1995) 'Governing for the Common Wealth? The World Bank's Approach to Poverty and Governance', *IDS Bulletin* 26 (2): 17–26.

Goldstein, J. (1993) *Ideas, Interests, and American Trade Policy*, Ithaca NY: Cornell University Press.

Goldstein, J. and R.O. Keohane (eds) (1993) *Ideas and Foreign Policy: Beliefs, Institutions and Political Change*, Ithaca NY: Cornell University Press.

Gore, C. (1996) 'Methodological Nationalism and the Misunderstanding of East Asian Industrialization', in R. Apthorpe and D. Gasper (eds) *Arguing Development Policy: Frames and Discourses*, London: Frank Cass, 77–122.

Goulet, D. (1971) *The Cruel Choice*, New York: Atheneum.

——(1995) *Development Ethics: A Guide to Theory and Practice*, London: Zed Books.

Gramsci, A. (1971) *Selections From the Prison Notebooks*, London: Lawrence and Wishart.

Green, R. (1980) 'Southern Africa Development Coordination: Toward a Functioning Dynamic?', *IDS Bulletin* 11: 53–58.

Greenblatt, S. (1991) *Marvelous Possessions: The Wonder of the New World*, Chicago: University of Chicago Press.

Grootaert, C. (1998) 'Social Capital: The Missing Link?', SCI Working Paper 3, Washington DC: World Bank.

Gupta, M.R. (1993) 'Rural-urban Migration, Informal Sector and Development Policies: A Theoretical Analysis', *Journal of Development Economics* 41: 137–51.

Gwin, C. (1994) *US Relations with the World Bank 1945–92*, Washington DC: Brookings Institution.

——(1997) 'US Relations with the World Bank, 1945–1992', in D. Kapur, J.P. Lewis, and R. Webb (eds) *The World Bank: Its First Half Century*, vol. 2, Washington DC: Brookings Institution, 195–274.

Gwynne, R. and C. Kay (1999) 'Latin America Transformed: Changing Paradigms, Debates and Alternatives', in R. Gwynne and C. Kay (eds) *Latin America Transformed: Globalization and Modernity*, London: Arnold, 2–30.

Gyohten, T. (1997) 'Japan and the World Bank', in D. Kapur, J.P. Lewis and R. Webb (eds) *The World Bank: Its First Half Century*, vol. 2, Washington DC: Brookings Institution, 275–316.

Haas, E. (1980) 'Why Collaborate? Issue-linkage and International Regimes', *World Politics* 32: 357–405.

——(1990) *When Knowledge is Power: Three Models of Change in International Organizations*, Berkeley: University of California Press.

Haas, P. (ed.) (1992) *Knowledge, Power and International Policy Co-ordination*, Columbia SC: University of South Carolina Press.

Habermas, J. (1987) *The Theory of Communicative Action: Critique of Functionalist Reason*, vol. 2, trans. T. McCarthy, Boston MA: Beacon Press.

——(1998a) *Between Facts and Norms: Contributions to a Discourse Theory of Law and Democracy*, Cambridge MA: MIT Press.

——(1998b) 'Remarks on Legitimisation Through Human Rights', *Philosophy and Social Criticism* 24 (2): 157–71.

Hacking, I. (1999) *The Social Construction of What?*, Cambridge MA: Harvard University Press.

Haggard, S. and Lee, C. (1993) 'The Political Dimension of Finance in Economic Development', in H. Lee and S. Maxfield (eds) *The Politics of Developing Countries*, Ithaca NY: Cornell University Press, 3–20.

Hall, P.A. (1989a) 'Conclusion: The Politics of Keynesian Ideas', in P.A. Hall (ed.) *The Political Power of Economic Ideas*, Princeton: Princeton University Press, 361–401.

Hall, P.A. (ed.) (1989b) *The Political Power of Economic Ideas: Keynesianism Across Nations*, Princeton: Princeton University Press.

Hall, R.B. (1997) 'Moral Authority as a Power Resource', *International Organization* 51: 591–622.

Hamlet, L.L. (2000) 'Co-operation Problems, Secretariat Solutions: States, International Secretariats and the Politics of Institutional Design', paper presented at the 41st Annual Convention of the International Studies Association, Los Angeles.

Hancock, G. (1989) *Lords of Poverty: The Free-wheeling Lifestyles, Power, Prestige and Corruption of the Multi-billion Dollar Aid Business*, London: Macmillan.

Hansen, S., M. Koch-Weser and E. Lutz (1988) 'Environmental Funding Options', internal draft working paper, June and November versions.

Hanson, M. and J.J. Hentz (1999) 'Neocolonialism and Neoliberalism in South Africa and Zambia', *Political Science Quarterly* 114: 479–502.

Haq, K. and U. Kirdar (eds) (1986) *Human Development: The Neglected Dimension*, Islamabad: North South Roundtable.

Haq, M. ul (1972) 'The Limits to Growth: A Critique', *Finance and Development* 9 (4): 2–8.

——(1976) *The Poverty Curtain: Choices for the Third World*, New York: Columbia University Press.

——(1995) *Reflections on Human Development*, Oxford: Oxford University Press.

——(1999) *Human Development in South Asia 1999*, Human Development Centre, Karachi: Oxford University Press.

Harr, J.E. and P.J. Johnson (1991) *The Rockefeller Conscience: An American Family in Public and Private*, New York: Charles Scribner's sons.

Harris, N. (ed.) (1992) *Cities in the 1990s: The Challenge for Developing Countries*, London: UCL Press.

Hart, K. (1973) 'Informal Income Opportunities and Urban Employment in Ghana', *Journal of Modern African Studies* 11: 61–89.

——(1982) *The Political Economy of West African Agriculture*, Cambridge: Cambridge University Press.

——(1985) 'The Informal Economy', *Cambridge Anthropology* 10: 54–58.

——(2000) *The Memory Bank: Money in an Unequal World*, London: Profile Books.

Hayek, F. von (1944) *The Road to Serfdom*, London: Routledge.

Hayter, T. and C. Watson (1985) *Aid: Rhetoric and Reality*, London: Pluto Press.

Helleiner, E. (1994) *States and the Re-emergence of Global Finance: From Bretton Woods to the 1990s*, Ithaca NY: Cornell University Press.

Hettne, B. (1995) *Development Theory and the Three Worlds*, London: Longman.

Higgott, R. (2000) 'Regionalism in the Asia-Pacific: Two Steps Forward, One Step Back?', in R. Stubbs and G. Underhill (eds) *Political Economy and the Changing Global Order*, 2nd edn, Toronto: Oxford University Press, 254–63.

Hill, P. (1986) *Development Economics on Trial: The Anthropological Case for a Prosecution*, Cambridge: Cambridge University Press.

Hobart, M. (1993a) 'Introduction: The Growth of Ignorance?' in M. Hobart (ed.) *An Anthropological Critique of Development: The Growth of Ignorance*, London and New York: Routledge, 1–30.

Hobart, M. (ed.) (1993b) *An Anthropological Critique of Development: The Growth of Ignorance*, London and New York: Routledge.

Hobsbawm, E. (1995) *Age of Extremes: The Short Twentieth Century 1914–1991*, London: Abacus.

Hodgson, D. (1983) 'Demography as a Social Science and Policy Science', *Population and Development Review* 9 (1): 1–34.

——(1988) 'Orthodoxy and Revisionism in American Demography', *Population and Development Review* 14 (4): 541–69.

Hodgson, D. and S.C. Wattkins (1997) 'Feminists and Neo-Malthusians: Past and Present Alliances', *Population and Development Review* 23 (3): 469–523.

Hoff, K. and J. Stiglitz (1999) 'Modern Economic Theory and Development', Washington DC: World Bank (mimeo).

Hoffman, P. (1970) 'Introduction', in C. Legum (ed.) *The First UN Development Decade and Its Lessons for the 1970s*, New York: Praeger, xxv–xxviii.

Hoksbergen, R. (1986) 'Approaches to Evaluation of Development Interventions: The Importance of World and Life Views', *World Development* 14 (2): 283–300.

Huq, H. (2000) 'People's Practices: Exploring Contestation, Counter-development, and Rural Livelihoods. Cases from Muktinagar, Bangladesh', Ph.D. dissertation, Wageningen University.

Hyden, G. (1997) 'Foreign Aid and Democratisation in Africa', *Africa Insight* 27 (4): 233–40.

ICTSD (1999) 'Acreditation Schemes and Other Arrangements for Public Participation in International Fora', http://www.ictsd.org/html/arcpubpart.htm.

Ikenberry, J.G. (1993) 'Creating Yesterday's New World Order: "New Thinking" and the Anglo-American Postwar Settlement', in J. Goldstein and R.O. Keohane (eds) *Ideas and Foreign Policy: Beliefs, Institutions and Political Change*, Ithaca NY: Cornell University Press, 57–86.

——(1996) 'The Myth of the Post-Cold War Chaos', *Foreign Affairs* 75: 79–91.

Ikenberry, J.G. and M. Doyle (1997) 'Conclusion: Continuity and Innovation in International Relations Theory', in J.G. Ikenberry and M. Doyle (eds) *New Thinking in International Relations Theory*, Boulder: Westview Press, 266–80.

Interaction Newsletter (February 1986) published by the Global Tomorrow Coalition

International Labour Organization (1972) *Employment, Incomes and Equality: A Strategy for Increasing Productive Employment in Kenya*, Geneva: ILO.

——(1976) *Employment, Growth and Basic Needs: A One World Problem*, Geneva: ILO.

——(1995) *World Labour Report*, Geneva: ILO.

International Monetary Fund (1997a) 'The Role of the IMF in Governance Issues: Guidance Note', 25 July, http://www.imf.org/external/pubs/ft/exrp/govern/govindex.htm.

——(1997b) 'Good Governance: The IMF's Role', http://www.imf.org/external/pubs/ft/exrp/govern/govindex.htm.

Jacobson, H. and D. Kay (1979) 'The Environmental Protection Activities of International Organizations: An Appraisal and Some Suggestions', paper presented at the annual meeting of the American Political Science Association, Washington DC, 31 August–3 September.

Jacobson, J.K. (1995) 'Much Ado about Ideas: The Cognitive Factor in Economic Policy', *World Politics* 47: 283–310.

Jain, A. (ed.) (1998) *Do Population Policies Matter?*, New York: Population Council.

Jain, A. and J. Bruce (1994) 'A Reproductive Health Approach to the Objectives and Assessment of Family Planning Programs', in G. Sen, A. Germain and L.C. Chen (eds) *Population Policies Reconsidered: Health, Empowerment, and Rights*, Cambridge MA: Harvard University Press, 193–209.

James, H. (1998) 'From Grandmotherliness to Governance: The Evolution of IMF Conditionality', *Finance and Development* 35 (4): 44–47.

Jervis, R. (1988) 'Realism, Game Theory, and Cooperation', *World Politics* 40: 317–49.

——(1998) 'Realism in the Study of World Politics', *International Organization* 52: 971–92.

Johnson, S. (1995) *The Politics of Population*, London: Earthscan Publications.

Jones, J. (1991) 'Farmer Perspective on Economics and Sociology of Coca Production in the Chapare', IDA Working Paper no. 77, Institute of Development Anthropology, Clark University.

Kahler, M. (1992) 'Multilateralism with Small and Large Numbers', *International Organization* 46 (3): 681–708.

——(1998) 'Rationality in International Relations', *International Organization* 52: 919–42.

Kaldor, N. (1957) 'A Model of Economic Growth', *Economic Journal* 82: 591–624.

Kanbur, R. and N. Lustig (1999) 'Why is Inequality Back on the Agenda?', paper presented at the World Bank's Annual Bank Conference on Development Economics, Washington DC.

Kanbur, R. and L. Squire (1999) 'The Evolution of Thinking About Poverty: Exploring the Interactions', Washington DC: World Bank (mimeo).

Kanbur, R. and D. Vines (2000) 'The World Bank and Poverty Reduction: Past, Present and Future', in C.L. Gilbert and D. Vines (eds) *The World Bank: Structure and Policies*, Cambridge: Cambridge University Press, 87–107.

Kappagoda, N. (1995) *The Multilateral Development Banks. Volume 2: the Asian Development Bank*, London: Lynne Rienner.

Kapstein, E. (1998–99) 'A Global Third Way: Social Justice and the World Economy', *World Policy Journal* 15 (4): 23–35.

Kapur, D., J.P. Lewis and R. Webb (eds) (1997) *The World Bank: Its First Half Century*, vols 1 and 2, Washington DC: Brookings Institution.

Kapur, D. and R. Webb (2000) 'Governance-related Conditionalities of the International Financial Institutions', G-24 Discussion Paper Series, no. 6, New York: United Nations Conference on Trade and Development/Center for International Development, Harvard University, August.

Katzenstein, P. (1996) 'Introduction: Alternative Perspectives on National Security', in P. Katzenstein (ed.) *The Culture of National Security: Norms and Identity in World Politics*, New York: Columbia University Press, 1–32.

Katzenstein, P., R.O. Keohane and S.D. Krasner (1998) '*International Organization* and the Study of World Politics', *International Organization* 52: 645–86.

Keck, M. (1998) 'Planafloro in Rondônia: The Limits of Leverage', in J. Fox and D. Brown (eds) *The Struggle for Accountability: The World Bank, NGOs, and Grassroots Movements*, Cambridge MA: MIT Press, 181–218.

Keefer, P. and S. Knack (2000) 'Polarization, Politics, and Property Rights: Links Between Inequality and Growth', Policy Research Working Paper 2418, Washington DC: World Bank.

Keet, D. (2000) 'Globalisation And Regionalisation: Contradictory Tendencies? Counteractive Tactics? Or Strategic Possibilities?', http://www.aidc.org.za/archives/dot.

Keohane, R.O. (1984) *After Hegemony*, Princeton: Princeton University Press.

——(1988) 'International Institutions: Two Approaches', *International Studies Quarterly* 32: 379–96.

——(1989) *International Institutions and State Power: Essays in International Relations Theory*, Boulder: Westview Press.

Keohane, R.O. and J. Nye (1987) 'Power and Interdependence Revisited', *International Organization* 41: 725–53.

Keyman, F. (1997) *Globalisation, State, Identity/Difference: Toward a Critical Social Theory of International Relations*, Atlantic Highlands NJ: Humanities Press.

Khundker, N. (1988) 'The Fuzziness of the Informal Sector: Can We Afford to Throw Out the Baby With the Bath Water? (A Comment)', *World Development* 16 (10): 1263–65.

Kiely, R. (1999) 'The Last Refuge of the Noble Savage? A Critical Assessment of Post-development Theory', *The European Journal of Development Studies* 11 (1): 30–55.

Kier, E. (1996) 'Culture and French Military Doctrine Before World War II', in P. Katzenstein (ed.) *The Culture of National Security: Norms and Identity in World Politics*, New York: Columbia University Press, 186–215.

Kindleberger, C. (1973) *The World in Depression, 1929–1939*, Berkeley: University of California Press.

Kjørven, O. (1992) *Facing the Challenge of Change: The World Bank and the Global Environmental Facility*, EED Publications, Lysaker (Norway): Fridtjof Nansen Institute.

Klotz, A. (1995) 'Norms Reconstituting Interests: Global Racial Equality and U.S. Sanctions Against South Africa', *International Organization* 49: 451–78.

Knack, S. (1999) 'Social Capital, Growth and Poverty: A Survey of Cross-country Evidence', SCI Working Paper 7, Washington DC: World Bank.

Knorr-Cetina, K.D. (1981) *The Manufacture of Knowledge: An Essay on the Constructivist and Contextual Nature of Science*, Oxford: Pergamon Press.

Koelble, T. (1999) *The Global Economy and Democracy in South Africa*, New Brunswick NJ: Rutgers University Press.

Kornegay, F. and C. Landsberg (1998) 'Phaphama Iafrika: The African Renaissance and Corporate South Africa', *African Security Review* 7: 3–17.

Koslowski, R. and F. Kratochwil (1994) 'Understanding Change in International Politics: The Soviet Empire's Demise and the International System', in R.N. Lebow and T. Risse-Kappen (eds) *International Relations Theory and the End of the Cold War*, New York: Columbia University Press, 127–66.

Kowert, P. and J. Legro (1996) 'Norms, Identity, and Their Limits: A Theoretical Reprise', in P. Katzenstein (ed.) *The Culture of National Security: Norms and Identity in World Politics*, New York: Columbia University Press, 451–97.

Kratochwil, F. (1989) *Rules, Norms and Decision Making*, New York: Cambridge University Press.

Kremer, M. (1999) 'A Purchase Fund for New Vaccines: Rationale and a Proposed Design', Cambridge MA and New York: Harvard University and Brookings Institution (mimeo).

Krugman, P. (1992) 'The Rich, the Right and the Facts: Deconstructing the Income Distribution Debate', *The American Prospect* 11 (fall): 19–31.

——(1995) 'Dutch Tulips and Emerging Markets', *Foreign Affairs* 74: 28–44.

Kuznets, S. (1955) 'Economic Growth and Income Inequality', *American Economic Review* 65: 1–28.

LaFalce, J. (1998) *The Role of the United States and the IMF in the Asian Financial Crisis*, Washington DC: Institute for International Economics.

Laffey, M. and J. Weldes (1997) 'Ideas and Symbolic Technologies in International Relations', *The European Journal of International Relations* 3 (1): 193–237.

Lancaster, C. (2000) 'Redesigning Foreign Aid', *Foreign Affairs* 79 (5): 796–815.

Lappé, F.M., J. Collins and D. Kinley (1980) *Aid as Obstacle*, San Francisco: Institute for Food and Development Policy.

Laserna, R. (1989) 'Coca Cultivation, Drug Traffic and Regional Development in Cochabamba, Bolivia', unpublished Ph.D. dissertation, University of California at Berkeley.

Latour, B. (1988) *The Pasteurization of France*, Cambridge MA: Harvard University Press.

Laudan, L. (1977) *Progress and Its Problems*, London: Routledge.

Lebow, R.N. and T. Risse-Kappen (eds) (1995) *International Relations Theory and the End of the Cold War*, New York: Columbia University Press.

Leftwich, A. (1993) 'Governance, Democracy, and Development in the Third World', *Third World Quarterly* 14 (3): 605–24.

Legro, J. (1997) 'Which Norms Matter? Revisiting the "Failure" of Internationalism', *International Organization* 51: 31–63.

Leons, M.B. and H. Sanabria (eds) (1997) *Coca, Cocaine, and the Bolivian Reality*, New York: State University of New York Press.

Lewitsky, J. (1985) 'Review of World Bank Lending to Small Enterprises', Industry Department, Washington DC: World Bank (mimeo).

Lipton, M. and M. Ravallion (1995) 'Poverty and Policy', in J. Behrman and T.N. Srinivasan (eds) *Handbook of Development Economics*, Amsterdam: Elsevier, 2551–657.

Litfin, K. (1994) *Ozone Discourses: Science and Politics in Global Environmental Cooperation*, New York: Columbia University Press.

Livingstone, I. (1974) 'Creating Employment in Kenya: The ILO Mission Report', *Journal of Administration Overseas* XIII (4): 374–82.

Lohman, M. (ed.) (1992) *Coca-Cronologia: Bolivia 1986–1992, Cien Documentos sobre la Problematica de la Coca y la Lucha contra Las Drogas*, Cochabamba: ILDIS-CEDIB.

Long, N. (2001) *Development Sociology: Actor Perspectives*, London: Routledge.

Long, N. (ed.) (1989) *Encounters at the Interface: A Perspective on Social Discontinuities in Rural Development*, Wageningen Studies in Sociology no. 27, Wageningen: Wageningen Agricultural University.

Long, N. and J.D. van der Ploeg (1989) 'Demythologizing Planned Intervention: An Actor Perspective', *Sociologia Ruralis* XXIX (3/4): 226–49.

Lubell, H. (1991) *The Informal Sector in the 1980s and 1990s*, Paris: OECD.

Lukes, S. (1974) *Power: A Radical View*, London: Macmillan.

Lund-Thomsen, P. (1999) 'The Politics of Trade and Environment in the World Trade Organization', M.A. thesis, Copenhagen Business School, Department of Intercultural Management and Communication.

Malthus, T.R. (1989) *An Essay on the Principle of Population: Or, a View of its Past and Present Effects on Human Happiness: with an Inquiry into our Prospects Respecting the Future Removal or Mitigation of the Evils which it Occasions*, Cambridge: Cambridge University Press.

Manzo, K. (1991) 'Modernist Discourse and the Crisis of Development Theory', *Studies in Comparative International Development* 26 (2): 3–36.

March, J.G. and J.P. Olsen (1989) *Rediscovering Institutions*, New York: Free Press.

——(1998) 'The Institutional Dynamics of International Political Orders', *International Organization* 52: 943–70.

Marglin, S.A. and J.B. Schor (1990) *The Golden Age of Capitalism: Reinterpreting the Postwar Experience*, Oxford: Clarendon Press.

Marx, K. and F. Engels (1996) [1848] *Manifesto of the Communist Party*, London: Phoenix.

Masujima, K. (1999) 'Europe, America, and Developing Countries: The Transformation of the OEEC to the OECD (1959–1961)', *Dokkyo Law Review* 49: 354–82.

Maxfield, S. (1990) *Governing Capital: International Finance and Mexican Politics*, Ithaca NY: Cornell University Press.

Mayo, M. and G. Craig (1995) 'Community Participation and Empowerment: The Human Face of Structural Adjustment or Tools for Democratic Transformation?', in G. Craig and M. Mayo (eds) *Community Empowerment: A Reader in Participation and Development*, London: Zed Books, 1–11.

McCloskey, D. (1983) 'The Rhetoric of Economics', *Journal of Economic Literature* 21 (2): 481–517.

McNamara, R. (1981) *The McNamara Years at the World Bank: Major Policy Addresses of Robert S. McNamara 1968–1981*, Baltimore: Johns Hopkins University Press.

McNeill, D. (1999a) 'Market Ethics as Global Ethics', *Forum for Development Studies* (1): 59–76.

——(1999b) 'On Interdisciplinary Research: With Particular Reference on the Field of Environment and Development', *Higher Education Quarterly* 53 (4): 312–32.

——(2000) 'The Concept of Sustainable Development', in K. Lee, A. Holland and D. McNeill (eds) *Global Sustainable Development in the 21st Century*, Edinburgh: Edinburgh University Press, 10–29.

Meier, G. (1993) 'Review of Development Research in the UK', report to the Development Studies Association (mimeo).

Mendez, R. (2002) *UNDP History Project*, http://www.yale.edu/unsy/UNDPhist.htm.

Milanovic, B. (1999) 'True World Income Distribution, 1988 and 1993: First Calculation Based on Household Surveys Alone', Policy Research Working Paper 2244, Washington DC: World Bank.

Mittelman, J. and M. Pasha (1997) *Out From Underdevelopment Revisited: Changing Global Structures and the Remaking of World Order*, Basingstoke: Macmillan.

Mohan, G. (1997) 'Developing Differences: Post-structuralism and Political Economy in Contemporary Development Studies', *Review of African Political Economy* 24 (73): 311–28.

Moore, D.B. (1995) 'Development Discourse as Hegemony: Towards an Ideological History – 1945–1995', in D.B. Moore and G.J. Schmitz (eds) *Debating Development Discourse: Institutional and Popular Perspectives*, London: Macmillan, 1–53.

Morgenstern, O. (1971) 'L'économie Est-Elle une Science Exacte? La Recherche', reproduced in *Problèmes Economiques* (2688–89): 2–6, November 2000.

Morgenthau, H. (1949) *Politics Among Nations: The Struggle for Power and Peace*, New York: Alfred A. Knopf.

Moser, C. (1994) 'The Informal Sector Debate Part I: 1970–1983', in C. Rakowski (ed.) *Contrapunto: The Informal Sector Debate in Latin America*, Albany: SUNY Press, 11–29.

Naim, M. (2000) 'Fads and Fashions in Economic Reforms: Washington Consensus or Washington Confusion?', *Third World Quarterly* 21 (3): 505–28.

Narayan, D. and L. Pritchett (1997) *Cents and Sociability: Household Income and Social Capital in Rural Tanzania*, Washington DC: World Bank.

National Herald (1993) 'India Not to Seek Further WB Loan', *National Herald (India)*, 31 March.

Nau, H. (1990) *The Myth of American Decline*, New York: Oxford University Press.

Neck, P.A. and R.E. Nelson (eds) (1987) *Small Enterprise Development Policies and Programmes*, Geneva: ILO.

Nelson, N. and S. Wright (1995): 'Introduction: Participation and Power', in N. Nelson and S. Wright (eds) *Power and Participatory Development: Theory and Practice*, London: Intermediate Technology Publications, 1–18.

Nelson, P. (2000) 'Whose Civil Society? Whose Governance? Decision-making and Practice in the New Agenda at the Inter-American Development Bank and the World Bank', *Global Governance* 6 (4): 405–31.

Ness, G.D. and S.R. Brechin (1988) 'Bridging the Gap: International Organizations as Organizations', *International Organization* 42 (2): 245–73.

New York Times (2001) 'World Briefing. Bolivia: Pact with Coca Growers', 5 May.

Nordström, H. and S. Vaughan (1999) 'Trade and Environment', *WTO Special Studies no. 4*, Geneva: WTO.

North, D.C. (1990) *Institutions, Institutional Change and Economic Performance*, Cambridge: Cambridge University Press.

Nunnenkamp, P. (1995) 'What Donors Mean by Good Governance: Heroic Ends, Limited Means, and Traditional Dilemmas of Development Cooperation', *IDS Bulletin* 26 (2): 9–16.

Nussbaum, M. and J. Glover (eds) (1995) *Women, Culture, and Development: A Study of Human Capabilities*, Oxford: Clarendon Press.

Nustad, K.G. (1996) 'The Politics of "Development": Power and Changing Discourses in South Africa', *Cambridge Anthropology* 19 (1): 57–72.

——(1997) 'The End of Development: Comments on an Obituary', *Forum for Development Studies* (1): 155–66.

——(1999) 'Community Leadership and Development Administration in a Durban Squatter Settlement', Ph.D. thesis, University of Cambridge.

——(2001) 'Development: The Devil We Know?', *Third World Quarterly* 22 (4): 479–89.

Nustad, K.G. and O.J. Sending (2000) 'The Instrumentalisation of Development Knowledge', in D. Stone (ed.) *Banking on Knowledge: The Genesis of the Global Development Network*, London: Routledge, 44–62.

Nyerere, J. (1968) *Freedom and Socialism: Uhuru na Ujamaa*, Dar es Salaam: Oxford University Press.

O'Brien, R., A.M. Goetz, J.A. Scholte and M. Williams (2000) *Contesting Global Governance: Multilateral Economic Institutions and Global Social Movements*, Cambridge: Cambridge University Press.

Odell, J. (1982) *US International Monetary Policy: Markets, Power and Ideas as Sources of Change*, Princeton: Princeton University Press.

OECD (1988) *Development Cooperation: Efforts and Policies of the Members of the Development Assistance Committee*, Paris: OECD.

——(1989) *Development Cooperation in the 1990s: Efforts and Policies of the Members of the Development Assistance Committee*, Paris: OECD.

——(1990) *Development Cooperation: Efforts and Policies of the Members of the Development Assistance Committee*, Paris: OECD.

——(1991) *Development Cooperation: Efforts and Policies of the Members of the Development Assistance Committee*, Paris: OECD.

——(1992) *Development Assistance Manual: DAC Principles for Effective Aid*, Paris: OECD.

——(1993) *DAC Orientations on Participatory Development and Good Governance*, Paris: OECD.

Office of the Special Coordinator for Africa and the Least Developed Countries (1995) 'Paper Prepared for the International Workshop on Development of Africa's Informal Sector', United Nations Headquarters, 13–15 June.

Olson, M. (1965) *The Logic of Collective Action: Public Goods and the Theory of Groups*, Cambridge MA: Harvard University Press.

——(1982) *The Rise and Decline of Nations: Economic Growth, Stagflation and Social Rigidities*, New Haven: Yale University Press.

Pantich, L. (1997) 'Rethinking the Role of the State', in J.H. Mittelman (ed.) *Globalization: Critical Reflections*, Boulder: Lynne Rienner, 83–113.

Peattie, L. (1987) 'An Idea in Good Currency and How It Grew: The Informal Sector', *World Development* 15 (7): 851–60.

——(1993) 'An Approach to Urban Research in the Nineties', working paper presented under the Ford Foundation funded research project, Urban Research for the Developing World.

Perotti, R. (1996) 'Growth, Income Distribution, and Democracy: What the Data Say', *Journal of Economic Growth* 1 (2): 149–87.

Piddington, K. (1992) 'The Role of the World Bank', in A. Hurrel and B. Kingsbury (eds) *The International Politics of the Environment*, Oxford: Clarendon Press, 212–27.

Pieterse, J.N. (1998) 'My Paradigm or Yours? Alternative Development, Post-development, Reflexive Development', *Development and Change* 29: 343–73.

Pijl, K. (1998) *Transnational Classes and International Relations*, London: Routledge.

Ploeg, J.D. van der (1989) 'Knowledge Systems, Metaphor and Interface: The Case of Potatoes in the Peruvian Highlands', in N. Long (ed.) *Encounters at the Interface: A Perspective on Social Discontinuities in Rural Development*, Wageningen: Wageningen Agricultural University, 143–63.

Polanyi, K. (1944/57) *The Great Transformation*, Boston MA: Beacon Press.

Population Council (1994) 'The Unfinished Transition', *The Population Council Issues Papers*, New York: The Population Council.

Porter, D.J. (1995) 'Scenes from Childhood: The Homesickness of Development Discourses', in J. Crush (ed.) *Power of Development*, London: Routledge, 63–86.

Portes, A. (1998) 'Social Capital: Its Origins and Applications in Modern Sociology', *Annual Review of Sociology* 24: 1–24.

Portes, A., M. Castells and L. Benton (eds) (1991) *The Informal Economy*, Baltimore: Johns Hopkins University Press.

Prebisch, R. (1971) *Change and Development: Latin America's Great Task*, New York: Praeger.

Presser, H. (1997) 'Demography, Feminism and the Science-Policy Nexus', *Population and Development Review* 23 (2): 295–331.

Prestre, P. (1989) *The World Bank and the Environmental Challenge*, Selinsgrove PA: Susquehanna University Press.

Pritchett, L. (1996) 'Where Has All the Education Gone?', Policy Research Working Paper 1581, Washington DC: World Bank.

Putnam, H. (1990) *Realism with a Human Face*, Cambridge: Cambridge University Press.

——(1994) 'Sense, Nonsense, and the Senses: An Inquiry into the Powers of the Human Mind', *The Journal of Philosophy* 91: 445–517.

Putnam, R.D. (1993a) *Making Democracy Work: Civic Traditions in Modern Italy*, Princeton: Princeton University Press.

——(1993b) 'The Prosperous Community: Social Capital and Public Life', *The American Prospect* 13: 35–42.

Rabinow, P. (1984) *The Foucault Reader: An Introduction to Foucault's Thought*, New York: Pantheon Books.

Rakowski, C. (1994a) 'The Informal Sector Debate Part II: 1984–1993', in C. Rakowski (ed.) *Contrapuntot: The Informal Sector Debate in Latin America*, Albany: SUNY Press, 30–50.

——(1994b) 'Convergence and Divergence in the Informal Sector Debate: A Focus on Latin America, 1984–92', *World Development* 22 (4): 501–16.

Ranis, G. (1997) 'The World Bank Near the Turn of the Century', in R. Culpeper, A. Berry and F. Stewart (eds) *Global Development Fifty Years after Bretton Woods*, New York: St Martin's Press, 72–77.

Rasnake, R. and M. Painter (1989) 'Rural Development and Crop Substitution in Bolivia: USAID and The Chapare Regional Development Project', *Institute of Development Anthropology* and Reports on work supported by Human Settlements and Natural Resources Systems Analysis, Bolivia: SARSA.

Rauch, J. (1991) 'Modelling the Informal Sector Formally', *Journal of Development Economics* 35: 33–47.

Ravallion, M. (1994) *Poverty Comparisons*, London: Harwood Academic Publishers.

——(1997) 'Good and Bad Growth: The Human Development Reports', *World Development* 25 (5): 633–38.

Rawls, J. (1971) *A Theory of Justice*, Cambridge MA: Harvard University Press.

Rein, M. and D. Schon (1991): 'Frame Reflective Policy Discourse', in P. Wagner *et al.* (eds) *Social Sciences and Modern States: National Experiences and Theoretical Crossroads*, Cambridge: Cambridge University Press, 262–89.

Rich, B. (1994) *Mortgaging the Earth: The World Bank, Environmental Impoverishment, and the Crisis of Development*, Boston MA: Beacon Press.

Richards, P. (1985) *Indigenous Agricultural Revolution*, London: Hutchinson.

Risse, T. (2000) 'Let's Argue: Communicative Action in World Politics', *International Organization* 54 (1): 1–39.

Risse, T. and K. Sikkink (1999) 'The Socialization of International Human Rights Norms into Domestic Practices: Introduction', in T. Risse, S. Ropp and K. Sikkink (eds) *The Power of Human Rights: International Human Rights and Domestic Change*, Cambridge: Cambridge University Press, 1–38.

Risse-Kappen, T. (1995) 'Ideas Do Not Float Freely: Transnational Coalitions, Domestic Structures, and the End of the Cold War', in N. Lebow and T. Risse-Kappen (eds) *International Relations Theory and the End of the Cold War*, New York: Columbia University Press, 187–222.

Rist, G. (1997) *The History of Development: From Western Origins to Global Faith*, London: Zed Books.

Ritchie, M. (2000) *Beyond Seattle: Getting Beyond No*, http://www.wtowatch.org/library/admin/uploadedFiles/Beyond_Seattle.htm.

Ritzen, J., W. Easterly and M. Woolcock (2000) 'On "Good" Politicians and "Bad" Policies: Social Cohesion, Institutions, and Growth', Policy Research Working Paper 2448, Washington DC: World Bank.

Robinson, J.A. (1996) 'When is a State Predatory?', Los Angeles: University of Southern California, Department of Economics (mimeo).

Robinson, M. (1999) 'Governance and Coherence in Development Cooperation', in J. Forster and O. Stokke (eds) *Policy Coherence in Development Cooperation*, London: Frank Cass, 408–28.

Rodriguez, F. (2000) 'Inequality, Economic Growth and Economic Performance', background paper for the *World Development Report 2000/2001*, College Park: University of Maryland.

Rodrik, D. (1998) 'Where Did All the Growth Go? External Shocks, Social Conflict and Growth Collapses', *Journal of Economic Growth* 4 (4): 385–412.

——(1999) 'Trade Policy and Economic Growth: A Skeptic's Guide to the Cross-National Evidence', *CEPR Discussion Paper* 2143, London: CEPR.

——(2000), 'Institutions for High-quality Growth: What They Are and How to Acquire Them', *NBER Working Paper* 7540, Cambridge MA: NBER.

Root, H. (1996) *Small Countries, Big Lessons: Governance and the Rise of East Asia*, Hong Kong: ADB and Oxford University Press.

Rörling, N.G. (1988) *Extension Science: Information Systems in Agricultural Development*, Cambridge: Cambridge University Press.

Rose, Nikolas (1999) *Powers of Freedom: Reframing Political Thought*, Cambridge: Cambridge University Press.

Rostow, W.W. (1961) *The Stages of Economic Growth: A Non-Communist Manifesto*, Cambridge: Cambridge University Press.

Ruggie, J.G. (1972) 'Continuity and Transformation in the World Polity: Toward a Neo realist Synthesis', *World Politics* 35: 261–85.

——(1982) 'International Regimes, Transactions and Change: Embedded Liberalism in the Postwar Economic Order', *International Organization* 36 (2): 379–415.

——(1983) 'International Interdependence and National Welfare', in J.G. Ruggie (ed.) *The Antinomies of Interdependence: National Welfare and the International Division of Labor*, New York: Columbia University Press, 1–39.

——(1998) 'What Makes the World Hang Together', *International Organization* 29: 557–83.

Sachs, J.D. (1999) 'Twentieth Century Political Economy: A Brief History of Global Capitalism', *Oxford Review of Economic Policy* 15 (4): 90–101.

Sachs, W. (ed.) (1995) *The Development Dictionary: A Guide to Knowledge as Power*, Johannesburg: Witwatersrand University Press.

Sahn, D., D. Stifel and S. Younger (1999) 'Intertemporal Changes in Welfare: Preliminary Results from Nine African Countries', Cornell University (mimeo).

Said, E.W. (1978) *Orientalism*, New York: Pantheon Books.

Sandholtz, W. (1993) 'Monetary Politics and Maastricht', *International Organization* 47: 1–41.

Santiso, C. (2001) 'International Cooperation for Democracy and Good Governance: Moving Towards a Second Generation?', *The European Journal of Development Research* 13 (1): 154–80.

Schimmelfennig, F. (1999) 'The Double Puzzle of Enlargement: Liberal Norms, Rhetorical Action, and the Decision to Expand to the East', *Arena Working Paper* 15.

Schmitz, G. J. (1995) 'Democratization and Demystification: Deconstructing "Governance" as Development Paradigm', in D.B. Moore and G.J. Schmitz (eds) *Debating Development Discourse: Institutional and Popular Perspectives*, London: Macmillan, 54–90.

Schmitz, H. (1982) 'Growth Constraints on Small-scale Manufacturing in Developing Countires: A Critical Review', *World Development* 10 (6): 429–50.

Schoute, S. (1994) 'Cultivating Illegality: The Case of Coca in Bolivia', unpublished M.Sc. dissertation, Wageningen Agricultural University.

Schraeder, P.J. (2000) 'Cold War and Cold Peace: Explaining US–French Tensions in Francophone Africa', *Papers on Africa* 40, Leipzig: University of Leipzig.

Schumpeter, J.A. (1954) *History of Economic Analysis*, London: Allen & Unwin.

Scott, W.R. and J.W. Meyer (1994) *Institutional Environments and Organizations*, Thousand Oaks: Sage.

Sen, A. (1997) *On Economic Inequality*, Oxford: Clarendon Press.

——(1998) 'Economic Policy and Equity: An Overview', paper presented at Conference on Economic Policy and Equity, 8–9 June, Washington DC: International Monetary Fund.

——(1999) *Development as Freedom*, New York: Alfred Knopf.

——(2000a) 'A Decade of Human Development', *Journal of Human Development* 1 (1): 17–24.

——(2000b) 'Consequential Evaluation and Practical Reason', *The Journal of Philosophy* 97 (9): 477–502.

Sen, G., A. Germain and L.C. Chen (1994) *Population Policies Reconsidered: Health, Empowerment and Rights*, Cambridge MA: Harvard University Press.

Serageldin, I. (1996) 'Sustainability as Opportunity and the Problem of Social Capital', *Brown Journal of World Affairs* 3 (2): 187–203.

——(1998) 'Foreword' in C. Grootaert, *Social Capital: the Missing Link?*, SCI Working Paper 1, Washington DC: World Bank, i.

Serageldin, I. and C. Grootaert (2000) 'Defining Social Capital: An Integrating View', in P. Dasgupta and I. Serageldin (eds) *Social Capital: A Multifaceted Perspective*, Washington DC: World Bank, 40–58.

Serageldin, I. and A. Steer (eds) (1994) *Making Development Sustainable: From Concepts to Action*, Washington DC: World Bank.

Sethuraman, S.V. (ed.) (1991) *The Urban Informal Sector in Developing Countries*, Geneva: ILO.

Sharpless, J. (1997) 'World Population Growth, Family Planning, and American Foreign Policy', in D.T. Critchlow (ed.) *The Politics of Abortion and Birth Control in Historical Perspective*, Pennsylvania: Pennsylvania State University Press, 72–102

——(1999) 'Population Science, Private Foundations, and Development Aid: The Transformation of Demographic Knowledge in the United States 1946–1965', in F. Cooper and R. Packard (eds) *International Development and the Social Sciences: Essays on the History and Politics of Knowledge*, Berkeley: University of California Press, 176–200.

Shihata, I. (1994) *The World Bank Inspection Panel*, Oxford: Oxford University Press.

——(1995) 'The World Bank and the Environment: Legal Instruments for Achieving Environmental Objectives', in I. Shihata (ed.) *The World Bank in a Changing World*, The Hague: Martinus Nijhoff, 175–89.

Sierra Club (1986) *Bankrolling Disasters: International Development Banks and the Global Environment*, San Francisco: Sierra Club.

Sikkink, K. (1991) *Ideas and Institutions: Development in Argentina and Brazil*, Ithaca NY: Cornell University Press.

Sindzingre, A. (1997) 'Institutions d'aide et Enquêtes sur la Pauvreté en Afrique', *Cahiers d'Economie et Sociologie Rurales* 42–43: 146–83.

——(2000) 'Les Bailleurs de Fonds en Manque de Légitimité', *Esprit* 264: 116–27.

Singh, J.S. (1998) *Creating a New Consensus on Population*, London: Earthscan.

Sjöberg, H. (1994) 'From Idea to Reality: The Creation of the Global Environment Facility', Global Environment Facility Working Paper 10, Washington DC: UNDP/UNEP/World Bank.

Solow, R. (1989) 'How Economic Ideas Turn to Mush', in D. Colander and A. Coats (eds) *The Spread of Economic Ideas*, Cambridge: Cambridge University Press, 75–84.

Soto, H. de (1987) *El Otro Sondero*, Lima: The Institute for Freedom and Democracy.

Squire, L. (2000) 'Why the World Bank Should Be Involved in Development Research', in C.L. Gilbert and D. Vines (eds) *The World Bank: Structure and Policies*, Cambridge: Cambridge University Press, 108–131.

Srinivasan, T.N. (1994) 'Human Development: A New Paradigm or Reinvention of the Wheel?', *American Economic Review Papers and Proceedings* 84 (2): 238–43.

——(2000) 'Growth, Poverty Reduction and Inequality', paper presented at the Annual World Bank Conference on Development Economics, Paris.

Standing, G. (2000) 'Brave New Words? A Critique of Stiglitz's World Bank Rethink', *Development and Change* 31: 737–63.

Stark, O. (1982) 'On Modelling the Informal Sector', *World Development* 10 (5): 413–16.

St Clair, A. and G. Skirbekk (2000) 'A Philosophical Analysis of the World Bank's Conception of Poverty', http://www.crop.org.

Stein, A. (1993) 'Coordination and Collaboration: Regimes in an Anarchic World', in R. Baldwin (ed.) *Neorealism and Neoliberalism: The Contemporary Debate*, New York: Columbia University Press, 29–59.

Stein, J.G. (1995) 'Political Learning by Doing', in R.N. Lebow and T. Risse-Kappen (eds) *International Relations*, New York: Columbia University Press, 223–58.

Stern, N. and Ferreira, F. (1997) 'The World Bank as an Intellectual Actor', in D. Kapur, J. P. Lewis and R. Webb (eds) *The World Bank: Its First Half Century*, vol. 2, Washington DC: Brookings Institution, 523–609.

Stewart, F. (1985) *Planning to Meet Basic Needs*, London: Macmillan.

Stiglitz, J. (1998) *Towards a New Paradigm for Development: Strategies, Policies and Processes*, UNCTAD, Geneva, Prebisch Lecture (World Bank website).

——(1999) 'Participation and Development: Perspectives from the Comprehensive Development Paradigm', paper presented at the Conference on Democracy, Market Economy and Development, World Bank and Government of Korea, Seoul, February (World Bank website).

——(2000a) 'Democratic Development and the Fruit of Labor', Boston MA: American Economic Association Meetings, Industrial Relations Research Association (World Bank website).

——(2000b) 'Introduction', in C.L. Gilbert and D. Vines (eds) *The World Bank: Structure and Policies*, Cambridge: Cambridge University Press, 1–9.

——(2002) *Globalization and its Discontents*, New York: Norton.

Stortingsproposisjon Nr. 65 (1993–94) *Om Resultatet av Uruguay-runden (1986–1993) og Samtykke til Ratifikasjon av Avtale om Opprettelse av Verdens Handelsorganisasjon (WTO)*, Oslo: Ministry of Foreign Affairs.

Strange, S. (1997) 'Territory, State, Authority and Economy: A New Realist Ontology of Global Political Economy', in R.W. Cox (ed.) *The New Realism: Perspectives in Multilateralism and World Order*, London: Macmillan, 3–19.

Streeten, P. (1984) 'Basic Needs: Some Unsettled Questions', *World Development* 12 (9): 937–78.

——(1993) 'From Growth, via Basic Needs, to Human Development: The Individual in the Process of Development', in S. Mansoob Murshed and K. Raffer (eds) *Trade, Transfers, and Development: Problems and Prospects for the Twenty-first Century*, Cambridge: Cambridge University Press, 16–33.

Streeten, P., S.J. Burki, M. Haq, N. Hicks and F. Stewart (1981) *First Things First: Meeting Basic Human Needs in the Developing Countries*, Oxford: Oxford University Press for the World Bank.

Suarez, F. (1999) 'The Developing Countries and the International Financial System: 25 Years of Hope, Frustration, and Some Modest Achievements', in E. Mayobre (ed.) *G-24: The Developing Countries in the International Financial System*, Boulder: Lynne Rienner, 3–25.

Swaminathan, M. (1991) 'Understanding the Informal Sector: A Survey', *WIDER Working Paper* 95, Helsinki: WIDER.

Szreter, S. (1993) 'The Idea of a Demographic Transition and the Study of Fertility Change: A Critical Intellectual History', *Population and Development Review* 19 (4): 659–701.

Tarrow, S. (1996) 'Making Social Science Work Across Space and Time: A Critical Reflection on Robert Putnam's *Making Democracy Work* ', *American Political Science Review* 90 (2): 389–97.

Taylor, L., S. Mehrotra and E. Delamonica (1997) 'The Links between Economic Growth, Poverty Reduction, and Social Development: Theory and Policy', in S. Mehrotra and R. Jolly (eds) *Development with a Human Face*, Oxford: Clarendon Press, 435–67.

Thacker, S.C. (1999) 'The High Politics of IMF Lending', *World Politics* 52 (1): 38–75.

Thomas, C. (2000) *Global Governance, Development and Human Security: The Challenge of Poverty and Inequality*, London: Pluto Press.

Toissaint, E. (1999) *Your Money or Your Life! The Tyranny of Global Finance*, London: Pluto Press.

Touraine, A. (1977) *The Self-production of Society*, Chicago: Chicago University Press.

Townsend, P. (1985) 'A Sociological Approach to the Measurement of Poverty: A Rejoinder to Pr. Amaratya Sen [Poor, Relatively Speaking]', *Oxford Economic Papers* 37 (4): 659–68.

Tsie, B. (1996) 'States and Markets in the Southern African Development Community (SADC): Beyond the Neo-Liberal Paradigm', *Journal of Southern African Studies* 22: 75–98.

Turnham, D., B. Salome and A. Schwarz (eds) (1990) *The Informal Sector Revisited*, Paris: OECD.

Udall, L. (1998) 'The World Bank and Public Accountability: Has Anything Changed?', in J.A. Fox and L.D. Brown (eds) *The Struggle for Accountability: The World Bank, NGOs, and Grassroots Movements*, Cambridge MA: MIT Press, 391–436.

UN (1995) *Report of the International Conference on Population and Development, Cairo, 5–13 September 1994* (sales no. E.95.XIII.18).

——(1973) *Renewing the Development Priority: Implementation of the International Development Strategy: First Overall Review and Appraisal of Progress during the Second United Nations Development Decade*, New York UN Development Committee for Development Decade.

——(1970) *Towards Accelerated Development: Proposals for the Second United Nations Development Decade*, New York: United Nations.

UNCDP (United Nations Committee for Development Planning) (1973) *Renewing the Development Priority. Implementation of the International Development Strategy: First Overall Review and Appraisal of Progress During the Second United Nations Development Decade*, New York: United Nations.

UNDP (1969) *A Study of the Capacity of the United Nations Development System*, 2 vols, Geneva: United Nations.

——(1975) *1975 Annual Report*, New York: UNDP.

——(1977) *UNDP: Why, What, How, Where*, New York: UNDP.

——(1984) *Annual Report of the Administrator 1983*, New York: UNDP.

——(1985) *Generation: Portrait of the United Nations Development Programme*, New York: UNDP.

——(1990) *Human Development Report*, New York: Oxford University Press.

——(1997a) 'Capacity Development and UNDP: Supporting Sustainable Human Development', http://magnet.undp.org/Docs/cap/BKMORG~1.HTM.

——(1997b) *Governance for Sustainable Development*, New York: Management Development and Governance Division, UNDP.

——(2000a) *Overcoming Human Poverty*, New York: UNDP.

——(2000b) *Human Development Report 2000*, New York: Oxford University Press.

UNDP/CSOPP (2000a) 'CSOPP Resource Centre: Toolbox-innovative Practices', www.undp.org/csopp/CSO/NewFiles/toolboxcase1.htm.

——(2000b) 'Peacemaking and Sustainable Development: Big Pictures or Small Projects: Collaboration betwwen UNDP and the Civil Society in Mali', www.undp.org/CSOPP/CSO/Newfiles/ipdoccasemali.html.

UNDP/SL (2000a) 'Rural and Urban Poverty: Similarities and Differences', www.undp.org/sl/Documents/General/20info/Rural_poverty/rural.htm.

——(2000b) 'Investing for Sustainable Livelihoods', www.undp.org/sl/Publications/Inv.pdf.

UNESCO (1998) *International Social Science Journal*, Paris: UNESCO.

USAID (1991) *Democracy and Governance*, Washington DC: Directorate for Policy, United States Agency for International Development.

——(1998) *Initiative for Southern Africa*, http://www.info.usaid.gov/pubs/cp98/afr/zz.isa.htm.

Veblen, T. (1953) [1899] *The Theory of the Leisure Class*, New York: New York American Library.

Vevatne, J. (2000a) 'WTO, NGOer og Seattle: En Analyse av Miljøbevegelsens Forsøk på å Øve Innflytelse ovenfor Verdens Handelsorganisasjon', M.A. thesis, Department of Political Science, University of Oslo.

——(2000b) 'Skilpadder og Tåregass: Miljøbevegelsen versus WTO', *Internasjonal Politikk* 58 (4): 527–57.

Vieira, P., J. Peña and M. Valeria (1997) 'The Limits and Merits of Participation', Policy Research Working Paper 1838, Washington DC: World Bank.

Wade, R. (2001a) 'Making the *World Development Report 2000: Attacking Poverty*', *World Development* 29 (8): 1435–41.

——(2001b) 'Showdown at the World Bank', *New Left Review* 7 (January/February): 124–37.

——(2002) 'US Hegemony and the World Bank: The Fight over People and Ideas', *Review of International Political Economy* 9 (2): 201–29.

Wæver, O. (1997) 'John G. Ruggie: Transformation and Institutionalization', in I. Neumann and O. Wæver (eds) *The Future of International Relations: Masters in the Making*, London: Routledge, 170–204.

Wagner, P. (1994) *A Sociology of Modernity: Liberty and Discipline*, London: Routledge.

Wagner, P., C. Hirschon Weiss, B. Wittrock and H. Wollman (eds) (1991) *Social Sciences and Modern States: National Experiences and Theoretical Crossroads*, Cambridge: Cambridge University Press.

Walker, R.B.J. (1987) 'Realism, Change and International Political Theory', *International Studies Quarterly* 31: 65–86.

Wallerstein, I. (1974) *The Modern World-system*, New York: Academic Press.

Waltz, K. (1979) *Theory of International Politics*, New York: Random House.

Wasserheit, J. and K.K. Holmes (1992) 'Reproductive Tract Infections: Challenges for International Health Policy, Programs, and Research', in A. Germain, K.K. Holmes, P. Piot and J.N. Wasserheit (eds) *Reproductive Tract Infections: Global Impact and Priorities for Women's Reproductive Health*, New York: Plenum Press, 7–33.

WCED (1987) *Our Common Future*, Oxford: Oxford University Press.

Weeks, J. (1975) 'Policies for Expanding Employment in the Informal Urban Sector of Developing Countries', *International Labour Review* 111: 99–117.

——(1996) 'Regional Cooperation and Southern African Development', *Journal of Southern African Studies* 22: 99–117.

Weiss, L. (1998) *The Myth of the Powerless State: Governing the Economy in a Global Era*, Cambridge: Polity Press.

Weiss, T.G. (2000) 'Governance, Good Governance and Global Governance: Conceptual and Actual Challenges', *Third World Quarterly* 21 (5): 795–814.

Weiss, T.G. and T. Carayannis (2001) 'Whither United Nations Economic and Social Ideas? A Research Agenda', *Global Social Policy* 1 (1): 25–47.

Welch, C. (1998) 'In Focus: The IMF and Good Governance', *Foreign Policy in Focus* 3 (33), October, http://www.igc.org/infocus/briefs/vol3/v3n33imf.html.

Wendt, A. (1987) 'The Agent-Structure Problem in International Relations Theory', *International Organization* 41: 435–70.

——(1992) 'Anarchy is What States Make of It', *International Organization* 46: 391–425.

——(1999) *Social Theory of International Politics*, Cambridge: Cambridge University Press.

Wihtol, R. (1988) *The Asian Development Bank and Rural Development: Policy and Practice*, London: Macmillan.

Williams, D. and T. Young (1994) 'Governance, the World Bank and Liberal Theory', *Political Studies* XLII (1): 84–100.

Williams, M. (1993) 'International Trade and the Environment: Issues, Perspectives and Challenges', *Environmental Politics* 2 (4): 80–97.

Williamson, J. (1993) 'Democracy and the "Washington Consensus"', *World Development* 21 (8): 1329–36.

Wilson, D. (1987) *A Bank for Half the World: The Story of the Asian Development Bank 1966–1986*, Manila: ADB.

Winters, L.A. (2000a) 'Trade, Trade Policy and Poverty: What Are the Links?', *CEPR Discussion Paper* 2382, London: CEPR.

——(2000b) 'Should Concerns about the Poor Stop Trade Liberalisation?', background paper of the *World Development Report 2000/2001* (World Bank website).

Wohlforth, W.C. (2000) 'Ideology and the Cold War', *Review of International Studies* 26 (2): 327–31.

Wolfe, M. (1996) *Elusive Development*, London: Zed Books.

Wolfensohn, J. (1997) 'People First', United Nations Development Program, Paul Hoffman Lecture, New York, 29 May.

Wolin, S. (1980) 'Paradigms and Political Theories', in G. Gutting (ed.) *Paradigms and Revolutions: Appraisals and Applications of Thomas Kuhn's Philosophy of Science*, Notre Dame IN: University of Notre Dame Press, 160–91.

Wood, A. (1996) 'Skill, Trade and International Inequality', *Institute of Development Studies Working Paper* 47, Brighton: University of Sussex.

Woods, N. (1999) 'Order, Globalization, and Inequality', in A. Hurrell and N. Woods (eds) *Inequality, Globalization, and World Politics*, New York: Oxford University Press, 8–35.

Woods, N. (ed.) (2000) *The Political Economy of Globalization*, London: Macmillan.

Woolcock, M. (1998) 'Social Capital and Economic Development: Toward a Theoretical Synthesis and Policy Framework', *Theory and Society* 27: 151–208.

World Bank (1981) *Accelerated Development in Sub-Saharan Africa*, Washington DC: World Bank.

——(1986) 'Involuntary Resettlement in Bank-Assisted Projects: A Review of the Applications of Bank Policies and Procedures in FY 1979–85 Projects', February, Washington DC: World Bank.

——(1989a) *Articles of Agreement*, Washington DC: World Bank.

——(1989b) *Sub-Saharan Africa: From Crisis to Sustainable Growth. A Long-Term Perspective Study*, Washington DC: World Bank.

——(1990) '*Summary Proceedings, 1990 Annual Meetings of the Board of Governors*', Washington DC, 25–27 September, report of the executive directors of IDA, para 17, p. 103, Operational Directive 4.02 (1992) formalizes Bank support for Environmental Action Plans (better known as National Environmental Action Plans), Washington DC: World Bank.

——(1991) *The African Capacity Building Initiative: Toward Improved Policy Analysis and Development Management*, Washington DC: World Bank.

——(1991) *Managing Development: the Governance Dimension*, Washington DC: World Bank.

——(1992) *World Bank Approaches to the Environment in Brazil: A Review of Selected Projects*, vol. 5, 'The Polonoroeste Program' , OED Report 10039, SecM92–64, 30 April, Washington DC: World Bank.

——(1993) *'The World Bank Inspection Panel'*, *Resolution 93–10*, *Resolution IDA 93–6'*, 22 September, Washington DC: World Bank.

——(1994) *The World Bank Group and the Environment, Fiscal 1994: Making Development Sustainable*, Washington DC: World Bank.

——(1994) 'An Overview of Monitoring and Evaluation in the World Bank', *OED Report* 13247, 30 June, Washington DC: World Bank.

——(1997a) *Expanding the Measure of Wealth: Indicators of Environmentally Sustainable Development*, Washington DC: World Bank.

——(1997b) *Development Report 1997: The State in a Changing World*, Oxford: Oxford University Press.

——(1998a) *Assessing Aid: What Works, What Doesn't, and Why*, Washington DC: World Bank.

——(1998b) 'The Initiative of Defining, Monitoring and Measuring Social Capital: Overview and Program Description', SCI Working Paper 1, Washington DC: World Bank.

——(2000a) *The Quality of Growth*, Washington DC: World Bank.

——(2000b) *World Development Report 2000/2001: Attacking Poverty*, New York: Oxford University Press.

World Health Organization (1991) *Creating Common Ground: Report of a Meeting Between Women's Health Advocates and Scientists on Women's Perspectives on the Introduction of Fertility Regulation Technologies*, report of a meeting jointly organized by IWHC and the World Health Organization, Geneva, February 1991. Geneva: WHO.

World Trade Organization (1994) *Trade and Environment Decision of 14 April 1994*, Marrakesh Ministerial (MTN7TNC/45(MIN), Geneva: WTO.

——(1996a) *Guidelines for Arrangements on Relations with Non-Governmental Organizations* (WT/L/162, 23 July 1996), Geneva: WTO.

——(1996b) *Procedures for the Circulation and Derestrictions of WTO Documents*, Geneva: WTO

Yasutomo, D.T. (1995) *The New Multilateralism in Japan's Foreign Policy*, London: Macmillan.

Yee, A. (1996) 'The Causal Effects of Ideas on Policy', *International Organization* 50: 69–108.

Young, O. (1986) 'International Regimes: Towards a New Theory of Institutions', *World Politics* 39 (1): 104–22.

Zakaria, F. (1994) 'Culture is Destiny: A Conversation with Lee Kuan Yew', *Foreign Affairs* 73 (2): 109–26.

Index